JEWISH CULTURAL STUDIES

VOLUME ONE

The Jewish Cultural Studies series is sponsored by the Jewish Folklore and Ethnology Section of the American Folklore Society in co-operation with the Council on the Anthropology of Jews and Judaism of the American Anthropological Association.

Members of the Section receive volumes as a privilege of membership. For more information see <http://afsnet.org/sections/jewish>.

The Section is also the sponsor of the Raphael Patai Prize, given to an outstanding student essay in English on Jewish folklore and ethnology. The chapter in this volume by Elly Teman of the Hebrew University of Jerusalem, entitled 'The Red String', received the prize in 2005. For more information, see the website listed above or <http://littman.co.uk/jcs/index.html>.

*This volume has benefited from
the financial support of*
THE ROTHSCHILD FOUNDATION (EUROPE)
and
THE TAUBE FOUNDATION FOR
JEWISH LIFE AND CULTURE

D0927513

THE LITTMAN LIBRARY OF
JEWISH CIVILIZATION

Dedicated to the memory of
LOUIS THOMAS SIDNEY LITTMAN
*who founded the Littman Library for the love of God
and as an act of charity in memory of his father*
JOSEPH AARON LITTMAN
יהא זכרם ברוך

'Get wisdom, get understanding:
Forsake her not and she shall preserve thee'
PROV. 4:5

*The Littman Library of Jewish Civilization is a registered UK charity
Registered charity no. 1000784*

JEWISH CULTURAL STUDIES

VOLUME ONE

Jewishness: Expression, Identity, and Representation

Edited by
SIMON J. BRONNER

Oxford · Portland, Oregon
The Littman Library of Jewish Civilization
2008

The Littman Library of Jewish Civilization

Chief Executive Officer: Ludo Craddock
Managing Editor: Connie Webber

PO Box 645, Oxford OX2 OUJ, UK
www.littman.co.uk

———

Published in the United States and Canada by
The Littman Library of Jewish Civilization
c/o ISBS, 920 NE 58th Avenue, Suite 300
Portland, Oregon 97213-3786

A catalogue record for this book is available from the British Library

Library of Congress Cataloging-in-Publication Data
Jewishness: expression, identity, and representation / edited by Simon J. Bronner.
p. cm.—(Jewish cultural studies; v.1) (The Littman library of Jewish civilization)
Includes bibliographical references and index.

ISBN 978–1–904113–45–4

1. Jews—Identity.   2. Jews—Civilization.   I. Bronner, Simon J.
DS143.J48 2008   305.892'4—dc22   2007038123

Publishing co-ordinator: Janet Moth
Proofreading: Kate Clements
Index: Bonnie Blackburn
Designed and typeset by Pete Russell, Faringdon, Oxon.
Production: John Saunders
Printed in Great Britain on acid-free paper by
Biddles Ltd., Kings Lynn

Editor and Advisers

Preface

AS THE INAUGURAL VOLUME of the *Jewish Cultural Studies* series, this book addresses a variety of ways in which Jewish culture is communicated and constructed. It sets out three major areas of concern in interpretations of Jewish culture: expression, identity, and representation. They have been placed in this order as the volume moves from close readings of texts to perspectives on social contexts and psychological processes. As the list of volumes in the series grows, I trust that readers will return to the essays here as benchmarks of these critical concerns.

The essays are, at a basic objective level, studies of Jewish culture. As cultural studies, they also deal subjectively with the way that Jewishness is perceived and created, by non-Jews as well as Jews. The essays show Jews to be a diverse lot, and give special attention to the expressions and representations of Jewishness that convey the plural identity of Jews among other Jews alongside questions of how the singular Jew is viewed, stereotyped, and appropriated by non-Jews. Individually, they contribute to the understanding of particular genres, whether film, folklore, music, literature, architecture, or art. Taken together, though, they represent a concern for cultural meaning as a theme of enquiry that cuts across genres and themes. Read alongside one another, the essays invite comparative enquiry into the patterns, and significance, of culture, and they force reflection on the intellectual legacy that makes culture central in human investigation. They use the label of Jewish cultural studies to discuss the importance of culture to the identity people call Jewish. We are aware that there is a movement of cultural studies devoted particularly to questions of media and power relations, and readers will recognize the influence of this movement on several writers. But our hope is that Jewish cultural studies can develop its own scholarly location rather than be construed as a sub-field.

This series is the first to be devoted exclusively to Jewish cultural studies, and will strive to articulate a distinctive understanding of Jewishness and the 'cultural Jew', and indeed culture generally. As my introduction explains, the interdisciplinary, hybridized field of Jewish cultural studies is of relatively recent formation, differentiated from both Jewish studies and cultural studies. The growing edifice of Jewish cultural studies is not without its disciplinary foundations: it draws largely on research in folkloristics, anthropology, cultural history, literary and media studies, communications, sociology, and psychology. Yet it often can disrupt disciplinary formalism with its discursive practice and extended reach. It treats culture not as something merely to be appreciated or entertained by, but as the central vessel for metaphors to live by, and die for. It unabashedly holds up the folk object and the popular subject as analytical opportunities; often dismissed in humanistic scholarship because they are 'ordinary' or unrefined, this object and subject open intellectual vistas on culture precisely because they are close to common human experience.

The purpose of this series is to present thematic volumes situating and interpreting the cultural dynamics of Jewishness in dominant societies, homelands, and ethnic communities around the globe. Contributors to the series will present studies on the ordinary life of Jewish communities and their often extraordinary circumstances. They will find exemplary expressions or texts of culture—in words, images, and things—and decode them as representations of identities, forces, and ideas. Concerned for the relative positions from which the ordinary is perceived, they will ask how people are 'ordinarized' as 'us' or 'them', and internalized as 'me'. Overall, the series will probe the very idea of Jewish culture as it has been symbolized, produced, communicated, and consumed in diverse contexts by both Jews and non-Jews, and some identities in between.

I want to thank Connie Webber, Managing Editor of the Littman Library of Jewish Civilization, for her help in turning this vision into a reality. Tim Lloyd, Executive Director of the American Folklore Society, deserves acknowledgement as well for his invaluable administrative support. In addition, my home institution, the Pennsylvania State University, provided me with staff assistance, for which I am grateful. I also worked on the volume while I had the benefit of a Fulbright Chair at Leiden University, The Netherlands, and I was flattered by the interest of colleagues there and at the Meertens Institute devoted to ethnological studies, which kindly extended me a research appointment. Oxford Brookes University in Oxford, England, graciously gave me travel support that allowed me to meet with the Littman staff on their home turf.

I have the privilege of working with a stellar international cast of advisers, who also served as reviewers of essays. I want to extend my special gratitude to advisers who served on the Raphael Patai Prize committee: Dan Ben-Amos, Haya Bar-Itzhak, and Steve Siporin. Other colleagues were involved in the evaluation and production of this volume: Itzik Gottesman, Galit Hasan-Rokem, Yelena Khanzhina, Neil Leifert, Andrea Lieber, and Joel Rubin.

My wonderful wife and Hebraist Sally Jo Bronner, as always, nurtured my work and opened my eyes to the potential of Jewish culture. She kept asking me why I was taking this series on, and forced me to reflect on my motives. I can share with you the answer I gave her. Intellectually, I cast this net of cultural study, drawing in a variety of experiences that define what it means to be Jewish, to make a difference in the thinking about, and with, tradition. It allows for a comparative cultural perspective and a fresh evaluation of being, and seeing, Jewish, or non-Jewish, and shades of in-betweenness and otherness. It identifies the many fragments of Jewish expressions, identities, and representations that need to be made whole or connected somehow to larger patterns and principles.

On a personal level, I know the emotions involved in the location of Jewish tradition, and its destruction and reconstruction. From my family's starting point in the town of Oświęcim or Auschwitz, covering a range of identities from *frum* to *frei*, survivors scattered to Israel, Germany, France, Russia, Sweden, Australia, and the United States. Varied landscapes, customs, and world-views well up in my mind's eye, as they may well do in the reader's, and a mixed, sometimes discordant chorus of languages fills my ears when I think about our collective, reconstructed 'us'. As a student of culture generally, I also felt that the Jewish subject was under-represented, and indeed misrepresented, in cultural studies, and there is something of a reformist agitation in the concept of the series. My hope is that, through the intellectual project represented in this series, sense will be made of both the disjuncture and linkage of Jewish experience, and perhaps provide a heightened sensibility of who 'we', or 'others', are.

Contents

PART III · REPRESENTATION

Note on Transliteration

THE transliteration of Hebrew in this book reflects consideration of the type of book it is, in terms of its content, purpose, and readership. The system adopted therefore reflects a broad approach to transcription, rather than the narrower approaches found in the *Encyclopaedia Judaica* or other systems developed for text-based or linguistic studies. The aim has been to reflect the pronunciation prescribed for modern Hebrew, rather than the spelling or Hebrew word structure, and to do so using conventions that are generally familiar to the English-speaking reader.

In accordance with this approach, no attempt is made to indicate the distinctions between *alef* and *ayin*, *tet* and *taf*, *kaf* and *kuf*, *sin* and *samekh*, since these are not relevant to pronunciation; likewise, the *dagesh* is not indicated except where it affects pronunciation. Following the principle of using conventions familiar to the majority of readers, however, transcriptions that are well established have been retained even when they are not fully consistent with the transliteration system adopted. On similar grounds, the *tsadi* is rendered by 'tz' in such familiar words as bar mitzvah, mitzvot, and so on. Likewise, the distinction between *ḥet* and *khaf* has been retained, using *ḥ* for the former and *kh* for the latter; the associated forms are generally familiar to readers, even if the distinction is not actually borne out in pronunciation, and for the same reason the final *heh* is indicated too. As in Hebrew, no capital letters are used, except that an initial capital has been retained in transliterating titles of published works (for example, *Shulḥan arukh*).

Since no distinction is made between *alef* and *ayin*, they are indicated by an apostrophe only in intervocalic positions where a failure to do so could lead an English-speaking reader to pronounce the vowel-cluster as a diphthong—as, for example, in *ha'ir*—or otherwise mispronounce the word.

The *sheva na* is indicated by an *e*—*perikat ol, reshut*—except, again, when established convention dictates otherwise.

The *yod* is represented by *i* when it occurs as a vowel (*bereshit*), by *y* when it occurs as a consonant (*yesodot*), and by *yi* when it occurs as both (*yisra'el*).

Names have generally been left in their familiar forms, even when this is inconsistent with the overall system.

The *Chutzpah* of Jewish Cultural Studies

SIMON J. BRONNER

THIS VOLUME, and the series of which it is a part, centrally places culture in an investigation of the social identities and textual expressions that are labelled Jewish. In an objective voice, the contents might broadly be called studies of Jewish culture, except that the essays present concepts swirling about the label of Jewish that are not lodged in the practices of Jews. The additional position, which might be called subjective in the sense of pertaining to attitudes, perceptions, and biases, considers the meaning of Jewishness as an idea, or a way of thinking, in different cultures, even those devoid of Jews. It not only includes the prejudices or affections of non-Jews, but also representations by Jews themselves, some of which may indeed be outside their awareness. Such representations are important in the consideration of how Jews view and differentiate themselves among other Jews, as well as the way they distinguish and align their cultural profiles to non-Jewish others. If studies of Jewish culture consider what Jews do, then the overarching concept of Jewish cultural studies takes in what is thought by and about Jews—and the idea of Jewishness in words, images, and things. The connection between the objective and subjective views is the quest for the meaning of being Jewish or representing 'Jewishness'. A way to fuse the standpoints into a conceptual whole is for scholars to refer to the cultural—those matters *related to* culture.

The volume proposes that the idea of Jewishness, or what people think of as Jewish, which may be distinct from the Jew or the things made by Jews, is revealed in the expressions of culture—speech, folklore, literature, art, architecture, music, dance, ritual, film, theatre, and so on. As contributors to cultural studies, the authors expand the scope of culturally related matters from the conventional artistic questions to their social relevance in politics, health, and economics. An implication of using 'cultural' as a keyword, therefore, is to declare that culture is not only to be studied for the sake of aesthetic appreciation but is also to be viewed as crucial to issues faced by societies and the individuals that compose them. Unlike many studies of culture that stop at the identification of the expressions of culture, the cultural studies here seek to interpret their meanings.

The contributors to the volume use various disciplinary perspectives to find meaning, and often use the opportunity of thinking broadly about culture to integrate approaches from history, anthropology, folkloristics, literature, psychology, and sociology. For them, Jewish cultural studies is at this juncture not so much a new discipline as a location for their existing work; for readers, it should be a common ground, a broad, fertile field, in which to make intellectual connections and sow new ideas. With the emphasis on cultural matters on this turf, writers in this volume, even if they identify themselves as anthropologists, folklorists, or historians, are naturally drawn to the guideposts set up by a scholarly movement called 'cultural studies'. Readers will find, however, that Jewish cultural studies as represented in this volume is being mapped out largely outside the departmental walls of 'cultural studies', for reasons I will outline in this introduction.

Studies of culture have various homes which usually slice off a piece of a subject—whether literature, music, or art—for their disciplinary pot. The effort in conceiving of Jewish cultural studies as a prime location for investigation is to be able to see culture as a whole panorama as well as a specific focus. A challenge to this endeavour is a legacy that has treated 'Jewish' narrowly as a religious identity. Is it surprising, for instance, that an august institution such as the sixteen-volume *Encyclopaedia Judaica* (1972) lacks an entry on 'culture'? The classic *Standard Jewish Encyclopedia* (Roth 1959) also leaves it out, while *The Book of Jewish Knowledge* (Ausubel 1964) deals with it by referring readers to entries on various disciplinary slices: art, Bible, folklore, language, music, and others. Indicative of a growing awareness of Judaism as a heritage as well as a religion, more recent reference works have drawn attention to culture, but nonetheless struggled with defining what constitutes culture and how its study is conceived. Introducing *The Blackwell Companion to Jewish Culture*, Glenda Abramson opines that of three signifiers that structure her reference work—'modern', 'Jewish', and 'culture'—culture is the most difficult to grasp, but she leans towards thinking of culture in terms of its components, particularly artistic activity (Abramson 1989: p. xii). David Biale's *Cultures of the Jews* (2002), despite its objectivist title, promotes a subjectivist 'cultural history' of the Jews. Admitting that 'culture is an elastic term', he introduces the concept of meaning into a modern definition, which this volume hopes to expand: 'manifold expressions—written or oral, visual or textual, material or spiritual—with which human beings represent their lived experiences in order to give them meaning' (2002: p. xvii).

In this definition, culture draws attention to itself because it is externalized through expressions. Biale also underscores that culture as a representation of experience is distinct from the experience itself. Scholars are attracted to culture, therefore, because it channels reality or offers fantasy as a discourse on life. The meaning it has is not just its documentation of an occurrence but its commentary on it, often elaborated with emotion and ideation. The expressions of culture, often recognized by their characteristics of being artistic or performed, are therefore *symbolic* representations of experience. They stand for something, which is often different from the thing it names. In folk speech, the heart may represent life, love, centrality, enthusiasm, or compassion, and the Jew, especially in various expressive combinations such as 'a good Jew', 'dirty Jew', and 'Jewish Jew', has various connotations—both positive and negative—which call for contextualization to illuminate their meanings. Since culture is shared among people, it often works to bind groups together and distinguish themselves from others. It gives insiders a sense of belonging and outsiders a reminder of difference.

Attention to the nature of expression, identity, and representation by contributors to this volume is at the heart of cultural studies. *Expression* refers to observable and collectible items—words, images, and things—that people offer to others to communicate something about themselves. The importance of these items lies not only in their content, but also in how they embed the beliefs and world-view of the giver. Accompanied by gesture and textured with style, words thus 'performed' reflect the cultures in which people operate. Images are the way that people picture themselves and others, whether in a signature or a movie. We are surrounded by images in advertisements, photographs, and logos that we 'read' for their message, see for their beauty, and critique for their representation (or stereotype). Things express the needs and feelings of their makers and users, and can be viewed as props in social exchanges and ritual displays. In a variety of hands, and across various landscapes, things enact culture for people to behold and interpret.

Identity shifts attention to the social and psychological functions of cultural behaviours that provide a sense of self or community. In the case of Jews, with their historical background of diasporization and victimization, a great diversity of identities have been acquired and discarded as they adapted to new times and places. Whereas studies written from a historical perspective frequently cover national traditions, in a cultural studies perspective attention is especially given to the situations of everyday life in which identity is negotiated and often divided between public and private personas. Indeed, one may find that contributors to the volumes in this series often deal with cultural identity apart from religious affiliation. As a matter of identity, being Jewish does not necessarily mean professing religious faith, but is revealed in what people do and how they think of themselves (or how others define them), whether in the street or the synagogue. Practitioners of cultural studies ask how people calling themselves Jews, and even those that do not, convey Jewishness, and how the larger, non-Jewish worlds they inhabit perceive, symbolize, and narrate their belonging.

The volume closes with *representation*, used in cultural studies to draw attention to symbolic, communicative systems mediating Jewish culture—in oral narrative, literature, and popular entertainment—often outside the awareness of participants. Contributors to this section analyse how the texts of a culture are symbolically encoded by their creators and then variously 'decoded', or read for meaning, by audiences and communities. They uncover the significance of culture as an arena for meaning-making in the struggles among groups for the power to dictate the readings, and images, a society favours. They also ask about the social and cultural structures which contain, and constrict, such readings, and the traditions that allow for the forms they take or the texts they inhabit. From a psychological viewpoint, the texts of a given culture are locations in which to air, and contest, often troubling dialogues that are difficult to broach in everyday conversation and formal institutional outlets. The definition of culture used in this series therefore refers to an expressive or artistic quality that draws attention to itself and is associative in identifying a people who relate to it.

Sensitive to the way in which meanings are conveyed through language and its social contexts, I should explain that the concern in cultural studies for the ordinary has multiple layers. It can shed light on the customs and traditions shared by people in their day-to-day existence to draw attention to the idea that culture is defined by expectations, often so ordinary that they do not need to be stated, of what is commonly done. Of great analytical benefit, the ordinary often signals what people believe, what they take for granted, what they do unselfconsciously. Where actions are self-conscious, when culture is organized, or communities mobilized, then ideas in discourse can be identified and analysed. Indeed, cultural studies often looks at *extra*ordinary instances when cultural practices are troubled, contested, or complicated to discern the forces that maintain or dissolve social conditions and to shed light on the intellectual construction of 'ordinary'.

In the case of Jewish cultural studies, such conditions are especially important to signify because of the variety of cultural contexts for a diasporic people with a long history and a legacy of power struggles in the face of persecution to maintain practices that exemplify Jewish identity. Jews are also an exemplary case of a group that has been 'ordinarized', in the sense that a precursor of cultural studies, Raymond Williams, described: a category essentialized by elites as *vulgus in populo*, meaning the unprogressive or incorrigible element of society. 'Ordinary' indicates for intellectual consideration the way in which people and their beliefs constitute, in Williams's terms, 'a generalized body of Others'. As a mode of enquiry that digs down for the various relative values held by different segments of society, cultural studies also seeks to discover how 'ordinary' can mean mainstream, popular, or normative. 'Ordinary' can signify 'us' rather than 'them', or what we consider 'sensible', 'right', and even 'decent'.

In sum, Jewish cultural studies untangles the ways in which meaning is created and received by different groups in various situations. Jews have a special position from which to comment on culture in such a study, since in their diasporic experience they have typically been part of, yet apart from, a dominant society. Thus, they have occupied a liminal space in which they comment as both observers of and participants in the larger society and its similarities of expres-

sion and identity, while also being concerned for the maintenance and representation of their cultural differences. Because this space is viewed as unbounded,
that Jewish commentary has often been viewed as incisive, bold, and even radical,
pointing out implications of which participants are unaware or unwilling to
admit. Jewish cultural studies is hardly content to be descriptive, as implied by
the rhetoric of 'studies of Jewish culture'; in staking out a location for interpretation, Jewish cultural studies has an edgy quality. Invoking a Jewish cultural
expression, it has *chutzpah*.

What does this word that draws attention to itself mean, as expression, identity, and representation? *Chutzpah* can make Jews cringe or crow, and for many
scholars hearing 'cultural studies' produces similar reactions, since it carries the
connotation of challenging assumptions and disrupting canons. Throw in 'Jewish' and one might just recoil as awareness of the tradition of critical enquiry in
Jewish hermeneutics doubles the bite. Upon reflection, that observation could
cause a worry that we are slipping into stereotype, essentializing Jews as obtru-
sive. Yet American intellectual Alan Dershowitz, for many readers the most public Jew they know, hardly shies away from *chutzpah*. In fact, he had the *chutzpah* to
make *Chutzpah* the title of one of his books, with the comment that, 'Notwithstanding the stereotype, we are not pushy or assertive enough for our own good
and for the good of our more vulnerable brothers and sisters in other parts of the
world' (Dershowitz 1991: 3). Calling for a post-Holocaust break with the old
world-view that Jews were guests in host countries, Dershowitz brought out the
irony that non-Jews associated Jews with *chutzpah* even though Jews themselves
decried it. It is in that acquiescence, he brazenly asserts, that we find a reason for
the diminishment of Jewish cultural identity and visibility (Dershowitz 1997).

But wait. What about the Jewish tradition of self-deprecation? Even an advertisement for the popular comedian Jackie Mason, characterized as full of *chutzpah* and with a voice that he boasts sounds genuinely 'Jewish' (with a slap at
Jewish celebrities worried about being cast as 'too Jewish') hooks buyers with the
pitch that he 'blends self-deprecating humility with abrasive chutzpah to acutely
dissect the differences between American Jewish and Gentile culture' (CD Baby
1991). Playing out in real life the storyline of the American-born son of immigrant parents who forsakes following the rabbinical line to go on the popular
stage and make it in the modern age, he nevertheless lends authenticity to the
role of the rabbi on the long-running television series *The Simpsons*, but in his
Broadway shows still reminds audiences that when he opens his mouth, they will
know he is ethnically different. From that position, he trenchantly comments on
the foibles of the *goyim*, literally non-Jews but also a metaphor for the dominant
society, as well as on the peculiarities of 'our people'. Mason has penned a book
instructing Jews 'How to Talk Jewish'—not necessarily because they have forgotten the language, but because they have lost its flavour—Yiddish words used to be

more 'expressive', he says. As a man of words, Mason drew attention to how the way one sounds and is understood is central to cultural identity.

Chutzpah naturally occupies a central role in Mason's book: he describes himself as someone who is 'brazen, brash, and has the gall to tell you off even when you did nothing to him', but he makes that sound like a good thing (Mason 1990: 34). After all, against the background of repression and discrimination, the humour of *chutzpah* can be rendered as a projection, maybe a fantasy, of a survival strategy, a way to triumph over adversaries. His explanatory narrative could even be read as a projective inversion in which the victim becomes victimizer: 'A guy with chutzpah takes out a gun and shoots you in the heart and then blames you for being in the wrong place at the wrong time.' For it is Jews who are often told they are in the wrong place and time, wandering, as the legend goes, looking for somewhere to rest and call home (Dundes and Hasan-Rokem 1986). Mason realizes the significance of his expressions for the identities and representations they suggest. He in fact inaugurated the Jackie Mason Lectureship in Contemporary Judaism at Oxford University in 1990, where he told the august gathering with self-deprecating humour, 'If the lecturers all start talking like me, the English language will be wiped out' (Anderson 1990).

Nobel prizewinning Yiddish writer Isaac Bashevis Singer, talking through his character Joseph Shapiro in *The Penitent*, was more philosophical than Mason about *chutzpah*. The story originally appeared in Yiddish in a daily newspaper read primarily by Jews from an east European background, but when it came time to produce an English version, the translator (his nephew Joseph Singer) left the Yiddish term *chutzpah* in. Sure, it is often explained by the nouns 'gall', 'impudence', or 'insolence', but it is usually considered untranslatable because it supposedly embodies a Jewish spirit. *The Penitent* illustrates *chutzpah* through a humorous story. Shapiro mulls over the idea of divorcing his wife, which leads him to muse, 'It's a principle among today's men that the unjust are always in the right. Chutzpah is the very essence of modern man, and of the modern Jew as well. He has learned so assiduously from the Gentile that he now surpasses him' (Singer 1983: 129). Does he mean, then, that *chutzpah* as a kind of arrogance is wrong, or that the unjust have been wronged? In a twist on the usual attribution, he seems to credit the dominant non-Jewish society of passing *chutzpah* on to modern Jews. 'Modern' here appears to mean secular or assimilated, judging by the way Singer contrasts it to traditional, Orthodox Jews (in the English edition *ḥasidim* is translated as 'the pious Jews') who maintain an obvious material separation from 'modern' Jews and non-Jews alike by adopting distinctive customs and dress: 'The truth is that the element of chutzpah was present even among the pious Jews. They have always been a stiff-necked and rebellious people. Well, there is a kind of chutzpah that is necessary, but I won't go into that now' (1983: 129–30). His implication is that they embody *chutzpah* in their everyday folklife rather than in their occasional folk speech or behaviour. As he explains in the author's note appended to the story, Singer has a personal sympathy for *chutzpah* as the rhetoric of secular protest: 'To me, a belief in God and a protest against the laws of life are not contradictory.' With a dash of *chutzpah*, he goes on: 'if I were able to picket the Almighty, I would carry a sign with the slogan UNFAIR TO LIFE!' (1983: 169).

The Yiddish word enjoyed a wide enough circulation in modern English to warrant an entry in the *Oxford English Dictionary*, which defines it in negative tones as 'brazen impudence'. The earliest example to supply the *OED*'s definition is British Jewish writer Israel Zangwill's use of the word in an essentialist characterization of Jews in *Children of the Ghetto* (first published in 1892), subtitled *A Study of a Peculiar People*. Like Mason's narrative, this could also be read as expressing a survival strategy. Zangwill's story depicts the condescension of Levi towards his younger brother Solomon: 'But it took a great deal to overawe Solomon, who, with the national humor, possessed the national *Chutzpah*, which is variously translated enterprise, audacity, brazen impudence and cheek' (Zangwill 1938: 77). The nation, or society, Zangwill means is Jewish, separated physically and culturally in a 'ghetto' from the dominant English society. The spirit represented by *chutzpah* could be positively rendered to suggest the promise of integration into that society (symbolized as a 'melting pot' in his 1908 stage play). But Zangwill looked down with disdain on the expression itself, probably because he had internalized the elitist opprobrium expressed towards a backward, 'oriental' civilization by members of Western industrial society (see Zangwill 1938: pp. v, ix; see also Kalmar and Penslar 2005). He associated these 'despised words', as he wrote, with 'superstitions grotesque as the cathedral gargoyles of the Dark Ages in which they had birth' (1938: pp. v, ix). The words, including *chutzpah*, remained intact in the many translations of *Children of the Ghetto*, which circulated world-wide in languages including Dutch (1896), Hebrew (1901), German (1913), and French (1921).

Disavowing Yiddish as a legitimate language for the redemption of the Jewish nation, Zangwill, in a Zionist polemic, reminds readers that 'most of these despised words are pure Hebrew; a language which never died off the lips of men, and which is the medium in which books are written all the world over even unto this day' (Zangwill 1938: p. v). In other words, Hebrew for Zangwill is the pure literary language of art and 'the rose of romance' from the land of Israel; Yiddish expresses 'The folk who . . . are children of the Ghetto' persecuted in, and corrupted by, European culture (1938: p. ix). Even if linguists point out that *chutzpah* (rendered as *khutspe* in Weinreich's modern orthography) in fact derives from Hebrew of late antiquity (*ḥutspah*), the popular perception remains that *chutzpah* is a Yiddishism, and a way to express Yiddishkeit (a Jewish cultural sensibility generally, but relating especially to east European heritage) (Steinmetz 1986: 60–1). In keeping with this concept of *chutzpah*, English speakers express a belief (or meta-folklore) that the word is untranslatable, implying that the culture which it represents is distinctive, although many English dictionaries do indeed translate it. In contrast to its meaning in Hebrew or Yiddish, *chutzpah* in English often has a positive value of self-confidence or initiative, unless modified by 'real', 'unbelievable', or 'the height of', in which case it negatively connotes effrontery (Steinmetz 1986: 61). Norman G. Finkelstein, for instance, blared *Beyond Chutzpah* in the title of his book critiquing Alan Dershowitz's assertions, thereby conveying the idea that Dershowitz's stance is unbelievable and idiosyncratic (Finkelstein 2005).

In English, use of *chutzpah* is not restricted to Jews, although its application by non-Jews can draw notice. When Italian Catholic Antonin Scalia, a justice of the United States Supreme Court, chastised the plaintiff in a decision (National Endowment for the Arts *v*. Finley, 1998) for a 'high degree of chutzpah', it drew commentaries from legal observers and internet bloggers alike. Even before Scalia's reportedly groundbreaking use of the term in the Supreme Court, Alex Kozinski and Eugene Volokh, writing in the *Yale Law Journal*, found that *chutzpah* had appeared in judges' decisions in a whopping 112 cases, mostly since 1980. They attribute its usage to the perception that Yiddish expressively underscores a point as no other language can, and *chutzpah* in particular needs no definition. In their words, Yiddish terms add 'spice' to dry 'American legal argot', but there is also the implication that Yiddish is safe to draw upon because it has become a classical language—much like Latin, which it has supplanted for legal flair. Yiddish more than Latin, though, provides a folksy spin appropriate to a democratic society (Kozinski and Volokh 1993: 463). It may be appealing in legal decisions because of the implication *chutzpah* carries of shamelessly or intentionally defying norms, with an echo of the Jewish tradition of the legalistic interpretation of religious texts. Is the mainstreaming of *chutzpah* a sign, or construction, of the loss of ethnic difference, since, as Jackie Mason observed, few people, at least in popular culture, 'talk Jewish'? And is it, too, significant in revealing how non-Jews 'see Jewish', even when they are not aware that they are doing it?

Even if the word *chutzpah* has entered common parlance, I have frequently heard Jews scornfully mock its mispronunciation by non-Jews as a signal that their ethnicity cannot be appropriated, indeed displaced, along with the word. Jews in conversation with one another observe that non-Jews reveal themselves by the inability to utter the 'ch' sound, found also in *challah* and *chanukah*, or they share stories associated with *chutzpah* as a kind of esoteric folklore, usually showing that use of the word is highly contextualized. The subtext is that Jewishness is a birthright, with local knowledge and a cultural continuity that cannot be mimicked. It is a familiar message, found also in legends that the Dutch Resistance uncovered German infiltrators during the Second World War by checking their ability to pronounce the name for a popular seaside resort, Scheveningen, interestingly boasting of their similar special ability to pronounce the 'ch' sound.

More than giving definitions or pronunciations, Jews are wont to tell stories of *chutzpah*. They may sound humorous, but in that play frame they allow for serious considerations of the limits of intrusion, perhaps placing the culprit in the role of trickster Jew. Probably the most frequently cited narrative, again giving the word a legal context, describes the man who murders his mother and father, and then asks the judge to forgive a poor orphan (Rosten 1982: 85). Renowned Jewish writer Leo Rosten liked to tell the story of the Jewish businessman who is distraught because a huge crate of black brassieres has been returned. His partner tells him to relax: 'What we can do is cut off the straps and sell them for *yarmulkes*' (Rosten 1982: 85). If this joke has a decided ethnic sensibility (or entrepreneurial stereotype) in it, the following story I have heard widely offers *chutzpah* as the strategy of the underdog or trickster:

A little old lady gets on to a crowded bus, then clutches her chest and says to the young girl seated in front of her, 'If you knew what I have, you would give me your seat.' The girl gets up and gives up her seat, then takes her magazine and starts fanning herself. The woman looks up and says, 'If you knew what I have, you would give me that so I could cool off.' The girl gives her the magazine. Several minutes go by, then the woman gets up and says to the bus driver, 'I want to get off right here.' The bus driver says she has to wait until he gets to the next stop, a block away. She clutches her chest again and tells him, 'If you knew what I have, you'd let me off right now.' The bus driver pulls over, opens the door and tells her she can get off the bus. As she steps down he says, 'Ma'am, I hope you don't mind my asking, but what is it you have?' And the woman says, 'Chutzpah!'

Various interpretative comments can be made on this story, such as the symbolic equivalence of *chutzpah* with 'old' and 'feminine', doubling the character's unlikelihood of holding power. The first person confronted is a 'girl', which in the narrative structure seems an easy mark. The more difficult challenge is the patriarchal bus driver, obviously in charge with his task of controlling the wheel. The literal vehicle for the story is the bus, indicating mobility, a microcosm of urban society, suggesting a competition among constituent social groups. What is first viewed as pathology turns out to be spirit, thus raising the question that someone posing Jewish cultural studies queries, such as Sander Gilman, might call the materialization of the Jew in the body as a device of Othering (Gilman 1991). In this story, unlike others suggesting dialect use of *chutzpah*, the term is a metaphor to live by. Instead of *talking* Jewish, she is shown to be *acting* Jewish, with the conclusion that she *feels* Jewish (without ever stating that she is) as a way to triumph over those who view her negatively or render her invisible. *Chutzpah* is her way of drawing attention to herself. Further, the ending of the story raises a crucial question for Jewish cultural studies of whether one can read Jewish, and for that matter think in, as well as with, Jewish (Bial 2005; Boyarin 1996; Gilman 1996).

Rendered positively or not, *chutzpah* in the twenty-first century or the post-modern age has been used in popular culture to convey an unshakable Jewish spirit in the absence of material difference. A few years ago, in fact, the comedy musical group Chutzpah made a splash in the media by drawing attention to the muting of Jewish intrusiveness, materially and musically, by making a comparison with African American ghetto youth, which gets ample mass-cultural notice. The three members of Chutzpah donned the garb associated with hip-hop rappers and belted out songs with titles such as 'Dr. Dreck', 'Chanukah's Da Bomb', and 'Shiksa Goddess'. They also produced a cult film (later turned into a DVD) called *Chutzpah, This Is?* (2005) with a parody of the 1927 film *The Jazz Singer* in the character of Master Tav, a cantorial student turned edgy rapper. Across the Pacific, *Chutzpah* (2000) is the title of an Australian animated short, again encapsulating Jewish identity, which challenges norms by featuring two ageing lesbians. Sometimes *chutzpah* does not have to be encoded by producers into a title to represent Jewishness. For example, in case theatre-goers did not recognize Wendy Wasserstein's Broadway play *The Sisters Rosensweig* as thematically Jewish, columnist Bill Marx titled his review 'Queens of Chutzpah' (Marx 2005), and the *New York Times* unapologetically characterized Jewish comedian Alan King, upon his death in 2004, as a 'Comic with Chutzpah' (Weber 2004).

So what does all this have to do with Jewish cultural studies? My intention in discussing *chutzpah* has been to draw attention to the questions, posed by the discipline, of representation and identity that arise from cultural communication. To be sure, other cultural expressions in words, images, and things could illustrate the layers of meaning that become apparent as people invoke tradition, and evoke cultural responses, in various social contexts. Maybe because I come out of a folkloristic background I am drawn to the rich narrative as well as linguistic aspects of a word with meanings constructed in diverse contexts. A yet wider link is to an inspiration for cultural studies in the work of Raymond Williams outlining keywords that are 'binding words in certain activities and their interpretation; they are significant, indicative words in certain forms of thought' (Williams 1983: 15; see also Bennett, Grossberg, and Morris 2005; Boyarin and Boyarin 1997: pp. vii–viii; Feintuch 2003). Cultural expressions, in other words, reveal meanings or ideas that are socially constructed, and often contested. People vie to dictate how they are represented in relation to Others, and especially in the conceptual terms that are considered essential to human existence: culture, society, tradition. At a behavioural level, keywords signify the experience that people describe through a shared vocabulary: they categorize the environment, create divisions, and characterize experience, thus setting up a nexus of expectations that people think of as 'culture'. At another level of thought revealed by discourse, keywords refer to themselves as part of a rhetoric of persuasion and performance. They thus invite efforts, often socially and politically driven, to give them meaning and shape and to direct the way people think and act.

Since Williams sparked this enquiry into keywords in the 1970s, the vocabulary of culture has expanded to include many forms of expression considered critical for guiding perception. Buildings, paintings, advertisements, films, jokes, and rituals are all symbolic representations meant to communicate ideas as much as they are modes of habitation or entertainment (Bartov 2005; Goldberg 2003; Hoberman and Shandler 2003; Kleeblatt 1996; Sachs and van Voolen 2004; Young 2000; Zurawik 2003). To be sure, recognizing the symbolic importance of cultural expression is not new. The social science of culture and tradition has been most notably pursued professionally for more than a century by folklorists, sociologists, psychologists, and anthropologists, before 'cultural' became a term for a mode of enquiry (Bronner 1998: 141–83). Practitioners using these labels, several of whom contribute to this volume, continue to identify and interpret the workings of culture with attention to social forces and contexts. Often devoted to the gathering of empirical evidence in culture, these disciplinarians distinctively invoke cultural studies to explore the idea of culture as it is conceptualized in 'ordinary' life and scholarship. Cultural studies is also a location to which we can bring mass-cultural evidence and objects closer to home (especially in modern complex societies), since traditional social science disciplines often call on analysts to detach themselves from their subject or choose topics that are unusual, even exotic.

The humanities have also made an important contribution to the knowledge of culture with the identification of artistic modes, forms, and styles of expression, usually by exceptional individuals. Humanists often approach expression as a portal through which to capture emotion and reveal spirit—indeed, to comment on the human condition. If it is not empirical or explanatory in the tradition of the social sciences, the humanistic mode of enquiry has been interpretative, offering speculations on the impressions made by artists and creators. But cultural studies advocates complain that the humanistic tradition has been to exalt uncommon, even unrepresentative, individuals in a culture for their 'genius' rather than choosing persons valued for their relation to 'ordinary' societies or communities. The humanistic search for *sui generis* creation rather than the process of creativity in everyday life means that emphasis is placed on production over consumption, writers over readers, performers over audiences, texts over processes. Another critique of classical humanities is the equation of culture with high art, rather than viewing the ordinary and traditional as a site for creative or artistic communication.

In response to these issues, cultural studies takes in, as the editors of *Cultural Studies* state, 'the entire range of a society's arts, beliefs, institutions, and communicative practices' (Nelson, Treichler, and Grossberg 1992: 4). It is often presented as a perspective that views material from a critical angle rather than lodging as a disciplinary alternative within the humanities or social sciences. This approach could be characterized as working from the inside out, as opposed to the conventional direction of coming from the outside and looking in, in the sense that the depth of experience of participants in a culture (particularly in multiple, often overlapping, subcultures) is valued. Meanings are sought that are generated by different, sometimes discordant, voices, as events unfold in human lives. Processes setting the multivocal tone, such as the formation of identity, the construction of collective memory, the fabrication of tradition, and the signification of imagery, invite comment (Du Gay, Evans, and Redman 2000; Hall 1997; Hall and Du Gay 1996). Power structures in which social hierarchies and cognitive categories operate are important to discern. Thus cultural studies can also entail asking a series of reflexive questions not posed from the detached position of the observer or the centralized vantage-point of the elite. It will intentionally chart the margins of a culture to find how the centre is maintained. To bring out the relativism and fiction of culture, it will ask what is *there*, to know what is *here*; it will discern rather than dismiss fantasies to better comprehend realities. Cultural studies often identifies the multiple dimensions of culture, and the world-views of its participants, instead of reducing each culture to a single trait. Reflexively, it probes the idea of culture—how it is used, who shapes it, and why.

In defiance of setting boundaries on their subject, many cultural studies proponents prefer to set out characteristics of enquiry. That perspective allows them to be more flexible in approach and responsive to the types of problems studied. The editors of *Cultural Studies* refer, for example, to cultural studies theory as 'sufficiently abstract and general that it can be moved [applied] to new contexts whenever it is helpful. It provides a way of describing the continual severing, realignment, and recombination of discourses, social groups, political interests, and structures of power in a society. It provides as well a way of describing the discursive processes by which objects and identities are formed or given meaning' (Nelson, Treichler, and Grossberg 1992: 8). All told, there is a characteristic interpretative strategy in cultural studies of reading and observing expressions that reveal the various stakes of, and identities in, a culture. Additionally proponents often cite a propensity to take a critical angle rather than a head-on or conventional approach, and to reflect ultimately on the structures and processes that frame such expressions (Shank 2001).

So why stake out a space for 'Jewish cultural studies' now? In announcing a 'new Jewish cultural studies' in the late 1990s, Jonathan and Daniel Boyarin answer forcefully that, for starters, non-Jewish academics have consistently devalued Jewish cultural difference since the Second World War (Boyarin and Boyarin 1997). They state a need for Jewish cultural studies to sight Jews on the academic radar and make possible a comparative ethnic perspective on culture. Other critics have also noted that the Jewish voice has been driven from or left out of the multicultural chorus, with the comment that since the Second World War many liberal academics have considered Jews inadequately racialized, problematized, colonized, or victimized to rate being featured on the public stage, with ethnicities such as those of Africans, Latinos, Arabs, and Asians seen as being more in need of advocacy (Biale, Galchinsky, and Heschel 1998; Brodkin 1999; Gilman 2006; Goldstein 2006). Typically omitted from the curricular roster of programmes for cultural studies and ethnic studies, Jewish studies typically stands on the margins of academic offerings or research into culture in departments for folklore, anthropology, psychology and sociology. One indication is that hefty flagship readers for the field, *Cultural Studies* (Grossberg, Nelson, and Treichler 1992, tipping the scales at 788 pages) and *The Cultural Studies Reader* (During 1999, 610 pages) make no mention of Jews. This omission is remarkable, considering the importance of Jews in the extensive historiography of race, othering, and subcultures. The Boyarins caustically comment that the deafness of cultural studies to Jewish voices has resulted from the politics of Jewish identity in the academy. With the balkanization of a Jewish studies pursued primarily by Jews, the Boyarins argue, 'few outside of the Jewish community have imagined that anything they said was worth listening to' (Boyarin and Boyarin 1997: p. ix). The cultural terms by which many Jewish scholars have presented the variety of Jewish societies and traditions—readings of ancient texts and languages, philological methods of interpretation, and cross-cultural comparisons over a diasporic history thousands of years in the making—were alien to a conventional presentist, nationalist mode of cultural studies enquiry. Sander Gilman adds to the case for Jewish alienation that, while cultural studies tends to situate its cultures in rooted settlements, the Jewish articulation of cultural meaning is often couched in terms of frontiers and movements as a result of the consciousness of dispersion and exile (Gilman 1999, 2003).

I would go further in stating that cultural studies, influenced by ideas of postcolonialism and orientalism, has often tended to frame Jewish groups as connected with imperial powers rather than as colonized or ghettoized subcultures affected by experiences of expulsion and Holocaust (Said 1994). In the usually presentist mode of cultural studies, Jews are often essentialized, and stigmatized, for example as Zionist exclusionists, or stereotypically cast as assimilated suburbanites fusing with the power elite. The roots of Jews in the Middle East, the expulsion of Sephardim from Spain in 1492 and their subsequent Mediterranean presence, and the derogatory orientalist images of Jews in Europe in discussions of the cultures of imperialism have been largely covered over. Writing in *Orientalism and the Jews*, Ivan Davidson Kalmar and Derek J. Penslar find that a crucial turn in perception of Jews occurred with the Balfour Declaration of 1917 committing the British empire to the establishment of a Jewish homeland in Palestine. They comment that, as a result,

the Jewish people became embroiled in imperialist intrigue, and the Zionist movement became from both the Western and the Arab point of view an instrument of European imperialism. Such was the beginning of the end of the story of the Ashkenazic Jews as a target of orientalism, and was no doubt what [Edward] Said had in mind when he suggested that the Jews, unlike the Arabs, were able to escape the stigma associated with the label 'Semite'. (Kalmar and Penslar 2005: p. xxxv)

Other factors besides this historical moment can be cited, including the assimilationist view that Jews have lost their difference, physically and spiritually, or that Judaism has been reduced to a religious faith rather than a cultural diversity. One can also hear references in academic conferences to the idea that Jews have become implicated by their economic and intellectual success with capitalist as well as imperialist intrigue, raising antisemitic images of the 'rich fat Jew'. Jews arguably, then, have not escaped a new form of antisemitism resulting from Western academic antagonism towards Israel or Jewish economic success (Chesler 2005; Wisse 1992).

If cultural studies is often guilty of the omission or stigmatization of Jews, or the Jewish subject, Jewish studies is often not a cosy home either for Jewish cultural studies. Treating Jewish studies as part of the classics, curricula typically steep students in the biblical and talmudic periods with special attention to readings of sacred texts. The study of 'Judaica' in this context equates Jewish identity with religion. The linguistic requirement is usually biblical Hebrew, rather than the languages in which Jewish culture is secularly expressed or represented— Yiddish, Ladino, Russian, German, French, English, Arabic. When the contemporary scene is discussed it is given a special designation of 'modern', often with reference to political and social thought, such as the history of Zionism, rather than cultural genres (music, art, folklore) or groups (hasidim, Sephardim, British Jewry). The huge *Oxford Handbook of Jewish Studies* (Goodman 2002), for instance, covering thirty-nine subjects in over a thousand pages, has no chapter on culture, but it discusses 'Modern Hebrew Literature' in a separate section and relegates 'Jewish Folklore and Ethnography' and 'Modern Jewish Society and Sociology' to the back of the book. To be sure, Jewish studies has evolved and there has been a movement to include more contemporary perspectives, particularly with reference to the great wave of immigration in the late nineteenth and early twentieth centuries, the Holocaust and its aftermath, and the Middle Eastern context of the state of Israel.

In its formation, Jewish cultural studies is something of a hybrid of Jewish studies and cultural studies, along with genetic relations to the social sciences and humanities, and, while it takes substance from these areas, like a hybrid it has characteristics that are distinct from the union of its parents. Following the inclusive range of cultural studies, Jewish cultural studies covers culture broadly in its local contexts, demanding a multilingual, multivocal comprehension. It gives more attention to the synchronic level of culture by ethnographically surveying contemporary groups and genres, but contextualizes its subject more than cultural studies has in its diachronic reference to the ancient past. Additionally, it delves into more folk and popular culture, particularly representations in the mass media, than does classically oriented Judaica work (Kirshenblatt-Gimblett 1998). It can also be said to open up the definition of 'Jewish' to what people do and feel, often outside the synagogue, rather than narrowly focusing on their faith. The texts of interest are also more broadly defined to include objects, images, gestures, and performances in addition to the written word.

I do not imagine Jewish cultural studies as putting up walls around itself, since as an open location for enquiry it works with, if not in, cultural studies and Jewish studies. For the former, the Jewish addition to the subject naturally involves commentary on culture generally, especially that of a dominant society. This is a function of Jewish diasporic experience involving a position typically part of, yet apart from, a dominant society. Thus, Jews have occupied a liminal space in which they comment as both observers of and participants in the larger society, with its similarities of expression and identity, while also being concerned for the maintenance and representation of their cultural differences. Liminality is evident, for example, in the position that Jews occupy in theories of orientalism and postcolonialism, since they have historically been racialized, ghettoized, primitivized, colonized, othered, and rooted in the Orient while also being depicted within fine arts as cosmopolitan generally, and European specifically. The processes of fragmentation and othering are also constantly under scrutiny in Jewish social processes given to schism and, especially, bifurcation (for example, in the essays in the present volume, the opposition of Zionism to Orthodoxy, or Hebrew to Yiddish). These processes are therefore not only viewed as a binary of Jew in relation to non-Jew, but also within Jewish social structures themselves— for example, Jewish perceptions of Mizrachi Jews (Hebrew *mizraḥi* meaning 'eastern', and by extension Jews from Arab countries), of ultra-Orthodox Jews known as *ḥaredim* (from the Hebrew *ḥaredi* meaning God-fearing), of Beta Israel (from the Hebrew *beit yisra'el*, house of Israel), and of Jews of Ethiopian origin, also socially constructed, often pejoratively, as Falasha (from the term meaning 'strangers' or 'exiles' used by non-Jewish Ethiopians) and *ḥabashim* (from the Hebrew *Ḥabash*, meaning Ethiopia). Even within the Jewish self, there is often a dialogue reported between public and private persona, past and present, tradition and modernity. Thus, the Jewish subject is often cast in psychological terms of 'double consciousness' in flux: citizen and Jew, public and private, ancient and modern, religious and secular.

Following postcolonialism, the ever-present consciousness of diaspora, movement, emancipation, frontier, and homeland in Jewish thought relates to the postmodern awareness in cultural studies of globalization and transnationalism as it crosses the boundaries of European–American nationalism. One of the issues within transnationalism—that cultural exchange and creolization can trouble politicized ideas of racial or cultural purity within the nation-state—is very much part of the Jewish historical experience. A social phenomenon within this deep historical experience related to diaspora is an ironic social immediacy, perhaps driven by a legacy of removals, for the discourse of heritage is often about a few generations rather than a tall family tree rooted deep in the soil of the nation-state. Cultural practice and synchronic social relations, relating children to their parents rather than to ancestors, characterizes much of the presentation of Jewish cultural studies.

In the context of this social immediacy, as many Jews pursue the Jewish subject as scholars of Jewish cultural studies, there is frequently a critical or reformist involvement in, and editorializing—some may even say *chutzpah*—about the conditions they observe. Perhaps this comes from the Jewish ethic of *tikun olam* ('repairing the world'), in which learning results in action for improving social welfare. Or it is a postmodern, counter-disciplinary move to craft research in terms of cultural criticism. Thus, the cultural politics of antisemitism, Zionism, self-hate, marginalization, invisibility, assimilation, Orthodoxy, intermarriage, genocide, hegemony, and capitalism are never far from the surface. Since the identity of Jewishness is often open to interpretation, a related discourse of Jewish cultural studies is on the authenticity of cultural practice and disputed claims to heritage, whether it is among the Lemba and Igbo groups in sub-Saharan Africa or the so-called crypto-Jews of the American Southwest. This discourse is also evident in the evaluation of Jewish revival, revitalization, and renaissance, constantly claimed throughout modern experience, whether set in the context of Lubavitch hasidism with its 'Mitzvah Mobiles' (drawing in Jews to put on *tefilin*) and their Chabad houses (outreach centres aimed at college-aged youth) or the contemporary klezmer music revival discussed in relation to the early twentieth-century Jewish 'national renaissance' in Germany.

For Jewish Studies, Jewish cultural studies helps to contemporize and contextualize Jewish experience. It provides an angularity characteristic of a wide-ranging approach to culture, because it gets beyond the literal content of sacred texts to their symbolic, performed meanings as they are constructed and communicated in everyday and ritual practice or mediated by cultural expressions, from speech to film. Whether as the people of the printed book or the oral joke, Jews have a long and diverse history of cultural expression, although much of it is still in need of recovery (for example the records of displaced persons camps, or DP camps, as they are known, featured in this volume) and the discovery of emerging patterns (for example new ritual uses of red string, also investigated below). Socially, Jewish cultural studies enquires not only into the many forms of Jewish communities across the globe, but also into the frames of mind and identities that individuals encounter for themselves and temporarily create (distinctive discourse with your 'Jewish friends', the yeshiva environment, or the Jewish summer camp, for example). Jewish cultural studies can also inform the expansion of the Jewish subject in Jewish studies by taking into account what non-Jews do with it, how they represent it, and even how they identify with or reject it.

Theoretically, Jewish cultural studies invites many angles of vision to arrive at a holistic picture of culture. But it is worth pointing out some prevalent sources of keywords and perspectives in its interpretative practices. I would first place in the field the big tent of communication. An organizing principle of concepts of communication is that culture arises from the interaction of individuals who construct symbolic systems communicated through expressions and mediated by social structures and contexts. With the emphasis on symbolic systems, analysts are concerned with the ways in which meaning is *encoded*, that is, embedded by the creator or performer, *mediated* by the means of communication (whether speech, ritual, film, or concert), and *decoded* by audiences (Hall 1992). In this approach, one can discern multiple 'readings' by participants in the cultural scene: these can be dominant (in accordance with the intentions of the creators or larger society), oppositional (contrary to the creators' or society's intentions), or negotiated (selected meanings from both dominant and oppositional readings). The point is that, rather than viewing culture as 'superorganic', an inherited, stable force dictating behaviour beyond the control of individuals, communication theory implies that culture is constructed by participants with strategic, instrumental goals in various situations. Culture is therefore what many cultural studies proponents call 'dynamic': it acts and reacts in relation to various forces present in a social scene. Indeed, in this view, culture is communication.

Complementary to the Jewish philological and hermeneutic tradition, I would argue, is the emphasis in communication theory on rhetoric and discourse. The key signifiers—whether in words, images, or things—used to encapsulate a position or people and persuade others through repeated or ritualized messages indicate broader concepts of culture. Often packed into expressions recognized because they draw attention to themselves as keywords or icons, the signifiers relate to a complex web of associations, referred to as the 'signified' meaning. As discourse, signified meanings are often contested and negotiated among participants, indicating the heterogeneous nature of society and the emergent character of culture. Whereas the classic Jewish philological interpretation would trace the history of a word's use, especially relating it to its original forms and subsequent variations, communication approaches call for scrutiny of a word *in use*, or its socially situated expression. The assumption is not made that someone Jewish always speaks or acts Jewish; instead, reference may be made to the cultural 'register' or 'performance' in which participants strategically enact a kind of communication that is appropriate to the immediate context (Kapchan 2003; Nicolaisen 2006). To get deeper into the underlying structures of everyday life, contributors to this volume may also refer to *praxis*, or cultural practice meaning behavioural patterns—in other words, the way a community expects things to be done (Bronner 1988).

In Jewish historiography, in addition to philological interpretation, there has also been an attraction to sociological and psychological explanation that has carried over to Jewish cultural studies. Using Freud's psychoanalysis as an analytical springboard or point of departure, many contemporary critics find embedded in the expressions people produce symbols that project often repressed or disturbing feelings and desires. These feelings and desires can be said to be externalized or 'projected'. According to this view, the frame of play or performance for many expressions allows outlets or 'fictive planes' for the coping mechanism of projection in which anxieties and ambiguities are dealt with. Although in a clinical context this theory is applied to individuals, in Jewish cultural studies the cognitive patterns drawn from readings of fictive planes are discerned in social groups. Informed by the lessons of cultural relativism and cross-cultural work by folklorists and anthropologists, psychoanalytically oriented researchers are careful to situate their symbolic interpretations within a particular culture or scene rather than universalizing meaning (Kirshenblatt-Gimblett 1975).

The roots of the related concept of 'projective inversion' come from Freud's 1911 paper 'Psycho-Analytic Notes Upon an Autobiographical Account of a Case of Paranoia', in which he posited that the repression of 'I hate him' becomes transposed to 'He hates me' (Dundes 1987: 36–7). Alan Dundes, frequently applying psychoanalytic theory to Jewish cultural subjects, has argued that the label 'projective inversion' is more appropriate than 'transposition', since desires are not only externalized but also inverted. Freud's projection, in a Dundesian perspective, can be interpreted as the symbolization of 'I hate him' in slurs or stories in which the object of hate is victimized. Dundes defines projective inversion this way: 'a psychological process in which A accuses B of carrying out an action which A really wishes to carry out him or herself' (1991: 353). Dundes distinguishes this kind of transposition from the transference of feelings onto an external object, which he calls projection. Dundes's projection is a way of dealing with anxieties or pent-up emotions, and involves disguising the object in the external expression. Dundes especially discusses examples of projection in jokes, myths, and rituals, for example 'Jewish American Princess' jokes (expressing unease over the independence of women generally, symbolized in the stereotype of the self-centred Jewish daughter), and the Creation myth in 'Genesis' (the appropriation of female procreative abilities in origin narratives of the male creation of the world) (Dundes 1987, 1997).

An example of Dundes's application of the Freudian concept of projection, for example, is the representation of Jewish murder in the 'blood libel' legend, which by implication provides a source of European antisemitism (Dundes 1991). In the legend, Jews kill a Christian child to furnish blood for their rites (Thompson 1975: motif V361). The story has been recognized as one of the most persistent antisemitic narratives among European Christians since the twelfth century. The legend is frequently recounted as a true event, in spite of its inherent incredibility and the fact that consumption of blood by humans is forbidden in Jewish law (Genesis 9: 4, Leviticus 3: 17 and 17: 12). Dundes purports to solve this puzzle of the story not jibing with the facts, and especially its coincidence around the Easter/Passover season, by pointing out in the narrative the *projection* of guilt onto another group and the *projective inversion* of Christians committing murder. As he explains,

For the commission of an aggressively cannibalistic act, participants in the Eucharist would normally feel guilt, but so far as I am aware, no one has ever suggested that a Catholic should ever feel any guilt for partaking of the Host. Where is the guilt for such an act displaced? I submit it is projected wholesale to another group, an ideal group for scapegoating. By means of this projective inversion, it is not we Christians who are guilty of murdering an individual in order to use his blood for ritual religious purposes (the Eucharist), but rather it is you Jews who are guilty of murdering an individual in order to use his or her blood for ritual religious purposes, making matzah. The fact that Jesus was Jewish makes the projective inversion all the more appropriate. It is a perfect transformation: Instead of Christians killing a Jew, we have Jews killing a Christian! (Dundes 1991: 354)

This example highlights the psychological interest in explaining the thinking behind apparently irrational antisemitic prejudice towards Jews by non-Jews. Psychoanalytical approaches have also been applied to ideas of 'self-hate' by Jews and to the cognitive processes involved in maintaining ethnic difference under pressures to assimilate or from being surrounded by hostile groups (an example in the present volume of such an approach is Elly Teman's discussion of the symbolism of red string in modern Israel). If irrational hate draws psychological enquiry, so too does puzzling love, or even philosemitism, in the representation of Jews in romantic and revival movements, as Jascha Nemtsov investigates here in his study of the discovery of Jewish folk music in Germany in the early twentieth century.

Many students of culture describe cultural expressions as performances of social structure rather than of repressed anxieties, in an interpretative concept of 'socioanalysis'. Intellectually, reverence (as well as citation) is often given to anthropologist Clifford Geertz's *Interpretation of Cultures* (1973) and his concept of 'thick description' in an 'interpretive theory of culture' which often hinges on events serving to enact and reinforce hierarchies and roles within a social structure. Representing interpretation through the analogy of a patient being diagnosed, he was particularly concerned that interpretation would not be predictive in the manner of psychoanalysis. Instead, it would anticipate a specific situation. His interpretation gave special attention to 'the meaning particular social actions have for the actors whose actions they are, and stating, as explicitly as we can manage, what the knowledge thus attained demonstrates about the society in which it is found and, beyond that, about social life as such' (Geertz 1973: 27). Geertz's 'interpretation' referred also to his background in literary study, because he conceived of actions as 'texts' that could be read differently by various observers, as well as by the participants in a cultural scene. Therefore the possibility exists—is even expected—of different, even simultaneous, meanings. The significance of this multivocal reading is that it offers a way to assess the sources of conflict within a society by examining the oppositional meanings of the same events or texts.

Dualistic terms spin off of the importance placed on the relationship of participants in a cultural scene to the meanings they construct and perceive. One is the distinction between 'esoteric' and 'exoteric' that will be encountered in several essays in this volume. Esoteric lore refers to texts that are told by members of a group about itself, whereas exoteric lore identifies narratives told about a group by outsiders (Jansen 1965). Thus, the blood libel legend told at Easter/Passover time is often presented as exoteric lore by Christians about Jews, while it may be argued that the legend of the prophet Elijah enacted at the Passover seder is an example of esoteric lore. One might also, as Dundes points out, see conflicting symbolic readings of matzah, between the socially constructed perception of it as corporeal following the Christian experience of the Communion host and the Jewish construction of it as experiential with reference to the narrative of Exodus. A related distinction is the linguistic one between 'etic' (from 'phonetic') and 'emic' (from 'phonemic') categories (Dundes 1962). Socioanalysis often looks for native categorization of expressions that are called 'emic' and refers therefore to the way that participants in a culture name and order their shared knowledge, while 'etic' approaches are those used by analysts to organize their material (Ben-Amos 1976; Bronner 2005: 31–41). *Chutzpah* can be called a native category for a type of behaviour that fits into an ethical order, but, as we have seen, judges have etically defined it as legal 'argot', and thereby given it a distinct meaning.

Despite the synchronic or ethnographic orientation of Jewish cultural studies drawing on the legacy of Jewish folkloristics and anthropology, a historicism adapted from Jewish studies is apparent. One can occasionally find a comparative project to relate contemporary practices to sources of customs in the ancient period revealed in biblical and talmudic sources. Yet Jewish cultural studies characteristically does not assume a causal link to religious precept and looks to evaluate the different functions of similar expressions across time and space. In other words, similar content does not translate into similar meanings, and that is why expressions are contextualized in localized cultural practices and social interactions.

Jewish historical periodization, organized by pivotal events and intellectual movements, informs ideas of social change in Jewish cultural studies. Moving backwards from the present, cultural processes are set in time against the backdrop of the emancipation of Soviet Jews, the founding of the State of Israel, the 'destruction' of the Holocaust and subsequent re-diasporization, the great wave of immigration from eastern Europe to the Americas, the eighteenth-century movements of the Haskalah (the Jewish Enlightenment) and hasidism, the expulsions from Spain and England, the Crusades and antisemitic agitation, the talmudic or rabbinical period, and the destruction of the Second Temple, among others. This periodization establishes processes of trauma, resistance, and resettlement that run through much of historical criticism and affect the Jewish preoccupation with questions of expression, identity, and representation as functions of diaspora and homeland, traditionalism and modernism, piety and secularism in Jewish consciousness and experience.

Part of the challenge, or *chutzpah*, of Jewish cultural studies is to craft a post-diaspora, as well as postmodern, angle by which to approach Jewish consciousness and experience (Aviv and Shneer 2005). This perspective focuses on the arrival of Jews and their cultures metaphorically and literally. Instead of recovering cultural practices that *came from* somewhere—with origins in central and eastern Europe, Spain and North Africa, ancient Israel, or the Bible—it considers the locations and situations they *go to*. This cultural enquiry is not just into the city or country in which Jews form intergenerational bonds, but the ritual space they create in the home and hall. Jenna Weissman Joselit, for example, has made a case for a 'singular' American Jewish culture unique in the Jewish world because of the ways in which the home, bar and bat mitzvah, and wedding were 'invented' and configured to suit the split away from a synagogue-centred life and to a locus in the Jewish family (Joselit 1994). An implication of this post-diaspora angle is getting away from the correlation of urban or ghetto density with a culture of poverty to foster an individualistic, dispersed Jewish culture. Instead of seeing the Jewish arrival in suburbia and holiday resorts as the end of Jewish history, Jewish cultural studies maps the sites and occasions where brands of Jewishness are organized, packaged, and consumed (Bronner 2001; Brown 2002; Diamond 2000; Moore 1994). Defying stereotype, small-town and rural Jews in modern industrial societies are being discovered as having a long history and distinctive cultures (Weiner 2006; Weissbach 2005). As the New Europe, New South Africa, and New Asia announce breaks from the past, Jewish cultural positions within these reconfigurations beckon scholarly scrutiny (Gilman and Shain 1999; Webber 1994). The places where Jews are from are incorporated into a Jewish imagination, part of heritage tourism, that has drawn the analytical 'etic' term 'virtually Jewish' from Ruth Gruber (Gruber 2002; see also Kugelmass and Shandler 1989; Shandler and Wenger 1997).

The challenge offered by Jewish cultural studies as a sensibility embedded in *chutzpah* can be discerned in the contents of this volume. Elly Teman opens Part I on 'expression' by acknowledging biblical references to the 'red string' evident at sites throughout Israel, but, taking a new angle, considers its function in the political context of, and psychological response to, terrorism in the region. Sergey Kravtsov follows by examining the way that a synagogue in eastern Europe is at the centre of memories maintained in narratives variously told by Jews and non-Jews. Miriam Isaacs, in 'Yiddish in the Aftermath', looks at the experience of survivors in DP camps as a cultural anomaly, when Yiddish language and literature formed the basis for cultural continuity in the aftermath of the Holocaust. Rounding out the section on expression is a look by Jascha Nemtsov at the way that Jewish folk music was presented as high art to concert audiences in early twentieth-century Germany and how that strategy was criticized.

Part II is devoted to questions of identity, opening with Joachim Schlör's enquiry into the meaning of objects inventoried and packed as emigrants prepared to leave Germany for Palestine after Hitler came to power. While Schlör uncovers documents from the period, Hannah Kliger, Bea Hollander-Goldfein, and Emilie Passow record survivors' stories told today not just as witness accounts, but as narratives expressing life stories that become integrated into family identities and are retold by succeeding generations. Contextualizing dilemmas of Jewish identity in post-perestroika Russia, Olga Gershenson offers close readings of films that enact conflicting attitudes towards Jews by Russians. She is drawn to questions arising from the unusual spate of films with Jewish themes in contemporary Russia, even as many areas there have been emptied of the Jewish presence. She suggests that the films reveal attitudes not easily discernible in the news—a simultaneous repulsion and attraction to Jews that bespeaks the dilemma of Russian–Jewish relations. Ted Merwin closes the section on identity-formation by viewing the correspondence of commercial establishments such as the American delicatessen to 'sacred spaces' for the establishment of secular Jewish identities and asks what happens when those spaces dissolve.

The final section, on representation, opens with stories collected by Ilana Rosen in Israel from Jews who lived in Carpatho-Russia. They craft plots out of the conflicts between hasidism and Zionism among Jewish community members in their pre-Holocaust homes to confront life in a new land. Their representation of community characters expresses a lingering ambivalence that needs to be resolved to form a new identity. The female character in French literature draws a critical reading from Judith Lewin, who contextualizes the material in French society and draws comparisons with other national literatures in suggesting that this character informed popular perceptions of the Jewish woman apart from men. Focusing more on popular culture are Holly Pearse and Mikel Koven, who respectively decode the often disguised Jewishness of modern radio comedy and Hollywood film.

The *chutzpah* of these studies is not in their effrontery, but in their Jewish sensibility, and sensitivity to meanings generated by cultural expressions. The contributors probe the Jewish subject for what it reveals of culture generally and the Jew specifically. Coming from a variety of learned backgrounds—literature, art, music, folklore, anthropology, religion, sociology, and media studies—they mobilize Jewish cultural studies to open common ground where the Jewish subject can receive the analytical attention it deserves.

References

ABRAMSON, GLENDA, ed. 1989. *The Blackwell Companion to Jewish Culture: From the Eighteenth Century to the Present*. Oxford.

ANDERSON, SUSAN HELLER. 1990 'Chronicle'. *New York Times* (19 Sept.). <http://nytimes.com>, accessed 26 Nov. 2006.

AUSUBEL, NATHAN. 1964. *The Book of Jewish Knowledge*. New York.

AVIV, CARYN, and DAVID SHNEER. 2005. *New Jews: The End of the Jewish Diaspora*. New York.

BARTOV, OMER. 2005. *The 'Jew' in Cinema*. Bloomington, Ind.

BEN-AMOS, DAN. 1976. 'Analytical Categories and Ethnic Genres'. In Dan Ben-Amos, ed., *Folklore Genres*, pp. 215–42. Austin, Tex.

BENNETT, TONY, LAWRENCE GROSSBERG, and MEAGHAN MORRIS. 2005. *New Keywords: A Revised Vocabulary of Culture and Society*. Malden, Mass.

BIAL, HENRY. 2005. *Acting Jewish: Negotiating Ethnicity on the American Stage and Screen*. Ann Arbor, Mich.

BIALE, DAVID. 2002. 'Preface: Toward a Cultural History of the Jews'. In David Biale, ed., *Cultures of the Jews: A New History*, pp. xvii–xxxiii. New York.

—— MICHAEL GALCHINSKY, and SUSANNAH HESCHEL, eds. 1998. *Insider/Outsider: American Jews and Multiculturalism*. Berkeley, Calif.

BOYARIN, DANIEL, and JONATHAN BOYARIN. 1997. 'Introduction/So What's New?'. In Jonathan Boyarin and Daniel Boyarin, eds, *Jews and Other Differences: The New Cultural Studies*, pp. vii–xxii. Minneapolis.

BOYARIN, JONATHAN. 1996. *Thinking in Jewish*. Chicago.

BRODKIN, KAREN. 1999. *How Jews Became White Folks and What That Says About Race in America*. New Brunswick, NJ.

BRONNER, SIMON J. 1988. 'Art, Performance, and Praxis: The Rhetoric of Contemporary Folklore Studies'. *Western Folklore*, 47: 75–101.

—— 1998. *Following Tradition: Folklore in the Discourse of American Culture*. Logan, Ut.

—— 2001. 'From *Landsmanshaften* to *Vinkln*: Mediating Community Among Yiddish Speakers in America'. *Jewish History*, 15: 131–48.

—— 2005. 'Menfolk'. In Simon J. Bronner, ed., *Manly Traditions: The Folk Roots of American Masculinities*, pp. 1–60. Bloomington, Ind.

BROWN, PHIL, ed. 2002. *In the Catskills: A Century of the Jewish Experience in 'The Mountains'*. New York.

CD BABY. 1991. Advertisement for Jackie Mason, 'Brand New', CD Baby website, <www.cdbaby.com/cd/jackiemason2>, accessed 7 Dec. 2006.

CHESLER, PHYLLIS. 2005. *The New Anti-Semitism: The Current Crisis and What We Must Do About It*. San Francisco.

DERSHOWITZ, ALAN M. 1991. *Chutzpah*. Boston, Mass.

—— 1997. *The Vanishing American Jew: In Search of Jewish Identity for the Next Century*. Boston, Mass.

DIAMOND, ETAN. 2000. *And I Will Dwell in their Midst: Orthodox Jews in Suburbia.* Chapel Hill, NC.

DU GAY, PAUL, JESSICA EVANS, and PETER REDMAN, eds. 2000. *Identity: A Reader.* London.

DUNDES, ALAN. 1962. 'From Etic to Emic Units in the Structural Study of Folktales'. *Journal of American Folklore*, 75: 95–105.

—— 1987. 'The Psychoanalytic Study of Folklore'. In Alan Dundes, *Parsing Through Customs: Essays by a Freudian Folklorist*, pp. 3–46. Madison, Wis.

—— 1991. 'The Ritual Murder or Blood Libel Legend: A Study of Anti-Semitic Victimization through Projective Inversion'. In Alan Dundes, ed., *The Blood Libel Legend: A Casebook in Anti-Semitic Folklore*, pp. 336–78. Madison, Wis.

—— 1997. 'Madness in Method Plus a Plea for Projective Inversion in Myth'. In Laurie L. Patton and Wendy Doniger, eds, *Myth and Method*, pp. 147–59. Charlottesville, Va.

—— and GALIT HASAN-ROKEM, eds. 1986. *The Wandering Jew: Essays in the Interpretations of a Christian Legend*. Bloomington, Ind.

DURING, SIMON, ed. 1999. *The Cultural Studies Reader*, 2nd edn. New York.

Encyclopaedia Judaica, 16 vols. 1972. Jerusalem.

FEINTUCH, BURT, ed. 2003. *Eight Words for the Study of Expressive Culture*. Urbana, Ill.

FINKELSTEIN, NORMAN G. 2005. *Beyond Chutzpah: On the Misuse of Anti-Semitism and the Abuse of History*. Berkeley, Calif.

GEERTZ, CLIFFORD. 1973. 'Thick Description: Toward an Interpretive Theory of Culture'. In Clifford Geertz, *The Interpretation of Cultures*, pp. 3–32. New York.

GILMAN, SANDER L. 1991. *The Jew's Body*. New York.

—— 1996. *Smart Jews: The Construction of the Image of Jewish Superior Intelligence*. Lincoln, Nebr.

—— 1999. 'The Frontier as a Model for Jewish History'. In Sander L. Gilman and Milton Shain, eds, *Jewries at the Frontier: Accommodation, Identity, Conflict*, pp. 1–28. Urbana, Ill.

—— 2003. *Jewish Frontiers: Essays on Bodies, Histories, and Identities*. New York.

—— 2006. *Multiculturalism and the Jews*. New York.

—— and MILTON SHAIN, eds. 1999. *Jewries at the Frontier: Accommodation, Identity, Conflict*. Urbana, Ill.

GOLDBERG, HARVEY E. 2003. *Jewish Passages: Cycles of Jewish Life*. Berkeley, Calif.

GOLDSTEIN, ERIC L. 2006. *The Price of Whiteness: Jews, Race, and American Identity*. Princeton, NJ.

GOODMAN, MARTIN, ed. 2002. *The Oxford Handbook of Jewish Studies*. Oxford.

GROSSBERG, LAWRENCE, CARY NELSON, and PAULA TREICHLER, eds. 1992. *Cultural Studies*. New York.

GRUBER, RUTH ELLEN. 2002. *Virtually Jewish: Reinventing Jewish Culture in Europe*. Berkeley, Calif.

HALL, STUART, 1992. 'Encoding/Decoding'. In Stuart Hall, Dorothy Hobson, Andrew Lowe, and Paul Willis, eds, *Culture, Media, Language: Working Papers in Cultural Stud-*

ies, 1972–1979, pp. 128–38. London.

—— ed. 1997. *Representation: Cultural Representations and Signifying Practices*. London.

—— and PAUL DU GAY, eds. 1996. *Questions of Cultural Identity*. London.

HOBERMAN, J., and JEFFREY SHANDLER. 2003. *Entertaining America: Jews, Movies, and Broadcasting*. New York.

JANSEN, WILLIAM HUGH. 1965. 'The Esoteric-Exoteric Factor in Folklore'. In Alan Dundes, ed., *The Study of Folklore*, pp. 43–52. Englewood Cliffs, NJ.

JOSELIT, JENNA WEISSMAN. 1994. *The Wonders of America: Reinventing Jewish Culture, 1880–1950*. New York.

KALMAR, IVAN DAVIDSON, and DEREK J. PENSLAR. 2005. 'Orientalism and the Jews: An Introduction'. In Ivan Davidson Kalmar and Derek J. Penslar, eds, *Orientalism and the Jews*, pp. xiii–xl. Waltham, Mass.

KAPCHAN, DEBORAH A. 2003. 'Performance'. In Burt Feintuch, ed., *Eight Words for the Study of Expressive Culture*, pp. 121–45. Urbana, Ill.

KIRSHENBLATT-GIMBLETT, BARBARA. 1975. 'A Parable in Context: A Social Interactional Analysis of Storytelling Performance'. In Dan Ben-Amos and Kenneth S. Goldstein, eds, *Folklore: Performance and Communication*, pp. 105–30. The Hague.

—— 1998. *Destination Culture: Tourism, Museums, and Heritage*. Berkeley, Calif.

KLEEBLATT, NORMAN L., ed. 1996. *Too Jewish? Challenging Traditional Identities*. New York.

KOZINSKI, ALEX, and EUGENE VOLOKH. 1993. 'Lawsuit, Shmawsuit'. *Yale Law Journal*, 103: 463–7.

KUGELMASS, JACK, and JEFFREY SHANDLER. 1989. *Going Home: How American Jews Invent the Old World*. New York.

MARX, BILL. 2005. 'Theater: Queens of Chutzpah'. WBUR website. <http://www.wbur.org>, accessed 27 Nov. 2006.

MASON, JACKIE. 1990. *How To Talk Jewish*. New York.

MOORE, DEBORAH DASH. 1994. *To the Golden Cities: Pursuing the American Jewish Dream in Miami and L.A.* New York.

NELSON, CARY, PAULA A. TREICHLER, and LAWRENCE GROSSBERG. 1992. 'Cultural Studies: An Introduction'. In Lawrence Grossberg, Cary Nelson, and Paula Treichler, eds, *Cultural Studies*, pp. 1–16. New York.

NICOLAISEN, W. F. H. 2006. 'Cultural Register'. In Simon J. Bronner, ed., *Encyclopedia of American Folklife*, 4 vols: i. 255–6. Armonk, NY.

ROSTEN, LEO. 1982. *Hooray for Yiddish! A Book about English*. New York.

ROTH, CECIL, ed. 1959. *The Standard Jewish Encyclopedia*. Garden City, NY.

SACHS, ANGELI, and EDWARD VAN VOOLEN, eds. 2004. *Jewish Identity in Contemporary Architecture*. Amsterdam.

SAID, EDWARD. 1994 [1979]. *Orientalism*, 25th anniversary edn. New York.

SHANDLER, JEFFREY, and BETH S. WENGER, eds. 1997. *Encounters with the 'Holy Land': Place, Past and Future in American Jewish Culture*. Philadelphia.

SHANK, BARRY. 2001. 'Culture and Cultural Studies'. In George T. Kurian, Miles Orvell,

Johnnella E. Butler, and Jay Mechling, eds, *Encyclopedia of American Studies*, pp. 443–8. New York.

SINGER, ISAAC BASHEVIS. 1983. *The Penitent*. New York.

STEINMETZ, SOL. 1986. *Yiddish and English: A Century of Yiddish in America*. University, Ala.

THOMPSON, STITH. 1975. *Motif-Index of Folk-Literature*, rev. and enlarged edn, 6 vols. Bloomington, Ind.

WEBBER, JONATHAN, ed. 1994. *Jewish Identities in the New Europe*. London.

WEBER, BRUCE E. 2004. 'Alan King, Comic with Chutzpah, Dies at 76'. *New York Times* online (9 May). <www.nytimes.com>, accessed 27 Nov. 2006.

WEINER, DEBORAH R. 2006. *Coalfield Jews: An Appalachian History*. Urbana, Ill.

WEISSBACH, LEE SHAI. 2005. *Jewish Life in Small-Town America: A History*. New Haven, Conn.

WILLIAMS, RAYMOND. 1983. *Keywords: A Vocabulary of Culture and Society*, rev. edn. New York.

WISSE, RUTH R. 1992. *If I Am Not For Myself . . . The Liberal Betrayal of the Jews*. New York.

YOUNG, JAMES E. 2000. *At Memory's Edge: After-Images of the Holocaust in Contemporary Art and Architecture*. New Haven, Conn.

ZANGWILL, ISRAEL. 1938 [1892]. *Children of the Ghetto: A Study of a Peculiar People*. Philadelphia.

ZURAWIK, DAVID. 2003. *The Jews of Prime Time*. Hanover, NH.

PART I

Expression

ONE

The Red String: The Cultural History of a Jewish Folk Symbol

ELLY TEMAN

AT THE CENTRAL BUS STATION in Jerusalem, an elderly Russian woman sits on a chair on the sidewalk in front of the station. She chants 'Mazel dir, Zai Gezunt' to passers-by, wishing them good luck and good health in Yiddish as she rattles a tin can in one hand and holds a fistful of red strings in the other. Some are plain and some are adorned with small blue heart-shaped evil-eye pendants. In exchange for a few coins in her cup she hands out a string and blesses the patron.

This kind of scene has been especially evident as a nationwide phenomenon in Israel since the late 1980s. In the first decade of the twenty-first century the number of male and female red string sellers standing on popular street corners in Jerusalem, and at cemeteries all over the country, is continuing to grow. They are especially prevalent at holy sites, such as Rachel's tomb in Bethlehem, where people can be observed measuring the tomb with red string. At the Western Wall and in the Jewish quarter of Jerusalem's Old City, up to half a dozen red string sellers can be seen plying their trade at any one time. In fact, they have spread to every corner of the country, from the Baba Sali's grave in the south to the many tombs of Jewish 'saints' in the north, where secular and religious Israelis make pilgrimages. Rabbis, such as the late venerated Yitzhak Kaduri, hand out red strings to those in need of protection against the evil eye or of medical or psychological help, especially for pain, infertility, or sickness.

Those given the string are told that it will protect them from the evil eye and bring them good luck. They are instructed to wear it until it falls off, and warned against taking it off on purpose, which would break their luck. The phenomenon seems to cut across all sections of the Jewish population in Israel. The attentive observer can spot the string on men and women of various ages, some in the traditional clothes of the strictly observant and some in jeans, some dark-skinned and some pale. Within Israeli cities, the string can be seen on the wrists of hospital doctors, schoolchildren at play, and bus drivers. It is worn by fashionably dressed teenagers on Tel Aviv's hip Shenkin Street, and young Israeli celebrities appear wearing it in newspaper photos and on television. The string is carried close to the body, usually tied around the wrist. Over the last decade I have met Jewish Israelis, both men and women, and of both Ashkenazi and Sephardi descent, who have tied it around an injured limb or placed it under their pillow. I have also met women who tie the thread around their waist and men who carry it in their shirt pocket or wallet.[1]

At the Western Wall an elderly Georgian-born woman named Sarah is such a familiar institution that red string sellers all over the country know of her. Sarah claims to have established her 'post' passing out red strings here with the unification of Jerusalem soon after the Six Day War in 1967. For a small donation in her cup she ties a red string to the patron's hand, blessing them in the names of the matriarchs and patriarchs with health, wealth, and fertility. She then adds a general blessing for all of the children of Israel, Israeli soldiers in particular.

When I interviewed her in 1997 Sarah told me that 'not just anyone can bless the red string'. According to her, only those 'who pray for the good of the people of Israel' are privileged with this role. She explained that she travels every few weeks to Rachel's tomb with a ball of red string, which she uses to encircle the grave seven times, begging Rachel for mercy: 'I ask her to prevent tears and to return her children to their borders.' Sarah's petition to the matriarch originates in the biblical verse Jeremiah 31: 14, in which the prophet visualizes Rachel weeping for her children as they are taken into exile. In what has become a theme of Zionist ideology, God comforts Rachel and tells her that her children will return to their land (Sered 1989). By way of association, the connection of Sarah's own name with another biblical matriarch supports her self-ascribed role as guardian of the people of Israel.

As our interview progressed, Sarah began to cry, relaying her sadness over the helicopter crash that had occurred a few weeks before near the border with Lebanon, in which seventy-three young Israeli combat soldiers had been killed. The accident had become a collective tragedy mourned by the entire nation, adding to the pattern of national mourning that the terrorist bombings of 1994–6 had created. Responding to Sarah with my own feelings of national solidarity, I concurred: 'It is so sad that you pray to return Rachel's children to their borders, but those boys will never return now from the border.' Sarah took both of my hands in her own, saying: 'Now let us pray together for the soldiers. We shall pray for all of the people of Israel. You repeat after me: *Mizmor ledavid . . .*'.

I repeated the verses of Sarah's prayer, line by line. Afterwards, she told me of her feeling of responsibility over the fate of those soldiers and of all of the people of Israel: 'I pray for the people of Israel. I will not praise myself, but I pray day and night for the wholeness of the land of Israel' (referring to territorial debates over Israel's geographical boundaries). Looking into Sarah's face, I asked her, 'Do you pray for the non-Jews as well?' Sarah answered with heightened emotion, pointing to the Temple Mount above us: 'I don't give red strings to non-Jews [*goyim*]. I bless the people of Israel, and may the golden calf ruin the others! We shall build another temple there!'

On my way home, the conversation with Sarah occupied my thoughts: the seventy-three soldiers, the terrorist bombings, the 1967 borders, the territorial wholeness of the land, and her prayers for the welfare of the children of Israel. It occurred to me that it might not be by chance that the red string had become so popular from the late 1980s onwards, reaching a climax during the 1990s. This was a period in Israel's history when Islamic extremist organizations were increasingly carrying out terror attacks on Israeli civilian targets, leading to a feeling of social uncertainty and vulnerability among all Israelis. This mood was amplified by the military conflict between Israelis and Palestinians living in Israeli-controlled territories in the aftermath of the first Palestinian uprising (the Intifada) in 1987.[2] In addition, the national sense of vulnerability was influenced by the failure of the Oslo peace talks between Israel and the PLO in 1995, and by the growing division within Israeli society on the issue of Israel's sovereignty over the territories that had been conquered in the 1967 war.

Could these political concerns, and a social reality marked by collective uncertainty, political threat to individual lives and to the nation's existence, and a preoccupation with the boundaries and borders of the land be connected to the heightened popularity of the red string?

Jewish Folklore Under Conditions of Stress

Folklorist Alan Dundes (1980) has suggested that, because folklore is an outlet through which anxieties can be vented, there is always new folklore being created in response to new anxieties. He explains the way in which this works in terms of 'folkloric projection'—a psychological mechanism in which an individual ascribes feelings or qualities of their own to a source in the external world. Even though the people who produce the folklore rarely recognize its projective nature consciously, the folklore still provides a socially sanctioned outlet for individuals to express psychological needs that cannot otherwise be articulated.

In the context of Jewish folklore studies, Israeli folklorist Aliza Shenhar (2000) identifies the creation of a particular type of folklore in response to the personal anxiety and social tension produced by war and military strife. She discusses this new folklore in relation to a realistic modern legend, about the long-awaited release from captivity of an Israeli air force pilot captured in the line of duty, which circulated among Jewish Israelis in 1982 during a period when Israeli society was internally divided by the first Lebanon war. Referring to this type of folklore as 'folklore under conditions of stress', Shenhar suggests that it is produced 'when reality becomes such that it can no longer be tolerated psychologically and socially' (2000: 114). She contends that this particular type of folklore has a healing effect on society by symbolically solving 'the conflict between wish and reality'; it reduces tension, creates a state of greater calm and ease, and serves as an instrument for group mental stabilization (2000: 106). In this sense, folklore under conditions of stress can be said to generate a type of 'symbolic closure' that reinstates a sense of collective order to the social body (Hertzfeld 1986). Shenhar suggests that in Israel the production of folklore under conditions of stress provides a 'group illusion' of unity when the collective is internally divided; unity has historically served as a staple in the Zionist ideology upon which the state was founded, and it is by creating the illusion of unity that the nation attempts to fortify its boundaries when they are threatened (Shenhar 2000: 104).

The question arises, however, as to why a particular folkloric expression comes into being in a particular group during times of stress. What symbolic properties enable this expression to heal the social body? And are there particular folkloric expressions that surface during times of strife among a given group repeatedly throughout that group's history? Dundes (1980) suggests taking a psychoanalytic semiotic approach to uncovering the way a particular folk symbol is used by a particular group in different historically related contexts. It is through this strategy, he proposes, that cultural studies can uncover the underlying cognitive reasons for a particular symbol's appearance at a particular moment in time. One may also discover a consistency in the use of that symbol within a culturally relative system of symbols that is not consciously recognized or articulated by the people who use it.

Here I will respond to Dundes's call by undertaking a symbolist analysis of the popularity of the red string in Jewish Israeli society. I begin by outlining the symbolic properties of the red string from a psychoanalytic semiotic perspective, suggesting that the string symbolically functions as a boundary marker between life and death. Next, I trace the history of the red string in Jewish tradition back to the Bible, where it consistently appears in situations of threatened personal and social boundaries and of symbolic closure. Finally, I suggest that the symbolic properties of the string, combined with its historic function in the Bible, contributed to its popularity in Jewish Israeli society throughout the tumultuous 1990s.

From the example of the red string, I expand on Shenhar's (2000) argument that folklore is produced under conditions of stress by adding that a particular group may call upon a set of images in the folkloric expressions it creates at such times. I am thus suggesting an approach to Jewish culture that pays close attention to the social context in which the folklore is created, to its psychologically embedded ramifications, and to the meanings attached to variations of it within significant Jewish texts.

The data presented in this essay are primarily based on textual references to red string in ancient Israel, in various periods among other world cultures, and in contemporary Israeli popular culture between 1996 and 2006. Its methodological framework is based on texts culled from folkloric records, ethnographies, websites, encyclopedias, newspaper articles, and academic journal articles that mention red string. I collected any mention of red, scarlet, or crimson thread, cord, or ribbon and classified it according to its culture of origin. I ran specific searches in Jewish and Hebrew-language sources for the Yiddish *roite bendel*, the

Hebrew *ḥut adom* and *serokh adom*, and the Hebrew *ḥut hashani* and the related term *ḥut hasikra*.[3]

Unravelling the Symbolism of the Red Thread

From a psychoanalytic semiotic perspective, the popularity of the red string in Jewish Israeli society may be viewed as a local version of a folk practice that has been widely documented in the historical and ethnographic records of many cultures. Indeed, the symbolic use of red thread, ribbon, cord, flannel, and wool is so widespread in world folklore that mentions of it can be found in Greek and Egyptian mythology,[4] ancient Chinese legends[5] and contemporary Chinese death rituals,[6] soul-loss rituals of the Lolo tribe of western China,[7] folk customs from England, Wales, and Ireland[8] as well as the United States,[9] Indian wedding traditions,[10] childbirth rituals in Romania[11] and Greece,[12] and Jewish fertility rituals.[13] There are also contemporary appearances of red string in such diverse cultures as those of the Dominican Republic[14] and Italy,[15] and even among American celebrities in Hollywood.[16]

The folk belief that the red string brings good luck and wards off harm is not particular to Jews or to Jewish Israeli society either. In nearly all of its local variations, it is believed to protect people, animals,[17] and houses[18] against the evil eye,[19] witchcraft,[20] illness,[21] the malignant powers of the dead (Trachtenberg 1970), and other forms of demonic attack (Opie and Tatem 1996; Simpson and Roud 2000). As my discussion so far has suggested, the symbolic behavioural use of the string is also strikingly similar among nearly all of its local variants, tied as it usually is to a part of the body or to the window or door of the home, and used as it is in many cultures during major life-cycle events (Trachtenberg 1970: 47). It is also commonly believed that the thread should be knotted a particular number of times, the most beneficial number of knots often believed to be seven (Hooper 1936).

What has made a simple piece of red string such a popular curative and protective symbol across such a wide range of cultures? I suggest that the string brings into play three important symbolic elements: redness, the act of tying and knotting, and the circular form it assumes when tied.

Redness

First, both the palliative and protective properties of the string partially derive from its redness. Red, crimson, and scarlet are all defined in most English dictionaries as 'the color of blood, or of a tint resembling that color' (*Webster's Dictionary* 1913; see also Wordnet 2003). Likewise, in Hebrew, the word for blood (*dam*) shares the same root as the word for man (*adam*) and for earth (*adamah*), suggesting a close linguistic connection between blood and life (Klein 1987).[22] The redness of blood links the colour to the living body—as opposed to the pale, bloodless corpse—and endows it with the boundary function of distinguishing the living from the dead. This makes 'red' a symbol of life that is traditionally associated with vitality, good luck, health, and joy (Beck 1969). These positive, life-giving qualities credit the colour with curative and protective powers, making red almost universally regarded as anti-demonic (Trachtenberg 1970: 133) and popularizing the use of red stones, particularly coral and ruby, as amulets.[23]

Conversely, the boundary function of the colour also stems from its modern symbolic association with danger and death, which does not seem to have folkloric roots (Weitman 1973). In this capacity, red connotes bloodshed, courage, military valour, readiness for sacrifice, revolt, and death (Simpson and Roud 2000). Weitman (1973: 349–50) and Wreschner (1980) note the extraordinary degree of consensus among contemporary cultures about the meaning of the colour, which is similarly used by the vast majority of modern nations in the symbolism of their national flags.[24] This life/death boundary quality of blood may also be gendered: as a feminine symbol, blood is associated with bleeding while creating life in the context of the reproductive life-cycle of menstruation, defloration, and childbirth. As a male symbol, blood is deliberately shed by men in rites associated with death, such as blood sacrifice and war (Bronner 2004; Ehrenreich 1997).

Knotting, Tying, Measuring, and Symbolic Closure

In addition to its colour, the knotting and tying of the thread has symbolic significance. Knotting thread is believed in many cultures to cure disease, bind evil spirits, and prevent or cause harm (Hooper 1936).[25] To tie a knot is to make something fast, to bind, hold, hinder or stop, while untying a knot signifies loosening, setting free, and releasing (Leach 1972: 586). Binding can shut out evil and force evildoers into inaction, transmute chaos into cosmos, and transform conflict into law and order (Cooper 1978: 92).[26] In terms of folkloristic projection, the tying and knotting of the string might be understood as a 'literalization of metaphor' (Dundes 1980: 45) in which societal disorder achieves 'symbolic closure' on a metaphorical level through the literal tying of a material string.

String is a powerful symbol when connected to any colour: rituals involving white (Weingrod 1990), green (Ben Ami 1984), black (Patai 1983), and blue (Jacobs and Jacobs 1958) threads have been noted by ethnographers. Rituals involving magic threads in locations as geographically varied as Egypt, the Shetlands, Russia, Rome, and Armenia share the basic principle that ritually binding and loosening thread can restrict or enable (Hooper 1936). This is the basis of many folk beliefs involving the tying and loosening of knots during weddings,[27] childbirth, and death.[28] Patai (1983) has recorded multiple fertility rites using threads of unspecified colour that share the idea that the body is an open receptacle and that tying the string 'locks' its openings, sealing it off from external attack and securing the pregnancy or life-essence within the skin boundary.[29] It is this same logic which might explain why contemporary red string wearers are warned not to intentionally break the string, lest the securely contained life-essence within its boundary be lost.

One of the best-known ritual acts involving string is 'magic measuring': the circumscription and containment of disease by measuring the body's physical limits (Hand 1980: 112).[30] In his study of magic measuring in a Grecian village, Hertzfeld (1986) suggests that measuring enables 'symbolic closure', restoring the body to a socially recognized wholeness and restoring the patient's environment to a unified order. Hertzfeld claims that such closure gives the individual the feeling of self-management and control by defining the boundaries of the body and metonymically sealing off its orifices. Bilu (1978) also views the ritual act of magic measuring by Moroccan folk healers in Israel as binding the body, and Hand (1980), summarizing Elfriede Grabner's work on the subject, observes that 'one's measure is a mysterious extension of oneself' (Hand 1980: 115).

Binding shares the duality of redness in its ability to represent the giving or taking of life. On the one hand, binding can seal off the body from attack and retain its life force within the bounded area, exposing it to chaos when the knot is loosened. Conversely, binding can choke the body and its abilities, and its potential is only enabled through loosening.[31]

Circular Boundaries

The third symbolic element that endows the red string with its curative and protective functions is the circle. As an ancient and universal magic symbol, the circle created by binding the red string around a body part enables a barrier to be erected between the encircled private domain and the external, public domain, providing a visible rampart that excludes demonic forces from entering the enclosed area. Nothing can trespass from the public to the private area, and the home or body that has been thus encircled becomes a private, forbidden precinct (Trachtenberg 1970).

Trachtenberg (1970) gives multiple examples of the magical application of circles: diviners and magicians during the Middle Ages would inscribe a circle upon the ground before beginning to evoke spirits;[32] protective circles were ritually drawn around the bed of those thought to be especially susceptible to attack, such as invalids or new mothers; in another rite of encircling, a diseased body part is encircled with an object, or a person or site is circumambulated while charms are recited.[33] What is common to all ritual applications of circles is the magical act of banning evil spirits to the circle's periphery.

Tying Folk Theories to the Red String

The three symbolic elements of red string elaborated above collectively endow it with the ability to signify crucial boundary distinctions between public and private, life and death, disorder and order, outside and inside. However, to understand how this symbolism is translated into practice, it is important to delineate the basic folk theories that inform the string's ritual use.

In his discussion of Jewish rituals of the Middle Ages, Trachtenberg (1970: 157) outlines three general categories of folk theories relating to warding off spirits: spirits are driven away or rendered powerless by a guard, such as an amulet, being posted over the threatened individual; spirits are deceived by disguising the intended victim, or by pretending that the situation is other than it actually is; spirits are bribed with gifts meant to placate them—in this case a substitute for the victim, in the form of a symbolic sacrifice, is offered to appease the powers that have decreed the impending bad luck.[34] Trachtenberg explains that, in the Jewish case, these methods can be employed together or separately.

Viewing red string rituals, symbolism, and functions through the lens of these folk theories can help illuminate the string's power as a traditional symbol across cultures. First, the circular form of the thread when tied to the body can be understood to guard the wearer by creating a symbolic private, impermeable arena within the circle. This marks the body as a protected, encompassed space, the string serving as the dividing line between the sacred and the profane. Second, the act of tying and knotting the string metonymically seals off the boundaries of the body, binding the life-liquid of the wearer within and keeping it from seeping out. This observation would concur with Dundes's (1981) theory of the evil eye, in which he claims that all evil-eye beliefs are based on the notion that life is liquid and death is dry. Dundes suggests that, because folk beliefs express the idea that a limited amount of liquid exists in the world, one person's increase of life-liquid is another person's relative loss of life. Having analysed hundreds of evil-eye practices, he articulated a theory that these rituals internationally employ liquid-related symbols such as fish, water, blood, and wine because the evil eye is believed to 'dry out' the victim's life-liquid. Dundes's theory may explain the nearly universal function of the red string in warding off the evil eye. Accordingly, it can be argued that, as a blood symbol, it symbolically covers the wearer in protective liquid, and that its binding symbolism seals the wearer's life-liquid within the body's boundaries. This may also explain the prohibition in Israel that purposely breaking the thread constitutes breaking your luck (Teman 1997).

Finally, the redness of the thread makes it serve as a symbolic substitute for the blood or life-maintaining liquid of the wearer, or may serve to 'fool' the evil eye into 'drinking' the external, visual blood mark instead of the life-blood of the wearer. Trachtenberg (1970: 135) relates the magical significance of the colour red directly to the idea that red amulets or red wine often substitute for the blood of sacrifice in folk rituals. Likewise, Murgoci (1981) interprets the use of red threads in Romanian folklore as a substitute for the blood of sacrifice, suggesting that the red strings tied to the threshold of the home may symbolize the blood mark on the doorpost during the tenth plague in the book of Exodus. One may thus conclude that by visually marking the body or home with surrogate sacrificial blood, the red string symbolically appeases the malignant force and saves the wearer as a symbolic sacrifice.

Together, these symbolic properties endow the thread with a boundary function, dividing the bound/enclosed/private/living/sealed/protected body from the public/dangerous/chaotic/external surroundings. The thread emerges as a symbolic sacrificial substitute for wearers, while binding and symbolically closing them off from demonic attack.

The Biblical Scarlet Thread

Having established the string's general symbolism and folk logic, I will now turn to the local, Jewish historical traditions associated with red string by tracing its appearances in the Hebrew Bible. It is through this culturally specific perspective that I wish to argue that the semiotic properties of the red string are not a sufficient explanation for its popularity in Jewish Israeli society in the post-Intifada period. Instead, I will suggest that the particular symbolic functions of red string within the biblical text contribute to its eminent suitability as a material expression of folklore under contemporary conditions of stress in this local context.

The Bible distinguishes between red (*adom*) and a particular shade of the colour referred to as *shani*. *Adom* describes such things as the newborn Esau's complexion (Genesis 25: 25), Jacob's porridge of lentils (Genesis 25: 30), Judah's eyes (Genesis 49: 12), the drunkard's eyes (Proverbs 23: 29), the sacrificial red heifer (Numbers 19: 2), a horse (Zechariah 1: 8), wine (Proverbs 23: 31), blood (2 Kings 3: 22), and bloodshed (Zechariah 6: 2). Conversely, *shani* describes a thread dyed red, crimson, or scarlet[35] that appears tied to Zerah's wrist (Genesis 38: 28–30) and to Rahab's window (Joshua 2: 18, 6: 25), worn by the rich (2 Samuel 1: 24; Proverbs 31: 21), and used in the textiles of the *mishkan* and later of the Temple (Exodus 25: 4, 26: 1, 31, 36, and 28: 5, 6, 8, 15) and in purification rituals (Leviticus 14: 4, 6, 51; Numbers 19: 6).

The crimson-dyed wool described in the Bible was produced by a mountain worm (Tosefta *Menaḥot* 9: 16), called *Coccus ilicis* by naturalists, *Kermes biblicus* by scholars, and *kermez* in Arabic, which infests oak trees in eastern Mediterranean countries (Easton 1897). In the Bible this small insect is referred to as 'crimson worm' (*tola'at shani*) because dye can be produced by squeezing the eggs from the females during the early spring, when they resemble red peas (Rashi on Isaiah 1: 18). Scarlet and crimson were thought in biblical times to be the most permanent dyes, not easily washed out (Easton 1897), and the fact that red was indelible (Jeremiah 4: 30) is alluded to in the figurative use of scarlet to signify sin at Isaiah 1: 18.

I suggest that, by following the scarlet thread (*ḥut hashani*) through the Old Testament, we can uncover two basic principles linked to its appearances: it is connected to situations of birthright, bloodshed, sacrifice, atonement, redemption, and protection, and it appears in situations where boundaries must be asserted between sacred and profane, forsaken and redeemed, those destined to live and those destined to die, those who belong to the Israelite nation and those who do not.

The first appearance of the red string in the Hebrew Bible is in the form of the *ḥut hashani* in the tale of Tamar and Judah in Genesis. Tamar is condemned to death by Judah, who then spares her life after realizing that he is the father of her child. As Tamar gives birth to her twin sons, one of the unborn infants extends his arm through the neck of the womb. The midwife grasps his outstretched hand and ties a scarlet thread around his wrist, announcing, 'This one came out first' (Genesis 38: 28). The twin then draws back his arm as his brother pushes through the birth canal to be born before him. The episode ends as Judah names the twins after their roles in the birth, naming one twin 'Perez' for his pushiness in 'breaking through' the womb before his brother, and the other 'Zerah'—literally 'shining'—for the brightness of the scarlet thread bound to his wrist. Zakovitch and Shinan (1992) comment that the name Perez is linguistically linked to the rupturing of a fence or a gate in biblical terminology, an observation that would accord with the symbolic closure effected by tying the string to counteract the disruption.

Several issues coexist within this account of the scarlet thread, including those of birthright, boundaries, and the reaffirmation of order out of chaos. In the issue of birthright, the scarlet thread serves as a mark on Zerah's wrist of the rights promised to him as the true firstborn son. The thread emerges as a sign, marked upon the body, of the rightful order of events, setting right this unsuccessful attempt of an unborn infant to 'push through' and break the 'natural' order of birth.[36] Second, the scarlet colour of the thread and its appearance following the sparing of Tamar's life only a few verses earlier, reminds us of a later account where a red mark appears at the hour when the Jews are redeemed from the threat of extinction. This incident, of course, is the marking of the doorposts with the blood of the sacrificial lamb during the tenth plague (Exodus 12: 6–7).[37] Taking into account the biblical appearances of red string so far, one can begin to formulate a symbolic pattern that connects it to the sparing of lives in face of danger, to reasserting the rightful order of events in face of upheaval, and to the protection of promises made to the one who is marked with the string.

The *ḥut hashani* next appears in the account of the harlot Rahab in the book of Joshua. Before Joshua and his army conquer Jericho, he sends two spies into the city. When the presence of the spies is discovered, Rahab hides them in her home, endangering herself and her family (Joshua 2: 1–11). In return for her kindness the two men promise to spare the lives of all those gathered within her home, and instruct her to hang a scarlet thread from her window so that they will recognize her house (Joshua 2: 18–21). One week later Joshua and his men begin their attack on Jericho by circling its perimeter for seven days until the walls collapse.

Before burning the city, the inhabitants of the home with the scarlet thread bound in the window are rescued (Joshua 6: 22–3); Rahab and her family become the sole survivors of the attack. Connecting this account with the story of Tamar and the twins, the red thread appears again, not only as a mark of a promise—whether Zerah's birthright or Rahab's salvation—but, as in Tamar's case, as a mark of protection from certain death.

Biblical scholars have identified additional parallels between these two accounts, linking the thread tied to Rahab's window directly to that tied to Zerah's wrist because they are both called by the same Hebrew name, *ḥut hashani*. Zakovitch (1975) has pointed out that *Midrash tadshe* 21 associates Rahab with Tamar because the scarlet thread is mentioned in both stories, while in *Midrash hagadol*, 'Hayei sarah', 94, the two spies hidden by Rahab are depicted as descendants of Tamar. Louis Ginzberg (1964: 36–7) extended this idea, suggesting that the spies Rahab saved were Tamar's sons Zerah and Perez and that the thread that they gave her was the very one that the midwife had tied to Zerah's wrist. Support for this idea can be found in an ancient Hebrew text quoted by Margalioth: 'There are those who say that Peretz and Zerah were those from whom she asked for a sign. Zerah said to her, "Take this crimson thread which was bound to me when I was in my mother's waters and tie it to your window"' (Margalioth 1975: 371).

Zakovitch and Shinan (1992) summarize the interpretations of the scarlet thread by various biblical scholars in their comprehensive study of Genesis 38. They conclude that the string is considered, first, a sign or memento of a promise made—the promise of the birthright to Zerah and the promise of protection to Rahab. Second, it is a sign of salvation and redemption that rescued Rahab from her city's destruction and saved Tamar and her sons from the death sentence laid upon them by Judah. Third, it is a sign of repentance, in that both Tamar and Rahab were forgiven for their sins of harlotry and the God of Israel blessed them with fertility, honouring them as the founders of the dynasty of King David.[38]

Interestingly, the scarlet thread serves in a similar capacity as a mark of protection in Proverbs 31: 21, in which the 'virtuous woman' is not fearful of any harm to her household, because its members are protected with scarlet wool: 'She has no fear of snow for her entire household is clothed in scarlet [wool].' Rabbinic commentators explain the woman of valour's lack of fear by associating her with Rahab, who does not fear the death of her family because of the scarlet thread bound to her window.

Whether marking the doorposts of the ancient Israelites, the wrist of a newborn, or the window of a harlot, blood, or its image in the scarlet thread, remains a mark of protection and promise, and represents a public pronouncement of faith in God and his promises to the individual and to the nation as a whole. Visible to all, it emerges as a sign of self-definition and loyalty, and defines the boundary between private and public, differentiating the redeemed from the damned and the protected from the condemned.

The colour *shani* appears in several biblical passages as a mark of beauty, status, and holiness. Scarlet robes were worn by the rich and the privileged (2 Samuel 1: 24; Proverbs 31: 21; Jeremiah 4: 30), and by the high priest of the Temple (2 Chronicles 2: 7, 14, 3: 14). Scarlet threads were woven into all of the high priest's sacred vestments, including the ephod (Exodus 39: 2–3), the ephod's attached belt (Exodus 39: 5), the breastplate (Exodus 39: 8), and the pomegranates on the skirt of the robe (Exodus 39: 24). These garments, which were designed to elevate Aaron and his descendants to the high level of sanctity required of those who serve before God in the Temple, themselves possess a certain holiness, powerful enough to sanctify all those who merely come into contact with them (Ezekiel 44: 19) and to atone for the sins of Israel in the Yom Kippur rite (BT *Zev.* 88*b*). Moreover, scarlet threads were one of the prescribed ingredients used to create the furnishings of the Holy Temple, including the curtains for the enclosure (Exodus 38: 18), the packing-cloths for sacred use (Exodus 39: 1), the ten large tapestries of the tabernacle (Exodus 26: 1), the cloth partition dividing the sanctuary from the ark (Exodus 26: 33), and the drapery for the tent's entrance (Exodus 36: 37). It is possible to interpret the inclusion of scarlet thread in the handful of symbolic ingredients that God instructs Moses to use in these ritual furnishings as reinforcing the idea that it was of special symbolic significance.[39]

The symbolism of the thread as a boundary marker can also be seen in the use of red string in items in the Temple that delineated the boundaries between holiness and impurity. Such items include the belt of the high priest, which was wrapped around his hips to separate his upper from his lower organs; the *parokhet* that separated the sanctuary from the ark; and the partition between the Temple's outer and inner sanctuaries. Similarly, it is said that during the forty years that Simon the Righteous was high priest, a crimson thread associated with his person always turned white when he entered the Temple's innermost Holy of Holies. Both the Jerusalem and the Babylonian Talmud note that this thread ceased to change colour from 30 CE until the destruction of the Temple in 70 CE.[40] In these capacities the thread marks the increasingly strong boundaries between the impure and the pure, beginning with the body of the high priest, moving out to the sanctuary, and then to the ark itself. In later writing we learn of the ritual sacrifice at the Temple and that a red thread, the *ḥut hasikra*, was bound around the centre of the altar to perform the boundary function of separating the kosher blood that appeared above the thread and the non-kosher blood below (JT *Midot* 3: 81; *Zevaḥim* 10).

As a marker of the boundaries of the pure and impure, it is not surprising that we find the scarlet thread as an integral element in the Temple's ritual purification rites, which distinguish between those who can and those who cannot enter the Israelite camp, where elaborate codes of purity governed behaviour.[41] *Parashat Tazria* details the procedure for purifying a person or a house from leprosy using two birds, scarlet thread, and a mixture of cedar wood, hyssop, and spring water (Leviticus 14: 1–7). The ashes of the red heifer, used in Temple purification rites, were also ritually mixed with cedar wood, a low-growing grass, spring water, and a crimson thread (Numbers 19: 2). The author of the apocryphal writings of Barnabas (late first or early second century CE) mentions that during the ritual of the red heifer on the Mount of Olives, the priests tied a crimson thread to a nearby tree.

Finally, as outlined in the Mishnah (*Yoma* 4: 2, 6: 8) and Maimonides' *Mishneh torah* ('Hilkhot avodat yom hakipurim'), red string was used in the Yom Kippur scapegoat ritual, in which the high priest would place his hands on the scapegoat, confessing the sins of Israel and asking for atonement. He tied a red string between the horns of the scapegoat and another strip around the neck of a second goat to indicate where it should be slaughtered. He then killed the goat with the red string around its neck as a sin offering and sent the first scapegoat out through the eastern gate into the wilderness. There, the person in charge of the scapegoat tied a heavy rock to the red thread strung between his horns and shoved the animal over the edge of a cliff. During this ritual a portion of the red wool was tied to the door of the sanctuary, and each year on Yom Kippur when the scapegoat reached the wilderness this wool turned white, as if to signify that the atonement of another Yom Kippur was acceptable to the Lord.

In sum, I have suggested that the red string evokes a particular set of culturally specific symbolic associations within the Old Testament. The two basic principles common to its appearances are that it is linked to situations of birthright, bloodshed, sacrifice, atonement, redemption and protection, and that it appears in situations where boundaries must be asserted between sacred and profane, forsaken and redeemed, those destined to live and those judged deserving of death, those who belong to the Israelite nation and those who do not. In the remainder of this essay I will argue that the principles outlined above can help to explain the popularity of the red string in the contemporary political context of modern Israel.

Red Threads in Contemporary Jewish Israeli Life and Imagination

In contemporary Israeli life, red strings are used in rituals tied to the Jewish Israeli life-cycle. To encourage conception, string is tied around the waist of a barren woman—sometimes this is done by the woman's rabbi, at others by her mother after the barren woman has immersed herself in the *mikveh* (Teman 1997). Red string is also used in new rituals established in the context of the Jewish feminist movement. For instance, at female-centred new moon ceremonies, women are sometimes instructed to bring a red string to the group meeting, bless it, and wind it around the members of the group who are pregnant. This is done while reading *midrashim* about Rachel (Adelman 1986: 49; Land 1989). Red strings are also tied on male children during the eight days between birth and circumcision (Teman 1997). This emphasis on the string's presence before the circumcision rite accords with Trachtenberg's (1970: 170) assertion that these eight days were believed to be especially dangerous for infants, and that the need for a heightened guard over the baby immediately subsided after circumcision. This idea leads Trachtenberg to suggest that circumcision may be considered a protective rite in itself, and accords with Hoffman's (1996) interpretation of circumcision as a protective rite that guards the child with a blood mark signifying symbolic sacrifice. In connecting this idea with the red string, it is significant that the string is believed necessary only during the first eight days of the male child's life, when it is replaced by another blood mark.

The final rite involving red string particular to the Jewish Israeli life-cycle is the custom of a mother tying the string to her son's right wrist, either before he enters the military or on her first visit to his military base during his initial training. This rite is also performed in some families by the soldier's grandmother or grandfather (Teman 1997). In the context of the sociopolitical reality of contemporary Israeli life, the blood and tying symbolism of the red string takes on particular connotations in relation to combat soldiers and bloodshed. During the years when the fear of losing one's son at the Lebanese border was a particularly stark reality, the practice of tying the soldier son with a red string allowed mothers to feel some semblance of control over his fate, binding him to her and simultaneously sealing him off from harm.

This is the idea behind a popular Israeli play called *Red Ribbons*, written by playwright Smadar Amitai in 1997. Amitai explained that she had written the drama 'almost as an exorcism, to ward off the evil eye as it were, because of my fears for my son who'll enlist in two years. It's very personal, yes, and very antiwar, especially the unnecessary wars we seem to fight with our eyes open' (Kaye 1997). The production focuses on a father who goes to visit his son's grave in a military cemetery six months after the young man has been killed in action. The father agonizes over his own less than heroic conduct in the Yom Kippur War, and the possibility that had his son known how his father had behaved then he might not have been killed. Amitai explains that 'the red ribbon of the play is more a thread really, a metaphor perhaps for blood flowing, and certainly for the amulets that are pushed on mourners at cemetery gates and which were peddled by Shas [a political party] during their election campaign'. The themes of blood, boundaries, order and chaos, and the need for protection against the evil eye became amplified at both local and national levels during the 1990s, when Amitai's play was produced. While many Israelis do consciously believe that actions they undertake individually are crucial to the very survival of the state, particularly combat soldiering for men and motherhood for women (Ben-Ari, Rosenhek, and Maman 2001), I refer here to the unarticulated, symbolic connection between the individual and collective bodies.

The idea that the individual body and the social body, or body politic, symbolic-ally mirror one another has been explored by Mary Douglas (2003) and further developed by Nancy Scheper-Hughes and Margaret Lock (1987). It is significant that Douglas explains this mirroring effect with an example drawn from ancient Jewry, claiming that the Jews have always been a threatened society, and that the threatened boundaries of their body politic have been mirrored in their pre-occupation with the integrity, unity, and purity of the physical body.

In the matter of blood, it is important to realize that, while the history of Israel's wars has linked blood to the idea of bloodshed, the post-Intifada period has linked it to terrorist attacks in the national imagination. In particular, blood has become linked to rupture—as in the blood of victims of the attacks spattered on sidewalks—and to national solidarity, as in the routine call to donate to the national blood banks in the aftermath of an attack (Seeman 1997; Weiss 2002). These particular associations are explored in Don Seeman's (1997) study of the Ethiopian blood case, in which Ethiopian immigrants to Israel reacted to the public disclosure that their blood was being discarded by the national blood bank with protests that evoked this dual blood symbolism. Some carried placards on which the slogan 'One People, One Blood' was written, using the blood metaphor to protest at the Israeli politics of who is included and who is excluded from the social body. Others lamented the idea that their blood was 'good enough' to be spilt with that of the rest of the nation in terror attacks, but not good enough to be included in the national blood bank. Through this case we can see how the connotations of blood as a mark of inclusion and exclusion, rupture and national solidarity, made it a popular public symbol to draw upon during those years.[42]

In addition to the particular meanings of blood, the symbolic closure related to tying became interconnected at this time with a movement towards closure at a national and collective level. From this perspective, it is readily apparent how the random danger of the malignant evil eye can be quickly replaced by the fear of national and personal catastrophe in a dangerous political reality. I would argue that the red string reached the height of its popularity at this time as it gave Israelis a sense of control over both the personal and the national.

In her book *The Chosen Body* Meira Weiss (2002) uncovers an underlying preoccupation in Jewish Israeli society with bodily wholeness and symbolic closure. In a chapter on the media treatment of terrorist bombings in 1994–6, Weiss outlines the ritualistic pattern in the aftermath of a bombing as a three-part sequence: the description of the chaos and rupture immediately following an attack, followed by images of regrouping, and then recovery (closure). Weiss argues that the images of the symbolic closure of the collectivity are used routinely by the media to realign the three ruptured bodies: those of individuals, that of the nation, and that of the land itself, and suggests that they serve to impose order and designate the boundaries between Israel and her Arab neighbours.

In the light of Weiss's findings, it is not surprising that in the post-Intifada period, in which the boundaries of individual bodies and of the nation as a whole were continually threatened by the attack of malignant forces that were all too real, one could find the spontaneous application of the red string as a metaphor for blood flowing in the wake of terror attacks. On a metaphorical level, the linguistic use of the scarlet thread underwent a significant transformation, from a metaphor of continuity, in such expressions as 'the scarlet thread running through' a series of ideas or events, to a metaphor of blood flowing: a 'red thread of blood'. For example, journalist David Landau of the Jewish Telegraphic Agency entitled his annual 'Year in Review' of 1995 'the Year of the Red Thread', claiming that '*Chut hashani*, a Biblical metaphor used in Modern Hebrew to mean a theme, literally means a red thread. For the past year, the *chut hashani* running through Israeli society has been an all too literal red thread: a blood soaked motif of terror attacks that has left dozens of arbitrary victims dead or maimed' (Landau 1995).

Interestingly, Weiss told me in a conversation about my research in 2002 that during her fieldwork at the National Forensic Institute, where the bodies of the victims of terror attacks are brought to be identified, many of the doctors and other staff wore red strings on their wrists. This strengthens the idea that the string performs a boundary function and provides symbolic closure, for it is the duty of the institute to identify and reassemble the ruptured pieces of the personal—and, by extension, the national—body. Moreover, it is significant that the strings are worn by the staff, for as she shows in her ethnography of the institute, much of their work focuses on maintaining symbolic boundaries between different sectors of Israeli society.

In addition, television reports on the progress of those injured in the attacks often included a brief close-up of the wrist of the patient, and a passing statement as to their belief that the red string may help them heal faster and protect them from further misfortune. This association of the red string with victims of terror was similarly embraced by the Kids for Kids organization, whose campaign to raise money for and awareness of the needs of Jewish children injured in terror attacks in Israel has focused on red string since 1998. The organization's website claims that it has 'taken the red string as an appropriate symbol to remember that in Israel there are thousands of children who are victims of Arab terrorism'. It sells the red strings to Jewish American youth to 'wear in solidarity with young victims of terror in Israel' (Kids for Kids 1998–2003). In this way the red string yet again signifies the boundaries of the collective, yet also extends beyond Israel, encompassing American Jewry and signifying its solidarity with the Jews of Israel against terrorism. A similar movement which promoted solidarity between Jews in Israel and in the United States appeared in the 1990s, with the routine wearing of red strings by participants in youth missions to Israel, both during their trip and upon their return home as a reminder of their connection with Israel. The Jerusalem curriculum of the March of the Living International (2002), an educational programme taking Jewish teenagers from around the world first to Poland and then to Israel, mentions the red strings worn by the marchers, as does the report on participants' experiences in the Birthright Israel project (Kelner et al. 2000).[43] The red string also appears in the online diaries and poetry written by participants in these programmes.[44]

The resurgence of the red string shows signs of continuing into the twenty-first century. Indeed, when I visited the Western Wall in July 2003 I asked several red string sellers there if there had been a change in their clientele in the past seven years. Three of them told me that there has been a steady rise in the number of customers since the millennium, forcing them to travel to Rachel's tomb more frequently and to purchase more string. A shop owner in Jerusalem's Old City, where many of the sellers buy the balls of string before they are blessed, confirmed that this was still happening during a conversation I had with him in December 2005, saying for example that 'it seems that they are coming to buy string from me every other day now'.

There are parallels between the spread of the red string ritual throughout the country and the heightened attention given to the boundaries of the Israeli nation-state around the turn of the century. Relating to public expressions in Israeli news media promoting the territorial wholeness of the Land of Israel, Weiss (2002) claims that the drive towards the wholeness of the individual body serves as a mirror of the embodiment of the land. The red string may illustrate this general pattern. Accordingly, the modern Jewish Israeli ritual use of the string was first documented in the day books of Rachel's tomb in Bethlehem during the 1930s, when it was primarily visited by those with fertility problems.[45] Seeming to disappear during the years when the tomb was under Jordanian jurisdiction, the ritual resurfaced when Israelis returned to the site following the Six Day War in 1967 (Sered 1989).

Susan Sered (1989) views the string as a fertility symbol particular to Rachel's tomb during the 1970s and early 1980s, an idea supported by both Eli Shiller (1977) and Zev Vilnai (1966), who note that it also appeared at the nearby grave of Huldah the prophetess on the Mount of Olives. Common to the tombs of Huldah and Rachel—other than their geographical proximity—is the fertility theme associated with Rachel overcoming barrenness (Genesis 30, 35) and the blessed fertility of Huldah's ancestress Rahab, whose dynasty produced King David.[46]

After the unification of Jerusalem in 1967, the red string began to appear at the Western Wall, and Sarah, the red string seller introduced at the start of this essay, claims to have begun her long station there then. In post-Oslo Israel, the red string became more associated with the Western Wall than with Rachel's tomb, as it became increasingly dangerous for Israelis to reach the tomb after it came under Palestinian jurisdiction. Moreover, the string's fertility theme became secondary, as its primary use changed to serving as a protective amulet.

Within the Israeli political and territorial context, Rachel's tomb took on the symbolic position of a guarded fortress on the border between Israel and the Palestinian Authority, evoking again the image in Jeremiah of Rachel weeping for her children as they are exiled and promising them that they will return to their land. This political association of the string is underscored by the fact that a political group called The Faithful of Rachel's Tomb now sells on its website red strings that have been blessed at the tomb in exchange for a donation to the group's political mission of upholding a Jewish presence at the tomb.

Through the 1990s, the red string found its way across the width and breadth of the country to nearly all the saints' graves in Israel, as if in an effort to geographically secure the territorial boundaries of the land. When I began my fieldwork on the string in 1997, I found red string sellers in cemeteries in Tel Aviv and its suburbs, at the Baba Sali's grave in Netivot; at Mount Meron where Rabbi Yohanan ben Zakai is buried; at Amoka where people pray to Rabbi Yonatan ben Uziel, and at the Western Wall. This spread of the red string may be interpreted as mirroring the concern over the boundaries of the nation at that time, when the concept of exchanging 'land for peace' was on the political agenda and the movement for securing the 'whole land of Israel' was prominent in the media. In this light, the movement of the red thread over the geographical area may be seen as the metonymic sealing off of the orifices of the nation's body. In this social context one might therefore conclude that, when Sarah the red string seller prays for the people of Israel and ties them with red strings, she is also symbolically marking the boundaries of the nation. The physical bodies of the 'children of Israel' then become mirrors of their 'body politic' (Scheper-Hughes and Lock 1987), symbolically marking the territorial boundaries of the land. Complying with the belief associated with the string that the wearer must not intentionally break it thus becomes an act of political significance.

I have argued that uncovering the culturally specific meanings ascribed to the red string in the Hebrew Bible can help to explain its popularity in contemporary Jewish Israeli life. In particular, I have suggested that the string appears in many cultures in an array of ritual contexts, and that these rituals draw upon the symbolism of the string's redness, the symbolic closure evoked when it is tied onto the body, and the magic circle it makes when tied. Moreover, I have suggested that the string is used across cultures as ritual protection against arbitrary harm, such as the evil eye, because its ritual use and its colour are linked to basic folkloric principles shared by many cultures.

However, beyond these general 'projective folkloristic' (Dundes 1980) qualities of the red string, I have posited that one can only account for its contemporary popularity in Jewish Israeli society by tying the practice to historic Jewish traditions and biblical images that might be beyond the awareness of participants, but are nonetheless embedded psychologically in the string's symbolic function. To make this argument I have suggested that in ancient Israel the red string was linked to particular biblical accounts of lives spared in face of danger and the reassertion of order out of chaos. I have also contended that the thread is connected to the theme of boundaries between the doomed and the redeemed, the sacred and the profane, those destined to live and those destined to die, and those who belong to the Israelite nation and those who do not. I have proposed that these culturally specific symbolic associations of the red string, together with its psychological ramifications, can answer the question of why this particular folk symbol has gained popularity as a form of 'folklore under conditions of stress' (Shenhar 2000) in the sociopolitical context of post-Intifada Israel.

The elements of blood and symbolic closure have carried particular politically related meanings during this period, and the red string, in line with its historic function in the Bible, has served on a collective level as a mark of the boundaries of the nation, who is included and who is excluded from the collective or social body, symbolic closure in the face of rupture, protection against personal and national catastrophe in a dangerous political reality, and even national solidarity. This metonymic effect of the red string is the result of the symbolic mirroring of the individual body and the body politic (Scheper-Hughes and Lock 1987). The symbolic closure on the collective level is therefore not dependent upon the specific personal reason for wearing the string. Thus, I end with the contention that it does not matter whether a contemporary Jewish Israeli wears the string to ward off the evil eye, to cure an illness, to promote fertility, to please their elderly grandmother who brought it home from a saint's grave, or because they want to be like Madonna, because the power of the symbol on a collective level is the same.

Notes

A version of this essay received the Raphael Patai Prize for best graduate student essay in Jewish Folklore and Ethnology in 2005. The prize is awarded annually by the Jewish Folklore and Ethnology Section of the American Folklore Society in conjunction with the Council of Anthropology of Jews and Judaism of the American Anthropological Association. Earlier versions of the essay were first written as seminar papers for courses taught by Hagar Salamon and Shalom Tsabar of the Folklore Department at Hebrew University. Special thanks to Professor Simon Bronner for his encouragement and helpful suggestions. I also appreciate comments towards improving the manuscript that I have received from Avi Shoshana, Chen Bram, Susan Sered, Harvey Goldberg, Eric Schulmiller, Eyal Ben-Ari, Meira Weiss, Susan Kahn, Naama Shay-Catrieli and Dov Noy. Finally, I would like to thank my parents, Rhisa and Nissan Teman, and my husband, Avi Solomon, for their unwavering support and advice.

1   One of the most interesting aspects of the red string phenomenon to emerge from my earlier study (see n. 3 below), and which continues to be expressed today in newspaper coverage of the red string, is that both Ashkenazim and Jews from Arab countries wear the

string, but that each group ascribes the practice to the other. Both groups told me that it was an oriental custom, whereas many of those from Arab countries, including their rabbis, told me that it was an Ashkenazi tradition. This aspect is beyond the scope of the present essay.

2 The first Intifada of Palestinians living in Israeli-controlled territories was characterized by civil demonstrations, riots, and terrorist attacks on Israeli civilian targets. Following the failure of the Oslo peace talks in 1995, the second Intifada broke out in 2000 and included the additional factor of organized guerrilla warfare by Palestinian Authority forces (Kaplan 2003: 269).

3 Although here I primarily take a historical approach to the cultural study of the red string, I also refer to an earlier study that I conducted on rituals and beliefs of contemporary Jewish Israelis regarding the string, in which I conducted thirty interviews with red string wearers and sellers (Teman 1997). Ten informants were sellers, four were rabbis, and the remainder were people who wore the string or had worn it in the past. I also conducted participant observation on the ritual preparation and selling of the string at holy sites across the country. The interviews, which lasted anywhere up to an hour, were structured, open-ended, and guided by a questionnaire I had developed referring to the origins, rituals, and magical qualities that informants ascribed to the red string. Briefly, data collected from the study included the following. I found that Jewish Israeli red string wearers believe that it protects them from evil and brings them good luck. They tie it to various parts of the body, most commonly the wrist. Informants gave a variety of reasons as to why it was more auspicious to tie the string to the left or right hand. Most had obtained the string from a holy site or believed that it had originally been blessed at one. One of the most essential ritual elements that informants associated with the string was that another person, preferably a rabbi or a female elder (such as a mother or grandmother) should tie it to them. All informants noted that, once tied, the string should not be deliberately broken or removed as this would break their luck.

4 Red threads are linked to divinities such as the 'god of boundaries' (Grimm RA. 182 and 809, cited in Grendon 1909) and the Egyptian divinity Hathor, who was 'adorned with strings of red thread' (Greene 1993: 497). In 1940s Egypt it was believed that red thread bound to a sore throat could cure it (Smith 1941).

5 The red thread as a sign of connecting people has gained momentum as a key metaphor in international adoption, where it is linked to a Chinese legend that when a child is born invisible red threads connect that child's soul to all the people whom it is fated to meet (Adoptshoppe 2000).

6 Gene Cooper (1998) has documented a funeral ceremony in Dongyang County, Zhejiang Province, in which one person carries a basket filled with loose red threads and paper; this is scattered along the way to the grave to demarcate the road for the mourners to find their way back home.

7 Among the Lolos the soul is supposed to leave the body in cases of chronic illness. A complicated ritual is then enacted in which the soul is called by name and besought to return. A red cord is then tied round the arm of the sick man to retain the soul; this cord is worn until it decays and drops off (Henry 1903).

8 The red thread has rich historical roots as a curing device in English, Welsh, and Irish folklore dating back to 1040 CE. Records from that time mention the use of a red thread bound

about the head to cure a headache, or wound about the neck to cure lunacy 'when the moon is on the wane'. In Ireland in 1887 red thread tied about the throat was said to cure whooping cough (Wilde 1887); in England in 1910 it was said to relieve a baby's teething pains when tied about the neck, while in 1954 a record states that it could cure a sore throat. According to John of Gaddesden, in 1314 a piece of scarlet cloth was even used to cure the king of England's son of smallpox. All these beliefs are recorded in Opie and Tatem 1996.

9   A large number of documents record the use of red threads in the US, especially to cure nosebleeds (see Simpson and Roud 2000): in Kansas, wearing a red string around the neck was believed to cure a nosebleed (Davenport 1898), and the same cure was recorded in Laharp, Illinois (Norlin 1918). In Detroit in the 1800s, tying a red thread around a child's neck was believed to prevent the mumps from 'falling' (Stekert 1970).

10   Gow (1901: 77) mentions a Hindu wedding tradition in India in which the bridegroom lays a red thread in the track on one wheel, a blue thread in the other, then recites a verse and drives over them.

11   The Serbs of Romania direct that a woman should wear a red thread tied around her middle finger during pregnancy, while in Macedonia it is believed that she should wear a twisted red and white thread around her neck. In eastern Europe, during childbirth the woman's body and the delivery room are both secured: in Bukovina, the midwife makes a red tassel and nails it over the door; in Moldavia she puts a needle with a red thread on the threshold; and in Macedonia she puts a twisted red and white thread over the door and a knife at the threshold (Murgoci 1981). In Romania and the surrounding areas mentioned above both mother and baby wear red ribbons or bows for many months following the birth. In the case of older babies the red bow is considered especially necessary when the baby leaves its own home. For further details of these beliefs see Murgoci 1981.

12   In Greece a mother still in childbed will tie a red ribbon around her arm (Jones 1981).

13   As far back as 1938 there are records of Jewish women encircling the tomb of the biblical Rachel with a red string and then wearing it around the neck or wrist to cure pain or infertility (Shiller 1977: 16; Vilnai 1966), or, in Israel since the 1980s, to relieve a protracted labour (Abramowitz 1992).

14   A group of American nurses studying the health beliefs of Dominicans found that in all the towns observed red strings were worn on the wrists of children to protect them from the evil eye (mal ojo) because 'there are evil spirits everywhere'. Another method of maintaining health by protecting against bad spirits was 'to take a thick or thin red string, burn it, and eat it' (Babington et al. 1999).

15   Pitrè (1981) notes that in his pre-1980s fieldwork in Italy he witnessed people tying red ribbons to their pipes, their spectacle cases, or the handles of their coffee pots, or even sewing them into the linings of their vests or jackets.

16   Made popular through the media, the string appeared in gossip columns as an accessory worn around the wrists of famous stars. The long list of celebrities who have worn the string includes Madonna, whose wrist has been adorned since 1997, and other famous followers of the Kabbalah Centre such as Roseanne Barr, Britney Spears, comedienne Sandra Bernhard, Marla Maples, Rosie O' Donnell, Dan Ackroyd, Mick Jagger, and Demi Moore (Addley 2001). Actress Winona Rider reportedly 'accessorized with the red string during her shoplifting trial' (Celebs on a String 2002); Sean 'Puffy' Combs and his Jewish

attorney wore them at the singer's murder trial (Leland 2001); Michael Jackson has worn one for several years as he has fought accusations of molesting children (Hyde 2003); Sharon Osbourne wore a red string while being interviewed by Barbara Walters about her battle with colon cancer (*Celebs on a String* 2002); Stella McCartney began wearing one after incurring a large loss for Gucci in her first year as a designer for the company (Lampert 2003); and singer Britney Spears began wearing a red string to help her recover from her emotional break-up with boyfriend Justin Timberlake (Farber 2003).

17   Red threads have also been documented in a wealth of cultures as a measure of protection for horses and cattle. Tied to the tail or a front leg of the cow, or hung from the forehead of a horse or woven into its tail, they were thought to protect grazing animals. Jones (1981) notes the Irish practice of weaving a red thread into a horse's tail where it cannot be seen but where its effectiveness will be great. Pitrè (1981) observed in Italian villages that horses, mules, and donkeys were decorated with red threads, and that some cab drivers had attached red threads to the headlamps of their carriages. Records from Aberdeen from 1851 give evidence of a common practice among housewives of tying a piece of red worsted thread around cows' tails to protect them from the evil eye as they grazed; a similar Scottish ritual of tying a red rag around a cow's front left leg served the same purpose (Opie and Tatem 1996). The Talmud even mentions crimson thread being hung on the forehead of a horse to protect it against the evil eye (Trachtenberg 1970: 133).

18   In order to protect the home and its inhabitants red threads are tied to apertures, such as windows or doorways. In Britain practices of this nature included winding a twig of the rowan tree with dozens of yards of red thread and placing it visibly in the window to keep witches away from the house (Opie and Tatem 1996). The belief in securing one's surroundings in order to metonymically protect one's family from demonic attack reaches a height in Italian folk practice where, Pitrè (1981) reports, red wool, braids, and kerchiefs can be spotted hanging in windows and tied to railings and gates. He further notes that he saw city dwellers attach red threads to the bell-pulls of gates or doors, to the small trees on their balconies, or to the potted plants on the stairs of their homes. He also observed peasants attaching red threads to trees, plants, and canes in their fields and orchards. Interestingly, the idea of protecting one's fields with red thread was also observed among the Pennsylvania Germans in 1819 (Hohman, Hohman, and George 1904).

19   Red thread was believed to protect a person from certain death or disability caused by the evil eye (Hone 1967; Opie and Tatem 1996).

20   Records from 1814 state that red thread was thought to protect the wearer from the spells of witches (Opie and Tatem 1996).

21   The curative properties of red string were released when it was bound about the head, neck, stomach, wrist, or toe to alleviate a long list of ailments, including whooping cough, infant teething pains, sore throat, fever, smallpox, rheumatism, 'water in the head', mumps, nosebleeds—particularly the nosebleeds of unmarried females—warts, hair loss, sickness caused by loss of one's soul, disability caused by the evil eye, and infertility.

22   It is also significant to note that the commonly used metaphor for Israel in contemporary spoken Hebrew is 'the land' (*ha'arets*). Likewise, the common term for homeland in spoken Hebrew is literally 'land of birth' (*erets moledet*). This term consequently adds to the symbolic association between the land, blood, and birth, through the association of blood with the reproductive life-cycle. I thank Simon Bronner for pointing out this connection.

23   Red has been used as a protective colour against haemorrhages and fluxes from time immemorial. Red stones attached to Hebrew amulets have long been used by those concerned with protection in childbed, or with illness and wounding (Shrire 1966). Red coral necklaces were worn for protection against the evil eye by Jewish and Christian children in the Middle Ages (Trachtenberg 1970), and have been documented in other cultures such as that of Burma, where children wear them as a protection against sickness (Hildburgh 1909).

24   Weitman (1973), who has studied colour associations in national flags, reports: 'The vast majority of nations use the colour red to symbolize such things as "wars fought against aggressors", "military valour", "courage", "blood shed in battle", "readiness to sacrifice", "revolt", "struggle for independence", "revolution", etc.'

25   For instance, as a harmful device knot magic was believed in ancient times to prevent the performance of the marriage act, inspiring precautions such as loosening the bride's hair before the ceremony and untying all the knots in the clothing of the bride and groom (Trachtenberg 1970: 127).

26   This is probably the symbolism behind the sacred cord worn by high-caste Hindus, the knotted strings of the prayer shawl and the knotted straps of phylacteries in Jewish ritual clothing, and the cords, sashes, bows, and braids worn by soldiers and officials in military ceremonies (Cirlot 1962: 317).

27   In English a common expression for getting married is 'tying the knot', but, as we have seen, in many cultures knots are believed to prevent the enactment of a marriage or its consummation (Cooper 1978: 22). Westermark (1972) notes the beliefs surrounding knotting and tying in Moroccan wedding folklore, where the groom is not allowed to wear a belt, and the bride's undergarment is knotted seven times before the ceremony, to be untied by her groom before they consummate the marriage.

28   Leach (1972) notes the folk belief that wearing knots can cause a man to suffer a long and agonized death, while Hill (1968) notes that all knots must be untied in a room where someone has died to prevent their newly freed soul from being trapped there.

29   Patai (1983: 363) cites several prescriptions recorded in ancient Hebrew manuscripts for securing a pregnancy by 'locking' it in with threads as a symbolic act of closing the 'gate' of the womb.

30   Hand (1980: 113, citing Pliny, *Natural History* 28.6.33–4) notes in the context of magic measuring with string that 'where colors are prescribed, red would appear to be favored'.

31   In the Talmud, magic itself is described as consisting of 'binding and loosening', while the book of Daniel (5: 12, 16) lists the ability 'to loosen knots' as one of the magician's accomplishments. Also, the Hebrew word for amulet (*kame'a*) has the root meaning 'to bind' (Trachtenberg 1970: 132). The Babylonian Talmud (*Shab.* 66*b*) refers to folk medicine in relation to sabbath practices: one is allowed to go out in the public domain on the sabbath with *Rubia tenuifolia*, a climbing plant, which is a remedy for jaundice; it is knotted and hung around the neck. Abaye expands on this and details the benefits of knotting the *Rubia*: 'My nanny told me that three knots stabilizes the patient so his situation does not worsen, five knots heals the illness, and seven knots works even against sorcery.' In the Jerusalem Talmud (*Eruv.* 10: 26) it is said that five or seven or nine knots help protect against sorcery.

32   According to Trachtenberg, one of the most picturesque of ancient Jewish miracle work-ers was Honi Hame'agel (1st cent. BCE), whose penchant for standing within a circle while he called down rain from heaven won him his title 'the circle drawer'.

33   Trachtenberg (1970) states that in the Orient the general practice at a funeral is for the mourners to encircle the coffin seven times, reciting an anti-demonic psalm. He also sug-gests that the custom among east European Jews (which also prevails in the Orient) for the bride to walk around her groom under the wedding canopy three or seven times was prob-ably originally intended to keep off the demons who were waiting to pounce on them (Trachtenberg 1970).

34   Trachtenberg (1970: 162) suggests that the *kaparot* rite can be reread in this context as a rite for transferring the sins of the individual to the fowl. By offering this substitute to the supernatural powers one saves oneself from the punishment decreed by heaven.

35   'Red' is usually used as a general term that includes many different shades or hues, including scarlet—a bright red tinged with orange and yellow—and crimson—a deep red tinged with blue (*Webster's Dictionary* 1913).

36   The connection between the scarlet thread and the struggle over the birthright in this case seems to symbolically set right the earlier story in Genesis (25: 30–1) wherein another pair of twins, Jacob and Esau, fight over their birthright. In that story justice is not served, for Jacob is born grasping Esau's heel and later tricks his brother out of his birthright in exchange for 'red porridge'. Through the parallels between the two stories of twin brothers and birthrights we can thus understand that the scarlet thread tied to Zerah's wrist is to be seen in the context of the red porridge with which Jacob tricks Esau: the red porridge helps the theft of the birthright from the red-faced Esau, while the red-hued thread sets things right in the case of Zerah and Perez. With the tying of the string to the infant's wrist, jus-tice and order are maintained, and the red string becomes a signifier or a mark of the blessing reserved for Zerah as Judah's true firstborn son.

37   It is no coincidence that in the Exodus story it is also the firstborn sons of the ancient Israelites whose lives are spared by way of the blood mark.

38   The book of Joshua informs us that Rahab later converted to Judaism, married, and was blessed with an unusually long life and remarkable fertility. Some say that she married Perez and that together they established the dynasty that led to the birth of David. Zakovitch (1975) has pointed out that rabbinic texts view Rahab as forerunner of the royal dynasty of Israel and credit her with being David's great-great grandmother: 'And Salmon begat Boaz, and Boaz begat Obed, and Obed begat Jesse, and Jesse begat David' (Ruth 4: 21, 22). He also points out that the New Testament explicitly sees Rahab as the mother of Boaz (Matt. 1: 5). Finally, Zakovitch informs us that in the Talmud (BT *Meg.* 10*b*, 14*b*), Rahab is viewed as the ancestress of 'Twenty prophets and Priests', including Jeremiah, Elkanah, Seraiah, Baruch ben Neriah, Hanamel, and even the prophetess Huldah.

39   The items that God instructs Moses to gather from the people of Israel as materials for building the sanctuary include gold, silver, copper, sky blue wool, dark red wool, and wool dyed with the pigment of the 'crimson worm' (Exod. 35: 4).

40   In the Jerusalem Talmud we read: 'Forty years before the destruction of the Temple, the western light went out, the crimson thread remained crimson, and the lot for the Lord always came up in the left hand. They would close the gates of the Temple by night and get up in the morning and find them wide open' (JT *Yoma* 6: 3). A similar passage in the Baby-lonian Talmud states: 'Our rabbis taught: During the last forty years before the destruction

of the Temple the lot ['For the Lord'] did not come up in the right hand; nor did the crimson-coloured strap become white; nor did the westernmost light shine; and the doors of the *heikhal* [Temple] would open by themselves' (BT *Yoma* 39*b*); both translations are taken from Neusner 1998.

41   The book of Leviticus cites three main causes of ritual impurity: leprosy, contact with the corpses of humans and certain animals, and the emission of fluids from the sexual organs. Verses in *parashat Tazria* and *parashat Metsora* detail a ritual process for purifying the individual so that they can again be allowed to enter the Israelite camp.

42   Salomon (1999) also discusses blood as a key symbol among the Ethiopian Jews before their mass immigration to Israel.

43   Operating on the belief that it is every Jewish person's birthright to visit Israel, the Taglit-Birthright programme has sent 110,000 young adults aged between 18 and 26, from fifty-one countries, on fully paid, ten-day educational trips to Israel.

44   One example of this is a poem entitled 'Values', written by 16-year-old Libi Molnar from New York, about her first visit to the Western Wall in Jerusalem during a youth group trip. The poem won third prize in the 2002 essay and poetry contest on the JVibe Jewish teen website (<www.jvibe.com>, accessed 30 Oct. 2002). Molnar uses the red string as a symbol of her growing sense of connection to Judaism and to Israel: 'I learned what Jewish values were that evening. I had never felt so connected to Judaism. As the handwritten request left my hand, I tied it to the bush growing outside of the wall. It reminded me of the life that lies within the great stones. I tied it with a red string. Then I tied a string on my hand. I kept it even when it fell off. It was a constant reminder of what I learned that night. And even when it fell off, it was okay. I had learned what my values were and they will never untangle from inside me.'

45   Sered (1989: 40 n.) cites one of her male informants who had lived in Jerusalem in the 1930s and 1940s, who recalled accompanying his father to the tomb in 1939 in order to perform the red string ritual on behalf of his sister, who was experiencing a difficult pregnancy.

46   As mentioned above, in addition to being granted long life, Rahab was also rewarded for her faith with the blessing of fertility, and she is credited with being the forerunner of the royal dynasty that included 'twenty prophets and priests' including Huldah and, finally, King David (Zakovitch 1975). I suggest that the connection of Huldah to Rahab's lineage may explain the fertility rite that came to be connected with her grave. Although I have yet to find a specific link which would explain the connection of the red string with Rachel's tomb—despite the prevalent belief that it is 'prescribed by the sages' or written in the Zohar—I can make a few suggestions as to its origin. The first would be the geographical proximity of Rachel's tomb to that of Huldah on the Mount of Olives, and the shared fertility theme linking their histories: the ritual could simply have migrated from one tomb to another—as, in Israel, it has moved to many different tombs during the past twenty years. Another possible explanation would be the combined symbolism of tying and redness in Rachel's personal history of infertility. Specifically, the biblical story of Reuben giving Rachel mandrakes to help her conceive could be behind the string's connection to her. To support this hypothesis we can note that Jerusalemite women in the 19th century would tie mandrakes around their waists to make them fertile, and that they would also consume ground ruby, a stone whose colour and linguistic link to Reuben's name gave it magical potency (Patai 1983).

References

ABRAMOWITZ, LEAH. 1992. 'Apples, Oil, String and Cookies to Ease Birth', *Jerusalem Post* (31 July), 8.

ADDLEY, ESTHER. 2001. 'It's Only Red Thread, But I Like It', *Guardian* (10 Dec.), 2.

ADELMAN, PENINA. 1986. *Miriam's Well: Rituals for Jewish Women Around the Year.* Fresh Meadows, NY.

ADOPTSHOPPE. 2000. 'The Red Thread'. Adoptshoppe website, <www.adoptshoppe.com>, accessed 1 July 2000.

BABINGTON, LYNN M., BARBARA R. KELLEY, CAROL A. PATSDAUGHTER, RUTH M. SODERBERG, and JAIME E. KELLEY. 1999. 'From Recipes to Recetas: Health Beliefs and Health Care Encounters in the Rural Dominican Republic', *Journal of Cultural Diversity*, 6: 20.

BECK, BRENDA E. F. 1969. 'Colour and Heat in South Indian Ritual', *Man*, NS 4: 553–72.

BEN AMI, ISSACHAR. 1984. *Saint Veneration among Moroccan Jews.* Jerusalem.

BEN-ARI, EYAL, ZEEV ROSENHEK, and DANIEL MAMAN. 2001. 'Military, State and Society in Israel: An Introductory Essay'. In D. Maman, E. Ben-Ari, and Z. Rosenhek, eds, *Military, State, and Society in Israel: Essays in Honor of Moshe Lissak*, 1–39. New Brunswick, NJ.

BILU, YORAM. 1978. 'Traditional Psychiatry in Israel: Visits of Moroccan Immigrants with Psychiatric Problems and Life Difficulties to Rabbis and Sages'. Ph.D. diss., Hebrew University of Jerusalem.

BRONNER, SIMON J. 2004. '"This Is Why We Hunt": Social-Psychological Meanings of the Traditions and Rituals of Deer Camp', *Western Folklore*, 63: 11–50.

Celebs on a String. 2002. <www.straitstimes.asia1.com.sg/women/story/0,1870,157376,00.html>, accessed 18 Apr. 2003.

CIRLOT, J. E. 1962. *A Dictionary of Symbols.* London.

COOPER, GENE. 1998. 'Life-Cycle Rituals in Dongyang County: Time, Affinity, and Exchange in Rural China', *Ethnology*, 37: 373–94.

COOPER, J. C. 1978. *An Illustrated Encyclopaedia of Traditional Symbols.* London.

DAVENPORT, GERTRUDE C. 1898. 'Folk-Cures from Kansas', *Journal of American Folklore*, 11: 129–32.

DOUGLAS, MARY. 2003 [1966]. *Natural Symbols: Explorations in Cosmology.* London.

DUNDES, ALAN. 1980. *Interpreting Folklore.* Bloomington, Ind.

——1981. 'Wet and Dry, the Evil Eye: An Essay in Indo-European and Semitic Worldview'. In Alan Dundes, ed., *The Evil Eye: A Folklore Casebook*, 257–98. New York.

Easton's 1897 Bible Dictionary. 1897. <www.eastonsbibledictionary.com/>, accessed 22 Nov. 2006.

EHRENREICH, BARBARA. 1997. *Blood Rites: Origins and History of the Passions of War.* New York.

FARBER, JIM. 2003. 'Just Like a Woman: Britney Spears Opens Up on Madonna, Justin and her "Not Sexy" New CD', *New York Daily News* (18 Nov.), 2.

GINZBERG, LOUIS. 1964 [1910]. *The Legends of the Jews*, ii: *Bible Times and Characters from Joseph to Exodus*. Philadelphia.

GOW, J. 1901. 'Latrans in Phaedrus (in Correspondence)', *Classical Review*, 15: 77–8.

GREENE, THOMAS M. 1993. 'Poetry as Invocation', *New Literary History*, 24: 495–517.

GRENDON, FELIX. 1909. 'The Anglo-Saxon Charms', *Journal of American Folklore*, 22: 105–237.

HAND, WAYLAND D. 1980. *Magical Medicine: The Folkloric Component of Medicine in Folk Belief, Custom and Ritual of the Peoples of Europe and America*. Berkeley, Calif.

HENRY, A. 1903. 'The Lolos and Other Tribes of Western China', *Journal of the Royal Anthropological Institute of Great Britain and Ireland*, 33: 96–107.

HERTZFELD, MICHAEL. 1986. 'Closure as Cure: Tropes in the Exploration of Bodily and Social Disorder', *Current Anthropology*, 27: 107–20.

HILDBURGH, W. L. 1909. 'Notes on Some Burmese Amulets and Magical Objects', *Journal of the Royal Anthropological Institute of Great Britain and Ireland*, 39: 397–407.

HILL, DOUGLAS. 1968. *Magic and Superstition*. Verona.

HOFFMAN, LAWRENCE. 1996. *Covenant of Blood: Circumcision and Gender in Rabbinic Judaism*. Chicago.

HOHMAN, CARLETON F. BROWN, JOHN GEORGE HOHMAN, and JOHANN GEORGE. 1904. 'The Long Hidden Friend', *Journal of American Folklore*, 17: 89–152.

HONE, WILLIAM. 1967 [1827]. *Every-Day Book*, 2 vols. Detroit.

HOOPER, VINCENT FOSTER. 1936. 'Geryon and the Knotted Cord', *Modern Language Notes*, 51: 445–9.

HYDE, MARINA. 2003. 'Comment and Analysis: This Week', *Guardian* (29 Nov.), <www.guardian.co.uk/diary/story/0,,1095804,00.html>, accessed 20 Dec. 2003.

JACOBS, WILHELMINA, and VIVIAN JACOBS. 1958. 'The Color Blue: Its Use as Metaphor and Symbol', *American Speech*, 33(1): 29–46.

JOHN OF GADDESDEN. 1314. *Rosa Anglica seu Medicinae Johannis Anglici*, ed. Winifred Wulff (1923–9), Irish Texts Society 25. London.

JONES, LOUIS C. 1981. 'The Evil Eye among European Americans'. In Alan Dundes, ed., *The Evil Eye: A Folklore Casebook*, 150–68. New York.

KAPLAN, DANNY. 2003. *Brothers and Others in Arms: The Making of Love and War in Israeli Combat Units*. Binghamton, NY.

KAYE, HELEN. 1997. 'Warding Off the Evil Eye', *Jerusalem Post* (10 Mar.), 5.

KELNER, SHAUL, LEONARD SAXE, CHARLES KADUSHIM, RACHEL CANAR, MATTHEW LINDHOLM, HAL OSSMAN, JENNIFER PERLOFF, BENJAMIN PHILLIPS, RISHONA TERES, MINNA WOLF, and MEREDITH WOOCHER. 2000. 'Making Meaning: Participants' Experiences of Birthright Israel'. In *Birthright Israel Research Report 2*. Waltham, Mass.

KIDS FOR KIDS. 1998–2003. 'What's Up with the Red String?'. Kids for Kids Red String Campaign website, <www.kidsforkids.net>, accessed 14 Dec. 1998, 5 Aug. 2003, 23 Nov. 2006.

KLEIN, ERNEST. 1987. *A Comprehensive Etymological Dictionary of the Hebrew Language for Readers of English*. Jerusalem.

LAMPERT, NICOLE. 2003. 'Stella Joins Band of Sisters', *London Daily Mail* (15 Oct.), , accessed 15 Oct. 2003.

LAND, RANDI JO. 1989. 'Religious Women Test/Create', *Jerusalem Post* (27 Jan.), 8.

LANDAU, DAVID. 1995. 'Year in Review: Israel's "Red-Thread" Year Marked by Terror, Turbulence and Rabin's Determination to Advance Peace Process', *Jewish News Weekly of Northern California* (22 Sept.), , accessed 5 July 2003.

LEACH, MARIA, ed. 1972. *Funk and Wagnall's Standard Dictionary of Folklore, Mythology and Legend*, 2 vols. New York.

LELAND, JOHN. 2001. 'Noticed: At the Combs Trial, an Unexpected Accessory', *New York Times* (18 Mar.), 6.

MARGALIOTH, MORDECHAI, ed. 1975 [1947]. *Midrash Hagadol: Genesis* [Midrash hagadol: al ḥamisha ḥumshei torah. Sefer bereshit], 4th edn. Jerusalem.

MURGOCI, A. 1981. 'The Evil Eye in Roumania and its Antidotes'. In Alan Dundes, ed., *The Evil Eye: A Folklore Casebook*, 124–9. New York.

NEUSNER, JACOB. 1998. *The Talmud of the Land of Israel: An Academic Commentary to the Second, Third and Fourth Divisions*, iv: *Yerushalmi Tractate Yoma*, South Florida Academic Commentary Series 112. Atlanta, Ga.

NORLIN, ETHEL TODD. 1918. 'Present-Day Superstitions at La Harpe, Ill.: Survivals in a Community of English Origin', *Journal of American Folklore*, 31: 202–15.

OPIE, IONA, and MOIRA TATEM. 1996. 'Red Thread Cures'. In Iona Opie and Moira Tatem, *A Dictionary of Superstitions*, online edn, <www.oxfordreference.com/>, accessed 25 Nov. 2002.

PATAI, RAPHAEL. 1983. *On Jewish Folklore*. Detroit.

PITRÈ, GIUSEPPE. 1981. 'The Jettatura and the Evil Eye'. In Alan Dundes, ed., *The Evil Eye: A Folklore Casebook*, 130–42. New York.

SALOMON, HAGAR. 1999. *The Hyena People: Ethiopian Jews in Christian Ethiopia*. Berkeley, Calif.

SCHEPER-HUGHES, NANCY, and MARGARET LOCK. 1987. 'The Mindful Body: A Prolegomenon to Future Work in Medical Anthropology', *Medical Anthropology Quarterly*, NS 1: 6–41.

SEEMAN, DON. 1997. 'One People, One Blood: Public Health, Political Violence and HIV in an Ethiopian-Israeli Setting', *Culture, Medicine and Psychiatry*, 23: 159–95.

SERED, SUSAN STARR. 1989. 'Rachel's Tomb: Societal Liminality and the Revitalization of a Shrine', *Religion*, 19: 27–40.

SHENHAR, ALIZA. 2000. *Jewish and Israeli Folklore*. Denver, Co..

SHILLER, ELI. 1977. *Rachel's Tomb* [Kever raḥel]. Jerusalem.

SHRIRE, THEODORE. 1966. *Hebrew Amulets: Their Decipherment and Interpretation*. London.

SIMPSON, JACQUELINE, and STEVE ROUD. 2000. *A Dictionary of English Folklore*, online edn, <www.oxfordreference.com/>, accessed 25 Nov. 2002.

SMITH, GRACE PARTRIDGE. 1941. Folklore from 'Egypt', *Journal of American Folklore*, 54: 48–59.

STEKERT, ELLEN J. 1970. 'Focus for Conflict: Southern Mountain Medical Beliefs in Detroit', *Journal of American Folklore*, 83: 115–47.

TEMAN, ELLY. 1997. 'The Red String: A Universal and Local Symbol', Archive of Jewish Folklore, Jewish Folklore Department, Hebrew University of Jerusalem.

TRACHTENBERG, JOSHUA. 1970. *Jewish Magic and Superstition: A Study in Folk Religion*. New York.

VILNAI, ZEV. 1966. *Holy Graves in Israel*. Jerusalem.

Webster's Revised Unabridged Dictionary. 1913. Springfield, Mass.

WEINGROD, ALEX. 1990. *The Saint of Beersheba*. Albany, NY.

WEISS, MEIRA. 2002. *The Chosen Body*. Stanford, Calif.

WEITMAN, SASHA R. 1973. 'National Flags: A Sociological Review', *Semiotica*, 8: 328–67.

WESTERMARCK, EDWARD. 1972 [1914]. *Marriage Ceremonies in Morocco*. London.

WILDE, LADY FRANCESCA SPERANZA. 1887. *Ancient Legends, Mystic Charms, and Superstitions of Ireland*. London.

WORDNET. 2003. 'Red'. In *Wordnet Online Dictionary*, <www.wordnet-online.com/>, accessed 4 Aug. 2003.

WRESCHNER, ERNEST E. 1980. 'Red Ochre and Human Evolution: A Case for Discussion', *Current Anthropology*, 21: 631–44.

ZAKOVITCH, YAIR. 1975. 'Rahab als Mutter des Boas in der Jesus-Genealogie (Matth. I 5)', *Novum Testamentum*, 17: 5.

—— and AVIGDOR SHINAN. 1992. *A Tale of Judah and Tamar* [Ma'aseh yehudah ve-tamar]. Jerusalem.

TWO

A Synagogue in Olyka: Architecture and Legends

SERGEY R. KRAVTSOV

DWELLING, belonging to a place and having a 'sense of place' that is socially and culturally constructed, plays an important role in the formation of human identity (Sheldrake 2001: 9–11; see also Tuan 1976). Identification with place, commonly associated with people rooted or settled over long periods of time in one location, extends to groups of diaspora people such as Jews, often viewed as being on the move (Bar-Itzhak 2001: 22). My thesis is that the creation of a narrative with local references is especially significant as a strategy for mobile Jews in Europe who seek identification with a place dominated by a non-Jewish majority. Further, I will argue that a sacred place, one related to a theological conception of time and space, is cognitively constructed through legends to root this experience in a usable past (Sheldrake 2001: 30).

Architecture arranges place for rituals, which perpetuate memory. Accustomed as it is to studying material objects, architectural history describes the physical attributes of a structure, and dates it. The work of architectural historians is linked to cultural studies in that the historians seek the meanings of the material as revealed in related verbal texts and visual iconography. A cultural approach reconstructs a building and its milieu as they were seen and understood by contemporaries, including the building's architects and their clients, the local authorities, and the community and its neighbours. Through such reconstruction we can often gain insights that are not available through literary or material means alone.

An example is a synagogue in Olyka, a Volhynian town which has successively belonged to the ancient Rus, the Grand Duchy of Lithuania, the Polish Kingdom, imperial Russia, the Second Polish Republic, and the Soviet Union.[1] At the centre of a fertile area populated by Ukrainians and ruled at different times by members of the Ruthenian/Ukrainian, Polish, and Lithuanian nobility, it attracted a community of Jews, who settled there and plied their various trades and crafts for three and a half centuries. Though these activities connected them to the local population and to the rulers of the city, the Jews preserved their identity in a local population dominated by Christian denominations, including Orthodox, Calvinist, and Greek and Roman Catholic. Central to both Jewish and Christian communities was the visible sacred symbol of the synagogue or church, and in their synagogue architecture Jews felt a need to substantiate a Jewish presence, organized around their sacred space, in their own eyes and in the eyes of other communities.

As a typical example of a shtetl, or town that in the Jewish imagination preserved a folk life, Olyka attracted the ethnographic expedition of S. A. An-ski (Shlomo Z. Rappoport, 1863–1920). In 1913 An-ski and his colleagues documented the Jewish community of Olyka as a living entity (Sergeeva 2001: 173–4); later, in 1925, its image was captured by the outstanding Polish photographer Henryk Poddębski (1890–1945). This community disappeared during the Holocaust. It is remembered in a collective memorial book (Livne 1972), and a work of personal reminiscence (Grinstein 1973). The only remaining vestiges of the town's Jews are an old brick house in the former Jewish quarter and a monument erected recently at the place of execution of more than 4,000 Jews in the summer of 1942.

Here my aim is to reconstruct Olyka's main synagogue, known as the Great Synagogue, as a virtual site of memory. It is remembered by both Jews and non-Jews, although in different ways. In certain matters, the memory of non-Jews constitutes a counter-narrative. For instance, Bohdan Chmielnicki (c.1593–1657), who played a role in the history of the town, is said to be 'of eternal memory' for the Ukrainians, while in the Jewish view his memory should be blotted out like that of Amalek (Deut. 25: 17, 19; see Hannover 1983: 25; Lindheim and Luckyj 1996: 54). Belarusian, Ukrainian, Russian, and Polish historiographies are informative concerning the Jewish past of Olyka, while Jewish sources are largely silent, or give a legendary narrative of events. Thus, both legend and history contribute to the construction of a place of memory. It can be imagined as a multi-storey building, a structure of meanings, whose floors and the links between them need to be mapped.

Architectural Record of the Synagogue in Olyka

Olyka is one of the oldest settlements in Ukraine, first mentioned in the Laurentian Codex in 1149 (p. 323). For almost four hundred years, from 1544, it was in the possession of the noble family of Radziwiłł. In 1564 it was granted a town charter following the pattern of Magdeburg (Chlebowski and Walewski 1888: 527–8). Jews had apparently begun to settle in Olyka by 1591, when Stanisław 'the Pious' Radziwiłł (1559–99) prohibited them from building houses in the market-place (Stecki 1887: 34). In 1637 they were allowed to rent wooden stores adjacent to the town hall, which stood in the marketplace, and from 1645 on they could replace their stores with new masonry ones on the western side of the market-place (Stecki 1887: 40–1). These changes occurred at a time when Prince Stanisław Albrycht Radziwiłł (1595–1656) was altering the town's layout. The Jews, together with the Catholics (mainly Poles), settled permanently in Olyka's downtown district, called Serednye Misto ('midtown' in Ukrainian). They avoided the eastern section of the town, called Zalisoche, and the southern suburb of Zavorottya, which was inhabited mainly by Ukrainians (Tersky 2001: 27).

The Ukrainian uprising led by Chmielnicki marked the beginning of a terrible time for Olyka. On 30 August 1648 Radziwiłł's serfs joined the rebels, plundering the town and its castle (Radziwiłł 1974: 47). In June 1651 about 18,000 Cossacks attacked Olyka again. This time, the peasants loyal to Radziwiłł burned down the suburban villages, and fortified their positions in the midtown area. They not only managed to withstand three assaults, but in a brave defence also slaughtered three companies of Cossacks. Furious Cossacks, who faced the approach of the Polish army, robbed the town, set it ablaze, then, on 19 June, retreated (Hrushevsky 1928: 276–9). At the outbreak of the uprising in 1648, thirty Jewish households had been listed in the town; by June 1649 only twenty survived.[2] These calamities halted the development of Serednye Misto, which by 1662 numbered only ten domiciles, compared to 107 in Zavorottya, and ninety-nine in Zalisoche.[3]

Restrictions on Jews in the city were not completely forgotten in later times. In 1686 the prince's commissar reconfirmed the prohibition on Jews erecting houses in the marketplace. Despite this, in many respects Jews had obligations equal to those of their non-Jewish neighbours: they were compelled to participate in the fortification of the town, working on ramparts and palisades, roads and dams with their own handcarts, spades, and axes, they had to keep watch over Radziwiłł's palace and the town hall during the night, and they were asked to delegate several men—'compromisers rather than quarrellers'—to help with the municipal accounting.[4] Development of the Jewish area was slow, and thirty-six plots still stood empty in Serednye Misto in 1719, while at this time the synagogue and the rabbi's house were taxable, from which we can infer that they were in use.[5] The surrounding community imposed order on the Jewish sector. Thus, after the source of a fire that broke out in 1752 was identified as the house of a mute Jewish tailor, the long blocks of residential housing were forcibly broken into smaller units as alleys were driven between them running from the marketplace to the river.[6] In 1787 the non-Jews accused the Jews of neglecting their obligations in respect of tidying the city and paying municipal taxes.[7] In January 1788, as if in response, the Jews complained to Prince Karol Stanisław Radziwiłł (1734–90) about the burden of high taxes and prices, and the bad economic situation in general. They calculated Radziwiłł 's debts to the Jewish community of Olyka, and concluded their epistle with an application for the reconstruction of the synagogue, which had been destroyed in a fire:

Since the synagogue burned down in 1787 the congregation has not yet acquired appropriate material for a new building, and will accept with gratitude the aid of His Great Princely Lord's Grace and merciful benefactor in procuring credit, and asks to issue orders also to His Grace Mr Przetocki the forester to allow the release of wood from the

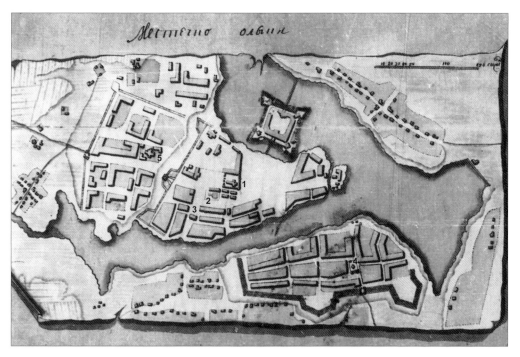

Figure 1 Plan of Olyka, last decade of the eighteenth century. (1) Catholic collegiate Holy Trinity church; (2) town hall; (3) the Great Synagogue; (4) church of the Presentation in the Temple; (5) the Orthodox Holy Trinity church. *Reproduced by courtesy of the Russian State Military Historical Archive, Moscow*

forest, as well as to His Grace the Manager of Olyka not to bar access to the sawmill. As soon as the rescued congregation enjoys the benefit of a new synagogue, it will take upon itself the new obligation of praying to the Highest Throne of God for the prolongation of the Prince's reign in good health, and will declare its continued loyalty . . . bowing its heads at the Prince's feet . . . the whole congregation of Olyka.[8]

The oldest known depiction of the Great Synagogue that was built as a consequence of this appeal is found in the town plan from the last decade of the eighteenth century (Figure 1), where it appears as a large, rectangular building, the construction material of which is not specified, though we know it was built of wood.[9] Two large fires which occurred in Olyka in 1803 and 1823 could have damaged this structure. The illuminated drawing by Napoleon Orda from 1874 shows the triple-tiered hipped roof of this synagogue rising above the roofs of the midtown district (Figure 2). Its age cannot be dated more accurately than somewhere between 1788 and 1874.[10]

Shortly after Orda made his drawing, the synagogue, which supposedly burned down, was replaced by another. Photographs of this new Great Synagogue were taken in the early twentieth century, in the last decades of its

Figure 2 View of Olyka: pencil drawing illuminated with watercolours, by Napoleon Orda, 1874. The huge structure on the right is the Catholic collegiate Holy Trinity church; the multi-tier hipped roof of the synagogue can be seen rising above the dwelling houses on the left. *Reproduced by courtesy of the National Museum, Kraków*

existence (Figures 3, 4, and 5). It was a large, though unpretentious, rectangular log structure. The building included a vestibule, the women's section on the second floor, and a double-height prayer hall in which four timber pillars supported the ceiling, which was divided into nine bays by wooden imitations of retaining arches. The extant photographs show a flat ceiling in the outer bays of the hall; we have no visual record of the central bay. A choir gallery occupied the rear of the hall, which had large, round-headed, paired windows cut into its southern, eastern, and northern walls. The building had exterior galleries on the first and second floors on the west, and was covered with a double-tiered hipped tin roof. There were two symmetrical, low, plastered half-timbered extensions under lean-to roofs in the south and north; these housed the craftsmen's synagogues (Livne 1972: 107). Inside, the prayer hall had an octagonal *bimah* (platform) at the centre; to the east was the *aron hakodesh* (holy shrine) flanked by barley-sugar 'Solomonic' columns, and topped by the Tablets of the Law and the hands of the high priest raised in blessing under a canopy. Here also was the *duḥan* (pulpit) for the *sheliaḥ tsibur* (public reader), decorated with a *mizraḥ* ('east' plaque) inscribed with the year 1879, thus giving an approximate date for the whole structure. The synagogue was similar to the one in the neighbouring town of Torhovytsya, built in the early nineteenth century, which similarly featured a

Figure 3 The Great Synagogue, exterior view from the south-east. Photo: Solomon Yudovin, 1913. *Reproduced by courtesy of the Petersburg Judaica Centre*

Figure 4 The Great Synagogue, exterior view from the south-west. Photo: Henryk Poddębski, 1925. *Reproduced by courtesy of the Instytut Sztuki, Polish Academy of Sciences, Warsaw*

double-tiered hipped roof, paired round-headed windows, and the nine-bay layout of the prayer hall with the ceiling divided by wooden imitations of retaining arches (Piechotka and Piechotka 1996: 353–4).

Figure 5 The Great Synagogue, interior view towards the *aron hakodesh*. Photo: Henryk Poddębski, 1925. *Reproduced by courtesy of the Instytut Sztuki, Polish Academy of Sciences, Warsaw*

It is not surprising that Holocaust survivors remember the Great Synagogue in general terms, if at all, and pay more attention to Olkya's eight hasidic synagogues (Livne 1972: cf. pp. 36 and 107). By the 1930s these synagogues had probably become more important, while the Great Synagogue—still a significant symbol of the Jewish presence in the town—was only used on special occasions. The structure was not well cared for: the logs at the corners were excessively long, and the exterior walls were not sided in planking, thus exposing the structure to rot (Figure 3). An elderly woman referred to in the sources as 'righteous Freydke' looked after the *aron hakodesh*, Torah mantles, and prayer books (Kremer 1972: 72). The Great Synagogue stood intact on the eve of the liquidation of the Olyka ghetto on 29 July 1942 (Livne 1972: 302). However, it did not survive the war. Its fate was shared by 404 dwelling-houses and 326 auxiliary structures in the town (Klymash et al. 1970: 286).

Legends of the Olyka Synagogue

The Jewish legends about the Great Synagogue of Olyka contrast with the documentary sources. All of them are narrated in Yiddish. One of these narratives was published in 1903, and in 1913 it was recorded by Abraham Rechtman (1880–1972), one of the participants in An-ski's ethnographic expedition (Biber 1903: 5–6; Rechtman 1958: 70–1). The legend tells how the Jews, together with the famous rabbi David ben Shmuel Halevi Segal (known as the Taz, 1586–1667) took refuge in the local fortified masonry synagogue during the Chmielnicki uprising:

In 1648, when Chmielnicki's Cossacks murdered thousands of Jews in Ostroh, the Taz managed to escape with his family to Alik, a small hamlet defended by a strong fortress with ancient cannons placed in its walls. Initially, Chmielnicki's men were afraid to approach the fortress of Alik; but later, in 1649, the Cossacks did make an attempt to overrun the fortress. They advanced on Alik and began to shell the town. The Jews of Alik cowered in their synagogue, which was built like a fortress, praying and fasting. Among the Jews of Alik gathered in their synagogue was the Taz, who was a frail man. As a result of the protracted praying, crying, and fasting he could barely stand on his feet. They say that, almost fainting from exhaustion, he leaned his head against a pillar and immediately fell asleep. He dreamt that a sweet voice was reciting the verse from 2 Kings 19: 34: 'I will protect and save this city for My sake, and for the sake of My servant David.' Waking up, he ordered all of them to keep praying and crying and wailing, for, he said, salvation was near. And indeed the miracle ensued: suddenly the old and rusty cannons began to fire, the murderous bands fled to the four winds, and the town of Alik was saved. In commemoration of the miracle that had occurred, the Taz composed special penitential prayers. The Jews of Alik had the custom of reciting them every year on the day that the miracle occurred, 26 Sivan. (Rechtman 1958: 70–1)[11]

Another version of this legend describes the same episode as taking place in the local castle, one of the most fortified in the vicinity, rather than the synagogue (Livne 1972: 19). The penitential prayer of 26 Sivan follows another one on 20 Sivan, allegedly composed by the Taz to memorialize the persecutions of 1648 in Olyka. The rabbinical authorities of Poland saw the attack of 12 Elul 5408 (30 August 1648), like other disasters of that year, as merely an extension of the persecutions in Blois nearly 300 years previously, so they marked the attack by reciting the prayer on 20 Sivan (Biber 1903: 7–10), the date of the initial attack. In a second conflation of historical events, I would suggest, memory further shifted the miracle of the retreat of the Cossacks from Olyka from 1651 to 1649 so that the attack could be seen as part of the disasters known collectively as *gezerot taḥ vetat*—the decrees (meaning 'the divine decrees', or the heavenly retributions) of the years 5408 and 5409, corresponding approximately to 1648 and 1649 (and therefore to the attacks perpetrated on the Jews by Chmielnicki in those years). In the oral tradition 1648 is of particular significance because the Zohar saw it as a year of messianic occurrences (Scholem 1973: 88). The Council of Four Lands, the Jewish self-governing body of the Polish–Lithuanian Commonwealth, fixed 20 Sivan (instead of the historically correct date for Olyka of 12 Elul 5408, corresponding to 30 August 1648) as the date for commemoration of the Chmielnicki massacres of 1648 and 1649, while the prayer of 26 Sivan was adopted to mark the historical salvation of the besieged community on 30 Sivan 5411 (corresponding to 19 June 1651).

The legend in its two versions makes little distinction between the fortified synagogue and a castle, both referred to by the biblical metaphor of the divinely saved city. In this context, such details as castle or a synagogue as the backdrop to the scene were unimportant. However, the narrative does supply the synagogue with an interior pillar, against which the exhausted Taz could lean his head, thus adopting the layout of the four-pier synagogues of neighbouring Ostroh or Lutsk (Kravtsov 2005a: 320–4). In this way memory fixes the chronology and topography in general terms, eliminating and changing secondary details and adding new ones to make the scene more vivid. In historical terms, it does not prove the existence of a masonry synagogue in Olyka in the mid-seventeenth century.

Another legend, recorded elsewhere in Ukraine, is known in two versions, published by An-ski and by Rechtman in 1925 and 1958 respectively. An-ski's version reads:

For a long while the Jews of Alik had been begging their nobleman to build them a synagogue, and the Christians had been pleading for a [Catholic[12]] church. He, for his part, wanted to build a town hall.

Well, one day the nobleman was taken so ill that it seemed no one could cure him. So he made a vow to build a large and beautiful church. But he remained as sick as ever; indeed, he grew weaker by the day. When he felt that he was at his last gasp, he made a vow to build a large and beautiful synagogue. Lo and behold, he felt better at once.

After he had fully recovered, he began to think about which of his vows he should keep first. If he built the church first, the Jews would take offence. If he built the synagogue first, he would provoke the Christians. If he followed his own wishes and built the town hall, the Jews and the Christians would all be angry. So he decided to have all three structures built simultaneously and to make them identical.

He hired a famous foreign architect and instructed him to erect the three buildings at exactly the same time, stone by stone. The architect drove three posts into the ground to indicate where the church, the synagogue, and the town hall were to be built. Then he stretched a rope from post to post and, balancing himself on it, went backwards and forwards, laying brick after brick in sequence. As the buildings rose, he tied the rope higher and higher up the posts. And that was how he was able to build the three structures simultaneously.

They were the most beautiful buildings in the world, so beautiful that the nobleman, worried lest the architect construct others as wonderful somewhere else, had the posts cut down just as all three were finished. As a result the architect fell from the ropes and died.

When I visited Alik, I came upon an old church, but I did not see either a [masonry] synagogue or a town hall.[13] I was told that these had both burned down some time ago. (An-ski 1925: 248–9[14])

Rechtman's version differs at a number of points:

The Count[15] of the shtetl Olik was a wicked and vicious man. He mistreated his own peasants and never allowed the Jews to get away with anything. Time and again the Jews petitioned him, asking permission to build a synagogue, but, just as he denied his peasants the right to build a church,[16] the Count repeatedly refused the Jews' request.

One day it happened that the Count became seriously ill. All the best physicians from the big city were summoned to his bedside, but to no avail; on the contrary, his condition worsened as the days passed and his life began to ebb away. Then the Count sent for the priest and asked him to pray to God for a cure. He promised the priest that if God would listen to his prayer and if he would recover he would build the church. However, the Count's health did not improve. He felt his strength continue to ebb and his life nearing its end. Finally, the Count ordered emissaries to go and fetch the rabbi, and to ask him to pray for his recovery. Again he made a promise: if the rabbi's prayers were answered he would build a synagogue for the Jews. And it happened that immediately after he had given his word to the rabbi, the Count began to feel better and after a couple of days he was totally cured. Leaving his sickbed, the Count did not forget his promises, neither to the Christians, nor to the Jews, and he was determined to fulfill both requests. Yet he could not decide which of the two promises he should keep first: if he began with the church, the Jews would complain; if he started with the synagogue, the Christians would feel wronged. Eventually he hit upon an ingenious solution; the Count ordered the two buildings to be built simultaneously. And so, the masons followed the Count's orders. They dug holes in the ground for both buildings simultaneously and began laying the foundations. Then they laid one brick on the wall of the church and the next on the synagogue's. After a short while both buildings were completed: they looked identical.

It was said that when the church and the synagogue were finally finished, the Count came to have a look. Inspecting the buildings, he could not take his eyes off them, the architecture was so sublime. The Count left feeling very troubled. The next day he called for the architect and had him put to death. The Count could not bear the thought that this architect might be invited by another count anywhere else to build anything as wonderful. (Rechtman 1958: 54–5)[17]

These two versions of the story are not identical with the original account, lost by Rechtman in his native Proskuriv during the Russian Civil War. An-ski's version was published posthumously in 1925. Rechtman wrote down his reconstruction of the original text in about 1918, and had an opportunity to make a comparison with An-ski's version before his own was published in 1958. 'I have therefore tried not to repeat the stories already published, unless my version is different in some way', Rechtman states in his introduction (1958: 25).[18]

In both permutations this narrative is a variant of the master builder tale—type 1099, 'The Giant as Master Builder', in Aarne and Thompson's Tale Type Index (Thompson 1957). In the most common version of the tale, a giant, a troll, or a devil who is a master builder builds a cathedral in a certain city, and has to accomplish the work by a certain deadline. As remuneration for this task he demands something impossible or horrible, such as the sun and moon, or the eyes of the person who has commissioned the building, unless somebody can guess his name (only the devil remains nameless). The name is guessed, and the giant loses not only his payment but also his life (Uther 2004: 37–8). The existence of the master builder tale is confirmed in the Snorra Edda (c.1220/30), while popular versions were widespread in the seventeenth and eighteenth centuries, mostly in Swedish, Norwegian, and German folklore. The tale is known in an Edda version, as well as in Scandinavian, Baltic, and west and south European sources (Taloş 1977). The legend of Olyka, with its motif of bricks laid one by one in two buildings simultaneously, is a variation of the west European tale of two giants building a church: both have the use of only one hammer, which they throw to each other each day.[19] Close analogues of the tale are known in Little Poland (Dobrzycki 1983: 11; Heyduk 1980: 57–8), west-central Poland, and in Vienna (Jaindl 1992: 27–8; Knoop 1909: 53–4). The narrative of Olyka mentions neither the builder's remuneration nor his name, and instead of the deadline we have the simultaneous construction of two buildings (in Rechtman's wording) as in the Viennese legend of St Stephen's towers.

Jewish legends often seek to assign antiquity to a synagogue, thereby establishing its legitimacy in the eyes of the law. They do this by making various fantastic claims, attributing the synagogue's origins to supernatural providence, a hoary past, or some factor in the non-Jewish realm: the synagogue always existed—it was unearthed centuries ago (Sataniv and many other places); it was built eight hundred years ago (Ostroh); it was built during the short period of Turkish occupation (Husyatyn); it used to be a Protestant church, prohibited in the early seventeenth century (Pidhaitsi); it used to be a part of an ancient fortification (Lutsk) (Bar-Itzhak 2001: 154; Kravtsov 2005b: 84–94). Jews' desire to establish the antiquity of a particular synagogue led them to use particular architectural styles suggestive of age, such as the Gothic Survival style used in the synagogues of Volhynia, Ruthenia, and Podolia well into the early eighteenth century (Kravtsov 2005b). In the Olyka story, such a claim is strengthened by associating the Great Synagogue with other venerable buildings, namely the town hall and the Catholic church in An-ski's version, or the 'peasants' church' in Rechtman's. Unlike the early twentieth-century narrator of the legend, the Jews of prewar Olyka believed that their synagogue was 'only' two hundred years old (Livne 1972: 107).

An additional theme in the Olyka story is jealousy, which causes the death of the builder.[20] Initially, the Count pretends to be a fair judge, willing to override the mutual jealousy ascribed to both Jews and peasants for the sake of peace in his Ukrainian city. However, ultimately it is the Count himself who is the jealous one, capable of killing the master builder, whose only sin is his excellence. The final section echoes the introduction, where the Count is described as a wicked and vicious man. This, and the central theme of the simultaneous construction of the synagogue with other ancient monuments, both appear to be related to competition among the religious communities of Olyka, each with a desire to prove the legality of its presence in the city.

The motif of a synagogue built as a sign of the Count's gratitude for Jewish prayers for his health is a reflection of the actual wording of the Jewish request for a new synagogue quoted above. The legend presents the prayer as the cause of the lord's recovery and hence the construction of the new synagogue, whereas the letter of 1788 mentions the construction of the synagogue as a precondition for a new prayer to be offered for his health. Both texts include so many similar elements, though in different causal configurations, that the legend can be perceived as an echo of the real application for a new synagogue. The need for wood was a story that was often repeated in Olyka, where the synagogue burned down more than once, and the forest was always in the nobleman's possession. However, the notion of a new obligation to pray for the lord's health makes this account unique, dating it to the late 1780s. Linking the building date to older structures could reflect the presence of the real synagogue in the same place for a long time, from about 1590 on, close to the historical facts. Nevertheless, it is hardly believable that a wooden synagogue ever replaced the masonry one that appears as a backdrop in the legend of the Taz.

The legend of Olyka's synagogue depicts it as a sublime and wonderful building, the most beautiful in the world. This is presented as a good thing, in contrast to the legends of the righteous women, the Golden Rose of Lviv and Mirale of Brailiv, who sacrifice themselves to expiate the excessive beauty of a synagogue (Bar-Itzhak 2001: 150–3). Moreover, the Olyka story does not express anxiety about the synagogue design being modelled on the non-Jewish pattern, suggesting the architectural taste of a narrator who lived in a magnate-owned town relatively tolerant of the Jews, away from the ghettos of the old royal cities with their fear of persecution and their notorious restrictions on the height and exterior decoration of synagogues. Such prohibitions regarding the construction of new masonry synagogues were generally in force in the sixteenth and seventeenth centuries (Kravtsov 2005b: 84–9).

An architect as the victim of the lord's jealousy was a recurrent theme in folklore in Radziwiłł's cities: it is said that Giovanni Maria Bernardoni (1541–1605), the architect of the Cathedral of Christ's Body at Nyasvizh (1593) was blinded by his jealous client (Shishigina-Pototskaya 1997: 12).[21] Vasyl Slobodyan, a student of Ukrainian architecture, relates a legend regarding an architect 'who had built the castle and the whole city of Olyka', and was put to death by Prince Radziwiłł.[22] Thus, the subject entered Jewish folklore from the narratives of the surrounding community.

It can be concluded that the legends of Olyka use categories of time and place for the aetiological explanation of vital matters, such as surviving a massacre or possession of a synagogue. The function of time and place in these narratives follows the rules of the genre, substituting days for years, synagogue for castle, and result for cause. The legend of a synagogue built at the same time as a church is a variant of the international master builder tale, which has a parallel in local Ukrainian folklore. The jealousy, though a universal motif, reflects real features of everyday life in multiethnic Olyka. The motif of bricks laid one by one is used to suggest the venerable age of the synagogue, which is a Jewish central European theme found in other local legends. The legend can point to a historical moment, when a new prayer for the prince's health as a thanksgiving for the wood for the new synagogue was introduced. The narrator appears to be free from concerns about the height of the synagogue or the material used in its construction, restrictions which derive from legislation in the royal Polish and Lithuanian cities of the sixteenth and seventeenth centuries. This points to the comparatively late origins of the legend.

Architecture Meets Legend

In his ethnographic essay An-ski reported that the legend of the Olyka synagogue provides important though controversial architectural information. Most striking are the differences between the three buildings situated in the midtown area, at a 'rope's distance' from each other, and described in the legend as identical. They were to some extent familiar to An-ski from his visit to Olyka. By a process of elimination, I propose to find a structure that might have supplied the model for the Great Synagogue among the public buildings of Olyka.

The Calvinist church—converted in 1580 to the Catholic church of the Holy Trinity, dedicated in 1592 to the Apostles Peter and Paul, and still standing to the west of the marketplace—could not have supplied a model for the synagogue building, since its plan is based on the Greek cross (Brykowska 2003: 41–2, 44).

The huge Holy Trinity collegiate church, which, though now abandoned, still dominates the midtown area, was sited on the advice of the Jesuit architect Benedetto Molli, designed by Giovanni Maliverna, and built between 1635 and 1640; it was modelled on Jesuit patterns, such as the Gesù church in Rome (Zharikov 1985: 81).[23] Founded by Stanisław Albrycht Radziwiłł, the Grand Chancellor of Lithuania and the overlord of Olyka, it was the place of worship for the Catholic citizens, including college students, as well as the residents and guests at Olyka's castle situated across the esplanade and moat. Its capacious crypt was designed to be the place of eternal rest for the princely Radziwiłł family. In contrast to synagogue architecture, both the exterior and interior of the church were richly decorated with sculptures.

The town hall was built between about 1637 and 1647, at the same time as the Holy Trinity collegiate church, and was much smaller than the latter, as can be

Figure 6 Engraving of Olyka. The large structure in the centre is the Catholic collegiate Holy Trinity church; the small one to the right is the Orthodox Holy Trinity church at Zavorottya; on the left is the town hall. *From Tygodnik Ilustrowany (1860), 586*

seen from an engraving of 1860 (Figure 6) (Anon. 1860: 586; Brykowska 2003: 45). Its design essentially followed that of the town hall of 1596 in Nyasvizh, another city in the possession of the Radziwiłłs, though its tower was much lower than that in Nyasvizh, and had very little in common with the sacred buildings of Olyka (Pashkow et al. 2001: 77, 527).

A third church, the Orthodox church of the Holy Trinity, which in 1886 took the place of its precursor in Zavorottya which was destroyed in a fire, is crowned with five domes, and is very unlike the synagogue architecture of Volhynia (Teodorovich 1889: 983–4). The remaining candidate for the Christian edifice that might have supplied a model for the Great Synagogue is the Greek Catholic, later Orthodox, church of the Presentation in the Temple (Figure 7) in Zalisoche,[24] the eastern district of Olyka, situated across the river Putylivka from the Jewish quarter. This area was bounded by the city fortifications of Olyka in the 1620s and 1630s. Later it became a separate village; however, its inhabitants continued to call themselves *mishchane* (townsmen). Their parish church was constructed in 1784 (Teodorovich 1889: 984). The extant church is masonry, with a wooden dome based on an octagonal plan after the Dome of the Rock in Jerusalem, in accordance with the theme of the Temple made explicit in the dedication of the church—Christians in medieval and later times often thought that the Dome (a Muslim structure) was actually Solomon's Temple, and therefore used it as a model for church architecture. The church of the Presentation is one

Figure 7 Church of the Presentation in the Temple at Zalisoche. Photo: Sergey Kravtsov, 2003

of a very small group of Volhynian churches to follow this design (Kowalczyk 1997: 400, 402; Zharikov 1985: 76–7), and was probably modelled on the octagonal cemetery chapel of All Saints (1773–5) in the Volhynian town of Pochayiv (Rychkov 1995: 87–8; Zharikov 1986: 76–7). Its decorative elements include paintings of the Four Evangelists in the cupola and eight icons of the remaining Apostles at the piers.[25] Thus the composition expresses 'the twelvefold completeness of the chosen people', a reference to the twelve tribes of the Old Testament, and explicit also in the twelve alabaster figures of the Apostles in Olyka's Holy Trinity collegiate church (Averintsev 1991: 355). During my visit in the town in 2006 I asked the priest, Father Mykolay—a local resident since 1962—about legends regarding the origins of his church. He said that it was erected on the parishioners' account. Asked whether Radziwiłł allowed the construction, he replied: 'The old prince would never prohibit such a comely thing', obviously referring to the collective image of the Radziwiłłs as Olyka's benefactors (see Teodorovich 1889: 984). An interesting legend explained the presence of a tank shell in the church's wall, a modern version of the story of a miraculously unexploded cannonball that hits a sacred building, known from the Maharsha synagogue of Ostroh and Lviv Cathedral. However, Father Mykolay could not remember any legend linking the church to a synagogue of Olyka.

The octagonal design of the church of the Presentation in the Temple could have been an acceptable model for synagogue architecture in the 1780s. In a responsum dating from 1788 Rabbi Ezekiel ben Judah Landau of Prague expressed no opposition to a plan to build an octagonal synagogue, as long as it was not intended to follow a non-Jewish model (Landau 1969: no. 18). The question had been submitted to the rabbi by the Ashkenazi community of Trieste, where an octagonal synagogue was never actually built. The idea emerged again in Berlin as a competition design for a synagogue in 1848, and was realized the same year in the German city of Hildesheim, and later in Paderborn (1881), and in Bad Driburg-Pömbsen (1886) (Birkmann and Stratmann 1998: 148–9, 192–3; Bothe 1983: 79, 81). However, in Olyka, this kind of synagogue design remained a purely theoretical possibility. It is my contention that the architectural element that suggests a comparison between the church and the synagogue in Olyka is not the octagonal shape but the cupola over the central bay of the wooden synagogue. It is not referred to in any document, but it could have been easily accommodated in the high, multi-tiered roof evident in Orda's drawing, as was the case in many other synagogues. The similar synagogue of Torhovytsya (Figure 8)—with its

Figure 8 Interior view of the synagogue at Torhovytsya. Photo: Szymon Zajczyk, before 1939. *Reproduced by courtesy of the Insytut Sztuki, Polish Academy of Sciences, Warsaw*

Figure 9 Hebrew printer's mark showing the Dome of the Rock as a messianic temple, printed in the books of Marco Antonio Giustiniani, Venice, 1552. The image shows the temple as a twelve-sided structure, though the Dome of the Rock is octagonal. The Hebrew inscriptions read as follows: on the banner, 'The [latter] glory of this house shall be greater [than the former], says the Lord of Hosts' (Haggai 2: 9); above and below the temple, 'For all the peoples walk each in the name of its god, but we will walk in the name of the Lord our God [for ever and ever]' (Micah 4: 5); on the temple itself, 'House of the Lord' (2 Chronicles 36: 7) (translations from the Standard English Edition). *Reproduced by courtesy of the Gross Family Collection*

wooden imitations of retaining arches which divide the flat ceiling into nine bays—accommodated a central, twelve-sided cupola decorated with the signs of the zodiac. This composition could have been repeated in Olyka. The centric structure of the Dome of the Rock, which tops the Temple Mount in Jerusalem, was also a recognizable messianic symbol in Jewish art from at least the sixteenth century (Figure 9; Sabar 1998). It is represented in the illustration of the messianic temple in the 1739 Passover Haggadah of Issachar Baer ben Yaacov Hayim of Olyka (Figure 10).[26] It could have served as the common denominator in the late Baroque Christian and Jewish sacred architecture of Volhynia. In the case of the synagogue it could only be seen from the interior, whereas in the case of the church it could be seen from the exterior. It appears only in the Jewish narrative.

The interpretation of an interior cupola as modelled on the Dome of the Rock, and hence alluding to the Temple at Jerusalem, is an alternative to the accepted view that such constructions refer to the Tabernacle, the portable sanctuary (Hubka 2003: 93–4; Piechotka and Piechotka 1996: 129–30), an interpretation that implies that the Jews saw themselves as nomads. However, the literary image of the Polish Jews as people wandering in the wilderness is a comparatively recent trend, evident in the writing of S. Y. Agnon (1888–1970) and Aaron Zeitlin (1898–1973); it would be anachronistic to attribute it to pre-Zionist times (Bar-Itzhak 2001: 37–8). The interpretation that I am proposing for the interior cupola would remove the apparent contradiction between most of the building, evidently an imitation of masonry architecture, and the cupola, which allegedly symbolizes

מין מוֹנזרן טמנין טירה · יוֹמ טירה · טוֹמ בוֹימ כוֹימ בוֹימ · מין · מין מ
מוֹנזרן טמנין טירה · בֿמריס הערלֿינֿר גֿלֿיט גֿרוֹטֿיר גֿמט ·
דֿ עַ אוֹטינֿר גֿמֿט · כוֹן בוֹים דֿיין טענֿמֿפֿיֿל טירה · מֿלֿוֹי טיר מוֹכֿ
מֿלֿוֹי בֿמֿלֿוֹד מין מוֹנזרן טמנין טירה יוֹמ טירה · כוֹן בוֹימ · כוֹן
בוֹימ דֿיין טענֿמֿפֿיֿל טירה · הֿכֿ3ֿיר גֿמֿט · 1 וערדֿינֿר גֿמֿט
יֿ פֿר גֿמֿט · דֿ עטֿר גֿמֿט · כוֹן בוֹימ דֿיין טענֿמֿפֿיֿל טירה ·
הֿלֿוֹי טיר מוֹכֿ/ מֿלֿוֹי בֿמֿלֿוֹד מין מוֹנזרן טמנֿן טירה · יוֹמ טירה
כוֹן בוֹימ כוֹן בוֹימ דֿיין טענֿמֿפֿיֿל טירה · כֿ וֿלֿ3ֿיר גֿמֿט יֿ דֿיטֿר
גֿמֿט כֿ רעֿ9ֿטֿינֿר לֿ עבֿנֿדֿיֿגֿר גֿמֿט · כוֹן בוֹימ דֿיין טענֿמֿפֿיֿל
טירה מֿלֿוֹי טיר מוֹכֿ מֿלֿוֹי בֿמֿלֿוֹד מין מוֹנזרן טמנֿין טיר · יוֹמ ·
טירה כוֹן בוֹימ כוֹן בוֹימ דֿיין טענֿמֿפֿיֿל טירה

Figure 10 Page from Issachar Baer ben Yaacov Hayim of Olyka's Passover Haggadah (1739), showing the messianic temple as an octagonal domed structure. MS Mic 8896, fo. 37v. *Reproduced by courtesy of the Library of the Jewish Theological Seminary*

a tent. The cupola would more likely emphasize the hope for the rebuilding of the Temple rather than the Tabernacle, a symbol of wandering.[27]

The four wooden pillars seen in photographs of the synagogue in Olyka were also a symbol of the Temple of Jerusalem. The four-pier, nine-bay synagogue layout was introduced into Polish masonry architecture during the 1620s in the synagogues of Lviv and Ostroh. It was based on the imaginary reconstruction of the Temple after Ezekiel's vision by the Jesuit theorist Juan Bautista Villalpando (Kravtsov 2005a: 317–24). The barley-sugar shape of the 'Solomonic' columns of the *aron hakodesh* in Olyka were another element thought to have been originally inspired by the Temple at Jerusalem: Catholics believed that the barley-sugar columns of St Peter's shrine in Rome had been brought there from the destroyed Temple, and the Jews then took this architectural element from the Christians (Ward-Perkins 1952). Thus, various applications of the same sacred prototype were somewhat tautological but convincing metaphors of the Temple. They pointed, elsewhere, to the Promised Land, the Holy City, and the rebuilt Temple, and to the eschatological future expected 'speedily in our days'. This connection between the actual place of residence and prayer and the sacred 'elsewhere' is expressed in Jewish legends of the subterranean passage to Jerusalem, the stones of the Temple being incorporated in the building of a synagogue, and the miraculous transfer of all the synagogues of the Diaspora to the Holy Land as taught in the Talmud (BT *Meg.* 29a (Epstein 1984); for a folkloric interpretation of this theme see Bar-Itzhak 1992, 2001: 38).

Figure 11 Interior of the Maharsha synagogue, Ostroh. Photo: Henryk Poddębski, 1922. *Reproduced by courtesy of the Insytut Sztuki, Polish Academy of Sciences, Warsaw*

Architecture states these links in its own language. The wooden synagogues of Olyka or Torhovytsya echo the masonry Maharsha synagogue of Ostroh (Figure 11); they should be interpreted not only in the physical terms of their design, or as wooden replicas of a masonry model, but also culturally and spiritually as a sequence of places where the Taz taught, took refuge, and saved a small community. Local, individual and collective salvation thus finds itself caught up in a wider story of redemption, and both the local and the universal are legible in the architecture of these synagogues.

The dates of the church of the Presentation in the Temple (1874) and of the application for the new synagogue (1788) coincide with the period when Prince Karol Stanisław Radziwiłł was lord of Olyka. Referred to by his nickname Panie Kochanku, he was one of the most colourful and controversial personalities of his time.[28] From a Jewish viewpoint he was definitely 'a wicked and vicious man', unlike most of his noble family. A long list of his 'feats' on the Jewish street is given by philosopher Solomon Maimon (1754–1800), who was born in Nyasvizh: the prince once jestingly opened the veins of the local Jewish barber; being drunk, he urinated on the church altar and then levied a tax of wax on the Jews as a sin-offering for the purification of the church; accompanied by his court, he went to a synagogue, smashed windows and stoves, threw the Torah scroll on the floor, and hit a pious Jew who tried to rescue it with a musket-ball (Maimon 1954: 63–5). A folk tale known from a Polish source tells how Panie Kochanku demanded the extermination of all the Jews of Nyasvizh (Maciejowski 1878: 136–7).[29] Other stories describe him ordering a Jew to climb a tree, shooting him, and then declaring himself happy with having killed 'a cuckoo'; or riding horses into a crowd of Jews returning from sabbath prayers, catching a Jew, and then releasing him in a field beyond the *eruv* (boundary), thus rendering him unable to return home before nightfall; or kidnapping Jewish girls (Stokfish 1976: 20–4).[30] There are many anecdotes about and by Panie Kochanku, in which he appears as a malevolent trickster or a spendthrift gentleman but a master of his word. Towards the end of his life he was possessed by a passion to relate fantastic stories (Michalski 1972: 260). I have not found, however, any analogue to the legend of the Great Synagogue of Olyka in Radziwiłł's legacy.

The architect who served Panie Kochanku was Leon Lutnicki. He signed his works as a 'warrant officer', 'architect', or 'surveyor'.[31] His most interesting project was the Altana Palace (1780) at the Alba Park by Nyasvizh (Figure 12). This was an extravagant, three-storey octagonal building with rusticated corners, and bucrania in the capitals of the pilasters and in the frieze that ran round the exterior of the building. It included minarets topped with crescents, and a concave

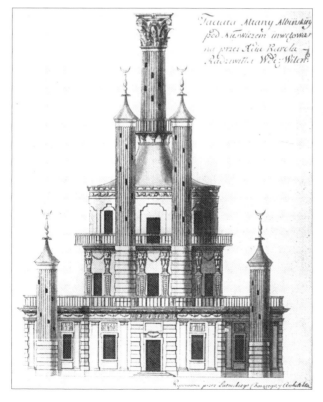

Figure 12 The Altana Palace, Alba Park by Nyasvizh. Drawing by Leon Lutnicki, 1780. *Reproduced by courtesy of the University Library, Warsaw*

'Chinese' roof crowned with an enormous Corinthian column. The local legend of Nyasvizh compares this building, destroyed in the Napoleonic Wars, to St Sophia in Constantinople (Shyshyhina-Patotskaya 2001: 35). The Corinthian order together with the octagonal plan suggest an affinity with the Temple of Solomon (Kravtsov 2005a: 315–16), thus glorifying the wisdom and divine inspiration of its founder. This design might be related to models from Freemasonry known to Panie Kochanku (who was apparently among the founders of the Masonic lodge known as 'Au Vertueux Voyageur') and his stepbrother Maciej Radziwiłł (1749–1800), the second steward of the 'Zum Tempel Weisheit' and 'Isistempel' Masonic lodges (Hass 1982: 107).[32] However, I do not see any direct link between the Freemasons' legend of Hiram as a master builder of the Temple, killed by his wicked apprentices, which circulated among the elite (see Curl 2002: 32–4), and the Jewish folk tale of the Olyka synagogue, mainly because of the considerable number of differences between the stories. Panie Kochanku is by no means seen in the legend as King Solomon, a client of Hiram, and his pretension to be a just judge is vain. As for Lutnicki's fate, he reconstructed St Michael's Catholic church and another church of the Eastern rite at Nyasvizh in 1790, the year of Prince Karol's death, and went on to serve his successor, Prince Dominik in 1793 (Michalski 1972: 260; AGAD, AR 21-L100, fo. 40).

Thus, the church of the Presentation in the Temple and the wooden synagogue of the late 1780s were the possible models for the legend. Their architectural elements could well have been similar, given the significant references to the Dome of the Rock and the Temple of Jerusalem. Since the dates of construction are known, we can identify the 'wicked and vicious' overlord of Olyka as Karol Stanisław Radziwiłł. However, his architect Leon Lutnicki could not have been the victim in the story as he was still alive three years after his client's death.

The Jewish memory of Olyka as expressed in local legends is related to its history. Legends adapt history to the rules of the genre, and to the knowledge of the sacred past and promised future. In this way, a castle and a synagogue can be interchangeable, years can become days, and a prayer miraculously saves the Jewish community and heals its benefactor. Here, in the circle of a narrator and his listeners, the Jews feel protected by their faith, able to survive the calamities in their native town.

The Jewish legends exploit diverse sources, including the Scriptures, as in the legend of the Taz, and the folkloric themes of the neighbouring non-Jewish communities, such as the master builder tale. Such a cultural exchange between Jewish and Ukrainian folklore is possible as long as the subject does not touch directly on the relations between these two groups but rather involves a third force, the wicked and vicious prince with his architect, and projects the evil onto them.

In the realm of architecture, communication between Jews and non-Jews is easier to assess, since the sacred buildings quote the same iconographical source or family of sources related to the Temple of Jerusalem. The Great Synagogue of Olyka was a sign of Jewish commitment to the place, even in the days when it was seen as less important in comparison to other, newer, houses of prayer. It was vital for the local Jews to convince themselves of its antiquity, and hence legality. At the same time, it spoke, through its architectural language, of other venerable places, such as Ostroh, from where it had borrowed its plan, and the Temple Mount in Jerusalem, the legendary source of inspiration and radiation of the divine beauty, the final spiritual destination.

Notes

I wish to express my profound gratitude to Mykola Bevz, Maria E. Brykowska, Judy Cardozo, Nati Cohen, Olga Goldberg, Maria Grobman, Sharman Kadish, Vladimir Levin, Benjamin Lukin, Roman Mohytych, Dov Noy, Vladimir Pervyshyn, Petro Rychkov, Dvora Sax, Irina Sergeeva, Vasyl Slobodyan, and Magdalena Tarnowska for their kind advice and help with my research.

1   Today Olyka belongs to the Volynska *oblast'* of Ukraine. Its Yiddish name is Olik or Alik; Ołyka is its Polish name.

2   TsDIAUK, collection 25, registry 1, file 263, fos. 675ᵛ–676.

3   *AYuZR*, pt 7, vol. iii, 121.

4   AGAD, AR 20-9-4, fos. 56–7.

5   Ibid., fos. 60–2.

6   AGAD, AR 20-12-3, fos. 4–5.

7   AGAD, AR 20-9-7, fos. 85–8.

8   The Polish text reads:

Po spaleniu w r. 1787 bożnicy, jeszcze dotychczas kahał nie wystarawszy się zdatnych materiałów na nowey zbudowanie, zebrze wspomagający od Jego Wielkoksiążęcej Miłości Pana i Miłościwego Dobrodzieja w uzyskaniu zaliceń tak i do Jegomości Pana Przetockiego leśniczego, o dozwolenie lasu na wypuszczenie drzewa, jako też y do Jegomości Ekonoma Ołyckiego o niewzbronienie tartaku.

Żądanych dobrodziejstw skorzystaniem pod ratowany kahał w nowozbudowanej mianej bożnicy y nowy zabierze obowiązek błagania Tronu Najwyższego Boga o przedłużenia dni pełnych miłego zdrowia Książę cemu Panowaniu, i ponowi chęci do wiernego zostawania w dozgonnym wyznaniu że razem z nami czoła swoje pod stopy książęce schyliaić—Prawdziwy.

Jaśnie oświeconey waszej książęcey mości | Pana Dobrodzieja | Podnózek y szczere życzący | Poddany | Cały kahał ołycki | Pisan na Ołyce | Dnia 25 januarij 1788 roku.

See NARB, collection 694, registry 2, fos. 9–10.

9   RGVIA, file 21546, fo. 1.

10   MNK, III-r.a. 4218 (file 'Volhynia'). The drawing is labelled *Ołyka*; the inscription in the underlay reads: 'Wołyń. Ołyka,—kościół parafialny 1874' (Volhynia. Olyka,—the Catholic parish church). See Piechotka and Piechotka 1996: 296–7 (the Piechotkas erroneously date Orda's drawing to *c.*1867).

11　　The translation is taken from Bar-Itzhak 2001: 136.

12　　The original Yiddish word is *kostsiol*, corresponding to the Polish *kościół* (a Catholic church). See An-ski 1925: 248.

13　　An-ski's expedition had definitely seen and photographed the wooden synagogue of Olyka.

14　　Translation from Weinreich 1988: 330–1.

15　　Yiddish: *dukas*.

16　　Yiddish: *kloister*. This could mean any denomination of church.

17　　Translation by Mikhail Nosonovsky from State Ethnographic Museum 1992: 71.

18　　Translation ibid. 15.

19　　Petzoldt 1978: 274–5 and 450, no. 446b. In west Ukraine I have heard a builders' joke about two carpenters. One throws the other an axe: 'Pass me the axe mate!—Catch it!—Ahhh!—What does "Ahhh" mean? Have you caught it or not?'

20　　It is classified as a universal motif W181.2 in Thompson 1957: 497.

21　　This theme can be identified as motif S165.7 according to Thompson 1957: 312.

22　　A local schoolteacher told this story to Vasyl Slobodyan in 1984.

23　　On Polish parallels to the Holy Trinity collegiate church in Olyka, see Brykowska 2003: 46–8.

24　　The Ukrainian term for the Presentation in the Temple is *Stritennya*.

25　　Actually, there are two tiers of icons of the Apostles, the older icons above the new ones, both depicting the same figures.

26　　New York, Jewish Theological Seminary, MS Mic 8896, 37ᵛ.

27　　For more criticism on Hubka's Tabernacle theory see Moshe Rosman's review of Hubka, *Resplendent Synagogue* (Rosman 2006: 165–8).

28　　'Panie Kochanku' means 'My Darling Lord'. On Karol Stanisław Radziwiłł see Borucki 1980; Jodłowski 2001; Królikowski 2000; Maciejowski 1985; Michalski 1972; Sidorski 1987; and Stępnik 2003.

29　　This subject was used by the Russian Jewish writer Lev O. Levanda (1835–88) in his novel *Gnev i milost' magnata* (Odessa, 1912).

30　　The motif of a 'cuckoo' is also found in a legend about Hieronim Florian Radziwiłł (1715–60): see Jodłowski 2001: 10.

31　　The Polish reads 'chorąży i architekt'. See Warsaw University Library's collection of graphics, Zb. Krol. P. 188, nos 1–3. The Polish word for surveyor is *geometra*. See ibid., no. 4.

32　　The stepbrothers were close from the late 1770s: see Anusik and Stroynowski 1972.

References

Primary Sources

AGAD. Archiwum Główne Akt Dawnych [Central Archives of Historical Records]. Warsaw.

AYuZR. Arkhiv Yugo-Zapadnoi Rossii [Archive of South-Western Russia]. Kiev, 1905.

MNK. Muzeum Narodowe w Krakowie [National Museum, Kraków].

NARB. Natsional'nyi arkhiv Respubliki Belarus' [National Archive of Belarus Republic].

RGVIA. Rossiiskii gosudarstvennyi voenno-istoricheskii arkhiv. [Russian State Military Historical Archives].

TsDIAUK. Tsentral'nyi derzhavnyi istorychnyi arkhiv Ukrayiny v misti Kyyevi [Central State Historical Archive of Ukraine, Kiev].

Other Sources

ANON. 1860. 'Ołyka', *Tygodnik ilustrowany*, 62: 585–7.

AN-SKI, S. 1925. 'Old Synagogues and their Legends' (Yiddish). In *Complete Works* [Gezamlte shriftn], vol. xv. Vilnius.

ANUSIK, ZBIGNIEW, and ANDRZEJ STROYNOWSKI. 1972. 'Radziwiłł, Maciej', *Polski słownik biograficzny*, vol. xxx, pp. 285–8. Warsaw.

AVERINTSEV, SERGEY S. 1991. 'Dvenadtsat' apostolov'. In Sergey A. Tokarev, ed., *Mify narodov mira*, vol. i, pp. 355–7. Moscow.

BAR-ITZHAK, HAYA. 1992. 'Space in Jewish Saints' Legends' (Heb.), *Tura*, 2: 191–233.

—— 2001. *Jewish Poland—Legends of Origin: Ethnopoetics and Legendary Chronicles.* Detroit.

BIBER, MENAHEM MENDEL. 1903. *Menachem's Anthology* [Yalkut menaḥem]. Vilnius.

BIRKMANN, GÜNTER, and HARTMUT STRATMANN. 1998. *Bedenke vor wem Du stehst. 300 Synagogen in Westfalen und Lippe*. Essen.

BORUCKI, MAREK. 1980. *Po radziwiłłowsku: O życiu i działalności politycznej wojewody wileńskiego księcia Karola Radziwiłła 'Panie Kochanku'*. Warsaw.

BOTHE, ROLF. 1983. *Synagogen in Berlin. Zur Geschichte einer zerstörten Architektur*, vol. i. Berlin.

BRYKOWSKA, MARIA. 2003. 'Urbanistyka i architektura Ołyki w XVI–XVII wieku'. In Alicja Sulimierska, and Alicja Szmelter, eds, *Studium Urbis: Charisteria Teresiae Zarębska Anno Iubilaei Oblata*, 37–50. Warsaw.

CHLEBOWSKI, BRONISŁAW, and WŁADYSŁAW WALEWSKI, eds. 1888. *Słownik geograficzny Królestwa Polskiego i innych krajów słowiańskich*, vol. vii. Warsaw.

CURL, JAMES STEVENS. 2002. *The Art and Architecture of Freemasonry*. London.

DOBRZYCKI, JERZY. 1983. *Hejnał Krakowski*. Kraków.

EPSTEIN, I, ed. 1984. *Hebrew–English Edition of the Babylonian Talmud. Megillah*, English trans., with notes, glossary, and indices, by Maurice Simon. London.

GRINSTEIN, MICHAEL. 1973. *Never Again*. Los Angeles.

HANNOVER, NATHAN BEN MOSES. 1983. *Abyss of Despair (Yeven Metzulah): The Famous 17th Century Chronicle Depicting Jewish Life in Russia and Poland during the Chmielnicki Massacre of 1648–1649*, trans. Abraham J. Mesch. New Brunswick, NJ.

HASS, LUDWIK. 1982. *Wolnomularstwo w Europie środkowo-wschodniej w XVIII i XIX wieku*. Wrocław.

HEYDUK, BRONISŁAW. 1980. *Legendy i opowieści o Krakowie*, 3rd edn. Kraków.

HRUSHEVSKY, MYKHAILO. 1928. *Istoriya Ukrayiny–Rusy*, vol. ix/1. Lviv.

HUBKA, THOMAS C. 2003. *Resplendent Synagogue: Architecture and Worship in an Eighteenth-Century Polish Community*. Hanover, NH.

JAINDL, ELISABETH. 1992. *Der Stephansdom im alten Wien. Geschichte und Geschichten*. Korneuburg.

JODŁOWSKI, ANTONI. 2001. *Legendy i bajki o bialskich Radziwiłłach*. Biała Podlaska.

KLYMASH, I. S., et al., eds. 1970. *Istoriya mist i sil Ukrayins'koyi RSR: Volyns'ka oblast'*. Kiev.

KNOOP, OTTO. 1909. 'Die Teufelskirche bei Dembe'. In *Ostmärkische Sagen, Märchen und Erzählungen*, 53–4 (no. 35). Leszno.

KOWALCZYK, JERZY. 1997. 'Elementy Świątyni Salomona w kościołach nowożytnych w Polsce'. In Piotr Paszkiewicz and Tadeusz Zadrożny, eds, *Jerozolima w kulturze europejskiej*, 395–406. Warsaw.

KRAVTSOV, SERGEY R. 2005a. 'Juan Bautista Villalpando and Sacred Architecture in the Seventeenth Century', *Journal of the Society of Architectural Historians*, 3: 312–39.

—— 2005b. 'Gothic Survival in Synagogue Architecture of the 17th and 18th Centuries in Volhynia, Ruthenia and Podolia', *Architectura. Zeitschrift für Geschichte der Baukunst*, 1: 69–94.

KREMER, H. 1972. 'R. Noah's Freydke of Olyka Tells An-ski the Tale of Dibbuk' (Yiddish). In Natan Livne, ed., *Memorial Book of the Community of Olyka* [Pinkas hakehilah olika: sefer yizkor], 69–72. Tel Aviv.

KRÓLIKOWSKI, BOHDAN. 2000. *Wśród Sarmatów: Radziwiłłowie i pamiętnikarze*. Lublin.

LANDAU, EZEKIEL BEN JUDAH. 1969. *Known in Judah: Questions and Answers on the Four Parts of the Shulḥan arukh* [Noda biyehudah: she'ilot veteshuvot be'arba ḥalkei Shulḥan arukh], vol. ii. Jerusalem.

Laurentian Codex. *Lavrent'evskaya letopis'*, ed. Aleksey A. Shakhmatov, 2nd edn. Leningrad, 1926–8.

LINDHEIM, RALPH, and GEORGE S. N. LUCKYJ, eds. 1996. 'The Bendery Constitution'. In *Towards an Intellectual History of Ukraine: An Anthology of Ukrainian Thought from 1710 to 1995*. Toronto.

LIVNE, NATAN, ed. 1972. *Memorial Book of the Community of Olyka* [Pinkas hakehilah olika: sefer yizkor]. Tel Aviv.

MACIEJOWSKI, MARIAN. 1985. '*Choć Radziwiłł, alem człowiek . . .': Gawęda romantyczna prozą*. Kraków.

MACIEJOWSKI, WACŁAW A. 1878. *Żydzi w Polsce, na Rusi i w Litwie*. Warsaw.

MAIMON, SOLOMON. 1954. *Autobiography*. London.

MICHALSKI, JERZY. 1972. 'Radziwiłł, Karol Stanisław', *Polski słownik biograficzny*, vol. xxx, pp. 248–62. Warsaw.

PASHKOW, H. P., et al., eds. 2001. *Pamyats' Nyasvizhski rayon*. Minsk.

PETZOLDT, LEANDER. 1978. *Deutsche Volkssagen*, 2nd edn. Munich.

PIECHOTKA, MARIA, and KAZIMIERZ PIECHOTKA. 1996. *Bramy nieba: Bożnice drewniane na ziemiach dawnej Rzeczypospolitej*. Warsaw.

RADZIWIŁŁ, ALBRYCHT S. 1974. *Memoriale Rerum Gestarum in Polonia, 1632–1656*, ed. Adam Przyboś and Roman Żelewski, vol. iv. Wrocław.

RECHTMAN, ABRAHAM. 1958. *Jewish Ethnography and Folklore: Memories from the Ethnographical Expedition Directed by Professor Shmuel An-ski* [Yidishe etnografie un folklor: zikhroynes vegn der etnografisher ekspeditsie, angefirt fun prof. sh. ansky]. Buenos Aires.

ROSMAN, MOSHE. 2006. 'Resplendent Book', *Ars Judaica*, 2: 165–8.

RYCHKOV, PETRO. 1995. 'Do istorii formuvannya arkhitekturnoho ansamblyu Pochayivs'koyi lavry'. In *Arkhitekturna spadshchyna*, vol. ii, pp. 78–89. Kiev.

SABAR, SHALOM. 1998. 'Messianic Aspirations and Renaissance Urban Ideals: The Image of Jerusalem in the Venice Haggadah, 1609'. In Bianca Kühnel, ed., *The Real and Ideal Jerusalem in Jewish, Christian and Islamic Art* [= *Jewish Art*, 23/4], 295–312. Jerusalem.

SCHOLEM, GERSHOM. 1973. *Sabbatai Ṣevi: The Mystical Messiah, 1626—1676*. Princeton.

SERGEEVA, IRINA. 2001. 'Kiev Collection of S. An-sky's Manuscripts'. In Alexander Kantsedikas and Irina Sergeeva, *The Jewish Artistic Heritage Album by Semyon An-sky*, 142–207. Moscow.

SHELDRAKE, PHILIP. 2001. *Spaces for the Sacred: Place, Memory, and Identity*. Baltimore.

SHISHIGINA-POTOTSKAYA, KLAVDIYA YA. (Shyshyhina-Patotskaya, Klawdziya Ya.) 1997. *Legendy Nesvizha*. Minsk.

—— 2001. *Nyasvizh i Radzivily*. Minsk.

SIDORSKI, DIONIZY. 1987. '*Panie Kochanku*'. Katowice.

State Ethnographic Museum. 1992. *Tracing An-sky: Jewish Collections from the State Ethnographic Museum in St Petersburg*. Zwolle.

STECKI, TADEUSZ J. 1887. 'Radziwiłłowska Ołyka', *Przegląd Powszechny*, 15: 33–41.

STĘPNIK KRZYSZTOF, ed. 2003. *Radziwiłłowie: Obrazy literackie, biografie, świadectwa historyczne*. Lublin.

STOKFISH, DAVID, ed. 1976. *Sefer niasvizh* [Book of Nyasvizh]. Tel Aviv.

TALOŞ, ION. 1977. 'Baumeister'. In Lotte Baumann, Ines Köhler, et al., eds, *Enzyklopädie des Märchens. Handwörterbuch zur historischen und vergleichenden Erzählforschung*, vol. i: 1394–8. Berlin.

TEODOROVICH, NIKOLAY I. 1889. *Istoriko-statisticheskoe opisanie tserkvei i prikhodov Volynskoi eparkhii*, vol. ii. Pochayiv.

TERSKY, SVYATOSLAV. 2001. *Olyka: Istorychnyi narys*. Lviv.

THOMPSON, STITH. 1957. *Motif-Index of Folk-Literature*, vol. v. Copenhagen.

TUAN, YI-FU. 2001 [1976]. *Space and Place: The Perspective of Experience*. Minneapolis.

UTHER, HANS-JÖRG. 2004. *The Types of International Folktales: A Classification and Bibliography. Based on the System of Antti Aarne and Stith Thompson*, vol. ii. Helsinki.

WARD-PERKINS, JOHN B. 1952. 'The Shrine of St. Peter and its Twelve Spiral Columns', *Journal of Roman Studies*, 42: 21–33.

WEINREICH, BEATRICE, ed. 1988. *Yiddish Folktales*, trans. Leonard Wolf. New York.

ZHARIKOV, NIKOLAY L., ed. 1985. *Pamyatniki gradostroitel'stva i arkhitektury Ukrainskoi SSR*, vol. ii. Kiev.

——ed. 1986. *Pamyatniki gradostroitel'stva i arkhitektury Ukrainskoi SSR*, vol. iv. Kiev.

THREE

Yiddish in the Aftermath: Speech Community and Cultural Continuity in Displaced Persons Camps

MIRIAM ISAACS

As Jews from various countries gathered in displaced persons (DP) camps in central Europe in the immediate aftermath of the Holocaust, talk, as well as writing, was preoccupied with how the recent past would be linked to, or unhinged from, a cultural future. Having witnessed the near-annihilation of their civilization, many survivors set about a rescue effort to preserve and reconstruct whatever they could, usually from memory, of their pre-war world and of their wartime experiences. They also contemplated how memory would be communicated. Language, a central aspect of cultural identity, was debated in the Yiddish press of the DP camps, and one issue was how Yiddish—associated with the destroyed, pre-Holocaust world of eastern Europe—would figure in a reconstructed, re-located post-Holocaust world. As emigration to British-controlled Palestine[1] grew, many survivors argued for Hebrew as the primary Jewish language. This discourse raised questions about the future cultural function of Yiddish, alongside the many other languages brought from former Jewish homelands, especially Polish, Hungarian, Czech, and Russian. In this essay I will reflect on this critical period of cultural reformation and ask how Jewish, and particularly Yiddish-speaking, survivors' attitudes and aspirations were connected with the language they used. I will also discuss the related contextual issue of how the use of English or German in the American and British zones of occupied Germany and Austria figured in the recovery of Jewish culture.

Jews in the DP camps produced a number of Yiddish publications whose aim was to renew Jewish cultural life. But even as the camp setting fostered the use of Yiddish as a lingua franca, survivors recognized that the role of the language and its culture was changing. Despite the efforts of Yiddishist writers and cultural activists to sustain it, Yiddish stood at a critical juncture: the debate over the adoption of a common language to unify Jewish civilization was not new, but in the DP camps it set the stage for the future development of Jewish culture. The Jewish

DP camps held the last sizeable Yiddish-speaking community in Europe, as survivors just out of the death camps or emerging from hiding gathered from across Europe in camps in occupied Germany, Austria, and Italy. At first the occupying forces grouped survivors by country of origin, but as an influx of refugees arrived Jews were housed together, whatever their country of origin, in makeshift camps, or settled in nearby cities and towns. Within these groups Yiddish speakers formed a significant speech community in which the familiar and homey vernacular served for daily communication, as well as being the language of literature and public discourse.

Living on rations, having lost all their books, with limited printing facilities, and with their schools and homes destroyed, salvaging their culture became largely an act of memory and will. By the late summer of 1945, about 146,000 Jewish DPs had officially registered in the American zone of occupied Germany. According to Joint Distribution Committee statistics, of these, over two-thirds, about 100,000, were living in DP camps, 36,000 were living in German towns and cities, mainly in the Munich area, 3,800 were in agricultural collectives (known as 'kibbutzim'), and over 4,000 were in children's homes (Dinnerstein 1990). The number of DPs was swelled in 1946 by Jews who had fled Poland and the USSR. At their peak, the two largest DP camps, Landsberg and Föhrenwald, each held some 3,000 Jews, while many smaller camps were scattered over the occupied zone. In these places Jewish DPs formed themselves into a new entity, calling themselves the *she'erit hapeleitah*, a Hebrew term meaning 'surviving remnant', whose members soon numbered some 200,000 to 300,000 (Brenner 1997). Jewish intellectuals as well as ordinary Jews understood the existential issues to be faced as more Jews from scattered locations came together in these centres. For example, David Volpe, a Yiddish writer originally from Lithuania, relates in his autobiography that the three years following liberation until the creation of Israel, from 1945 to 1948, were 'a great constructive time for the survivors in Germany . . . an active, creative historical period [where] many-faceted nationalist organizations were on the way to exodus to Israel and to the wide world' (Volpe 1997: 300).

Cultural continuity is in large part a function of language choice. The many Yiddish publications in the DP camps provide ample evidence of Jewish efforts to salvage and transform Ashkenazi culture. Survivors' memories, now carefully preserved in archives, memoirs, and interviews, provide a vivid portrait of the era. YIVO, the Yiddish Research Institute, has carefully preserved most of the Yiddish DP camp publications on thirty-three reels of microfiche, making available the words and images of the writers and artists who created them. I have used this material to interpret the choices and loyalties that shaped the language practices of the time and the policies the intelligentsia of the camps articulated. I look, first, at factors internal to the DP camps and, second, at external factors influencing language use, especially political and Zionist organizations and agencies.

Languages in Cultural Reclamation

Material losses are easier to enumerate but do not cut as deeply as personal and cultural ones. When disaster struck the Jews of eastern Europe in the Second World War, little of material worth remained. After the cataclysm, survivors took stock of what had been lost and then had to decide what to rebuild, what to save, what to replace, and what to leave irretrievably behind. Languages were part of the cultural dilemma, for languages linked one in inextricable ways to one's country of origin and identity. Every effort to communicate revealed where one came from and who one was socially and religiously.

David Adler, in an almanac written in 1947 to record daily life in the camp, described the survivor dilemma in the following vivid terms:

Several weeks after liberation, barely sobered from the drunkenness of feeling liberated, sobered from the rush to satisfy the demands of the flesh, we began to look around us to see where in the world we were. We began to take stock of ourselves, our physical freedom being unbelievable, but a fact. But what about our souls, our spirits? What about the inheritance that our parents gave us and our duty to perpetuate it as Jews? (Adler 1947: 3)

Adler and many of his contemporaries, religious and non-religious alike, felt obliged to bring about a restoration of Jewish spiritual life for fellow survivors. He expressed loyalty to a shared heritage that was inextricably linked to prior generations by a 'golden chain' (in Yiddish *di goldene keyt*). Time and again in survivor literature we find the survivors referring to themselves as the 'last Mohicans', the remnant of a disappearing culture. Writing and publishing served them as an outlet for expressing their condition and, partially, as an instrument to overcome their helplessness. In this way the public use of Jewish languages was a key to psychological recovery.

A key part of the process of identity formation and recovery was an angry rejection of former loyalties. But this was a mixed phenomenon, for some continued to use Polish or Hungarian, not knowing Yiddish or still preferring their former national languages. Most remaining Jews sought to leave Germany as soon as they could, or to leave Europe altogether. They felt that, unless one converted to Christianity, staying was too dangerous, and too painful a reminder of recent betrayals. The bulk of the survivors were eager to remain Jews and so sought to leave Europe, with its history of pogroms and antisemitism.

While the drive to leave was strong, survivors had few practical options in the early years. Palestine had been closed by the British, Israel was not created until 1948, and the United States and most other countries had restrictive entry requirements for Jews. The survivors were bitterly disheartened by this state of affairs. They had imagined that once the world learned of what had happened, countries would welcome them with open arms. Instead, they had no place to go. Their old homes were no longer there for them; many had been destroyed, and reports filtered through of antisemitic riots and other actions by local popula-tions. If the numbers of the remaining Jews killed and injured in anti-Jewish events were not huge, they still loomed large in psychological terms in the overall context of the war. Many Polish Jews became convinced that they should not try to re-establish life in Poland after the violent pogrom in Kielce in July 1946, which resulted in the death of over forty Jews. Another factor was the refusal of the com-munist authorities to return pre-war property to Jews. Survivors deeply resented having to remain in Germany, where, again, there were acts of anti-Jewish vio-lence. One notorious instance, broadcast widely in the DP press, involved the murder of a Jew, Shmuel Danziger, in 1946 by Germans, and the failure of Am-ericans to protect him. According to noted Yiddish author H. Leivick, the Ameri-can authorities did not do enough to protect the surviving Jews, and even after Danziger's murder seemed more concerned with controlling the indignant Jew-ish survivors than with bringing the perpetrators to justice. Arriving in Stuttgart from America in the spring of 1946, Leivick had learned that a United Nations Relief and Rehabilitation Administration (UNRRA) director there, Harry Lerner, had been dismissed from his post for being too sympathetic to the Jews. Leivick's description of this event, much recorded in the Yiddish and DP camp press of the time, was forthright:

a squadron of new German policemen, taking advantage of the appeasing stance of the American occupation forces, invaded the courtyards of the DP camp buildings to try to see if they could, even under occupation, try a Nazi-style pogrom. The DP camp Jews opposed them. They went out, bless them, against the invaders, with anything they could grab in their hands. (Leivick 1947: 281)

As reported in the *Landsberger lagertsaytung* (Oct. 1946, p. 12), the event led to marches and protests, all of which were put down by American military person-nel concerned about worrying local Germans.

Yiddish writers protested against living on the 'blood-soaked German soil', but ironically that was nevertheless where they could find relative safety while they waited in hope of a passage elsewhere: obliged to wait out a transitional period while their condition was assessed, they were in an environment in which they could reclaim a modicum of self-determination (Gruber 2000). Their for-mer home countries had proven inimical to Jews, and so their local languages and cultures became simply irrelevant, a habit continued from the pre-war years but now of limited use.

During the war years Jews had little opportunity to control their collective cul-tural survival. Those who had once felt strong connections to their homeland were generally embittered and sought to sunder old cultural loyalties. Already deracinated, they had no real alternative but to fix up their barracks, educate themselves, and wait for a better future outside Europe. Eventually almost all left for a wider Jewish diaspora that had already developed in the wake of the pogroms and impoverishment that had begun in the 1880s and continued through the First World War; this diaspora became central rather than peripheral. Survivors ultimately voted with their feet and migrated to places as far flung as Australia, South Africa, China, South America, and Canada. Most, though, ultimately settled in the United States and Erets Yisra'el. Estimates of the number of Jewish survivors leaving Poland between 1945 and 1948 ranged from 100,000 to 120,000 out of a figure around 180,000. Added to this number were approximately 50,000 survivors from Hungary, Czechoslovakia, and Yugoslavia who left their homelands.

Those Jews who had never fully assimilated to European cultures had the easiest time with respect to identity. Some returned to Orthodoxy, established *ḥeders* and yeshivas, and observed a traditional Jewish way of life. These communities soon formed themselves into the nucleus of the Orthodox and hasidic enclaves of today. Of these, the hasidim continued to speak Yiddish. By contrast, those Jews who embraced European cultures faced more complex identity issues. Some turned to a definition of Yiddish nationalism, others to other variants of nationally or culturally oriented Judaism.

A multilingual person can choose his or her language. Written language is the visible expression of such a choice. To this end, most Jews who had languages to choose from could express their rejection of Europe and its languages in linguistic terms. Most of the DP publications after the war were in Yiddish, a few in Hebrew, and a small number in Polish, German, or Hungarian. Although Yiddish was not familiar to all displaced persons, it was the language most widely known among Polish, Romanian, Lithuanian, Ukrainian, Russian, and Slovakian Jews who predominated in the camps. Yiddish was also a language that was not associated with any particular country or region and so was suited to become a transnational language.

Issues of language and the rejection of European languages surfaced explicitly time and again in the Yiddish press. In an Austrian DP camp, the survivor Itzkhak Weiner wrote: 'we must . . . certainly once and for all forget about what divided us and separated us. Polish, Romanian, Hungarian, Czech and other Jews now have one and the same goal, to become a people equal to others, one language. Let us now learn Hebrew!!!' (Weiner 1946). With renunciation of the old ways there were still differences and divisions, some major and others seemingly trivial. Actor David Rogoff, who toured the DP camps with his troupe, recalled, during a lecture presentation at YIVO in autumn 2004, quarrels among the performers over whether their gefilte fish should be peppery or sweet, Lithuanians preferring the former and southern Jews the latter.

In a more serious vein, there were earnest calls for unity, for a collective identity to counter European enemies. Wolf Kur, writing from the Feldafing DP camp in 1945, expressed his bitterness towards Europe and his annoyance at the Jews who still preferred Polish and other languages to Yiddish. He challenged a then prevalent, though now outdated, view that European languages were a sign of higher status:

Everywhere it is the same story. It is an infection. Even here in our camp, one looks at the other. How long will we go on speaking Polish, Hungarian and other languages, the languages of our enemies? Is it a matter of showing that we are intelligent? If we were intelligent we would be ashamed to use the languages of those who made us suffer. There are those who speak miserable Polish. Is it not better to speak good Yiddish than bad Polish? (Kur 1945: 4)

For Kur, listening to European languages was 'like being stuck with pins'. He continued with a call to battle: 'Let us be real intellectuals and not be ashamed of our own language and speak in Yiddish or Hebrew and draw from the fount of Jewish culture and not from other wells that are poisoned with hatred against Jews' (1945: 4)

Discomfort with what were seen as enemy languages was even more intense in the German-language surroundings of the DP camps. Even though Yiddish was sufficiently cognate with German to be used when talking to local people, Jews could, and did when needed, obscure meanings through its Hebrew-Aramaic component. An elaborate code was developed in the camps during the war, recorded in Israel Kaplan's book-length glossary of codified terms (Kaplan 1949).[2] Kaplan was almost hanged for mere possession of the bit of pencil and paper which he used to make notes: the Germans made him stand with a noose around his neck for two hours, then commanded a very tall fellow inmate to hold up the rope and serve as his gallows. But the rope slipped, and Kaplan lived to tell his story (Leivick 1947: 199).

One of the first to publish a newspaper in the DP camps was Dr Rudolf Valsonok, a Lithuanian Jew. In the pre-war years he had strongly supported solidarity with Poles and Lithuanians, but afterwards his attitude altered dramatically. In an article entitled 'Where Is their Land?', he joined the chorus urging Jews to live as Jews and to demand a homeland. Having been twice disappointed, first by the Poles and later by the Lithuanians, Valsonok abandoned his desire for coexistence with non-Jews. The unrelenting antisemitism he had encountered in both countries drove him to embrace Jewish causes and languages (Valsonok 1945: 8).

Cultural Continuity in a Temporary Community

How do you hold on to your culture in a temporary community, far removed from your place of origin and amid strangers? Yiddish was needed for practical purposes as a lingua franca for people of scattered origins, for communicating needs for food and medical care or for searching for lost friends and relatives as, in the press and on walls, survivors posted information on the dead and missing. To these ends it proved logical and effective to use Yiddish.

It was through language, written and oral, that the survivors would locate themselves in the radically altered world into which they had been thrust. Jewish languages served emotional ends as the language of lost parents and grand-parents. Upon liberation, survivors first functioned individually or in ad hoc groups, but they soon formed speech communities. Yiddish, as the most com-monly spoken language of the DP camps, could span former national boundaries to link Jews of various backgrounds, including some individual Jews from the Soviet Union and in the American army.

Although Yiddish is usually written in Hebrew letters, it was printed in Latin script in almost all the early DP camp publications. In this form it proved useful because it could be more easily read by those who did not know the Hebrew alpha-bet but who could read Polish or German. As a transnational language that had never had its own country or official existence Yiddish was well suited to commu-nicating to a wide range of refugees. Having only a few years before boasted mil-lions of speakers and a thriving, well-established press, it offered a tradition of writing and a newly developed literary vocabulary. It had a history of high and low culture and an array of cultural institutions. In the aftermath of the war, Yiddish-speaking journalists and readers returned to these cultural habits. People had been accustomed to obtaining information from Yiddish sources and wanted news oriented to their particular needs. Still, despite the widespread use of Yid-dish in the DP camps, it was clear that its continuity was endangered as more ambitious survivors went on to study languages that might help them in their future lives.

Yiddish was not only useful; for Yiddishists, it was also romanticized. The poet H. Haymovitz urged loyalty to Yiddish in an ode, 'A Poem about the Yiddish Word':

> Yiddish word, you were liberated together with us!
> We will again hear your silvery sounds,
> You will help us braid the golden chain.[3]

For Haymovitz and many others, Yiddish became associated with martyrdom as the 'language of their mothers'. He praised Yiddish, perhaps because he feared the language was endangered. Not all felt as he did. Many Jews held that Yiddish was a lowly jargon connoting backwardness and poverty; to a cosmopolitan set, it was an embarrassment, a corrupted form of German.

Linguistic habits, abilities, and attitudes from before and during the war figured largely in post-war language attitudes, and the languages they chose to use in many ways articulated the social directions individuals would take later. During the war, languages that favoured survival were, in some instances, the languages that helped people hide their identity and, in others, those that helped an individual blend in as a Jew. Jews leaving the Soviet army and those who had survived in various ways in the USSR were better off not speaking Russian in the

Allied areas as the Cold War took hold. Those who had been partisans in the east European areas and Russia had used local languages to keep themselves hidden, and the more assimilated Jews could pull this off when unassimilated Yiddish-speaking Jews could not.

What happened to the Ashkenazi Jews of Europe linguistically in the post-war era constituted a sea-change. Initially multilingual, in preparation for life in Erets Yisra'el they increasingly used Hebrew, not only for prayer and religious study, as had previously been the case, but also in daily conversation, as an expression of their Zionist aspirations. Even as Yiddish was still the day-to-day language of the majority of Jews, Hebrew was rapidly gaining ground. Still, Hebrew and Yiddish each had important symbolic as well as communication functions.

Demography was an important factor in what happened in the refugee communities. In a chaotic Europe, traumatized Jews had lost their previous family or community groupings and were forced to try to build new communities. This entailed renegotiating their sense of individual and collective identity: normal demographic patterns had in large measure been destroyed by the Nazi policy of systematically killing Jewish children and older people, those who could not do their slave work. With many survivors having no family left at all and many more having lost most of their family members, connections to past and future generations took on new weight (Brenner 1997: 22). The implications in human terms are described in H. Leivick's account of his visit to a small rural camp near Munich, in 1946, where he was struck by the absence of children and old people. Many people there told him of how they had lost their children, or of how they had put them into hiding with local Christians who later refused to return them and who chased the parents away. With the oldest and youngest generations wiped out in the Nazi plan, survivors were mainly young adults, or adolescents who had lost critical years of learning, cultural literacy, and acculturation. Filling the cultural gaps for the young required organized effort. They needed to catch up, to make up for the wasted years. Meanwhile, many began to create new families. This happened rapidly: DP newspapers were full of announcements of marriages and births. Sometimes the newly-weds did not share a common language. Decisions had to be taken as to what the future culture and language of their children was to be.

The generation that came of age in the DP camps was different culturally from the pre-war generation. Many had lived in hiding or as partisans; many were orphans. They had had a disrupted childhood. According to Leivick (1947), the young DPs had different tastes from the older generation, as was demonstrated at the regular Friday-night gatherings sponsored by the US Jewish military chaplains in an effort to reintroduce religious customs: Leivick found that the young people hung together at the back and were not interested in the old-style singers and poets. They sought out the new literature and songs in Hebrew circulated by Zionist organizations rather than the more established, pre-war Yiddish literature. He concluded that they were cut off from the greater Yiddish cultural world generally and from Yiddish literature specifically. A political exploration of identity began to play itself out. According to historian Mark Wyman, 'Groups were choosing their futures; thousands thought, pondered, discussed and made decisions that would direct the flow of their people for generations' (1989: 131–2). There was an awareness that the past had ended abruptly and for ever. Yiddish culture was part of a pre-war past that was to be left behind. In the diverse mix of ethnicities that characterized the DPs, a pluralistic survivor subculture emerged. It was a hybrid community and only partly connected to the transplanted pre-war culture. Older survivors, in fact, tried to rebuild many of the institutions of Jewish cultural life: theatres, schools, and concerts. This continued to be a culture in flux and on the move, but where it was going was not immediately clear.

Societal shift was taking place. Jews were sorting themselves out by political orientation and in part by former geographical origin. Survivors reasserted their sense of collective self by forming associations based on their place of origin, supported by established *landsmanshaftn*, mutual aid societies based on home towns. Many memorial services were organized, and these brought together survivors with others from their own town or region. These gatherings evoked a sense of their former east European places of origin but in a new setting. An early post-war census conducted by UNRRA found 80,000 Polish Jewish survivors of camps; a later census added another 130,000 Polish Jews who had fled to Russia, and to that was added another 90,000 from Hungary and 100,000 from Romania (Wyman 1989).

One factor in social unification was the call to create a Jewish state. The president of the Landsberg DP camp, Samuel Gringauz, noted that the Nazis' targeting of Jews had produced a sort of Jewish universalism that had not been present before: 'An important difference [of] the new Zionism was that it temporarily overwhelmed divisions that had been rife among European Jews, divisions that earlier had left them almost incompetent to meet the challenges of the Hitler era' (Wyman 1989: 134). Yet there was little real uniformity, as evidenced by the great variety in the DP camp press, the many political voices and loyalties.

Cultural Transmission in Publishing

Right from the outset, Jews in the DP camps began to produce newspapers, books, and pamphlets—publications by survivors for survivors. According to historian Michael Brenner (1997), 'The Jewish press was especially significant in the cultural activity of this extraterritorial entity, the DP. Between 1945 and 1951, over a hundred newspapers and magazines—often short-lived—existed in the DP camps and among the Jews living outside the camps'. Newspapers, literary journals, and bulletins became so numerous that in those first years after liberation bibliographers began the task of keeping track of them (Baker and Warnke 1990).

In these publications one can readily observe that survivors faced considerations of religious, linguistic, and national identity.

The overwhelming majority of these publications, over two-thirds, were in Yiddish (Baker and Warnke 1990), which had a solid modern tradition of journalism. Even during the war, in the ghettos and camps, some Jews managed to write in secret. In the DP camps, wartime events were carefully documented, deep emotions expressed, and Jews' present lives and needs were given voice. The open use of Yiddish had a defiant quality, especially in Germany, near Hitler's headquarters (Leivick 1947: 156): to publish in Yiddish was an assertion of survival. This period of Yiddish publication can be seen as one of achievement, but also of great frustration and disillusionment. The writing provided emotional catharsis for survivors, but it did not get through to the outside world beyond the confines of the small cadre of Yiddishists and recent emigrants in the United States and elsewhere (Brenner 1997: 12).

Cultural reclamation was a matter of urgency. It meant honouring lost family. The earliest publications, mainly single sheets or bulletins, were usually the product of individuals or small groups eager to engage in cultural rescue. This early writing was often produced with minimal means: some was even hand-penned by calligraphers and included evocative artwork. Its content reflects the terrible emotions of the time. Poignantly, it was produced in makeshift housing erected on the sites of concentration camps or former enemy barracks, its authors still surrounded by former Nazis, as the camps of Buchenwald, Bergen-Belsen, or Dachau were transformed into DP camps.

The core of Yiddish writers and intelligentsia in the American zone was of Lithuanian origin, among them Levi Shalitan, Israel Kaplan, Yosef Gar, and David Volpe (Volpe 1997: 286). Volpe, still in a German hospital suffering from his recent tortures and depressed and haunted by nightmares, stated in his memoirs that writing had re-energized him and given him hope and vitality. Writing in a familiar Jewish language restored a sense of community and continuity (Volpe 1997). In July 1945 Volpe was still recovering in St Ottilien hospital in Geltendorf when an American rabbi informed him that Levi Shalitan wanted to create a newspaper. Volpe wrote in his memoir: 'I began to climb out from my solitary shell and saw other survivors looking to new generations. I wanted to do, to rush, to run.' He began to read books and papers and to get himself well. The only member of his family to survive, he was given hope by news from Erets Yisra'el and the establishment of the 'Jewish brigade' (Hahayil in Hebrew) by the British War Cabinet in 1944 as the only Jewish military unit to fight the Axis powers. Before the brigade was disbanded in 1946, its approximately 5,000 members assisted the Allied authorities in searching for Holocaust survivors and often provided assistance to get survivors to Erets Yisra'el. Before the war Volpe had been with the Zionist group Hashomer Hatsair in Lithuania; now he met two friends from that group, and together they went to Munich. When Volpe had been in a hospital near Munich, his doctor had brought him a notebook of his own writing that had survived from the concentration camp at Dachau: he had left it in his prison jacket when he went to shower. Volpe's friends, other writers who had traced him through the ID number on this jacket and who had literary tendencies, encouraged Volpe, while he was still in recovery and very ill, to pick up writing again, and this gave him the courage and desire to keep living and writing. This cadre formed one of several core groups that formed nuclei of literary life. 'It was the first summer of becoming people with our own will' (Volpe 1997: 276).

The founders of the two most widely distributed Yiddish DP weekly newspapers in the American zone of occupied Germany were both from Lithuania. In October 1945 Rudolf Valsonok, together with Baruch Hermanowicz, created the *Landsberger lagertsaytung* (Landsberg Camp Newspaper) and Levi Shalitan (who later used the Hebraized form 'Shalit') formed the Munich-based weekly *Unzer veg* (Our Way). In October 1946 the Landsberg paper came under the auspices of the Central Committee of Liberated Jews and UNRRA. Journalists on these papers at first faced great hardships, and the papers had so few writers that they wrote both under their own names and also under a number of pseudonyms to promote the illusion of a staff.

Their stories are tragic. Rudolf Valsonok died of war-related illnesses at the end of 1945, while Shalitan was deposed by the Central Committee of Liberated Jews in late 1946, in large part because his Zionist views differed from those of the 'tone setters' (Gar 1971: 61). But the papers grew in strength: their writers aspired to high standards and at their height these two weekly publications grew in length, from a page or two to about ten to twelve pages. For a time a third paper, the *Yidishe tsaytung* (Jewish Newspaper), which continued into the 1950s, was reaching 10,000–15,000 readers. Many other Yiddish-language periodicals and single titles appeared, as well as assorted party-affiliated publications, organs of assorted political movements, and papers of organizations for former partisans.[4]

By giving voice to particular Jewish needs the Yiddish press became a means to autonomy and empowerment. Survivors held mass demonstrations to voice their displeasure at their treatment by the US administration after the war. Wanting better housing, living conditions, exit visas, and greater security at Landsberg DP camp, a mass gathering of 3,000 survivors in October 1945 published a list of demands in the *Landsberger lagertsaytung*. They were outraged that a full six months after liberation they lacked what they saw as basic rights, including 'contacts with the Jewish and non-Jewish world'. They were eager to express their will, to help in the struggle for a Jewish homeland, to emigrate, to have Jewish self-government, and to see improved material, cultural, and moral conditions. Zishe Shaykovsky, for example, described the position of writers as follows:

For many survivors, silence was not an option. Language, suppressed in the war years, became a means for reassertion of peoplehood and a means of discovering renewed aspirations. Many had survived in order to keep the memory of the dead alive, to accuse the murderers, and bring about justice. The strongest weapon in their arsenal was, after all, memory and their impulse was to get their words down immediately. (Shaykovsky 1948)

Actor David Rogoff remarked further that Yiddish radio in Munich was broadcast from the very station that had not that long ago broadcast Hitler's speeches (personal communication). Leivick noted the irony that the very same printing press that put out the *Landsberger lagertsaytung* had also printed Hitler's venomous speeches in a publication of the same name. But now, instead of the Nazis, four Jewish typesetters were employed to publish the words of Jews in Yiddish.

The titles of the publications reflect empowerment and community-building. Some proclaimed a collective continuity through use of the pronoun 'our': *Unzer shtime* (Our Voice), *Unzer veg* (Our Way), *Unzer velt* (Our World), *Unzer front* (Our Front),[5] *Unzer mut* (Our Courage), *Unzer lebn* (Our Life), and *Unzer gerangl* (Our Struggle).[6] Some of the names pronounced Jews to be fighters rather than victims, as in the strident *Unzer front* and *Eyner kegn alemen* (One Against All), or the Hebrew *Lenitsaḥon* and Yiddish *Tsum zig* (To Conquest). Just surviving meant victory. *Tkhiyes hamesim* (The Dead Arisen) voiced the sad fate of the Jews in the very first DP paper from Buchenwald in 1945. *Mir zaynen do* (We Are Here) was the anthem of the survivors, as was *Lebedik amkha* (Your People Are Alive). Many titles suggest transformation and forward movement, *Ibergang* (We Passed Through), *Unzer veg*, *Bederekh* (On the Way), *Bafrayung* (Liberation), and *Oyf der fray* (We Are Free) evoking images of movement, freedom, strength, and peoplehood.

It was not only to affirm their survival that survivors wrote but to satisfy a spiritual need. B. Kosovski, in a bibliography of Jewish publications from the British zone of occupied Germany, endowed the act of writing with mystical powers. He claimed that the German destruction of the great Jewish libraries meant that, though the books had been burned, only their physical aspect had really been destroyed. He claimed that, in keeping with an old hasidic legend, the Jewish letters 'flew into the air and right after the bloody nightmare, the letters found new attire and hope' (Kosovski 1950).

One of the very first papers, *Oyf der fray*, was elaborately and lovingly written out by hand and included drawings. The December 1945 issue contains an anonymous article featuring a drawing of a cemetery with rows of tombstones and a weeping willow. The text above it says *Shema Yisroel* (Hear, O Israel), the words of a prayer of affirmation but also the words traditionally spoken by a Jew who is about to die. The text of the article reads, in part:

They were martyrs when they had *Shema Yisroel* on their lips as their holy spirits expired. With this they wanted to touch the consciousness of the world and remind people of their unforgettable murdered brothers and the needed rescue for the tiny number of survivors. The future historian will surely find the right word. We now stand before their graves with a great respect and deep sorrow, bent over, and say, *Yisgadal veyiskadash*.

At times the newspapers helped to console the survivors. Moyshe Edelstein, the editor of a short-lived Leipheim newspaper, articulated his vision of the role of the newspaper in healing; 'an inner quiet, pleasant joy creeps into your tormented heart, warms and spreads over your feelings, though you are broken from suffering. It makes this grey, cloudy time easier, giving you new lust for life and courage, new hope and striving for lovelier, better days.' The paper was ironically called *A heim* (A Home), though the writer was conscious that this was a temporary shelter for the homeless dwellers of former Luftwaffe barracks, gallingly near the home town of the infamous Josef Mengele: 'This paper is to give courage to the spiritual being, so that when you return to your troubled, grey, dark barracks, in the cold, tight quarters of your unheated, poorly lit home [*heim*] you can work to create, build, and fight for your great, holy, and heartrending task.' This publication, which lasted less than a year, had an entertaining humour section. One poem was dedicated to the pleasure of chewing (and eating) and what one does to gain that pleasure. There were chess games, advice to women on how to make themselves attractive, and a sports column—all illustrating an effort to achieve normality.

Even as the writing of these Yiddish papers took shape their momentum began to wane. By 1948 and 1949 many Jews had emigrated, while the writers had organized and formed a DP camp writers' union. They felt they had become established enough to focus on the attributes of a formal language, including a uniform Yiddish orthography (Kahn 1948). Such developments in language policy had little impact on the average survivor.

Yiddish publications reflected the complex mosaic of survivor life. They voiced the particular social agendas of their sponsoring organizations and the competition for political and religious affiliation. Some were for fellow partisans and ghetto fighters, others were organized by nationality. Some survivors were not impressed with the newspapers of the time, viewing them as mouthpieces for various interests. One survivor told me that she noticed that a certain weekly had doubled its circulation in a given month and she assumed this was because a newly available but very messy *schmaltz* herring needed extra wrapping. She saw the paper as an organ for the administration of the camps and she did not find its content especially interesting. Reports of cultural events did have an audience. Thousands of Yiddish-speakers, for example, turned up at Leivick's literary lecture in Landsberg, during his five-week visit in the spring of 1946 (Leivick 1947).

Leivick's expressions of sympathy endeared him to his thronging audiences but made him unpopular with UNRRA in Munich. His request for an extension to his visa was rejected, and his movements and speeches were monitored. The authorities refused to allow DP camp journalists to attend a conference of Yiddish journalists in New York, with the result that the DP press remained isolated (Gar 1957: 150–8).

External Forces

The development of a survivor subculture was not just an internal matter. Social contact with other survivors—Jews of many different ethnic backgrounds, from many lands and many cultural traditions—led to new ways of interacting but still with a foundation, a common base of history and suffering. But there was also contact with assorted Jewish and non-Jewish outsiders: for example individuals associated with the rescue agencies, or with administrators.

A social and political landscape was evolving in which many forms of Zionism competed for survivors' allegiance. In addition, American military chaplains and relief workers were introducing survivors to Reform and Conservative forms of religious practice and ritual that had developed in the United States. Both these developments led to a need for Hebrew literacy. The military chaplains, and the administrators and agents of assorted agencies, were all involved in determining what was to happen culturally. As well as developments in the use of Hebrew and Yiddish, there were opportunities for the older youths to study in German universities which opened them up to new influences. In another vein, the leftists had their own sources. Many survivors had fled from the Soviet Union and its sphere after the war and were influenced by Russian culture. A Bundist paper, *Unzer shtime* (Our Voice) was published in Paris and brought into the DP camps. It continued publishing in Yiddish until the mid-1990s.[7]

Activists from Erets Yisra'el travelled to Europe to work with Zionist survivors. David Ben-Gurion came to speak to the refugees and was warmly greeted. Zionist agencies established schools and kibbutzim, and organized cultural events. Many varieties of Zionist groups remained active, among them the General Zionists, Revisionists, Hashomer Hatsair, Mapai, Mizrachi, Aguda, and Poalei Zion. Some groups had their own newspapers, mostly in Yiddish. Berihah ('Flight' in Hebrew), founded by Jewish partisans and Zionists in January 1945, worked to smuggle survivors trapped in eastern Europe to Allied occupied zones as a step towards immigration to Erets Yisra'el. The Jewish Agency was actively supporting Zionist ideas already present among the survivors by building schools and cultural institutions to promote the idea of Israel. Across the spectrum, there was a philosophical shift towards Zionism, partly because the popular pre-war Bundist vision of Yiddish nationalism within Europe had been shattered by the Holocaust (Wyman 1989: 168–9).

But support for Zionism was tempered by harsh realities in the aftermath of the war. Zionist groups arranged transport to a land still closed off by the British, and frequently survivors wound up imprisoned in Cyprus in British camps.

Reports from Palestine of violence between Arabs and Jews reached the camps. And when, in 1948, the State of Israel was finally born, there was no place in it for Yiddish culture. Yiddish and Hebrew, which had for centuries coexisted in an integral system, became rivals (Weinreich 1980). After the war, having a Jewish language and the cultural habits associated with Yiddish proved instrumental. Yiddish had become associated with high culture—it had a press, a literature, and was used in performance arts—and yet it was held in low esteem by many, in contrast to the values associated with European languages.

Hebrew ultimately won out in the post-war years. In many ways Yiddish, already in a steady state of decline before the war, was associated with the misery of the European condition. Assimilated Jews had already shifted their loyalty to the language of the country they inhabited; Yiddish was associated with the world of the shtetl, with old folks and the traditional life many were abandoning. Many educated Yiddish writers knew both Hebrew and Yiddish: Volpe, for example, wrote in both languages (Volpe 1997: 300). But in Israel, Hebrew became the national language and Yiddish came to be mocked, a relic spoken, or occasionally sung, behind closed doors by that last generation of survivors.

Even as Yiddish was being used as the lingua franca of the camps, it was showing signs of obsolescence. Note the distinction on the part of an anonymous journalist for *A heim*, the Leipheim DP camp paper, in which he urged the learning of Hebrew even as Yiddish was being spoken: 'We must shed the mould of the years of exile, foreign names, foreign manners, to learn Hebrew and speak Yiddish, to acquaint ourselves and steep ourselves in the sources of a Jewish past and be ready to begin anew in our new, healthy, free land' (*A heim*, no. 8 (1946), 7). Writers like this one, who felt there was room for both languages in the Jewish future, were to be disappointed in Israel. Whether Zionist sentiments grew organically, out of conviction, or whether they took root because there were no alternatives, the linguistic impact of its success was that Hebrew supplanted Yiddish entirely. Zionists used Yiddish as an expedient but their agenda was clear. Once survivors arrived in Israel they were actively discouraged from using Yiddish in any circumstances, and the language was not even granted minority status.

In the newspaper *Dos vort* (The Word) in October 1946, a writer decried the divisiveness over Hebrew and Yiddish, calling Yiddish the 'language of the holy martyrs'. The writer had hoped that the catastrophe of Europe had erased the difference between the old and new Yiddishkeit, between orthodox and secular Judaism, between Hebrew and Yiddish. Instead roles were reversed and Yiddish was associated with martyrdom, and Hebrew associated with broad practical use and ideological value.

Cultural contact with American Jews influenced the DPs as they pondered their course. Notably, there was no effort to impart English to the survivors. Various aid workers were sympathetic and helpful, but they were removed from the survivors' day-to-day existence except in their capacity to grant favours. Survivors were desperate for visas out of Germany. For a time there was not enough food or supplies: some was being siphoned off by black marketeers. More influential at the personal level were the Jewish military chaplains bringing in prayer books and establishing ritual life. But even helpers who knew some Yiddish did not get close to survivors at a personal level (Baumel 1989).

In the memoir of his visit in 1946, Leivick expressed shock at the generally negative attitude of the American authorities he encountered, especially the Jewish ones. He found that survivors were far removed physically and socially from the officials who came through. The extent of this alienation is brought home in an interview with a Jewish former official of the State Department who, even though he had heard Yiddish as a child, chose to speak German in Munich. This individual knew Yiddish and could have associated with survivor Jews, but he said that he avoided them, describing them as unpleasant, dirty, and dishonest.

Survivors were dependent on the authorities and so were in no position to criticize their overseers. The publications were in great measure funded and distributed with the permission and perhaps funding of these organizations, so little was published about any friction. But Leivick, upon entering the grounds of the Landsberg DP camp, found that those in charge lived in luxury, behind gates that separated them from the camp. The DPs were subject to dangers, but the Jewish police who were to keep order among them had no live ammunition to protect the community. In contrast, the German police and the American soldiers were well armed. It was ironic that the Germans were better equipped than those who had been their victims. Leivick found the American administrators unsympathetic. He had expected a Jewish son of someone he knew from Baltimore to be more helpful and was disappointed:

It didn't take a moment and we saw before us, to our astonishment, a hardened, ill-disposed bureaucrat. Inherited from his father no Jewish feelings, warmth or friendliness. All this was mud in his eyes, and to those like him who come to Munich only to work their way up at the expense of the DPs, upon whom they look as from far above. (Leivick 1947: 56)

Upon his arrival in Munich Leivick had to report to a Dr Glasgold, the director at UNRRA official headquarters. He was sickened that an UNRRA official, a director of a Jewish camp, himself a Jew, should lack any sense of a connection with the suffering or extraordinarily tragic circumstances of his fellow-Jews. UNRRA headquarters was a mansion outside the camp, and there officials lived in luxury, served by German servants, the walls hung with deer heads from aristocratic hunting expeditions. Meanwhile the survivors lived in cold and cramped quarters. Leivick's encounters with survivors had to be reported in writing to the officials. Glasgold accused him of identifying too much with the DPs. As he left after his failure to have his visa renewed, Leivick concluded that their stance towards the survivors was 'unsympathetic' and that officials treated survivors as if they were of 'low moral worth' (Leivick 1947: 76–83).

Survivors appreciated any help they received. Those who ultimately left for the United States and Canada were given little help to prepare for what awaited them culturally. The *landsmanshaftn* played a prominent role for many in their new homes, but otherwise they were mainly left to their own devices.

After the Aftermath

The DP experience involved the establishment of a new role for Yiddish as a transnational subculture rather than a Yiddish that was rooted in established communities. Except in old jokes, the conventional divisions of Galitzianer, Litvak, and Romanian lost their force. The DP camps were not just a historical moment, in which the once great flame of Yiddish flickered before being eclipsed by the light of better and greater times ahead, but a highly formative period, where a smelting of diverse elements shaped what was to come in significant ways. There were powerful internal and external social forces at work in the years that the DPs were in limbo. Indeed, the refugees were living with their mental suitcases packed as they worked out their cultural issues. Still they actively anticipated their life after the camps, writing, retrieving old cultural treasures, and creating new ones.

Linguistically, the rejection of European culture meant that European languages, and with them old identities, were to be eliminated from public discourse. The emotional impetus to extend the use of Hebrew at the behest of Zionist movements was reinforced even as daily life was still conducted in Yiddish.

Despite the best efforts of the intellectuals among the DPs, the idea of cultural Judaism began to recede to the background. The operation to rescue, restore, and revive cultural Yiddish continued in the camps, and later some of the same people continued this effort in the United States, Argentina, Australia, South Africa, and Canada, and, with even greater constraint, in Israel. However, with the exception of the hasidim, who lived in tight-knit communities, Yiddish could not be passed on to the coming generations. The efforts to keep the language alive and to connect the survivors and their offspring to their emotional and cultural past were only a small-scale, though earnest, attempt in the context of a changing world. The many Yiddish organizations, schools, camps, and publications that survive exemplify this phenomenon, as does the revival of interest in Yiddish music. Jeffrey Shandler aptly views post-Holocaust Yiddish as a form of performance (Shandler 2006). Indeed, much of what happened with respect to Jewish languages in the camps led them to be used less as a vehicle for expression and more as an enactment of which the whole point was the fact of their voicing by

Jews. Hebrew and Yiddish became the locales in which to regenerate a revived Jewish presence in the world. Jews had to negotiate how to express themselves, and to figure out the boundaries of their society—who were the insiders and who the outsiders. What languages to take with them and what their attitude towards these languages was to be remained for them to play out in a later era.

The evolution of the role of Yiddish in the aftermath of the Second World War can be viewed in the context of the emotional turmoil of its speakers. The spate of Yiddish publications in this period reflects a sense of great achievement, but there is also evidence of frustration and disillusionment. The many literate, articulate, and prolific authors ultimately had no one to write for but themselves and a core of sympathizers in outlying countries dispersed across the world. At the time these authors understood that Yiddish culture stood on the brink. Indeed, notwithstanding the increased interest in Holocaust studies, much of what was published in those years has remained ignored and known only within a small community.

For the brief years of the DP camps, writers as social and community activists were working to effect change through their writing. As David Adler has noted, 'The history of the Jewish community in post-war Germany may be likened to a meteor that has fallen to earth. It has neither a past nor does it want to have a future. But it will, in the continuum of Jewish history be noted as an important period of transition' (Adler 1947: 3). The literary writers expressed the powerful currents of sorrow and anguish and invoked the lost world of Yiddish, and in doing so provided readers with a sense of a common past and shared fate. Yiddish did not end with the Holocaust. What happened in the DP camps was that a temporary community not only used the Yiddish language but adapted it socially to form a new set of cultures in the new diaspora.

Notes

1   From 1948 the State of Israel; referred to below as Erets Yisra'el.

2   Kaplan, among the first editors of one of the central Yiddish newspapers in the US zone of Germany, later wrote of the *katzet* (an acronym for *Konzentrationslager*—camp) lingo.

3   The poem was published in the *Landsberger lagertsaytung* (Sept. 1945). The author was Haymovitz (in YIVO transliteration, Jachimowicz).

4   These were *Unzer front* and *Per il popolo,* partly in Italian.

5   Published once only from Bergen-Belsen, 1948.

6   The transcription of *undzer* versus *unzer* is one of the many battles over seemingly small things that seem to loom large to Yiddishists and which is still debated.

7   Itzak Niborski. Information courtesy of the Medem Library in Paris, which houses copies of *Unzer shtime.* It was originally published by the socialist Bund organization.

References

ADLER, DAVID. 1947. 'Poalei Agudath' (Yiddish), *Israel Almanac*. Munich.

BAKER, ZACHARY, and NINA WARNKE. 1990. *A Guide to the Microfilm Editions of Jewish Displaced Persons Periodicals from the Collections of the YIVO Institute*. Microfilm. New York.

BAUMEL, JUDITH TYDOR. 1989. 'The Politics of Spiritual Rehabilitation in the DP Camps', *Simon Wiesenthal Center Annual*, 6: 59–79.

BRENNER, MICHAEL. 1997. *After the Holocaust: Rebuilding Jewish Lives in Postwar Germany*. Princeton, NJ.

DINNERSTEIN, LEONARD. 1990. 'The United States and the Displaced Persons', *She'erit hapletah, 1944–1948*. 347–64.

FELDSHUH, BEN ZION. 1945–8. *Sheyres, H. Bibliography. 1945–1948*. Stuttgart. Published by the Directorate of Education and Culture in Germany. [Feldshuh's series of bibliographies document the flowering of writing in the DP camps.]

GAR, JOSEPH. 1957. 'Newspapers, Publications, Press of the American Zone of Germany'. In *Fun noentn ovar* [one of a series of volumes produced by the Conference on Jewish Claims Against Germany], 150–90. New York.

—— 1971. *Echoes: Autobiographical Accounts* [Viderklangen: oytobiografishe fartseylungen], vol. ii. New York.

GROSS, JAN T. 2006. *Fear: Anti-Semitism in Poland After Auschwitz*. New York.

GRUBER, RUTH. 2000. *Haven: The Dramatic Story of 1,000 World War II Refugees and How They Came to America*. New York.

KAHN, BERL. 1948. 'Yiddish and the Yiddish Press'. *In gang: zshurnal far literatur un Kunst*. Rome.

KAPLAN, ISRAEL. 1949. *Jewish Folk-Expressions Under the Nazi Yoke* [Dos folksmoyl in nazi klem]. Munich. Repr. as 'Jewish Jargon Under the Nazis: Selections'. In *A Glossary of Yiddish and Hebrew Slang and Code Words in Ghettos and Concentration Camps*. Tel Aviv, 1982.

KOSOVSKI, B. 1950. *Bibliography of Yiddish Publications in the British Zone of Germany, 1945–50* [Bibliografye fun di yidishe oysgabes in der britisher zone fun daytshland, 1945–1950]. Published by the Culture Office of the Central Committee of Liberated Jewish of the British zone.

KUR, WOLF. 1945. In *Dos naye vort: Feldafing*, Oct.

LEIVICK, H. 1947. *Among the Survivors* [Tsvishn di sheyres hapleytim]. New York.

ROGOFF, DAVID. 2004. Lecture at YIVO. New York.

SHANDLER, JEFFREY. 2006. *Adventures in Yiddishland: Postvernacular Language and Culture*. Berkeley, Calif.

SHAYKOVSKY, ZISHE. 1948. 'The Yiddish Press in Germany, Austria, Italy, and Sweden' [Di yidishe prese in daytshland, estraykh, italye un shvedn], *YIVO Bleter*, 28(2).

VALSONOK, RUDOLF. 1945. *Landsberger lagertsaytung*, Oct.: 8.

VOLPE, DAVID. 1997. *Me and My World: Autobiographical Pages* [Ikh un mayn velt: autobiografishe bleter], vol. i. Johannesburg and Jerusalem.

WEINREICH, MAX. 1980. *The History of the Yiddish Language*, trans. from the Yiddish. Chicago.

WEINER, YITZKHAK. 1946. In *Der Admonter Hajnt* (July).

WYMAN, MARK. 1989. *DPs: Europe's Displaced Persons, 1945–1951*. Ithaca, NY.

FOUR

'National Dignity' and 'Spiritual Reintegration': The Discovery and Presentation of Jewish Folk Music in Germany

JASCHA NEMTSOV

IN JANUARY 1901 the first issue of the journal *Ost und West* (East and West) appeared in Berlin. It served as the most important organ of cultural Zionism for the next two decades, and, as its title suggests, it attempted to bridge the cultural divide between east and west European Jews with the aim of creating an ethnic nationalist goal. The leading article of the first issue of this 'Illustrated Monthly for Modern Judaism' explained the editors' intentions:

East and West—to bring elements of Judaism that are far away from one another not just geographically but also culturally closer again by emphasizing everything that unites us or could unite us, by showing our common past and the efforts and achievements of the Jews today. We want to promote . . . Jewish solidarity, justified Jewish self-awareness, by bringing knowledge of all Jewish endeavour and all Jewish ability into as wide a circle of members of our house as we possibly can.

The new Jewish art definitely belonged here, 'being not something that comes from Jews only by chance or which at best cursorily rehashes a page of the Bible. It is art that sobs in the soul of the Jewish people and sings, art that will shape the fate of our people in its content and form.'[1]

The first issue contained, among other things, an article by the renowned Jewish philosopher Martin Buber entitled 'Jewish Renaissance'—a term that was to characterize this movement. Critical to this renaissance, following ideas of ethnic nationalism since the time of Johann Gottfried Herder (1744–1803) and the Grimm brothers (Jacob, 1785–1863, and Wilhelm, 1786–1859), was the establishment of a common spirit binding a modern nation, which drew on the folklore of ordinary, even peasant, society. But unlike that of the other Romantic nationalist movements sweeping across Europe in the nineteenth and early twentieth centuries, the agenda of *Ost und West* was distinctively Jewish in its Zionist concerns and its sensitivity to the diasporic character of Jewish society. Although based in Germany, the leaders of the movement envisioned that this spirit would be found not in the Grimms' German peasantry but in the 'authentic folk' of eastern Europe and the ethno-poetry of the folk song. My purpose here is to uncover the often overlooked story of these leaders, particularly Leo Winz (1876–1952) and Fritz Mordechai Kaufmann (1888–1921), and the significance of their renaissance movement for modern Jewish thought and culture.

'A Precept of our National Dignity and our Self-Awareness': Leo Winz

Ost und West was founded by two young Zionists: Davis Trietsch (1870–1935) and Leo Winz. Trietsch devoted himself chiefly to the work of Zionist colonization; his involvement was brief. In 1902 he left the journal, and from then on Winz was the sole editor and publisher,[2] but although he made an unusual contribution to Jewish culture in this and other areas, Winz's name was later forgotten. His biography and varied activities have never been reviewed, and there is not even an entry for him in the *Encyclopaedia Judaica*.[3]

Leo Winz's migration and cultural experience are reflected in the title of *Ost und West*. He came west from Russia, where he was born. As a young man he was a member of a Hovevei Zion group.[4] In the 1890s he studied in Zurich, where he was active in the Jewish student society Hessiana (named after the German Jewish philosophical precursor of Zionism, Moses Hess).[5] In 1898 he moved to Berlin to continue his studies, and made contact with leading German Zionists such as Heinrich Loewe and Max Bodenheimer. In the same year he joined the Berlin Zionist Organization.[6] He was still a student in 1901 when he founded *Ost und West*, and, a year later, the Kunstverlag Phönix Leo Winz (Phoenix Leo Winz Art Publishers), which was the first publishing company in the world to print 'postcards and pictures of works of art with Jewish content'.[7] Winz was the manager of both companies until he dissolved them in 1923. As a Russian citizen, he had to leave Germany after the outbreak of the First World War, and during the war he lived in Copenhagen. In 1921 an old friend, Meir Dizengoff, the long-time mayor of Tel Aviv, invited him to Palestine, where he was appointed as the 'representative of the interests of Tel Aviv'.[8] Presumably this meant business enterprises, which Winz described as follows:

In the years after the war, on the advice of friends who had emigrated to Palestine, I invested significant sums in the export of building materials. This business, which was not wound down until four years later, cost me thousands of pounds. A few years later I devoted myself to tobacco plantations, which also brought anger and disappointment.[9]

His business failures forced Winz to come back to Germany at the end of 1926. At the start of 1928 he bought the *Gemeindeblatt der jüdischen Gemeinde zu Berlin* (Community Newspaper of the Jewish Community in Berlin), which under his management achieved the largest circulation of all the German Jewish newspapers. Although 87,000 copies were distributed free of charge it was financed exclusively by advertisements and managed without being subsidized by the community. During the period when Winz owned the *Gemeindeblatt* he travelled every year to Palestine, and in November/December 1933 he undertook a 'journey through all of Syria on order of the Syrian government and in the company of high Syrian dignitaries'.[10] The goal of the trip was a project for the settlement of Jewish immigrants from Germany; however, it was not realized. In 1935 Winz sold the *Gemeindeblatt* back to the community of Berlin and moved to Palestine, where he became co-owner of the oldest newspaper in the country, *Doar hayom* (Daily Post). However, he was massively defrauded through false accounting and lost all his money. Unable to gain access to the money he had in Germany, in subsequent years he lived in extreme poverty, selling books and pawning valuables— in a letter of 1938 he relates how he even had to pawn his wife's wedding ring.[11] He died in 1952, after suffering a stroke at the funeral of his friend Sammy Gronemann.[12]

In 1926, on the occasion of Winz's fiftieth birthday, a tribute appeared in the Berlin Zionist newspaper *Jüdische Rundschau* (Jewish Review) characterizing him as an important promoter of Zionist culture and enterprise: 'He combines the energy and daring of a real businessman with great perseverance, animation, and intelligence.' His love for Palestine was particularly emphasized, competing with an 'almost unbelievable tenacity in serving the land'. He was 'one of the first party members to see the "practical work" in Palestine as the most important political means of reaching our ideal and to draw personal consequences for himself from this' (Dyk 1926: 118). Indeed, Winz was very closely tied to Palestine. As he related himself, after 1919 he spent a good deal of time studying it: 'I crossed the country every year in all directions with like-minded friends. There must be few people here in Palestine who know all the parts of the country geographically and topographically as well as I do.'[13]

In a letter to someone we know only as Buck, Winz described his most important creation, the journal *Ost und West*, as 'known to be the most widely distributed and respected Jewish magazine in the world'.[14] This was no exaggeration: in the first fifteen years of its existence the journal attracted the best Jewish publicists, academics, and artists in Germany. Yet its influence extended far beyond the German borders: in addition to the readers it boasted in Germany and Austria-Hungary, it also had many subscribers in Russia. In the west, *Ost und West* made a significant contribution to the formation of what Steven Aschheim (1982) called the *Ostjudenkult* (cult of east European Jews). According to Inka Bertz, who mounted a retrospective exhibition on the Jewish renaissance, 'The idealization of the east European Jewish world and its inhabitants, who for a long time were at best social care cases if not despised, became the alternative to the assimilated, bourgeois German Jewish world' (1991: 37).

For many Jews in the west, *Ost und West* initially offered the only opportunity to learn something about the Jewish culture of the east, regularly publishing as it did articles on the works of the *jungjüdisch* (young Jewish) poets and artists,[15] who devoted themselves to the east European Jewish tradition or who came directly from it. *Ost und West* was the first and for a long time the only medium in the west to express consistent support for the Yiddish language and to celebrate Jewish folk song. 'If someone wants to understand our people . . . he should learn the Jewish German [Yiddish] language, much reviled, foolishly hated and faithlessly abandoned', declared Theodor Zlocisti in an article he wrote for the journal (Zlocisti 1902).

During the early twentieth century one could also experience new Jewish art at different events, in part organized by the editorial staff of *Ost und West*. In 1902 the journal reported on the first 'young Jewish evening' in Berlin, which took up on a similar initiative by Martin Buber in Vienna:

For many of those present a whole new world opened up, a totally new area of litera-ture—that of the jargon [Yiddish]—a completely new folk song: the Jewish one. Many people, who until then had thought of the Jewish German dialect as *gemauschel* ['mut-tering', as in esoteric speech], went home the richer this evening, for having discovered previously unknown beauty. What was known as a jargon became 'socially accept-able'.[16]

On this evening, probably for the first time, Jewish folk songs rang out in an art concert in Berlin—including two songs from the Palestinian Jews and five Yiddish songs.

'Finally the first collection of Jewish folk songs has been given to us, songs that were really created from the mouth of the people', raved *Ost und West*'s reviewer, of *Evreiskie narodnye pesni v Rossii* (Jewish Folk Songs in Russia) by Saul Ginsburg and Pesach Marek (Bar-Ami 1904: col. 149; Ginsburg and Marek 1901). The review was signed with the pseudonym Bar-Ami ('Son of My People'), but the reviewer's real name was Leo Winz. He continued, 'With the feeling of joy at own-ing this beautiful and rich book there was a bitter sensation: why so late? Should not research into "folk literature"—in the broadest sense, i.e. folk song, folk music, folk sayings, popular beliefs, popular customs—have been one of the first and most important tasks of academic research?' (Bar-Ami 1904: cols 150–1). Winz was responding to the focus of Judaica studies at the time on ancient his-tory, particularly that of biblical Israel, while contemporary Jewish life was mostly ignored. The thoughts he expresses here were not only new in the West: for Winz it was a matter of urgency to collect evidence of Jewish folk culture because it was acutely endangered, in his words, by 'the storms of recent decades'—emigration, assimilation, and modernization. He predicted that it could soon be irretrievably lost (Bar-Ami 1904: col. 151).

This idea of the urgent need to document the vanishing folk roots of Jewish culture is found in almost the same words in the writings of S. A. An-ski (Shlomo Z. Rappoport, 1863–1920), the founder of Jewish folklore studies in Russia. Four years after Winz's essay, An-ski wrote: 'Every year, every day even valuable works of folk art are disappearing . . . We have an urgent task: to systematically and comprehensively collect works of all kinds of Jewish folklore and cultural monuments' (1908: 277). These sentences constituted a manifesto for An-ski, a declaration of intent for his future project—the Jewish ethnographic expedition (1912–15). Winz, however, could already in 1904 look back on his own successful activities in the field: in his review he mentions his collection of manuscripts of 1,200 Jewish folk songs from Galicia, Bukovina, and Romania (Ginsburg and Marek's collection contained only 376 songs). Winz's collection included not only texts but also melodies, and can thus be considered the first Jewish folk-music collection.[17]

Winz expressly described Ginsburg and Marek's collection as being 'of the greatest importance to cultural history, social psychology and linguistics' (Bar-Ami 1904: col. 155). However, his review also contained several criticisms. Even the title of the collection was wrong: as most of the published songs it contained were also known outside Russia, they belonged to the common cultural heritage of all Ashkenazi Jews: 'The borders of Russia do not in any way constitute a dividing border for folklore' (1904: col. 156). Four-fifths of the songs could also be found in his own collection. Furthermore, Winz criticized the texts as being 'unreliable and imperfect', and bemoaned the fact that the authors had not collected them themselves: they had largely been supplied by people who had in part outgrown the traditional Jewish milieu. For this reason many of the texts were fragmentary and apparently often the product of lapses in memory. Winz was even more critical, however, of the fact that they were published in Latin transcription, seeing this as an embarrassing concession to the non-Jewish public that greatly reduced the collection's academic value: 'Any attempt at a transcription of this sort is a horror—and this transcription in front of me is the strongest evidence of this' (1904: col. 159). According to Winz, Yiddish was a natural and living language from which several dialects had developed. While the Hebrew script was the same for all dialects, the Latin script could at best only reproduce a certain local dialect. The article closed with an appeal to Jewish educated circles to devote themselves to collecting Jewish folk songs and an admonition not to neglect the melodies in the rush to recover traditional texts (1904: col. 160).

Winz's essay is significant as an early statement of the goals of Jewish musical folklore studies in western Europe. It shows that at that time Winz had a considerable advantage in this area over his colleagues in Russia. His collection was not only quantitatively far superior to the Russian one; his approach was also more systematic and more academic.[18] In comparison to Winz's programme of work, the first experiments in the study of Jewish musical folklore in Russia seem chaotic and almost naive. Four years before the founding of the Society for Jewish Folk Music (Obshchestvo Evreiskoi Narodnoi Muzyki) in St Petersburg, Winz developed two fundamental ideas: first, he spoke of the need to make a systematic and comprehensive collection of and to evaluate Jewish folk music; second, he planned an equally systematic integration of this folklore into the concert repertoire and amateur music-making—the melodies were to be arranged by professional composers. Both ideas also caught on a few years later in Russia: An-ski organized the first folklore expeditions on an academic basis, and the founding of the Society for Jewish Folk Music prompted a large number of folk-song arrangements for art music.

Jewish music became an important focus of *Ost und West* after 1905. In its first four years the journal had mainly been committed to national Jewish poetry and the visual arts. Dozens of artists were introduced, with large feature articles and many illustrations. At the same time, Winz also expanded the Kunstverlag Phönix, publishing postcards and prints of artists' work that had been featured in the journal.

Jewish musical publications were still rare in the years 1901 to 1904. Those that were available were composed pieces with Jewish themes rather than arrangements of folk pieces. An example is the song 'War ein kleines stilles Haus' (There Was a Small Still House) by James Rothstein from his song cycle *Judenlieder* (Jewish Songs) based on texts by Adolph Donath.[19] In a brief article on this, Rothstein was described as 'one of our most talented young Jewish composers', who, in addition to many songs, had created an opera, a work for male choir and orchestra, piano sonatas, and chamber music (Heller 1903: col. 643). Born in Königsberg in 1871, Rothstein studied under Max Bruch in the composition master class of the Royal Academy of Art in Berlin, and he spent the rest of his life in that city. In the 1930s he took part in the activities of the Berlin Jüdischer Kulturbund (Jewish Cultural Association), which honoured him with a portrait in 1934. As late as May 1941 the Kulturbund orchestra played, under the direction of Rudolf Schwarz, Rothstein's Suite in C minor (Op. 28). 'This orchestral suite is an early work of the elderly Jewish composer who is with us [i.e. who attended the concert]', announced the *Jüdisches Nachrichtenblatt*, the last Jewish newspaper allowed to operate by the Nazis. 'The warm and heartfelt applause that the listeners gave him may be taken as an indication of their gratitude for his rich creation' (Stompor 2001: 169). The concert was to be a double farewell: the orchestra was playing for the last time, as the Nazis subsequently dissolved the Kulturbund; James Rothstein was deported a few months later to the Łódź ghetto, where he died soon afterwards.

The text of 'War ein kleines stilles Haus' describes a sabbath celebration in a Jewish home, filled with longing for Zion: 'Fly away, fly away, my prayer, to the far-away latitudes, where the temple of Zion stands.' The Zionist hope is especially connected to the child dreaming of the cedar trees of Palestine. The musical language of this simple, fervent song is to a great extent early Romantic, with clear echoes of Schubert, but individual elements of synagogue music in the style of Louis Lewandowski[20] can be identified.

Indicating the growing importance in Winz's agenda of folklore and ethnology as part of a Jewish cultural renaissance, the first issue of *Ost und West* in 1905 opened with the article 'On Jewish Ethnology'. Here, Winz called on his readership in different countries to become involved in a unique project. It concerned the collection of Jewish folklore (which he called 'the neglected, shabbily treated Cinderella of Jewish studies'), but the spectrum was unusually broad: customs and traditions, proverbs, anecdotes, and children's games, popular beliefs and folk medicine, folk songs and melodies of every kind, legends and fairy-tales. Winz considered this task to be 'our duty, a precept of our national dignity and our self-awareness'.[21]

From this issue onwards almost every issue of the journal included Jewish musical works, mainly arrangements of folk music. The few composed pieces were closely linked to folklore. Almost all the arrangements published used melodies from Winz's collection. The only exception was the 'Berühmte Melodie des Wilnaer Balebessel' (Famous Melody of the Balebessel of Vilna), which was 'taken from a song by a Jew from Vilna and arranged for piano' by Arno Nadel.[22] Nadel came from Vilna, where he was born in 1878. At the age of 12 he went to Königsberg, where he studied Jewish liturgical music with Eduard Birnbaum.[23] From 1895 he lived in Berlin and was a student at the Jewish teacher-training college there. Nadel was multi-talented, equally gifted as a poet, painter, and musician. He wrote poems and stage plays, and he translated An-ski's play *Hadibuk* (The Dybbuk) into German. From 1916 he led choirs at various Berlin synagogues, for which he also wrote liturgical works. Besides these creative activities, he made a name for himself as a music reviewer for various Jewish newspapers and journals.

It was Leo Winz who suggested that Nadel adapt Jewish folklore for his compositions. Nadel became one of Winz's closest musical collaborators, and Winz's folk-song collection became his most important source in the early years. Later he published two collections of arrangements of Jewish folklore for voice with piano accompaniment—*Jontefflieder* (Festival Songs) and *Jüdische Volkslieder* (Jewish Folk Songs)—as well as a collection of folk poetry, *Jüdische Liebeslieder* (Jewish Love Songs).[24] In 1918 Nadel composed incidental music for Stefan Zweig's anti-war play *Jeremiah* using traditional Jewish motifs. The music was played for the last time in 1934 at a performance at the theatre of the Berlin Jüdischer Kulturbund under the direction of Leopold Jessner (Stompor 2001: 43). In 1943 Arno Nadel was deported to Auschwitz, and murdered there (*EJ* 1971: xii, cols 752–3; Rothmüller 1951: 150).

Many other young Jewish composers besides Nadel belonged to the circle around *Ost und West*. Apart from James Rothstein, they included Hirsch Lifschütz (the dates of whose birth and death aren't known), Bogumil Zepler (1858–1918), Janot Roskin (1884–1946), Jacob Beymel (1880–1944), and Leo Kopf (1888–?). They were all commissioned by Leo Winz to arrange the folk melodies from his collection. These arrangements thus became Winz's (or *Ost und West*'s) property; they were subsequently published in the journal, and, above all, performed at many events organized by its editorial staff.

Among the composers commissioned by Winz were several members of the Society for Jewish Folk Music in St Petersburg. The concert programmes of *Ost und West* contained the names of Lazare Saminsky, Alexander Zhitomirsky, Joel Engel, Ephraim Shklyar, Moshe Shalyt, Hirsch Kopyt, and Boris Levensohn. There was active co-operation between *Ost und West* and the society, and it was mentioned explicitly on every occasion that all the folk melodies came from Winz's collection. On 11 November 1908, even before the society had started its work, two arrangements for violin and piano —*Ch'ssidisch* (Hasidic) by Saminsky and *Dem reben's nigun* (The Rebbe's Tune) by Zhitomirsky—were performed in Berlin; they were later published by the society in 1910 and 1912 respectively.[25] Leo Winz's collection became—alongside the melodies made available by Zusman Kiselgof, the pedagogue and collector of Jewish folk music—an important source for the work of the society in its early phase (Nemtsov 2004: 54). Further proof of this is the well-known *Lieder-Sammelbuch für die jüdische Schule und Familie* (Jewish School and Family Songbook), which Kiselgof was commissioned to compile by the society, and which was published in 1912 by *Ost und West*. It is specially noted in the anthology that seven of its melodies came from Leo Winz's collection, including 'Die alte kasche' (The Old Question), 'Chazkele', 'Alef-bejs' (Alphabet), and 'A retenisch', which belonged to the repertoire of the St Petersburg society. It is also noticeable that many other folk songs which appeared in the first two series of the society's publications in 1910 and 1912 had previously been performed in other arrangements in the *Ost und West* concerts. The second series of 1912 (which had nineteen issues) had been published by the *Ost und West* publishing house as well. The society's composers received the material, which had already been arranged in Berlin, from Winz.

Jewish Folk Music on the Concert Stage

The first big musical event sponsored by *Ost und West* occurred on the eve of Purim, 21 March 1905. It was actually organized by two other Jewish societies—the Verein für jüdische Geschichte und Literatur (Society for Jewish History and Literature) and the Verein jüdische Lesehalle (Jewish Reading-Room Society),[26] but *Ost und West* was entirely responsible for the content. The programme focused equally on Jewish music and art, and several poems were also recited.[27] The works of art were projected onto the wall with the aid of an optical apparatus called a Skioptikon. There were nearly eighty pictures by thirty-one artists, including Jozef Israëls, Lesser Ury, Hermann Struck, Samuel Hirszenberg, Mark Antokolski, Boris Schatz, Max Liebermann, and Leonid Pasternak. All the pictures had been published by Kunstverlag Phönix and had been printed in *Ost und West*. The musical part of the programme consisted mainly of folk-song arrangements by various composers. According to the review in the journal,

This was something completely new for Berlin. Individual songs raised veritable storms of applause. Particularly appreciated were the folk songs, from which now rejoicing high spirits, now deep longing, now moving melancholy rang out . . . The . . . hasidic melodies, those original 'songs without words', were a joy to hear for lovers of singing. All the performances were also greeted with enthusiastic applause.[28]

The concert programme had accompanying notes for five of these arrangements, including 'Chazkele', 'Geh ich mer spaziren (Verlassen)' (When I go for a walk (Alone)), and 'Chassidisches Lied' (Hasidic Song; without words) by Arno Nadel, 'Wer es kenn afn fidele spilen' (Who Can Play the Fiddle) by Hirsch Lifschütz, and 'Her nor du schön mejdele' (Listen, Pretty Maiden) by M. Gibianski. The pieces that had previously been published in *Ost und West* thus received further publicity. The musical style of the arrangements was almost identical to that of the Society for Jewish Folk Music's pieces, or to the style of those by Joel Engel: the accompaniments were conventional, they were based on classic harmonies and also doublings and thirds, and sometimes second voices were used. The compositions were simple and could also be played by amateurs without difficulty.

Despite the success of the Purim performance the journal did not immediately continue its concert-giving activities. The organization of regular concerts was only resumed at the end of 1906. In the following two years *Ost und West* cooperated in this area with the newly established Verein zur Förderung jüdischer Kunst (Society for the Promotion of Jewish Art) in Berlin. The first joint concert took place on 12 December 1906, and contained only musical acts. The well-known Zionist activist and poet Theodor Zlocisti[29] delivered the opening lecture, on 'The History, Sources, and Psychological Character of the Jewish Folk Song'. The composer Bogumil Zepler took on the artistic direction and also presented the programme. Zepler, who also conceived most of the other concert programmes in subsequent years, became, with Arno Nadel, one of the most important members of the music circle revolving around *Ost und West*. In addition to composers, there were several performers who belonged to this circle: first and foremost the soprano Vera Goldberg and the tenor Leo Gollanin, who were initially involved in most of the concerts. They were joined later by the singers Claire Dawidoff-Spiwakowski, Bella Falk, Susy Lipsky, Michael Magidson, and Janot Roskin, as well as many other musicians such as the violinist Betty Tennenbaum and the Spiwakowski brothers —Jascha (piano), Tossi (violin) and Albert (violoncello or piano accompaniment)—who could be heard in several *Ost und West* concerts.[30] Arno Nadel, James Rothstein, Bogumil Zepler, or Ludwig Mendelssohn usually accompanied the songs.

The concert programme for 10 December 1906 was divided into several sections presenting different spheres of Jewish music. Arrangements of Yiddish folk songs for voice and piano dominated; in addition there was 'liturgical house music'—traditional prayer motifs in Hebrew, and some Sephardi and Ashkenazi melodies arranged for violin and harmonium (including the melody of the Vilna Balebessel arranged by Nadel)—as well as what was known as 'art music using Jewish motifs', including works by Rothstein (the song 'War ein kleines stilles Haus'), Anton Rubinstein (an aria from the opera *Die Makkabäer* (The Maccabees)), Karl Goldmark (an aria from the opera *Die Königin von Saba* (The Queen of Sheba)), and Bogumil Zepler. 'Jewish art music' referred to a mixture of works that contained compositions with elements of traditional Jewish music, works with Jewish subjects by composers of Jewish origin, and sometimes also pieces by non-Jewish composers with Jewish themes (such as oratorios by Handel or songs by Rimsky-Korsakov and Mussorgsky). Similar ideas dominated in the first phase of the St Petersburg Society for Jewish Folk Music, whose concerts during 1908–10 exactly repeated the organizational principles of the *Ost und West* concerts.

Some of the composers in the *Ost und West* circle creatively pushed the boundaries of Jewish art music. In the concert of 10 December 1906 a song by Bogumil Zepler rang out, 'Wo du hingehst . . .' (Whither thou goest . . .), for voice and harmonium, based on a text from the biblical book of Ruth. In May of the following year the song was published in *Ost und West*. The composer created two parallel versions of the voice part—in German and in Hebrew—that differed considerably and which were therefore able to translate the rhythmic peculiarities of both languages optimally. The Jewish colour is created both by the rich instrumental ornamentation in the style of biblical cantillation and by the voice part, whose arrangement—'in a free recitation tempo' according to the score—create clear associations with the traditional recitation of biblical texts.

The December concert was followed on 9 January 1907 by a literary programme of 'Modern Jewish Poetry' with the legendary Rudolf Schildkraut.[31] A projected evening of 'Jewish Fairytales and Legends' did not take place. Instead *Ost und West* organized its first guest performance outside Berlin in April 1907: at the invitation of the Society for Jewish Art in Breslau the December programme was repeated there.

In the next season of 1907/8, two concerts with different programmes, staged in co-operation with the Berlin Society for the Promotion of Jewish Art, were organized (on 13 October 1907 and 19 February 1908); in addition a concert took place in the Hamburg Concert House, where the works that had already been performed in Berlin were presented. The repertoire had been considerably broadened: along with many folk-song arrangements several new works by Jewish composers were performed, including *Divertissement über chassidische Melodien* (Divertissement on Hasidic Melodies), for violin and piano, by Arno Nadel (with variations on the song 'Alef-Bejs' as the finale), as well as songs by Jacob Beymel, Ignaz Brüll,[32] Bogumil Zepler, Diamant,[33] and Hirsch Lifschütz.

A concert on 20 September 1908 was to be the last event organized jointly with the Jewish Art Society (as it came to be called); the other concerts of this season were directed solely by *Ost und West*. On 27 December the concert team gave a guest performance in Halberstadt at the invitation of the local Zionist organization Tikwath Zion, and in the following season, on 9 May 1909, at the Libanon-Loge (of the Jewish fraternal organization, B'nai Brith) in Insterburg in East Prussia.

Various events were held in the following seasons, but in 1912/13 the staging of concerts intensified. In the space of less than three months, at least fourteen concerts took place: on 27 October 1912 in Berlin (in the National Jewish Women's Union), on 31 October in Leipzig, on 2 November in Breslau, on 5 November in Frankfurt am Main, on 7 November in Cologne, on 9 November in Munich, on 11 November in Nuremberg, on 16 November in Berlin, on 18 November in Hamburg, on 21 November in Posen, on 24 November in Hanover, on 1 December in Berlin, on 16 December in Berlin again (as part of the Maccabi celebration of the Berlin Zionists), and on 15 January 1913 in Leipzig (a benefit concert 'for the Israelite Society for Supporting of Sick People Bikur Holim'). Compared to other contemporary Jewish cultural events, the programmes of these concerts developed in a distinctive direction. While, in Jewish music concerts in Russia at this time, art music was increasingly played and a distinctive Jewish style crystallized in the works of the most talented members of the Society for Jewish Folk Music (Achron, Saminsky, Milner, Rosowsky) (Nemtsov 2004: 55–6), developments in Germany followed another course. After several very promising attempts, art music completely disappeared from the concerts initiated by *Ost und West*, which from then on exclusively presented arrangements of Jewish folk melodies. There were apparently at least two reasons for this: the creative potential of the group of composers around Leo Winz was considerably weaker than that of the society in St Petersburg, and the German circle lacked the continual artistic exchange that the Russian society and its music committee could guarantee.

Although the artistic ambitions of the circle around *Ost und West* were in the end reduced to the promotion of traditional Jewish music, and although even of this only a part—the secular songs of east European Jews—was really represented, the significance of their work cannot be underestimated. Not only the Jewish audience but also the general public felt the concerts of *Ost und West* to be first-class cultural events, which presented—for the first time in Europe, to a broad audience, and in a convincing artistic way—a folk-music tradition that was hardly known. According to reports at the time the concerts, which were consistently sold out, prompted storms of enthusiasm and left a long-lasting impression in which amazement at the high musical and poetic quality of the songs was combined with the wish to hear more in the genre. A complete edition of the folk melodies and their arrangements was often requested. Evidence of these reactions can be found in the reviews (largely from non-Jewish newspapers) of the concert tour in autumn 1912 with the singers Bella Falk, Claire Dawidoff, and Michael Magidson, violinist Betty Tennenbaum, and Arno Nadel as accompanying pianist. A collection of these reviews was printed in *Ost und West*, and also appeared in the form of a brochure.[34]

After the 1912/13 season the concert activities of *Ost und West* suddenly stopped, for unknown reasons. No more events were organized until 1917. The few performances of songs from the proven repertoire of *Ost und West* were staged on the initiative of individual musicians from the group. The singer Leo Gollanin was involved in a concert on the occasion of the eleventh Zionist Congress in Vienna, which took place on 7 September 1913; the Jewish Choral Society from Czernowitz and the English Jewish violinist Margery Bentwich also took part.[35] Several arrangements by Nadel and Zepler were performed on 7 February 1914, as part of a 'Jewish student evening' in Berlin. On 25 December 1916 Arno Nadel himself organized a concert, mainly of his folk-song arrangements from Leo Winz's collection, in the Berlin Klindworth-Scharwenka Hall. At this time Winz had already been living in Copenhagen for two years, from where he supervised the editing of *Ost und West* as before. On 6 December 1917, he organized, by himself, a large-scale concert of Jewish folk music, in which the young Polish Jewish soprano Susy Lipsky took part. The concert was compered in Danish, and all the texts were translated. Again, the response was positive, and there were nine reviews in the Danish newspapers. 'For the many people, who attended the concert yesterday, the evening became a great musical experience', *København* (Copenhagen) reported the next day. The reviewer raved that 'throughout one feels a glow and an inventiveness in the expression of all of these changing, brightly coloured moods, that raise the artistic value of this unique music to a very high level'.

In Germany the musical activities of *Ost und West* were resumed as soon as Leo Winz returned to Berlin after the war. The *Jüdische Rundschau* published a whole-page advertisement on 3 October 1919 which included details of the establishment of the Verlag für Volksmusik (Folk Music Publishing Company) under the artistic direction of Winz and Janot S. Roskin. The publication catalogue included around 300 arrangements of Jewish folk melodies from Winz's collection, of which forty-eight had already been published at this time. The company was presumably directly connected to *Ost und West*, since both operations had the same address. As part of its activities a 'concert department' was formed, which according to the advertisement was to take over 'the arrangement of folk songs and other Jewish art evenings in Berlin and the provinces in grand and modest style in co-operation with outstanding permanently engaged artists'.[36] The first series of folk-song evenings was also announced in the advertisement. It consisted of no fewer than seven large-scale concerts in Berlin (in the Oberlicht Philharmonic Hall, the Blüthner Hall, the concert hall of the College of Music in Fasanenstrasse, and in the Teachers' Union House), as well as further concerts in twelve other German towns: Frankfurt, Cologne, Mannheim, Stuttgart, Nuremberg, Munich, Hanover, Dresden, Leipzig, Hamburg, Breslau, and Königsberg. In organizing these programmes the circle around *Ost und West* (as well as the members of the St Petersburg society) assumed that presenting authentic performers, or songs as they were performed in their original context, could not play a role in the national renaissance. They firmly believed that folk music had to be refined and adapted for the concert stage to be culturally significant in the modern era.

The first of the announced concerts took place on 13 October 1919, in the Oberlicht Philharmonic Hall. An insert in the concert programme testifies to the difficult conditions in which the concerts were given in the post-war period: 'We ask that you make allowances for the artists who are suffering from heavy colds due to their unheated apartments.' Those who took part in the series included seven singers, among them Leo Gollanin, Janot Roskin, and Susy Lipsky, and several instrumentalists. The participation of the Spiwakowski brothers was of particular note. Two of them—Jascha and Tossi—were to go on to formidable international careers a few years later. At this time Tossi (his name was later written as Tossy Spivakovsky) was still appearing as a child prodigy; at the age of 19 he became the concert master of the Berlin Philharmonic Orchestra under the direction of Wilhelm Furtwängler. He gave concerts around the world together with his brother, the pianist Jascha; they were giving guest performances in Australia when they learned in 1933 of the Nazi takeover. Jascha remained permanently in Melbourne, where he distinguished himself at the Academy of Music; Tossi later went to the United States, where he taught at the prestigious Juilliard School in New York City. Evidence of the popularity of this concert series can be found in the journal *Schlemiel*: 'While Jewish diplomacy rests on the laurels of its advance [referring to the Balfour Declaration of 1917 stating British support for a Jewish national home in Palestine], for lack of other state actions the tiny [*winzige*—a play on Leo Winz's name] affair of the Jewish folk song is raised to the level of one [a state action].'[37]

After Winz's departure for Palestine in 1921 no further concerts by *Ost und West* are documented. Two years later the journal disappeared from the Jewish cultural scene. However, the Russian Jewish musicians who had immigrated to Germany continued to undertake engagements. They presented the German public not only with performances of Jewish folk music but also with the art music of the New Jewish School.[38] From the mid-1920s the pianist and publicist Alice Jacob-Loewenson, who was an active member of the Zionist Organization, became the main disseminator of Jewish music in Germany (see Nemtsov 2005), while many other Zionist-oriented musicians in Austria and other central and east European countries rendered outstanding service in disseminating Jewish music (see Nemtsov and Schröder-Nauenburg 2004). The effects of Zionist cultural thinking on Jewish music influenced the organization of events of the Jüdischer Kulturbund in Germany in the 1930s (see Nemtsov forthcoming: ch. 6).

'Spiritual Reintegration into our own Nation':
Fritz Mordechai Kaufmann

Late in 1916 the well-known businessman and patron of the arts Zalman Schocken (1877–1959), who had been involved in the Zionist movement since 1910, addressed the Zionist Organization of Germany with an extensive paper entitled 'Organization and Content of Zionist Work in Germany'. Schocken was at the time closely associated with the circle of cultural Zionists around Martin Buber, according to whom the most important aspect of the Zionist project was the rediscovery of Jewish spiritual values as the means of the renewal of the people (Schreuder and Weber 1994: 26). The practical measures that Schocken proposed in his paper included the establishment of the Ausschuss für jüdische Kulturarbeit (Committee for Jewish Cultural Work). This suggestion was accepted. With Schocken as chairman, Martin Buber, Moses Calvary, Kurt Blumenfeld, Hugo Bergmann, and Max Brod were elected as members of the committee. Its most important task was to be editorial or, in Schocken's words, 'the creation of books for the Hebraization and Judaization of German Jews' (Schreuder and Weber 1994: 27). Only a few publication projects could be realized, including a Hebrew textbook, a German–Hebrew phraseology, and a few stories for Jewish youth. In July 1918 the Committee for Jewish Cultural Work initiated a musical project: Fritz Mordechai Kaufmann was commissioned to produce a Jewish songbook. As a result two works by Kaufmann were published: *Das jüdische Volkslied. Ein Merkblatt* (The Jewish Folk Song: A Leaflet) in 1919 and, a year later, *Die schönsten Lieder der Ostjuden. 47 ausgewählte Volkslieder* (The Most Beautiful Songs of the East European Jews: 47 Selected Folk Songs), both released by the Jüdischer Verlag in Berlin.

Inspired by Saul Ginsburg and Pesach Marek's 1901 collection of Jewish folk songs in Russia, several other publications had come out before the First World War: Zusman Kiselgof's *Lieder-Sammelbuch für die jüdische Schule und Familie*, the two-volume *Jüdische Volkslieder* (Jewish Folk Songs) by Jehuda Leib Cahan from Warsaw (New York, 1912) and the collection of folk songs by Noyech Prilutzki, also in two volumes (Warsaw, 1911 and 1913). Many folk melodies were arranged by composers for concert repertoires and private musical performances, published by *Ost und West*, the Society for Jewish Folk Music in St Petersburg, and also by Joel Engel and some others. Numerous concerts of Jewish folk music took place in Russia and Germany, but also in other European countries,

Figure 1 Portrait of Fritz Mordechai Kaufmann

exposing a broader audience to this tradition for the first time. This diverse activity had great national-cultural significance, but the extent of its artistic and academic achievement was sometimes doubtful. Most of the activities were inspired by nationalist enthusiasm, by the wish to spread the newly discovered Jewish folk music by all possible means and in this way promote a Jewish nationalism bringing together traditions across the European diaspora. Only a short time before it had seemed natural that the Jews had no folk music of their own that could be taken seriously, so at this stage it seemed more important to prove the reverse, and in this way strengthen national self-consciousness, than to undertake a systematic analysis of the material.

The enthusiasts for Jewish folk song lacked criteria with which to judge folklore. It was not easy, for instance, for the St Petersburg society to realize that the artistic value of the collected folk songs varied. In the west there was no such analysis at all. The melodies published and performed by *Ost und West* were for this reason heterogeneous: besides recognized folk melodies, material was also promoted whose roots in tradition were doubtful. In addition no distinction was made in east or west between authentic folk melodies and arrangements; folk music was played in concert arrangements that were often foreign to the character and nature of Jewish melodies. It was believed that the folk songs could only achieve their effect when they were improved and cultivated by accompaniments composed in the European style. In fact, this belief arguably caused the characteristic nature of these songs to be lost. The problem was not only the lack of an

Figure 2 First song from Fritz Mordechai Kaufmann's *Die schönsten Lieder der Ostjuden* (1925). The Yiddish orthography follows the system of Solomon Birnbaum

appropriate stylistic means, but above all the lack of understanding of the distinctiveness of Jewish musical folklore. Hardly anyone made a serious theoretical study of its special features, and the few attempts to do so were amateurish and naive, such as the brochure *Das jüdische Volkslied* (The Jewish Folk Song) by Zusman Kiselgof (translated from Yiddish and published by the Berlin Jüdischer Verlag in 1913).[39] An appropriate academic approach was only to be found in the articles and lectures of Lazare Saminsky (see Saminsky 1914, 1915), but these remained unknown outside Russia. So nationally minded musicians and cultural activists integrated Jewish folk music into the new Jewish renaissance, largely without scholarly guidance.

The work of Fritz Mordechai Kaufmann—who produced the first collection of Jewish folk songs to follow scholarly standards of Jewish ethnology—seems all the more important against this backdrop. In contrast to all the previous works in the Jewish renaissance which had emphasized accessibility, simplicity in performance, and popularity, Kaufmann turned his attention to matters of authenticity and the traditions of musical-poetic style.

Kaufmann was born in 1888 in Eschweiler in the Eifel and studied medicine in Munich and Marburg before he went to Leipzig in 1910. His time in Leipzig shaped his career in many respects. It was there that he became a member of the Zionist Organization and became intensively interested in east European Judaism, which he perceived as 'the living body of Judaism' (Kaufmann 1923: 11). It was there that he learned, among other things, the Yiddish language, in which he later became fluent. Leipzig was also the place where he met his future wife, Rachel (or Rahel) Kaganoff from Odessa, the daughter of a Torah scribe. The pair were musically inclined: Kaufmann played the violin, and Rachel was a singer; they shared a love for east European Jewish song.

Another important encounter for Kaufmann was with Nathan Birnbaum, who became his spiritual mentor. According to Kaufmann's friend and brother-in-law Ludwig Strauss, 'Birnbaum's greatest personal achievement as an east European Jew, who landed in the West and was brought up in German culture, was to reconquer the home. Kaufmann followed him as the first western Jew to feel at home in east European Judaism and to learn to think and feel in its language' (Kaufmann 1923: 12). Under the influence of Birnbaum, who was opposed to political Zionism, Kaufmann also left the Zionist Organization in 1913.

Kaufmann's first published works appeared in the *Jüdische Rundschau*. From spring 1913 he and his brother Julius published their own journal, *Die Freistatt. Alljüdische Revue* (The Free State: All-Jewish Review). The title was intended to be polemical, since part of the journal was devoted to countering political Zionism, which Kaufmann viewed as a restriction of the national Jewish idea (Kaufmann 1923: 67–118). *Die Freistatt* asserted its entitlement to represent this idea in its entirety. It made east European Jewish culture its focus. It published many works of Yiddish poetry in the original Hebrew orthography and in German translation. In addition, it informed its readership about different aspects of the folk life of east European Jews.

Kaufmann distinguished his cultural Zionism, building Jewish social unity on the foundation of shared cultural roots in folk life, from political Zionism, associated with Theodor Herzl's call for the immediate creation of an independent Jewish state. Kaufmann's criticism in this respect had much in common with the position of Ahad Ha'am, who argued that before a Jewish state could be established enthusiasm for nationalist sentiment and culture needed to be spread among Jews in the Diaspora. They both polemicized against the arrogance of the political leaders of the Zionist Organization, pointing out their aloofness from the mass of Jewish people and their effort to create a political apparatus without first building a cultural foundation.[40] They both demanded that attention should be given to living Judaism and practical cultural work; while Ahad Ha'am saw the task as the revival of Hebrew culture, Kaufmann was a follower of the Yiddish cultural renaissance. Both these views caught on increasingly in the Zionist Organization: Hebrew culture became established in Palestine, while Yiddish grew within Zionist activities in the Diaspora.

It was logical that Kaufmann, after his front-line action during the First World War, which had interrupted his publishing activity for two years, came back to a now changed Zionism and was integrated into the circle of cultural Zionists around the journal *Der Jude* (The Jew) that was established and led by Martin Buber. From 1916 on, Kaufmann's articles appeared again mainly in the Zionist press.

In 1920 Kaufmann became the head of the Jüdisches Arbeiterfürsorgeamt (Jewish Workers' Welfare Office), which had been created the previous year in Berlin. This institution supported east European Jewish refugees and emigrants in many different ways.[41] In March 1921, however, possibly driven by chronic depression, he committed suicide.

Kaufmann's musical-ethnographic studies are still relevant today. They culminated in the works published between 1918 and 1920, including *Die schönsten Lieder der Ostjuden* and the accompanying leaflet *Das jüdische Volkslied*. However, his serious research into east European music and folklore had started much earlier, in 1911 in Leipzig. The impulse came from a concert by an ensemble of the St Petersburg Society for Jewish Folk Music under the direction of the singer Jakov Medwedew, who was performing on its first European tour. It was on this occasion that Kaufmann was 'shaken up by a few old songs' (Kaufmann 2001: 11). In the following years he sought out authentic folk singers in the field and documented a range of Jewish folk music.

In his articles Kaufmann analysed previous work in this field, mainly concentrated in the efforts of *Ost und West* and the St Petersburg society. He subjected them to a negative critique. In his opinion the folk songs that had been presented up to that point should mostly be described as falsifications: they did not represent the best of what the Jewish musical folk genius was capable of, but were merely a randomly assembled mixture in which, alongside authentic folk songs, other material—melodies from Jewish operettas, insipid popular songs, and 'all kinds of oversentimental art songs'—had been fabricated with hardly any connection with genuine folklore (Kaufmann 1923: 247). Furthermore he objected to the kind of adaptation used to introduce such songs to the public; these arrangements were mostly unfavourable to the style:

The folk song, so rounded and complete, that can only have its effect by virtue of the unsurpassable expression that is captured in it, is arbitrarily dislocated and decorated ... This is the case for most of the song supplements in the 'Ost und West' journal and many individual publications of the Society for Jewish Folk Music, not to speak of the sorry musical productions from Mazin & Co. (London), Hübner (Nadworna) and those printed in America. (Kaufmann 1923: 230)

The third important point of criticism was the Yiddish language, which was hopelessly distorted in these publications and, worse, became like German. The result was a 'language that is neither Yiddish nor German but *gemauschel*' (Kaufmann

1923: 247). Finally he criticized the performance milieu; he considered the concert atmosphere and the performers, who had either been trained at the opera or
came from the east European Jewish operetta, hardly appropriate to rendering
folk culture, and had little feeling for the contexts of the folk song.[42]

Kaufmann advocated ending the creation of high art out of folk material and
replacing this with the goal of authentic reproduction of the Jewish folk song,
which he considered to be an art form on its own terms and the purest expression
of the soul of the Jewish people. For this reason he detested everything that
clouded the original folk forms as 'dissipation' of the folk song. Referring to the
highly regarded 'Hebrew Melody' by Joseph Achron and the piano trio 'Fantastic
Dance' by Solomon Rosowsky, he remarked: 'A few simple melodies even became
virtuoso pieces for violin and piano; Yiddish songs feature as "Hebrew Melody"
or "Fantastic Dance". I cannot see an enrichment of Jewish folk music in this'
(Kaufmann 2001: 32).

In his article 'Performing Jewish Folk Music for West European Jews'[43] Kaufmann describes in detail his goal for the collection, publication, adaptation, and
performance of Jewish folk music. He was forced to admit, however, that under
the conditions prevalent in the West his vision would be difficult to achieve in all
its aspects in the foreseeable future. Nevertheless, he made a contribution
towards the goal of preserving authentic folk culture in an exemplary collection,
the forty-seven songs in *Die schönsten Lieder der Ostjuden*, which he had personally
gathered from east European Jewish folk singers.[44] The largest category com-
prises ten religious and hasidic songs; in addition there are lullabies, children's
songs, wedding songs, family songs, and soldiers' songs. For Kaufmann, the contextual relationship between the songs and religion was an important consideration in distinguishing between authentic folk material and tasteless 'pseudo-
folklore'. As he wrote, 'The formal elements of these songs are the same ones that
we find in traditional synagogue song . . . That means that the musical form . . . is
a kind of a recitative . . . The recitative has . . . stayed dominant until recently, even
in many lullabies and some love songs, that are clearly outside the religious
sphere' (Kaufmann 1923: 254). To be sure, Lazare Saminsky expressed similar
ideas in Russia around the same time. He also viewed the religious melodies as
the touchstone in judging the national and artistic value of even secular songs
(Nemtsov 2004: 70–1). In the following passage Kaufmann's words are almost
identical to Saminsky's, of which it can be proved that Kauffman was unaware:
'Without doubt those folk songs which do not come directly from liturgical music
are more comprehensible for the public, which is not on close terms with it . . .
The truly grandiose things, however, are those which are absolutely Jewish, from
the realm of the religion' (Kaufmann 1923: 255). In another place he emphasized
the 'inner connection between the old strict synagogue music and these songs,
that extended and internalized the melodic line of the religious song in an amaz-
ingly bold and independent way' (Kaufmann 2001: 12).

Kaufmann's leaflet contains valuable tips on authentic performance practice. Among other things, he concentrates on the correct pronunciation of the Yiddish texts, using a phonetic system that had been developed shortly before by Solomon Birnbaum[45] that reproduced the sound of all three important dialects of the Yiddish language—Polish, Lithuanian, and southern Russian. For details of correct pronunciation the reader was referred to the relevant publications in *Die Freistatt*. Since the Jewish folk song has a purely vocal character, Kaufmann argued in principle against instrumental accompaniment; if an accompaniment seemed indispensable, it had to be very sparing and could not contain any polyphonic elements.[46] Likewise, he warned against choral singing, which was unsuitable for many types of Jewish folk music. Jewish choral singing (for example that of the hasidim) was in all cases different from the German norm:

The Germans prefer to sing in a tight, disciplined mass; the Jewish mass has a completely different, freer collective form. It does not know how to sing in iron rhythm. It is under the influence of the singing in the house of prayer . . . the individual does not violate his rapture, his joy. The total effect of such a song, impossible for disciplined, Prussian disposition, is purely oriental; it produces a long-lasting, shattering effect' (Kaufmann 2001: 37).

The rhythmic aspects of the Jewish folk song were also significant for Kaufmann. Here as well a particular freedom is offered: 'In reality the art of playing and singing to time consists of ignoring the score at crucial points, inserting a minute pause here, there a barely noticeable speeding-up' (Kaufmann 2001: 14). However, in practice all these tips were only supposed to help beginners find their bearings; Kaufmann recommended in any case that people should listen to the authentic song of east European Jews and learn directly from folk singers.

Despite Kaufmann's great love for this art, the fostering of the Jewish song and Yiddish poetry was not a purely cultural affair for him, but—in the sense of cultural Zionism—part of the essential task of the national renaissance. He turned to those west European Jews who acknowledged that they were part of the Jewish Diaspora but were disconnected from a nationalist cultural identity. A nationalist rebirth could not happen, he argued, through 'repeating parrot fashion' the Zionist formulas, but only by overcoming cultural uprooting and by every individual internalizing the living spirit of the people. The spirit finds its most intense expression, according to Kaufmann, in east European Jewish culture, and particularly in music. He considered the Jewish folk song to be the best means to achieve the 'spiritual reintegration into our own nation' (Kaufmann 2001: 17).

More than eighty years after Kaufmann's statement and sixty years after the Holocaust, a remarkable revival of Jewish music is taking place in North America and Europe generally, and in Germany in particular, where a new movement calling itself klezmer is attracting a large non-Jewish audience. The 'king of klezmer', clarinettist Giora Feidman, as well as numerous klezmer bands, most of them consisting of non-Jewish musicians, evoke an idealized image of east European Jewry and its music. This image has little in common with the historical reality and the intentions of the national Jewish renaissance at the beginning of the twentieth century. Instead of the ethnological and aesthetic authenticity which characterized the goal of the renaissance, the crucial point of the klezmer movement in Germany is a sort of psychological effect. Through the popularization of this music some Germans can identify with the victims of National Socialism as a way of coming to terms with the past. It is therefore no wonder that neither Leo Winz nor Fritz Mordechai Kaufmann is present in the cultural memory of modern Germany. Even the reprint of Kaufmann's song collection in 2001 was barely noted in klezmer circles. This situation highlights the importance of recognizing in Jewish cultural studies the legacy of the pioneers of the Jewish musical renaissance who dedicated their lives to studying and fostering genuine Jewish folklore rather than what eminent American folklorist Richard Dorson (1971, 1974, 1976) later called 'fakelore'.

Translated from the German by Sarah Prais

Notes

1   'Ost und West', *Ost und West. Illustrierte Monatsschrift für modernes Judentum*, 1 (Jan. 1901), cols 1–4.

2   From October 1906 *Ost und West* was officially published as the organ of the Deutsche Conferenz-Gemeinschaft der Alliance Israélite Universelle; see *Ost und West*, 10–11 (Oct./Nov. 1906), cols 633–6. The Alliance, founded in 1860 in Paris, was the first international Jewish welfare organization. The focal point of its activities was in the area of secular Jewish education. It supported the first modern Jewish schools in Erets Yisra'el.

3   David A. Brenner admits that 'to date, there exists no biography of Winz or his main associates at *Ost und West*' (1997: 55). He nevertheless supplies—without referring to the sources—a few pieces of biographical information about Winz, most of which are incorrect.

4   Hovevei Zion (Lovers of Zion), an early Zionist movement in Russia, formed in 1884, which promoted Jewish colonization in Palestine. The leaders were Moses Leib Lilienblum and Leon Pinsker. Most branches later joined the Zionist Organization.

5   Information on the organization can be found in LWC, A 136/218. Moses Hess (1812–75) was an early Zionist writer.

6   Letter from the Berlin Zionist Organization and the Central Committee of the German Zionist Organization (LWC, A 136/218).

7   Letter from Winz to Buck, Tel Aviv, 31 Dec. 1937 (LWC, A 136/101/1).

8   See the obituary of Winz in *Jüdische Wochenschau* (Buenos Aires) (17 June 1952), 7.

9   Letter from Winz to Bernard de Vries, Tel Aviv, 20 Dec. 1938 (LWC, A 136/101/1).

10   Letter from Winz to Arthur Meyerowitz, Tel Aviv, 14 Oct. 1934 (LWC, A 136/101/2).

11   Letter from Winz to Kullmann, Tel Aviv, 1 Aug. 1938 (LWC, A 136/101/1).

12   *Jüdische Wochenschau* (Buenos Aires) (17 June 1952), 7. Sammy (Samuel) Gronemann (1875–1952) was a journalist, dramatist, and lawyer, a leading German Zionist, and a member of the Action Committee of the Zionist Organization.

13   Letter from Winz to Arthur Meyerowitz, Tel Aviv, 15 Sept. 1938 (LWC, A 136/101/2).

14   Letter from Tel Aviv, 31 Dec. 1937 (LWC, A 136/101/1).

15   On the term *jungjüdisch* see Gelber 1986.

16   'Jungjüdische Abende in Berlin', *Ost und West*, 9 (Sept. 1902), cols 211–12.

17   The collection, which was probably started before the establishment of *Ost und West*—at the end of the 19th century—is in the Leo Winz Archive (LWA).

18   In addition to Ginsburg and Marek only Zusman Kiselgof (1878–1939), who had just started collecting Jewish folk songs at that time, can be mentioned in this connection.

19   *Ost und West*, 9 (Sept. 1903), cols 639–42. Rothstein's *Judenlieder* cycle is published in Rothstein 1916.

20   Lewandowski (1821–94) was one of the most important composers of synagogue music in the 19th century.

21   'Zur jüdischen Volkskunde. Ein Wort an unsere Leser', *Ost und West*, 1 (Jan. 1905), cols 1–6.

22   *Ost und West*, 2 (Feb. 1905), cols 103–6. The Wilnaer Balebessel was the nickname of the famous Jewish cantor from Vilna who was the author of the melody.

23   Birnbaum (1835–1920) was a prominent cantor and pupil of Salomon Sulzer. He was also known as a musicologist and pedagogue.

24   *Jontefflieder*, 12 vols (Berlin: Jüdischer Verlag, 1919). *Jüdische Volkslieder*, vol. i, nos. 1 and 2 (Berlin: Jüdischer Verlag, 1920); no further volumes were published. *Jüdische Liebeslieder* (Berlin and Vienna: Benjamin Harz, 1923). The available bibliographical details for these collections are inaccurate. I should like to thank Jürgen Gottschalk (Berlin) for the relevant guidance to sources. The *Jüdische Volkslieder* collection contains thirty Yiddish poems with German translations and only five musical works.

25   Dritter Jüdischer Konzert-Abend veranstaltet von der Redaktion der Zeitschrift 'Ost und West', Berlin, 11 Nov. 1908 (in LWA). In the concert programme the names of the two composers are mixed up.

26   These were non-Zionist organizations for promotion of German Jewish culture. See Brenner 2000: 31–2, 69.

27   All quoted concert programmes of *Ost und West* are in LWA.

28   'Ein jüdischer Künstlerabend in Berlin', *Ost und West*, 3 (Mar. 1905), col. 214.

29   Zlocisti (1874–1943) was a doctor, a poet, and one of the first German Zionists. He was born in East Prussia and studied medicine in Berlin, where he became the secretary of the Young Israel club in 1893 and two years later co-founded the first Jewish Students Society. From 1921 he lived in Palestine. See *EJ* 1971: xvi, cols 1188–9.

30   Tossi Spiwakowski (b. Odessa, 1907; d. 1998), a child prodigy and violin virtuoso; Albert (b. 1899); Jascha (b. 1896). See *Lexikon der Juden in der Musik* 1940: 261; this infamous Nazi reference book is the only source where all three brothers are mentioned.

31   Schildkraut (1862–1930) was an outstanding Jewish actor; during this period he was

working at the Deutsches Theater under the direction of Max Reinhardt; later he played (also in Yiddish) in the USA.

32   Ignaz Brüll, b. 1846 in Moravian Prossnitz, d. 1907 in Vienna.

33   Probably the composer and choirmaster Jankel (Jakob) Dymont (1880–?).

34   This brochure can be found in LWA.

35   Margery Bentwich, who emigrated to Palestine in 1920, together with her sister, the cellist Thelma Yellin-Bentwich, was one of the pioneers of concert life in Palestine. See Hirshberg 2000: 125–6.

36   *Jüdische Rundschau*, 70 (3 Oct. 1919), 550.

37   *Schlemiel. Jüdische Blätter für Humor und Kunst*, 15 (1920), 204. *Shlemiel* is an idiomatic Yiddish word meaning 'bungler' or 'dolt'.

38   The New Jewish School is the usual name for the Jewish national movement in music in the first third of the 20th century, which was initially represented by the composers around the St Petersburg Society for Jewish Folk Music, and which later became active internationally (see Nemtsov 2004, esp. 111–12).

39   On the reception of this presentation in Germany see Barber 1913: 64–6.

40   Kaufmann accurately analysed the connection between political Zionism and the Haskalah (the Jewish Enlightenment), and criticized it for being 'strange and removed from the people and the national cultural community, with a lack of respect that turns into contempt, seeks to break up or distort all that is peculiarly Jewish in procrustean style, for the sake of norms that are borrowed from foreign nations' (Kaufmann 1923: 101).

41   The Jewish Workers' Welfare Office even published its own periodical, *Ostjuden in Deutschland. Schriften des Arbeiterfürsorgeamtes der jüdischen Organisationen Deutschlands* in the Philo-Verlag Berlin. Issue 2 (1921) contains an obituary of Kaufmann (pp. 3–4).

42   Kaufmann's critique gave the journal *Schlemiel* an opportunity for a satirical text entitled '*Shlemiel*'s Message about the "Jewish Folk Song"', which read: 'Now the unwitting reader will ask: what is the positive nature of the *Jewish* [underlined in the original] folk song? What distinguishes it from German folk songs? The eager concertgoer will produce an answer just like that and say: if one sings "Schlaf, Kindchen, schlaf, dein Vater ist ein Graf", then it is a German folk song; but if one sings "Schlof, mein Jingele, schlof, dein Tate is a Grof", it is a Jewish folk song. There is not much one can say against this: however, the condition is, that it has to have been sung for the first time in a Lithuanian small town. And besides: if a worker sings it, it is a folk song, but if it is sung by a bourgeois, then it is kitsch. With this we are hard on the heels of the condition, and a principle has been created, according to which a clear distinction can be made. This is necessary, before the people and its songs are transferred to Palestine'. *Schlemiel*, 15 (1920), 204.

43   'Die Aufführung jüdischer Volksmusik vor Westjuden'. First published in *Der Jude*, 12 (1917/18), 759–68.

44   Ludwig Strauss composed similar standard works in the area of Yiddish folk poetry: *Ostjüdische Liebeslieder* (Berlin, 1920) and *Jüdische Volkslieder* (Berlin, 1935). In the postscript to the *Ostjüdische Liebeslieder* Strauss thanked his 'dear friends Fritz Mordechai and Rahel Kaufmann, who opened the way to the world of this book in word, script and song' (p. 88). The collection *Jüdische Volkslieder* is dedicated to Rachel Kaufmann and the memory of Fritz Mordechai Kaufmann.

45   Birnbaum (1891–?), the son of Nathan Birnbaum, was a philologist and palaeographer.

46   This type of accompaniment was composed for example by Lazare Saminsky.

References

Primary Sources

LWA. Leo Winz Archive, Music Department, Jewish National and University Library, Jerusalem.

LWC. Leo Winz Collection, Central Zionist Archives, Jerusalem.

Other Sources

AN-SKI S. 1908. 'Evreiskoe narodnoe tvorchestvo', in *Perezhitoe* [anthology], 277–98. St Petersburg.

ASCHHEIM, STEVEN A. 1982. *Brothers and Strangers: The East European Jew in Germany and German Jewish Consciousness, 1800–1923.* Madison.

BAR-AMI [pseud. of Leo Winz]. 1904. 'Das jüdische Volkslied', *Ost und West*, 3 (Mar.), cols 149–60.

BARBER, PINKUS [pseud. of Fritz Mordechai Kaufmann]. 1913. 'Das jüdische Volkslied', *Die Freistatt*, 1 (Apr.), 64–6.

BERTZ, INKA. 1991. 'Eine neue Kunst für ein altes Volk'. In *Die jüdische Renaissance in Berlin 1900 bis 1924*, exhibition catalogue. Berlin.

BRENNER, DAVID A. 1997. '"Making Jargon Respectable": Leo Winz, *Ost und West* and the Reception of Yiddish Theatre in pre-Hitler Germany', *Leo Baeck Institute Year Book*, 42: 51–66.

BRENNER, MICHAEL. 2000. *Jüdische Kultur in der Weimarer Republik.* Munich.

DORSON, RICHARD M. 1971. 'Fakelore'. In Richard M. Dorson, *American Folklore and the Historian*, 3–14. Chicago.

—— 1974. 'Folklore vs Fakelore—Again and Again', *Folklore Forum*, 7 (1974), 57–63.

—— 1976. *Folklore and Fakelore.* Cambridge, Mass.

DYK, S. 1926. 'Leo Winz fünfzig Jahre alt', *Jüdische Rundschau* (26 Feb.), 118.

EJ (Encyclopaedia Judaica). 1971. Jerusalem.

GELBER, MARK H. 1986. 'The *jungjüdische Bewegung*: An Unexplored Chapter in German-Jewish Literary and Cultural History', *Leo Baeck Institute Year Book*, 31: 105–19.

GINSBURG, SAUL M., and PESACH S. MAREK. 1901. *Evreiskie narodnye pesni v Rossii.* St Petersburg; repr. Jerusalem, 1991.

HELLER, LEO. 1903. 'Ein junger jüdischer Tondichter', *Ost und West*, 9 (Sept.), col. 643.

HIRSHBERG, JEHOASH. 2000. *Music in the Jewish Community of Palestine 1880–1948: A Social History.* Moscow.

KAUFMANN, MORDECHAI. 1923. *Fritz Mordechai Kaufmann. Gesammelte Schriften*, ed. Ludwig Strauss. Berlin.

—— 2001. 'Das jüdische Volkslied. Ein Merkblatt'. In Achim Freudenstein and Karsten Troyke, eds, *Fritz Mordechai Kaufmann. Die schönsten Lieder der Ostjuden—Siebenundvierzig ausgewählte Lieder*, 11–32. Edermünde.

Lexikon der Juden in der Musik. 1940. Berlin.

NEMTSOV, JASCHA. 2004. *Die Neue Jüdische Schule in der Musik*. Wiesbaden.

—— 2005. 'Eine Berliner Vorreiterin der neuen jüdischen Schule. Alice Jacob-Loewenson (1895–1967)'. In Jascha Nemtsov, ed., *Jüdische Kunstmusik im 20. Jahrhundert. Quellenlage, Entwicklungsgeschichte, Stilanalysen*, 121–35. Wiesbaden.

—— forthcoming. *Der Zionismus in der Musik. Jüdische Musik und nationale Idee*. Wiesbaden.

—— and BEATE SCHRÖDER-NAUENBURG. 2004. 'Zwischen Zionismus und Antisemitismus. Der Wiener Verein zur Förderung jüdischer Musik'. In Karl E. Grözinger, ed., *Klesmer, Klassik, jiddisches Lied. Jüdische Musikkultur in Osteuropa*, 49–59. Wiesbaden.

ROTHMÜLLER, ARON MARKO. 1951. *Die Musik der Juden*. Zurich.

ROTHSTEIN, JAMES. 1916. *Judenlieder*. Berlin: Berlin Music Publishing House for National Art; new edn published in *Gesammelte jüdische Lieder*, vol. i. Berlin: Hatikvah, 1921.

SAMINSKY, LAZARE. 1914. *Ob evreiskoi muzyke*. St Petersburg.

—— 1915. *Evreiskaya muzyka, ee proshloe i nastoyashchee, ee perspektivy*. Petrograd.

SCHREUDER, SASKIA, and CLAUDE WEBER, eds. 1994. *Der Schocken Verlag/Berlin. Jüdische Selbstbehauptung in Deutschland, 1931–1938*. Berlin.

STOMPOR, STEPHAN. 2001. *Jüdisches Musik- und Theaterleben unter dem NS-Staat*. Hanover.

STRAUSS, LUDWIG. 1920. *Ostjüdische Liebeslieder*. Berlin

—— 1935. *Jüdische Volkslieder*. Berlin.

ZLOCISTI, THEODOR. 1902. 'Grundakkorde jung-jüdischer Kunst', *Ost und West*, 4 (Apr.), col. 232; speech on the announcement, at the Jewish art evening on 26 Feb. 1902, of the Jewish Students Society.

PART II

Identity

'Take Down Mezuzahs, Remove Name-Plates': The Emigration of Objects from Germany to Palestine

J O A C H I M   S C H L Ö R

STUTTGART, 10 MAY 1936. Leopold Frank, a sales representative for a stocking firm in Bavaria and Württemberg and a married man with two children, moved to this city only a short time ago; now he faces the task of packing a so-called 'lift' (a container) and making an exact list of all the belongings that he plans to take with him. To Palestine. Going to Palestine, possibly for ever, is not something that Leopold Frank and his family had ever contemplated. Their story, and the cultural themes and problems it suggests, form a portal in this essay through which to contemplate the distinctions between cultural studies, Jewish cultural studies, and *Kulturwissenschaften*.

The story has to be placed in the context of a complex web of associations. One of those associations, emigration, for example, is a radically disruptive event in a person's life. Many branches of research concern themselves with its various aspects—flight into exile, expulsion, migration to a particular place or migration continued over a long period. These have become the subjects of historical investigation, sociological analysis, and also of literature and the study of literature, and not just in the last few years. Within the overarching concept of migration studies, migration as both a theme and an individual fate has been presented as a paradigm of the experience of modern humanity: the migrant has been interpreted as a representative figure whose experiences—the loss of a homeland, the breaking of ties, an impermanent existence, but also mobility—are those that, in an age of globalization, individuals and societies at large must expect to face.

The image of flight and expulsion has been seen as encapsulating major strands of world history, and chains of causality have been suggested which do indeed present the outlines of a grand narrative of the twentieth century: the expulsion of the Jews from Germany and Europe as the start of the deportations and acts of genocide; the expulsion of the Germans from the east European countries and the forced resettlements under the Stalinist regime; the expulsion of the Palestinians from Haifa and Jaffa and the whole conflict in the Middle East. This prompts the question: might it be possible to examine these events not only in relation to their significance for historical developments and the contemporary

European and Middle Eastern political situation, but also 'from the point of view of their *cultural significance*' (Weber 1988: 165)?

If so, we would be concerned less with the events themselves than with, for instance, the forms of their transmission—in stories, descriptions, or documentary accounts; we would be enquiring into the media through which this transmission takes place and its crystallization into symbolic forms; we could begin to investigate, on the basis of specific examples, how the individual and the collective memory store, modify, and process a given event. Then what we do could certainly be called *Kulturwissenschaft* (cultural science), in Max Weber's sense of the term. For in Weber's view the social sciences were definitely to be counted among those disciplines 'which study the events of human life from the point of view of their cultural significance' (Weber 1988: 165). In the context of Jewish studies, not much use has been made of Weber's work, and indeed sociology and the social sciences are not yet a well-established part of interdisciplinary Jewish studies. More influence can be attributed to Georg Simmel, especially his 'The Metropolis and Mental Life' (Simmel 1950: 409–24) and the short but important 'The Stranger' (Simmel 1950: 402–8), and the works of Walter Benjamin and Siegfried Kracauer, but also to Sigmund Freud, considering his preoccupation with Jewish expressions such as the joke and the roots of antisemitism, and some of his followers who, like Theodor Reik, took up the question of Jewish cultural practice.

The many discussions that have taken place in the last decade around the concept of *Kulturwissenschaften* (cultural sciences or cultural studies) and the attempts to promote a dialogue between various theoretical and methodological approaches deriving from the humanities as well as from the social sciences compose what Lutz Musner of the International Research Centre for Cultural Studies (IFK) in Vienna has called a 'process which is open in many directions'. This debate, Musner observes, 'is proving productively unsettling not just at the margins but right at the heart of the academic institutions' (Gerbel and Musner 2003: 10). Any project undertaken in the field of cultural studies is by definition interdisciplinary and even transdisciplinary. Not only are the individual disciplines opening up to each other and actively seeking ways of working together, but they are also broadening their field of vision to include subjects outside the traditional canon of high culture.

I also observe not only different disciplinary versions of cultural studies, but also variations on national models. The phrase 'cultural studies', coming out of work at the University of Birmingham and extended in historiography to a 'British model', seeks to discover how people's everyday lives are defined by and through 'culture'. Its aim—not so very different, incidentally, from that of earlier work in the 'sociology of culture'—is to find out how culture is constructed, how it is practised, what relationship it bears to social change, what power structures shape it, and how culture can influence or even alter those power structures. And it asks what part is played by academic scholarship in all these processes. Its attention has been focused mainly on the working class and, following the disappearance of that class, on the social and ethnic minorities, and migration is certainly one of its themes.

Cultural studies in the United States also focuses on migration, in a way that is perhaps less obviously leftist and yet is actually more radical in a different way. Whereas, according to representatives of the cultural studies movement, the American academic tradition is—here I will add the word 'allegedly'—conservative, closely tied to the military-industrial complex, and enabling upper-class, white homogeneity and elite culture, cultural studies, by contrast, pursues counter-hegemonic projects in women's studies and gender studies, as well as Native American and African American studies, that disrupt or trouble the establishment. As an ideological tool for the manipulation of the oppressed classes by their rulers (here one cannot fail to recognize the influence of the Frankfurt School), mass culture and America's role in producing it is a major subject of research, notably in the context of media studies. Here, too, the theme of migration is present—as well as being, in many cases, part of the personal experience of the researcher. Race, and to an extent sexuality, appear paramount in the United States. In relation to physical difference and social status, there is abundant rhetoric about identity politics and 'othering' in American discourse. A key context for American scholars is the tension between disenfranchised groups in a multicultural society and elite interests in promoting nationalism. For many practitioners of cultural studies, multiculturalism in regard to the discourse on race has meant the relation of African Americans, Native Americans, Latinos, and Asian Americans to the body politic. Where does that leave Jews, often viewed historically as a continuously 'othered' group in American history? An impetus towards a distinctive strain of Jewish cultural studies in response to the omission of Jews from multicultural discourse has been created by the question of Jews as a special case of community and transnational formation. This can be seen vividly in the frequently cited titles of the new Jewish cultural studies, such as *Multiculturalism and the Jews* (Gilman 2006), *Insider/Outsider: American Jews and Multiculturalism* (Biale, Galchinsky, and Heschel 1998), and *Jews and Other Differences: The New Jewish Cultural Studies* (Boyarin and Boyarin 1997).

By way of contrast, the emergence of the new *Kulturwissenschaften* in Germany may be viewed primarily as 'a demand for a change of direction in academic research, a call for reform addressed to the traditional humanities disciplines'. The 'modernizing role' of this new subject area is 'an opening to the developments taking place internationally', the 'provision of a frame of reference for the study of people's *Lebenswelt* ['life-world']', and an 'interdisciplinary approach' (Musner 2001: 264–5). Following this exhortation, which was formulated by Wolfgang Frühwald, some of the traditional disciplines have started to redefine themselves as *Kulturwissenschaften*. Those, like Hartmut Böhme, who argue in favour of having a separate and distinct subject area called *Kulturwissenschaft,* tend to be scholars with an interest in such fields as historical anthropology, historical research into media culture, the study of cultures of knowledge, historical gender studies, or the study of ideas about nature and technology as historical products of culture. A conflict seems to be developing between the text-based disciplines, especially the various branches of philology, on the one hand, and the historical and ethnological disciplines on the other. From the vantage-point of the contributors to Metzler's *Lexikon der Literatur- und Kulturtheorie* (Lexicon of Literary and Cultural Theory)—in this case specifically the perspective of the editor, Ansgar Nünning—the disciplines that count as *Kulturwissenschaften* are chiefly distinguished by their understanding of 'culture as text', which derives from cultural anthropology and cultural semiotics (Bachmann-Medick 1996). There is also an oddly arrogant attitude towards other disciplines: 'Clarity of definition is not helped by including anthropology or European ethnology among the cultural sciences' (Nünning 1998: 299). My own opinion is that this deliberate exclusion of other views and conceptions of what culture is and how it should be scientifically studied places too much of a restriction on the discipline. In any case, 'culture as text' is long past its heyday. It is an important field for Jewish studies, though. Textual deconstruction as a cultural studies method is appealing because of the talmudic tradition of close reading and the multivocality of texts. But one could argue that the Jewish social science tradition has been one to emphasize context, perhaps because of the Diaspora experience. 'The latest approach, which sees culture in terms of practice and not as a system of symbols or as a discourse', states the historian Paula Hyman, 'makes it possible once again for historical analysis to take social factors and concrete experience into account' (Hyman 2002: 168). When culture is approached as practice and process, the dimensions of time and space, which are obscured by 'culture as text', once again become visible.

A matter of some dispute is where the field of Jewish studies is deemed to belong. Susannah Heschel has urged that it be integrated into cultural studies and has called Abraham Geiger the 'first post-colonialist' (Biale, Galchinsky, and Heschel 1998; Heschel 2001), but normally in the United States, Jewish studies has a firm place among the established 'inter' disciplines. In Germany it seems that the jury is still out on this. The new field of Jewish cultural studies is distinct from cultural studies in general and will remain in close co-operation with the traditional fields of religion (Bible, Talmud, rabbinic literature, hasidism, etc.) and history; but it can be opened towards new fields such as Diaspora studies, transnationalism, cultural transfer, and—in my view—especially studies of the *spatial dimension* of history and culture (forms of settlement; images of Jewish spaces such as the shtetl, the Jewish quarter in big cities, or even the ghetto; the relationship between Diaspora communities and Israel).[1] The study of Jewish identity (or identities) in 'host societies' will remain crucial, but it can be enriched with new approaches such as inter-ethnic or inter-cultural contact/conflict between minorities (with—or against—Weber's notion of the 'pariah' as 'a guest people who were ritually separated': Weber 1967: 417).[2]

It is probably political commitment that constitutes the main difference between cultural studies and the German *Kulturwissenschaften*: 'The critical engagement with marginalization, discrimination, and the concomitant self-images is a central topos of cultural studies and determines the subject's basic— and political—ethos' (Musner 2001: 263). It is, as one of the most eminent theoreticians of cultural studies, Lawrence Grossberg, has put it, 'interventionist' (Grossberg 1999: 55) and aims to translate theoretical work into political practice. Like the cultural anthropology of, say, Clifford Geertz (or sociological analysis such as Don Slater's examination of consumerism), cultural studies constantly endeavours to contextualize such concepts as class and gender, and attaches importance to the relationship between the producer and the recipient of a text or of any other media message. This strongly influences its methodology and treatment of sources. Because cultural studies and *Kulturwissenschaften* came into being in different ways, they also have a tendency—I will put it no higher than that—to use different methods: 'Whereas significant strands of *Kulturwis-senschaft* focus on key concepts such as "memory", "symbol", "system" and "mediality" and frequently employ methods taken from philology, hermeneutics and historiography, many contributions to cultural studies concentrate on the analysis of discourses and cultural practices without paying very much attention to historical context in the true sense of the term', according to Lutz Musner (2001: 265).

Precisely in Germany, where the memory of National Socialism and the Holocaust is never far from the surface and strongly influences the direction taken by research, questions of memory and experience are central to research in the *Kulturwissenschaften*. Such research therefore often deals with what causes the breakdown of a civilization, taking as its starting-point the fragmentation of the subject by the contradictions caused by the modern age and modernization as described by Freud or Proust. It also often asks 'questions—analogous to those concerning memory—about the nature of an archive and the logical principles underlying its storage of material' (Musner 2001: 269). If we are prepared to try and avoid the double pitfall and devise research methods and lines of questioning which are suitable for dealing with both history *and* memory, and which take lived experience no less seriously than the interpretation of symbolic forms, this may well lead us to look in a different way at the things packed by Leopold Frank in May 1936.

Kulturwissenschaft asks what *meaning* particular cultural goods have for a particular social group or for individuals, in what *social uses* the things were embedded, what *contexts* are thereby generated, transformed, or reproduced. Here it is important to remember that, in the societies that we examine, individuals and social groups do not only confront each other as antagonists. Cultural studies has tended to concentrate on the study of such antagonism—but different groups can also have common ideas and attitudes. In the situation where a German Jew is packing his bags in May 1936 because he has been turned into a foreigner, and is in the process of finding a new home in what to him is still a foreign land, this is particularly apparent.

So an analysis of the material objects of emigration like the one that, in a very tentative way, I am presenting here involves the merging of two distinct research traditions. On the one hand, we have memory and remembering as a central theme. The consideration of individual and collective forms of memory is a classic subject of German *Kulturwissenschaft*: one thinks of the work of Jan Assmann, Aleida Assmann, and others who have followed on, closely and in a spirit of constructive criticism, from Émile Durkheim and Maurice Halbwachs, that is to say from a kind of sociology that saw itself as *Kulturwissenschaft*. But at the same time we are talking of a very concrete experience of the kind of marginal-ization and exclusion that lead to emigration. These are classic areas of migration research as conducted within the social sciences, but also in cultural studies, for instance in the work of the cultural anthropologist James Clifford. The customary distinction between forced and unforced migration proves not to be especially helpful; had it not been for the persecution of Jews by the National Socialists, Leopold Frank would not have left Germany; on the other hand, if one thinks of the fate of those who emigrated later or those who missed their chance to emigrate, one can almost regard him as being among the lucky ones.

Frank was able to save his own and his family's lives, and he was able to take his things with him. Eugene Halton and Mihaly Csikszentmihalyi have given us new insight into the meaning of material things: their project, 'The Meanings of Things: Domestic Symbols and the Self' investigated 'the ways people carve meaning out of their domestic environment' (Csikszentmihalyi and Rochberg-Halton 1981: 1); but we have to go a step further. What happens when the 'domes-tic environment', the home, is threatened, destroyed, dissolved? What happens to the things and to the interpretations of their meaning? Many émigrés, in their memoirs, describe the homes, the furniture, the objects that they had to leave behind almost as lovingly as they describe the members of their family—this could surely be a theme for literary scholarship, which has already made a major contribution to exile studies, but which (like historical scholarship) has largely ignored this particular aspect. Private property has, for both the individual memory and the collective memory, a deep emotional significance. The exclu-sion of the Jews from German society started with the National Socialist policy of 'Aryanization', the expropriation of property. The émigré has to abandon, to leave behind, the private dwelling which, in contrast to the public space of the street, still provides shelter and protection. In the process he loses more than just the object itself: around 1800 the British philosopher and legal theoretician Jeremy Bentham drew attention to the importance of the *relationship* between an object

and its owner: ownership forms the basis of a hope. Only the law is able to ensure that this relationship can be carried forward into the future, to the next
generation—Bentham speaks of 'an assurance of future ownership'. If this sense
of assurance is attacked or threatened, more is involved than just the object as
such: 'Every attack upon this sentiment produces a distinct and special evil,
which may be called a *pain of disappointment*' (Bentham 1871: 111).[3] This 'pain of
disappointment' is especially obvious in our context: the 'things' are Leopold
Frank's *cultural* capital. The threat of losing them is symbolic of the loss of all
hope of a continued life in Germany and as a German; the link with the future—
when his children would receive their parental inheritance and, as Goethe's Faust
puts it, 'make it their own, in order to possess it'—is broken. Aryanization and
confiscation were a symbolic theft of identity. And in these cases even the legal
system was no longer capable of protecting property rights. Those who emigrated
in good time were able to take at least some of their property with them. It seems
to me that there is a kind of gap between studies undertaken in the field of the
new cultural studies—text-oriented, and concerned with questions of discursivity
and performativity—and those that remain close to more traditional academic
scholarship with its continuing preference for the calmly methodical interpretation of archive sources. Leopold Frank's personal story, which happens to be well
documented, is just one of many which can be viewed as part of the history of
German Jewry after the cataclysm of 1933, or equally well as the story of a migration taking place in those specific circumstances. Lists of things! What, I hear
many a traditional historian ask, can they possibly have to tell us? Nor does
Frank's story quite fit into that romantic type of cultural science that sees its
mission as being to preserve cultures from any and every assimilation into Western civilization (a tendency which has recently been persuasively rejected by
Roger Sandall in his critique of the 'Culture Cult') (Sandall 2002; cf. Tallis 2002).

Back, then, to 10 May 1936. A story unfolds before our eyes: a man packs up
his things, moves out of an apartment, goes with his family to the station, and
travels from Stuttgart to Munich (a route he knows well), and then on into the
unknown, to Milan and Trieste. There he boards a ship and in barely a week
arrives in a town called Jaffa, where he and his wife Betty and the children, Adolf
(soon to be renamed Abraham) and Hannah, together with their luggage, are
taken off the big ship and put into a small boat, under a hot, dazzlingly bright sun.
From there a horse-drawn cab takes him to Tel Aviv, but he soon leaves that city
again to travel on to an agricultural settlement on the Sea of Galilee. The story
seems very familiar, because we have already read or been told it so often, in
slightly different versions, that it has become almost like a film that we have seen.
Leopold Frank is only one of many whose lives took this course. And so we are all
too ready simply to slot this story into one of our existing stereotypes.

But I would like to go back and pause the film at a particular moment, the
moment when Leopold Frank is sitting in his flat in Stuttgart and starting to

gather together the objects that he wants to take with him—and to put to one side other objects that he is going to leave behind. As he embarks on this task, he is not wholly unprepared. In a letter sent from Tel Aviv to Stuttgart on 23 January 1936, his sister-in-law Netta Fürth had given him her views on the suitability of different objects for the whole difficult business of emigration (all the following quotations are taken from this letter):

It's very hard to answer your question about which things to take, given that we don't yet know whether you will be living in the town or the country, whether you will have two rooms or three, whether you will have any additional space (there are no attics or cellars here). So it's hard to give advice. . . . Since it's possible that you may have to make do with only two rooms, I wouldn't bring an actual suite of bedroom furniture if I were you, but buy a steel-framed sofa-bed or some beds and one or two modern wardrobes and linen cupboards. . . . Don't bring more than one big carpet, and some runners; if need be you can always exchange a big carpet for some rugs. The electricity here is 220 volts, so 220-volt vacuum cleaners can be used here, as well as irons and electric cooking-pots.[4]

Irons and vacuum cleaners? The idea is clearly to make life as normal as it can possibly be. The Frank family, who practise their religion, have a further problem, that of keeping a kosher kitchen, with *milkhik* (dairy) and *fleishik* (meat) foods and utensils kept separate. Perhaps this problem seems greater viewed from Stuttgart than it does in the reality of Palestine: 'I don't know whether in your place I would bother to cart along crockery for everyday *and* for "best". We have just one thing for milk and two for meat. But I haven't needed them.' The important items are the practical ones: 'To sum up again: you need to work out how you can furnish three moderately sized rooms with your things, and not bring a single thing more than necessary. As far as vases and unnecessary things like a punchbowl are concerned, only bring what you think you need. Do bring an axe, a saw, a bucket, maybe a washboard.'

Things, possessions, are starting very gradually to change in value, in function, in meaning. A thing that in Stuttgart is valuable and functional, a thing that *means* something to a man like Herr Frank, may turn out, in the place where their journey is taking them, to be wholly superfluous. And conversely the washboard gains significantly against the punchbowl—in terms not only of usefulness but also of meaningfulness. In the course of these few days a kind of revaluation takes place in Leopold Frank's flat, a reassessment of the value and the significance of objects which up to now have led a no doubt respectable and proper, but largely unheeded, existence. You could say that he now looks at them with different eyes.

Among the documents relating to Leopold Frank there is a duplicated list with 'Frank' written in pencil in the margin; this is the list sent to prospective emigrants by the Berlin branch of the Palestine Office. 'Above all else it is important to ensure beforehand that all objects are in perfect condition', the letter states. This is followed by long lists of things to be taken: first household articles, from pedal bins, through glass measuring jugs and milk jugs—for which the list, evidently produced in southern Germany, uses a regional word—through sets of bowls, buckets, stepladders, mousetraps, nails, tools, and 'a quantity of brushes of the best quality', to medicines, lint and shoe-scrapers, 'not of wire but with iron bars'. After this comes a list of electrical goods, and then clothes and underwear—'it is advisable to include underwear and especially outer clothing that is in quite poor condition, since for work even the most badly worn things can still be used'. Then garden tools, 'only those made of the best materials!' Finally there are some general pieces of advice:

(1) Have all quilts, pillows and blankets cleaned and mended (this should be done as early as possible)

(2) Have mattresses reconditioned

(3) Do not give away wooden boards or poles for washing lines, but take them with you. The wood in Palestine is very poor

(4) Any prams you may have are very useful as trolleys for moving washing-baskets, etc.

(5) Take some home-made cakes in tin boxes sealed with sticking-plaster. In the early days one is very glad of these.

(6) Don't forget:
    Fetch prayer books from the synagogue
    Collect fur coats from storage
    Remove thermometers from windows
    Take down mezuzahs
    Remove name-plates
    Cancel newspapers in good time
    Cancel electric light, water and gas in good time
    Arrange for telephone to be disconnected
    Cancel club memberships.

They might have added: dismantle a life. Be prepared for things to become more difficult—there is, for instance, the discouraging sentence (item 19 on the list, in between 'Bring all smaller items of furniture' and 'Put washable covers on sofa cushions'): 'Do not bring a great many testimonials, they are no use anyway.' This list is based on experience, no doubt on reports from immigrants, and it tells of what awaits those who are about to come to Palestine. But it also tells of a life in Germany, of standards that should be maintained: 'Bring good quality coloured pencils for the children. Unobtainable in Palestine', or, 'American drill overalls (available from Breuninger's in Stuttgart)'.

Look at the list again. It is almost a poem, with an *abba* structure: the two *a*s speak of one half of life, the Jewish half, the two *b*s of the other, German, half:

    Fetch prayer books from the synagogue
    Collect fur coats from storage
    Remove thermometers from windows
    Take down mezuzahs

I can hardly attribute any poetic intentions to the compiler of the list, but the reader recognizes in it the flipside of—perhaps even the precondition for—Günter Eich's famous poem *Inventur* (Inventory), which lists the few meagre possessions still remaining to a soldier returning home from the war. But 'synagogue' and 'mezuzahs' tell us that it is a Jewish life in Germany that is being wound up. The cases are being packed. We picture Leopold Frank standing in his flat, looking at the list.

In his own person he is experiencing a double sense of not belonging, of being a stranger: as a German, a German Jew who has to leave his country, but also as a future resident of a country that wants to become a state. The historical situation is crystallized, symbolized in the things he takes with him and those he leaves behind, and in the lists of them that he draws up. The things become embodiments of conditions and circumstances—bearers of memories, of hopes. And these mediators of memory lead a life of their own. They change their nature, that is to say they change the *meanings* they bear: over the years; and with each new generation; and of course (and this is a form of self-reflection that cultural studies can learn from ethnology) through the work of the researcher who finds them and tries to understand them.

One of the many things that Leopold Frank takes with him—an item that is clearly so significant in terms of family memories that his son, Abraham, still has it in his possession—is an accounts book. Lying on top of the bundle of his father's papers is a book with pages ruled for income and expenditure. The stamp on the title page reads: 'Leo Frank, Stuttgart, Bismarckstr. 118, Tel. 60726'. For anyone who is not a commercial representative or travelling salesman it takes a little while to get into it. The first page is dated 1934 and has the brief headings 'Balance', 'Day's takings', and 'Total'. The sum total reached by the end of the year is 11,100 Reichsmarks. '1935' appears on all the following pages except for one, and entries dated 'December 1936' have been inserted—in pencil—on the intervening page: evidence of a disruption to the normal, well-ordered routine. By January 1937 the family is far from Stuttgart; handwritten notes on bits of paper are clipped to the page, and they reflect new concerns: 'Purchases', 'Plot', 'Health insurance'. And 'Move'. At some point in all this, the decision has been taken which has changed a well-regulated life beyond recognition. For each succeeding month of 1937 such interim accounts are noted on pieces of paper; the 'Purchases' category grows and grows, and so does 'Miscellaneous' (which probably barely existed before). March sees the addition of 'Household' and 'Building', and by May there is 'School', 'Bananas', and then 'Cow'. Not 'Cows'; no, a single cow is apparently being added to a household—and to its accounts.

The collection of documents belongs to Abraham Frank. In his father's accounts book he still appears, early on, as the item 'Adolf—school'. From Adolf to Abraham, from Germany to Israel. When Abraham hands them to the inquisitive researcher to study, he does so with mixed feelings, and he is not alone in having them. What do you people want them for? Do you want to claim us, or at any rate our fathers' generation, for yourselves? That is not possible. Do you really want to know how it was for us? Can you even begin to imagine what it was like then? No, we cannot. All we can achieve is a reconstruction. In a book which up to then had matter-of-factly recorded his takings, sometimes good, sometimes not so good, a man suddenly starts to enter things like 'KKL' (a contribution to the land fund Keren Kayemet Leyisra'el), or 'Water meter', 'Interest payments on plot', 'Roofer', and then 'Seed' and 'Maize'. The items change position. 'School' now moves up into first position, but immediately after it—in April 1937—come 'Bananas', 'Cow', 'Chickens', and only then 'Purchases'. Even the solitary cow gives rise to considerable expenditure: planks, wood, a brush, fodder. Why does he do this, his son wonders sixty years later. Why does he persist in an exercise that was not designed for circumstances like these? Does continuing to keep this record give him a sense of security? When 'Calf' is added to 'Cow'—quite quickly, in June—should we see this as a success or only as a new burden? At least the 'Income' column now includes the item 'Milk'.

Memories—and that is what we are dealing with in our lists and our things—are recorded in certain media, and they change their meanings and associations over the course of years and with each new generation. Prevailing ideologies and discourses, but also political and social changes or personal experiences, surround and reshape the original memory (if it ever did exist in a pure form) as the amber encloses the fly; but this outer layer is invaded by what one might call foreign bodies—'traces of other texts, the traces of difference and alterity, of confrontations with what is alien and of traumas that have not been fully worked through'.[5] *Kulturwissenschaft* seeks a 'relational, process-orientated understanding of culture, an understanding whose conceptualization of the social goes beyond functional-structuralist or simplistically materialist approaches', according to Gotthard Wunberg and Lutz Musner (Musner and Wunberg 1999). Putting this in my own words, the aim of studies produced in this field is indeed to contribute to depicting society, but not by drawing a static picture of that society (for instance by concentrating on an analysis of its structures or trying to describe the relative importance of the economy and political power), but rather by making visible the development and change inherent in its social conditions. One way of doing this is to examine 'people's habitual practices and the many kinds of artefacts that play a part in their life-worlds' for their symbolic content, since 'it is this alone that gives actions, rituals and artefacts purpose and meaning' (Musner and Wunberg 1999). The incidental stories, the footnotes, the interpolated quotations and comments, the shifts of perspective, the debris of history are also to be found in our lists and our objects. No doubt these could form the basis of a museum, but turning them into museum exhibits does not seem to me the only, or even the best, way to engage with the objects of emigration. Memory requires a balance between solid form (in a museum or monument) and moving, fluid flow, in continued narration and ever new, renegotiated interpretation. Nowadays we no longer interpret the history and the experience of exile solely in terms of persecution and exclusion: research into emigration and migration in general is able to broaden its scope to include experiences that cross countries and borders, by looking at transnational migration and the consequent transformation of the individual.[6] In his study of the private possessions of an American family, Bill Christian identified the following patterns: 'Dimensions that differentiate between households in keepsake accumulation; objects handed down through male or female lines, exotica, the impact of wars and family trauma, gendered displays—public and private, collection, storage, and display rotation, and systems of memory transmission' (Christian 2002). If I try, specifically in the light of that last concept—'systems of memory transmission'—to tease out some of the dimensions that lie within these objects, I arrive at the following models:

- objects can be seen, like earlier life-forms enclosed in amber, as the nuclei of a narrative, and can be investigated—if the investigators are able to remove the outer layers acquired through preservation, change of owner, or oblivion;

- objects, assuming that they have not become museum exhibits, undergo changes of ownership (which for our present purposes include being stolen, destroyed, hidden away, sold or exchanged, or possibly restored to their original owners) and so come to be the bearers of various narratives, various memories, and are not fossilized but, as it were, fluid;

- the meaning and the interpretation of objects change according to historical circumstances, and the objects have different valences in different places;

- objects, things, can sometimes tell—if we know what to ask them—the *other side* of a historical narrative, and may sometimes contradict the memories of their owners;

- however, objects are hardly capable of narration by themselves; interpretation and careful explanation are necessary;

- objects preserve a certain order (and habit); they take longer to become Other than do their owners;

- a surprising number of people make lists of their objects, not only when faced with an imminent change of place (such as a move to an old people's home) or following the death of relatives, but more or less continually and in the midst of life: wedding lists, birthday lists, lists for insurance purposes, lists of objects given away, lists of objects returned to them, lists of lists.

I am thinking here of more than a merely technical relationship to things; in the words of Gottfried Korff, 'Things do not just depict, they also have the power to *form*, merely by being there' (Korff 1999: 279). And once again we have to add: they *also* do this even when—and precisely because—they are no longer there, no longer needed, cannot be taken along with their owner because they are too big, too awkward, too German for a new life. The writing of a list itself produces the beginnings of a system, but one to which we should probably not pay too much attention, since such lists are so dependent on their time and situation. All the same, the image of the *list* does suggest the idea of an incipient order into which the individual object is integrated; an accumulation of lists, and directories of further lists, and catalogues giving access to yet further directories, lists, and individual objects may, for instance, give rise to a museum or an archive, places where the memories are preserved. It is only in the last few years—probably far too late—that a start has been made on preserving the personal documents and testimonies of ordinary as well as prominent people.

For some time now students in Germany, like their contemporaries in Israel or the United States, have been members of the third generation and will no longer have much opportunity to talk to their grandfathers and grandmothers about their experiences during the National Socialist era and the war. The media through which history is transmitted, including objects, will gain in significance. In his ecstatic review of Gabriele Goettle's *Erkundungen im Lande* (Explorations of the Land [of Germany]), with its fascination for everyday life, Frank Schirrmacher makes the following comments on the text 'Personal Effects of a Teacher, Put in Order by his Sister':[7]

This article . . . is purely statistical. It conveys no sense of literary or even journalistic ambition. And yet it is more suggestive, more breathtaking than any complex literary prose could be. . . . It is literature in the most authentic sense. It *counts* things. The further the reader gets into this strange *account* of things, the stronger is his feeling of having crossed a line of intimacy. It is as if he were looking not at the text but at the ownerless property itself. And the longer he dwells on it, the more the everyday reality of that life that has come to an end is recreated on the page. Suddenly the things are linked to stories, hopes, plans—and the fragmentary detail of that life becomes visible again. (Schirrmacher 1991)

So 'reverence for the insignificant', for which folklore research has occasionally been derided, has now received its *literary* accolade, at any rate. Even though, in the debates about 'historical truth and the narrative structures of historiography' a 'return of narrativity' has been observed (Noiriel 2002), this manner of presenting history cannot escape the accusation of being fragmentary. At an initial, superficial level—and yet one that should not be underestimated—the fact that it has become impossible to return to the telling of complete stories points to a failure on the part of the institutions of memory. Neither the Leo Baeck Institutes in New York, London, Jerusalem, and now Berlin, nor the Central Archives for the History of the Jewish People, nor the Zionist Central Archives have managed to preserve the legacy of the supposedly unimportant people whose names are not famous.

Yet the material assembled here for its historical interest is also relevant to research on the situation of migrants today. In a project conducted at the Ludwig-

Uhland-Institut für Empirische Kulturwissenschaft (Ludwig Uhland Institute for Empirical Cultural Science) in Tübingen, Bernd Jürgen Warneken and a group of students investigated the 'movable property' of twenty-three migrants who had been living in the Tübingen area for some time, producing a study intended as a contribution to the 'ethnography of migration' (Warneken 2003). The project was inspired by a visit to the Immigration Museum on Ellis Island, New York, and the sight of the 'mountain of cabin trunks and suitcases, bundles and bags' there. Two things made a particularly strong impression:

The *range* of luggage, from the large trunk made of solid oak to the meagre cloth bundle, indicates social differences between their owners; the differences in material, shape and labelling reflect the various cultures and regions from which they came. At the same time this collection of luggage as a whole shows that despite the obvious differences in the amount and value of what they brought, ultimately what most immigrants transferred from their old world to the New World was very little.

And this observation leads to the very question that drew me to the case of Leopold Frank, namely, 'Which things were chosen, when people migrated, as being indispensable for material and cultural survival?' (Warneken 2003: 7).

Accordingly, the twenty-three interviewees were asked which objects were 'particularly important', and which were their 'favourite things'. Tilman Habermas places these in several different categories: 'objects fostering reflection' can help individuals to reflect upon themselves; 'mementoes' help to ensure a continuing link with their personal past; 'symbols of identity' underline the 'feeling of being at one with oneself'—or lack of such a feeling—in the new environment.[8] Personal objects may trigger memories and stories. Putting a question about the meaning of a thing may set one on a trail leading to fragments of biography that might otherwise not have been told. The Tübingen project confirms the thesis of an 'increase in meaning' in the case of some individual objects; they now stand as representatives of 'a former or a threatened social identity' and they symbolically replace the presence of people and situations that are now absent. An important role is played by religious objects, since many of those questioned had been persecuted or threatened with persecution on account of their religion. Among the Jewish migrants from the CIS states—as with the German Jewish immigrants to Palestine in the 1930s—great importance was attached to 'famous scientific, literary or musical works'. These are migrants, the study suggests, 'who see themselves as cosmopolitan and have multiple contacts with others who share the same worldwide culture; this can make migration far easier, but can also foster expectations which may be cruelly disappointed' (Warneken 2003: 13).

This being so, the investigation of *things* as vehicles of memory seems to me to be a good example of research on the subject of cultural transfer: 'Memory', writes Michel Espagne, 'becomes crystallized in particular places and around particular structures of thought or, it may be, particular social rituals' (Espagne 2003:

71). In our example it would be possible to see the objects which Leopold Frank takes with him or leaves behind as a crystallization of that kind. His emigration does involve 'more than one national space'—and those two very different national spaces, Germany and Palestine, prove, when we read them through the history of these emigrants, to possess more elements in common than one might at first suppose. One could certainly analyse those common elements within the framework of an analysis of cultural transfer, as Espagne states, 'without limiting our observations about them to a mere juxtaposition, a comparison or simple enumeration' (Espagne 1999: 1).

In the two countries—and certainly in this one man Leopold Frank (as in his generation as a whole)—I find concentrated the 'parallel acknowledgement of a set of values and symbols deriving from what is recognized as a shared prehistory', to use Matthias Middell's phrase (Middell 2000: 17). But Leopold Frank was forced to perform this act of transfer in his own person. 'Willingness to import' was not a notable characteristic of Jewish Palestine. As Middell further observes, 'Individual and collective experiences, ideas, texts, cultural artefacts take on a wholly different function in the new context of the receiving country; they are incorporated as foreign elements into its *own* culture' (Middell 2000: 20–1).

This incorporation was a long process, which has only in recent years received due attention. Throughout the period when it did not, but when the German Jews continued to feel isolated and alien in the Jewish society of Palestine, the things they had brought with them were the guarantors of their deeply undermined—but not lost—identity. And here we are faced once again with the question—the urgent question—about the role of the archive as 'the indispensable starting point for the study of a cultural area or of the joining of two cultural areas', as Espagne suggests (Espagne, Middell, and Middell 2000: 331, 335). What is to happen to the *things*?

Objects that perform a bridging function preserve the link with a person's place of origin; but there is also the phenomenon of a deliberate 'letting go of possessions, creating a space into which something new can flow'. This could form the basis for a project that pays more attention to the in-betweenness of emigration and immigration, the sense of passage, of being in transit, than museum displays in which, looking at the objects on exhibit, we may lose sight of the life-histories that lie behind them.

Notes

The first draft of this chapter was translated from the German by Helen Atkins. The text of the chapter is based on the author's lecture delivered, in the course of his habilitation, to the Philosophical Faculty of the University of Potsdam on 24 April 2003. An earlier, German, version is published in Wolfgang Schmale and Martine Steer (eds), *Kulturtransfer in der jüdischen Geschichte* (Frankfurt am Main: Campus Verlag 2006), 153–72.

1   See the postgraduate programme, 'Makom: Place and Space in Judaism' at Potsdam University: <www.makom-potsdam.de>.

2   For Weber see Abraham 1992 and Momigliano 1980. Maria Vassilikou's forthcoming study on Greek–Jewish relations in the city of Odessa will, I hope, supply a good example of an inter-ethnic study. Vassilikou was also part of the Makom team at Potsdam.

3   I am indebted to Lisa Silverman, Junior Fellow at the Internationales Forschungszentrum Kulturwissenschaften in Vienna, for this information on Bentham. She herself discusses the relationship between 'owner' and 'property' in her as yet unpublished paper, 'Repossessing the Past?' (Silverman n.d.).

4   Letter in the possession of Abraham Frank, of Jerusalem, whom I would like to thank here once more for allowing me access to these memories of his family.

5   Editor's contribution to a website dedicated to the critical memory of the Habsburg empire, <www.kakanien.ac.at/weblos/editor/11120332819>, accessed on 21 Mar. 2003. In a review of a new volume of essays—Borso, Krumeich, and Witte's *Medialität und Gedächtnis*—the *Süddeutsche Zeitung* took a hefty sideswipe at the dominance of the Assmanns' views on the theory of memory: 'A spectre is stalking this land of ours. Having escaped from a scholar's closet in Heidelberg, it is presiding over the discourses about memory that are proliferating so wildly among cultural scientists. In every place and every discipline, cultural memory is the topic of the hour. The republic of academe is entirely occupied by the Assmanns. Well, not entirely . . . One small pocket of resistance . . .'. With this allusion to the Asterix books (an obeisance to mass-appeal reading matter which is very much the norm in the new-style cultural sciences) the reviewer points to the arguments put forward in that 'pocket of resistance', Düsseldorf, urging the need for a critique of the Assmanns' concept and even for it to be given a firmer historical basis; he also refers to the hope, which I genuinely share, that Walter Benjamin may at last 'be liberated from the esoteric dungeons of Benjamin research' (Müller 2002).

6   An exhibition which dealt with this subject in a contemporary context, 'Bewegliche Habe. Ausstellung zur Ethnographie der Emigration' (Movable Property: An Exhibition Relating to the Ethnography of Migration), was held at the Ludwig Uhland Institute in Tübingen from 14 February to 16 March 2003. The research project studied the 'cultural luggage' of twenty-three individuals from twelve countries, and showed how the objects they had taken with them represented 'key symbols in relation to migration situations and individual coping strategies'.

7   Gabriele Goettle, 'Nachlass eines Lehrers, geordnet von seiner Schwester', in *Deutsche Sitten. Erkundengen in Ost und West* (Nördlingen, 1991).

8   Habermas 1996: 328; the formulation of the concept of identity as a 'Gefühl der Übereinstimmung mit sich selbst' (the feeling of being at one with oneself) was coined by Hermann Bausinger (Bausinger 1978).

References

ABRAHAM, GARY A. 1992. *Max Weber and the Jewish Question: A Study of the Social Outlook of his Sociology*. Urbana.

BACHMANN-MEDICK, DORIS, ed. 1996. *Kultur als Text. Die anthropologische Wende in der Literaturwissenschaft*. Frankfurt am Main.

BAUSINGER, HERMANN. 1978. 'Identität'. In Hermann Bausinger, Utz Jeggle, Gottfried Korff, and Martin Scharfe, *Grundzüge der Volkskunde*. Darmstadt.

BENTHAM, JEREMY. 1871. *The Theory of Legislation*, trans. from the French of Étienne Dumont by R. Hildreth. 2nd edn. London.

BIALE, DAVID, MICHAEL GALCHINSKY, and SUSANNAH HESCHEL, eds. 1998. *Insider/Outsider: American Jews and Multiculturalism*. Berkeley, Calif.

BORSO, VITTORIA, GERD KRUMEICH, and BERND WITTE, eds. 2001. *Medialität und Gedächtnis. Interdisziplinäre Beiträge zur kulturellen Verarbeitung europäischer Krisen*. Stuttgart.

BOYARIN, JONATHAN, and DANIEL BOYARIN, eds. 1997. *Jews and Other Differences: The New Jewish Cultural Studies*. Minneapolis.

CHRISTIAN, BILL. 2002. 'Households as Memory-Arrays'. Paper given at the Collegium, Budapest, on 7 March.

CSIKSZENTMIHALYI, MIHALY, and EUGENE ROCHBERG-HALTON. 1981. *The Meaning of Things: Domestic Symbols and Self*. Cambridge.

ESPAGNE, MICHEL. 1999. *Les Transferts culturels franco-allemands*. Paris.

—— 2003. 'Der theoretische Stand der Kulturtransferforschung'. In Wolfgang Schmale, ed., *Kulturtransfer. Kulturelle Praxis im 16. Jahrhundert*, 63–75. Vienna.

—— KATHARINA MIDDELL, and MATTHIAS MIDDELL, eds. 2000. *Archiv und Interkulturalität. Studien zur interkulturellen Überlieferung*. Leipzig.

GERBEL, CHRISTIAN, and LUTZ MUSNER. 2003. 'Kulturwissenschaften, ein offener Prozess'. In Lutz Musner and Gotthard Wunberg, eds, *Kulturwissenchafte. Forschung—Praxis—Positionen*, 9–23. Freiburg.

GILMAN, SANDER L. 2006. *Multiculturalism and the Jews*. New York.

GROSSBERG, LAWRENCE. 1999. 'Was sind Cultural Studies?'. In Karl H. Hörning and Rainer Winter, eds, *Widerspenstige Kulturen. Cultural Studies als Herausforderung*. Frankfurt am Main.

HABERMAS, TILMAN. 1996. *Geliebte Objekte. Symbole und Instrumente der Identitätsbildung*. Berlin.

HESCHEL, SUSANNAH. 2001. *Der jüdische Jesus und das Christentum. Abraham Geigers Herausforderung an die christliche Theologie*. Berlin.

HYMAN, PAULA. 2002. 'Die Theorie und ihre Grenzen'. In Michael Brenner and David N. Myers, eds, *Jüdische Geschichtsschreibung heute. Themen, Positionen, Kontroversen*, 163–71. Munich.

KORFF, GOTTFRIED. 1999. 'Dinge: unsäglich kultiviert. Notizen zur volkskundlichen Sachkulturforschung'. In Franz Grieshofer and Margot Schindler, eds, *Netzwerk Volkskunde. Ideen und Wege*, 273–90. Vienna.

MIDDELL, MATTHIAS. 2000. 'Kulturtransfer und Historische Komparatistik—Thesen zu ihrem Verhältnis', *Comparativ*, 10(1): 7–41.

MOMIGLIANO, ARNALDO. 1980. 'A Note on Max Weber's Definition of Judaism as a Pariah-Religion', *History and Theory*, 19(3): 313–18.

MÜLLER, TIM B. 2002. Review in *Süddeutsche Zeitung* (13 Aug.), 16.

MUSNER, LUTZ. 2001. 'Kulturwissenschaften und Cultural Studies. Zwei ungleiche Geschwister?', *KulturPoetik. Zeitschrift für kulturgeschichtliche Literaturwissenschaft*, 1(2): 262–71.

—— and GOTTHARD WUNBERG. 1999. *Kulturwissenschaft/en—eine Momentaufnahme*. Beiträge zur historischen Sozialkunde. Beihefte. Vienna.

NOIRIEL, GÉRARD. 2002. 'Die Wiederkehr der Narrativität'. In Joachim Eibach and Gunther Lotts, eds, *Kompass der Geschichtswissenschaft*, 355–70. Göttingen.

NÜNNING, ANSGAR ('AN'). 1998. 'Kulturwissenschaft'. In Ansgar Nünning, ed., *Metzlers Lexikon der Literatur- und Kulturtheorie*, 299–302. Stuttgart.

SANDALL, ROGER. 2002. *The Culture Cult: Designer Tribalism and Other Essays*. Oxford.

SCHIRRMACHER, FRANK. 1991. 'Aus dem Nachtgebet der Genoveva Kraus', *Frankfurter Allgemeine Zeitung* (8 Oct.), Literaturbeilage zur Frankfurter Buchmesse, 1.

SILVERMAN, LISA. n.d. 'Repossessing the Past? Property, Memory, and Austrian Jewish Narrative Histories'. Unpublished paper, Internationales Forschungszentrum Kulturwissenschaften, Vienna.

SIMMEL, GEORG. 1950. 'The Metropolis and Mental Life', adapted by D. Weinstein from *The Sociology of Georg Simmel*, trans. Kurt Wolff, 402–24. New York.

TALLIS, RAYMOND. 2002. 'Dreamers of Paradise', *Times Literary Supplement* (16 Aug.), 6.

WARNEKEN, BERND (project director). 2003. *Bewegliche Habe. Zur Ethnographie der Migration*. Book accompanying the exhibition by the project group at the Ludwig-Uhland-Institut. Tübingen.

WEBER, MAX. 1967. *Ancient Judaism*. New York.

—— 1988. 'Die "Objektivität" sozialwissenschaftlicher und sozialpolitischer Erkenntnis'. In Johannes Winckelmann, ed., *Gesammelte Aufsätze zur Wissenschaftslehre*, 146–214. Tübingen.

Holocaust Narratives and their Impact: Personal Identification and Communal Roles

HANNAH KLIGER,
BEA HOLLANDER-GOLDFEIN, AND
EMILIE S. PASSOW

SCHOLARLY ATTENTION within the humanities and social sciences has converged on aspects of trauma and its aftermath, especially the effect of trauma on personal and cultural formations of identity. Studies that range in perspective from the anthropological, the sociological, and the historical to the literary, the psychological, and the philosophical examine the long-term consequences of the experience of trauma on human beings and how their constructions of traumatic memories shape the meanings they attribute to these events (Brenner 2004; Lifton 1993; Van der Kolk, McFarlane, and Weisaeth 1996). Researchers from a variety of perspectives have investigated the history of the concept of trauma, and have offered their observations on the impact of overwhelming life experiences on those affected by genocidal persecution (Caruth 1996; Leys 2000).

For the Jewish historical and cultural narrative, particularly of the last century, the experience of trauma and dislocation is communicated on two levels, as family discourse and as communal oral history. Friesel (1994) has noted the ways in which the Holocaust affects contemporary Jewish consciousness. Bar-On (1999) describes the interpretative strategies that survivors and their children employ to communicate real and imagined lessons of the Holocaust. From these and other studies, the forms of recording and transmitting the experiences of Jewish Holocaust survivors offer lessons in the modes of adaptation and meaning-making in the aftermath of trauma. Ethnographic and autobiographical materials have thus become rich resources for research devoted to issues of survival and identity, providing an insider's view of the suffering endured by trauma victims as well as the processes by which these ordeals are experienced, incorporated, mediated, constructed, and transcended.

The Transcending Trauma Project

This essay traces the communicative practices of individuals and families, utilizing deepened life histories to examine the experiences of groups in society who have had to cope with uncontrollable and unavoidable traumatic events. The Transcending Trauma Project of the Council for Relationships at Thomas Jefferson University centres on one particular community, Holocaust survivors, defined as Jewish individuals whose lives were threatened during the Second World War because they resided in countries controlled by Nazi Germany. By eliciting testimonies that are fluid rather than fixed, open to the expression of deeper personal meaning and self-exploration, our enquiry focuses on the negotiability of narrative and its systemic impact. As survivors' narratives are heard, particularly within the family, their stories about traumatic events teach the listeners more than just how to cope with trauma; more broadly, they teach about how to be in the world. The historical accuracy of autobiography is less the point than the ways in which the traumatic events and meaning of survival are remembered, reported, and assimilated as part of the core identity of the listener.

Through our effort to gather a deeper life history, meanings heretofore unarticulated because they are more personal and, therefore, relegated to the private domain of human experience which our society has preferred to leave unexplored, are generated in a context and environment that is co-created by the interviewee and the interviewer. Participants in this process have expressed appreciation for the questions that 'no one has ever asked before' and welcome the opportunity to share their meaning systems. Our study interprets the individual Jewish life stories we have collected as more than testimonies that convey information. Rather, we understand these Holocaust narratives as components in a process of identity formation and expression, with the power to transmit and transform cultural values through their influence on the second generation.

Although invaluable in their own right, the documentation of survivor oral histories to date has largely concentrated on the period preceding and during the Second World War. Typically, the testimonies stop with liberation or emigration. Rarely do they include extended descriptions of life before the war, nor do these testimonies purposefully investigate the broad range of reactions that were part of the survivor's inner life during and after the war. These oral histories allow for spontaneous expressions of emotion on the part of the survivor, but they do not explore the meaning system within which the narrative is embedded. Documentation and bearing witness are the overt goals, whereas the Transcending Trauma Project seeks self-revelation and self-explanation.

Based on a range of sources, especially in-depth interviews, the project we describe in this essay shifts the angle of vision from documenting external conditions to recording and analysing the internal realities of survivors' lives, especially the personal and emotional significance of events before, during, and after the Holocaust. We ask, along with Hoffman (1994: 5), about the memory practices of survivors in order to probe 'not only what happened to them, but primarily what happened within themselves'. We are interested in how their memories tell us the story, and how their memory practices within the nuclear family convey to us the cultural impact of their stories.

In order to achieve the combined goal of eliciting self-explanation as a means of learning about the reconstruction of life after trauma and exploring the impact of memory practices on listeners, three methodological innovations are featured in the Transcending Trauma Project. First, whereas previous studies of survivors and children of survivors have worked with unrelated groups, our subjects, wherever possible, are families of survivors, their children, and in some cases even grandchildren. The opportunity to study ongoing, intergenerational dynamics within Holocaust survivor families is particularly promising for understanding the transmission of cultural values, meaning systems, survival mechanisms, and identity.

Second, our orientation recontextualizes these family groups into their past and present psychosocial and communal backgrounds to look at individual differences and why they exist. We adopt the imperative that the writer Aharon Appelfeld identified in his lectures collected in *Beyond Despair*, to 'make the events speak through the individual and his language, to rescue the suffering from huge numbers, from dreadful anonymity, and to restore the person's given and family name, to give the tortured person back his human form which was snatched away from him' (Appelfeld 1994: 39). We also give voice to the rebuilding process and how survivors put together the pieces of their shattered lives. These are the stories not recorded in the public archives.

Third, by asking survivors and their family members about their subjective responses, self-explanations, and meaning systems, our study explores factors and themes which mediate the impact of the trauma through processes of coping that serve to reconstruct disrupted lives and shattered identities. Sufficiently open-ended to allow interviewees to incorporate issues and descriptions significant to them, our interviews include discussions of family of origin, key life events, cultural affiliations, and religious and moral belief systems. These factors invariably influence the individual representations of memory, the construction of meaning, and the development of coping strategies.

Our questionnaires are geared not simply to accumulate facts, but to use questions that, in a social constructionist mode, 'provide the opportunity for participants to become observers of their own interactive patterns . . . Data gathered through this questioning method quickly become information about connections among people, ideas, relationships, and time. Thus information about patterns and process . . . emerges in this context' (McNamee 1992: 195). In resurrecting and vocalizing the memories of the past, personal testimonies may themselves contribute to the transformation of the trauma not, in this case, from the vantage point of bearing witness, but from the vantage point of self-revelation. More than 'this is my story and the story of those destroyed', what surfaces is 'this is who I am' (see Agger and Jensen 1990; Kestenberg and Fogelman 1994; Langer 1991). The numerous excerpts from deepened life histories that we have studied, and the sample of these stories that we bring here, demonstrate the impact of traumatic memories on the identity formation of children of survivors. These findings, in turn, provide a more realistic picture of intergenerational cultural impact based on identification with survivorship.

Narratives of Survival, Themes of Identity

In asking survivors for their life histories, our query focuses on how they rebuilt their lives, the methods they used to cope, and the ways in which their beliefs, attitudes, and values affected their will to live and, later, to start over and rebuild. To elicit these accounts by Holocaust survivors and their families, our research team developed semi-structured, open-ended questionnaires covering the years before, during, and after the war. Facts have been collected not as an end, but rather for the sake of understanding the context of the survivor experience. Process questions tell us how survivors perceived their ordeals. The interviewer deepens the story and asks questions about coping and adaptation that others have not posed before. Answering the questions posed, for the first time, out loud in words, brings to light the guiding forces of survival. What is shared is not new to the survivor, but the sharing of it is new. Speaking from one's inner self for the first time is a powerful, often affirming, experience. Thereby, the interviewer and interviewee are both transformed by the interpersonal process.

The methodological guidelines employed in this study of how realities can be recalled, recorded, and received are based on the assumption that the researcher or hearer of extreme human suffering is a participant in a dialogic discovery of the inner experience of the trauma. Our premise is that stories in the direct voice of those who actually endured what they are describing can provide insights into the experiential quality of these ordeals, how they are remembered, and what the possibilities might be for transcending them. Laub (1992) has written eloquently of this innovative route to deciphering what is being told in the testimony, a mode of research that underscores the important role of the listener, not only as witness to the recording of events but as recipient of value-laden, affectively charged belief statements. As Van Langenhove and Harre (1993) point out, people develop an integration of their external and internal experiences as they answer the new and different questions that arise in their conversations with others. The rhetorical redescriptions that spontaneously emerge may for ever change the retelling of the memories incorporating the inner voice as the narrator of life events. In the case of Jewish Holocaust survivors, we witness the power of their testimonies to reveal the value systems of those who share the memories of survival, as well as the impact on the value systems of those who hear the stories of survival.

As researchers have attested, this consideration of the untapped reservoirs of information surrounding conceptualizations of past traumatic events and post-trauma developments expands our understanding of survivorship. From this perspective, speakers listen to themselves and watch others listen acceptingly to their narratives that incorporate, often for the first time, their inner private experiences. There is self-validation, a sense of connection instead of aloneness. Bearing witness, in and of itself, is a profound experience. How much more so when the testimony is a sharing of 'who I am', not just 'what happened to me'.

The enduring legacy of the Holocaust that surfaces in both the difficulties and the successes that survivors pass on to their children includes not merely the damaging and haunting effects of living in the shadow of the Holocaust but also the adaptive and auspicious outcomes of growing up in families where survivorship is a pervasive theme (Davidson 1980; Halik, Rosenthal, and Pattison 1990; Rosenman and Handelsman 1990). The shift in focus from observations about groups of survivors to a consideration of how individual survivors construct their past, from the pre-war years, through the war, to their post-war encounters, and from the recording of testimony to an examination of how others hear the themes and lessons of these survivor narratives, reveals a more realistic picture of the broad impact of trauma and recovery. The methodological commitment to studying family units (i.e. survivors and their own children and grandchildren) means that we have a way to illustrate the intergenerational impact of narratives about war and survival within the Jewish community. Ordinarily, listeners attend to the details of the Holocaust by confronting the poignant existential issues raised in the telling. Yet, at another level, the story becomes something the listeners can identify as a source of important messages about Jewish identity.

For the children or grandchildren of survivors, listening to the experience of their parents or grandparents has multiple consequences. The second and third generations listening to traumatic memories are hearing not only what their elders went through and incorporating the constructed meanings of these events; they are also hearing who the parent or grandparent is. The normative developmental process of identification yields the incorporation of how the parent or grandparent is portrayed in the shared memory. When a particular attribute of a survivor parent or grandparent is clear and emotionally compelling, this attribute can become an organizing value system in the developing identity of the child. The workings of this process emerged in the analysis of intergenerational interviews. We call this process the transmission of pivotal narratives.

The Transformative Power of Pivotal Holocaust Narratives

In the cases that follow, we trace the metamorphosis of pivotal family memories recalled and now recounted by children of survivors in order to examine the cultural transmission of these narratives. In each example, the stories that filled the household relayed messages about the specifics of the trauma experienced by the particular person in the past, but the stories also compel the listeners to erect guideposts for positive functioning within contemporary Jewish settings, be it within the family or in the community. We find a range of Jewish identities emerging from the interpretation of these narratives.

The first example is the story told in Iris's family, one of several narratives that have had a profound effect on how she describes herself . The memory begins with the long death march towards the end of the Second World War. Iris's grandmother, as the story has been passed on, put her shawl over her head and simply walked out of the line to separate from the group, and get back to her children:

And she takes her shawl and puts it over her head and walks away from the hundreds, perhaps, women, that are being marched at gunpoint. And she took an out, she took the choice, she took control of her destiny, and as I interpret it, very calmly decided how she's going to determine the rest of her life, whatever it is.

As the interviewer asks Iris to consider the meaning of this choice, she reflects:

And she has said and has written that you know, she consciously made this very logical decision. If she turns around and walks away she'll get shot in the back and it will be over. And if she makes it, she'll get to be with her kids. And there is some courage in that . . . that incident evokes for me courage, control, solitude, the self-reliance that I think informs a lot of what I do in my life.

Asked to probe further about her own life, Iris underlines her own intuitive sense of being separate, the imperative to not be part of a crowd.

I see that scene, and I imagine her as being, if there are four or three women across in a line, she was obviously on the edge. So I know that whenever I'm in a crowd, I am reluctant to get into the center. I always stay on the edge. I'm conscious of where the exits are all the time. All the time.

Throughout her life, Iris has been cast as an oppositional rebel for her refusal to adhere to the rules. She shares her awareness of this judgement of her behaviour with resentment and pain, as revealed by tears welling up in her eyes. But, in the context of the pivotal memory of the grandmother who had had enough and left, Iris's behaviour needs to be understood as a strong and suitable reaction. Her apartness is less defiance than it is her inherited mode of survival. Making this connection, spontaneously, in the course of the interview provided an inner sense of self-recognition. For Iris, the recognition provided a much-needed salve for private doubts about her inner motivations. She knew she was not an oppositional rebel but could not explain the compelling drive within her. She continues later in the interview:

There's a defiance in general about rules and especially in crowds. But it sort of filters in all parts of my life. That following what everyone is supposed to be doing somewhere in my consciousness means sure and certain death. That it's up to me, if I want to survive,

I have to be on my own as a solo player, away from the crowd. I think that plays out a lot in my life. It's not, I have not consciously done this, but if I were to outline the path my life has taken, in terms of career, for instance, I manage to do things in a roundabout way, not from start to finish. I'm not assigning this experience of my grandmother's as the reasons I live the way I do. But it is interesting to note—and I think there's a connection that . . . that nothing in my life has been start to finish . . . And there's something that I still hold, that if you keep running, you're safe.

Establishing her own path and finding the routes of her choosing are pieces of Iris's legacy. In fact, when asked by the interviewer to connect this most profound and resonant memory to 'a trait of yours, an aspect of yours, a defining quality of you. Not just you reacting to war stories, but a war story that became, as you say, a self-defining aspect of your identity', she states:

That would be it. And as I mature and understand myself more with each passing month and year, and as I fine-tune my truths, it becomes more and more clear. [*crying*] And I feel like I'm on that . . . I'm behind her in those footsteps. In a way, the path has been paved. I'm not rebelling; I'm following a path.

In the telling of that story, in the context of the research interview, a critical clarification of self in relation to story occurred. The memories became messages about how one's core values, while rooted in a past that is painful, move forward to a more valid interpretation and a purpose rooted in moral and personal choices.

In a second example, Beth reviews a story she has always known about her mother's war experience:

It is at that first selection . . . that the drama of what happened between my mother and her mother and her baby took place . . . There were . . . three groups. One was the people sent to the trains into the death camp. Another group was the young people who could work, and then another group were those family members of the people in the work camp . . . So anyone connected to the people in the work camp were still being allowed to re-enter the work camp. And they had children, that group. So my grandmother, in I think the chaos of that moment, I can't imagine it feeling anything other than terribly frightening, my mother was holding my brother . . . in her arms. He was eight months or nine months at the time. Her mother . . . was trying to take the baby away from my mother, saying to her, 'I'll take care of the baby, you can go work.' Well . . . the unstated reality was, my grandmother knew she was going to her death, and that the baby would go with her, but at least my mother would have a chance to live.

Hearing her mother recapture the moment yet again on a recent occasion, Beth is reminded of her mother's choice to refuse to relinquish her infant child. She describes this latest retelling: 'But what she said poignantly, clearly, in words this summer which I knew was always part of the story whether she said it or not, [*pause, crying*] was the unwillingness on my mother's part to have any role in her mother's death.' For Beth, the daughter of the woman who could not tolerate any role in another's suffering, the message is clear. It is clear even without the explication of a larger meaning system by the parent about how the decision was made. The interview process defined what she sees as a 'very deeply embedded part of me'. She continues: 'It was like looking in the mirror when she told me that. And again, it's like I always knew it, and I always knew the message, but there's something when you take the time to really focus on it and pay attention and put all the words on it.' The pivotal memory assumes its place as a guiding principle for her own standard of behaviour. In the unfolding of her own narrative, Beth is drawn to the abiding power of the unspoken but ever-enacted value statement acquired from her mother's testimony: 'But I think I was very . . . [*pause, crying*] I'm not sure why this is so emotional. [*pause*] But I think I was even more exquisitely attuned to and avoidant of and unwilling to cause anybody pain. [*pause*] At all. In any way.' Her essential identification with the central principle of empathy for people, what her interviewer terms 'a universal, governing, dominant law in your very core being', is enunciated in numerous examples throughout her interview. With the interviewer as guide, Beth contemplates her own choices as lifelong continuities emergent from the pivotal telling of trauma.

The impact of telling the trauma is contrasted, in the next case, with the powerful legacy of not telling, where silence about deeply held painful secrets pervades the family. Lisa, a daughter of Holocaust survivors, claims not to have 'a memory of a story told to me by either of them that I would say was a pivotal one'. Only in adulthood did Lisa learn that her mother had a husband and a child who died of starvation in Siberia during the war, and with that knowledge came a clearer understanding of her mother's withdrawal and her distance. Lisa confirms the sentiment of other children of survivors, that the most important event in her life happened before she was born, yet in this instance 'the way [these] memories and stories were transmitted . . . was through silence'. The interviewer offers the possibility that 'the impact was not what she told you, it's who she was because she didn't tell you'. 'Right', Lisa responds. 'I could not make sense of her inability to connect emotionally, physically, and so I internalized bad feelings about myself.' Had the stories been made available earlier, she admits, 'it would have generated quite a bit of sadness . . . perhaps even overwhelming sadness, but I think it would have helped me be more compassionate of her and of myself'. Pivotal narratives, verbally communicated or non-verbally conveyed, play a role in identity formation.

In the transmission of traditions and beliefs about self and society from generation to generation, we can also trace how the historical memory of victimization is shaped and preserved as a life-affirming model for survival. Broadening the lens from a pivotal memory to a family theme, the focus shifts from the process of identification which can operate on an unconscious level, to survival strategies consciously chosen by the survivor parent and imparted to the next generation. We have also traced these legacies in the third generation, where possible, and interviews with grandchildren of survivors so far indicate a compelling continuity in how family narratives of trauma and resilience are listened to and recalled with great sensitivity. Moreover, the individual cases we have illustrated so far fall in a continuum of behaviours that also reflects the spectrum of communal responses to the legacy of the Holocaust found in the Jewish cultural tapestry overall. Iris is the differentiated community activist prone to political progressiveness and intergroup outreach, while Beth maintains a social service orientation aimed at personal growth, family connection, and communal responsibility. Lisa, whose pivotal narrative was absent, remains an outsider looking in. Further examples elucidate this link between distinctive life stories and the corollary patterned responses found in the communal domain.

Contending with Coping: Converging Past and Present

In the following narratives focused on coping styles, collected from a mother and her three daughters, powerful and far-reaching messages are revealed when the family unit is examined. The survivor mother sets the stage for a multiplicity of reactions as she recounts:

I calmed myself down a little bit. I always tried all my life to get a hold of myself. I have always had this strong will to survive. Being that what I went through I had to live, always had the will to live . . . I wanted to live for now and I wanted to bring up my children, they should not have the sadness and the pain that I went through. I didn't want to fill their hearts with pain.

In the same interview, we hear:

I wanted to protect them. But you know what? No matter how much you try to protect your children they see through you, they feel they are different than other children. Holocaust children are different than other kids. I don't think my children had as many good times maybe as the other kids did. They did not grow up in a home where it was all happy and vacations and everything else. But, you know, this is what life is. You've got to accept whatever it is. Can't change it.

In their own revelations, each of the three daughters interweaves her own stance with the parental legacy about survival. The eldest daughter speaks of her approach to life in relation to her mother's concerns: 'I feel like because of the miracles that happened to my mother, because of her faith and her giving me the feeling that I could accomplish whatever I needed to, I am pretty, pretty positive.' A middle daughter responds to the message about continuity:

Well, you know I somehow, my mother and her sisters just gave me a sense that I can do anything. They are such strong willed, powerful, believing people. I just think if you are someone who makes up your mind that I will overcome this or anything that gets in my way that's half the battle. It's a sense of survival that they all have and nothing is going to knock me down. They are just extremely strong and courageous.

Further on:

Yeah, oh my mother always just picked up her chin and said, 'It's going to be alright "mamale", don't worry and you'll do it.' You'll make it. She provided that outlook. Thank G–d she did. Yeah, I think that's where it comes from although now things are different. But as a child, she certainly gave us the encouragement.

The youngest daughter affirms her mother's resilience and resolve:

I think it forced me to give all I could to a situation. I work hard at pretty much every-thing I do. I'm committed to, I mean if I say that I am going to be somewhere at a certain time I am always there on time and it bothers me that someone, my husband, is always late and we argue constantly about it because what is ten minutes? To me it's a lot that I am expecting you at a certain time and if I have to work to be there at that time so should you, you know, you are disappointing me. So I mean even in terms of things like that, my work, parenting, I give things pretty much everything.

These vignettes of interview material demonstrate congruence in the transmis-sion of coping strategies from one generation to the next. And here, the function of repeating Holocaust testimony in contemporary Jewish culture is to express the power of resilience, affirmation, and courage not just in the past, but also in the future.

In another interview conducted with a child survivor who was with her parents in a Russian POW camp, we hear about a mechanism that enabled her to keep the pain of the war at a distance and to focus on the present. Only later in her life did she realize the price. The same mechanism which minimized pain could also minimize joy, and it was her children who alerted her to this potentiality.

I am an expert at viewing events and feelings through the wrong end of a telescope, a trick in manipulating perspective that I learned as a child in World War II. For a long time, I assumed the Holocaust had no effect on me because I am luckier than most Jew-ish survivors of World War II and I've always known it. We were in a Russian prisoner of war camp, but never in a concentration camp; I was not separated from my mother, my parents and sister also survived the war and even some aunts and uncles did. I thought of myself as fortunate.

She continues:

When the Diary of Anne Frank was published, I read it in one night without stopping, absorbed but not overwhelmed by it. When a group of my friends wanted to see the play on Broadway, I joined them eagerly. It was in the last few minutes of the play, when they read her lines about believing people are basically good, that's when I lost it. It's accept-able to shed tears in a theater, but I had to cross my arms and concentrate on breathing slowly in and out to keep from sobbing. With my telescope trick, I can shrink troubles and pain making them smaller, more distant and less important by comparing them with the worst things I can think of. At the lowest point of a migraine, with nothing left to retch, my head still pounding, when I am too restless to lie down for the sleep which is necessary to end the pain, I hear myself saying, 'You know you'll survive this. The

Nazis couldn't kill you, a migraine won't. This is your own bed; you have a home, nobody is chasing you.' I am not stoic, I complain, but I compare my pain to what I know my relatives suffered before they perished and it becomes almost insignificant.

Later, she adds:

It may be a good thing to have perspective, even to this extreme degree. Being able to shrink your problems is useful and gives you a certain pride in having overcome. I've heard about survivor guilt, which I'm not aware of having, maybe because I was a child. I've never heard of survival pride, which I am aware of feeling, though I know it's irrational. I did not survive because of my own skill or virtue, though I know of several actions each of my parents took which were crucial in saving my life.

And, finally:

Because I assumed the Holocaust had no effect on me, I had no concern about its impact on my children. Only recently, as they approach adulthood, they have shown me that my 'survivor's pride' and the toughness it demands, exacted a price from me and from them. Life is easier when pain is not measured against the yardstick of the Holocaust. I first glimpsed this when Anne Frank's story tampered with my telescope, returning to full size what I had made smaller. Even when it works, the telescope has a way of going into automatic mode. Sometimes, but only sometimes, it slips from my grasp and points at happy events and joyful feelings, making them small and far away, and so I cheat myself.

Here, the common thread linking this narrative with the earlier one is the focus on coping through acceptance and appreciation of what is. The survivors' narrative strategies lead the listeners, their children, to adopt a stance that shapes their intrapersonal reality, their interpersonal relations, and their relationship with the Jewish world. The three sisters quoted above recently celebrated their mother's birthday publicly at a local Conservative synagogue with a special dedication ceremony in her honour. Their bond with their mother, based on positive attachment, not guilt, enables them to celebrate both her survival and their shared communal sensitivities.

Choosing Leadership, Choosing Life

The analyses of the intergenerational interviews conducted by the Transcending Trauma Project reveal over and over again that when the second generation listened to their parents' traumatic memories they were not only hearing the story of what their parents went through, they were also hearing who their parents were as people. In Aron's story, which follows below, we witness his wrestling to understand the forces that brought about his mother's survival, as if they contained the secrets to how to be in this world. Aron recounts how his mother, in several incidents, actively chose to change her fate. For example, she took the risk of placing herself in the line requiring identification though she did not have any authentic documents. She explains:

So I thought I'll try. I'll just gamble, and I went there and just mixed with the crowd and just—and we had to stand in fives and I wore a shawl just to pretend that it covered the thing, the identification, and then the Germans came in and I looked them straight in the eye. They looked everybody straight in the eye and they started counting the people, and they counted me along with them.

Eventually she found out that everyone from the first group was executed by the SS men. On another occasion, after the SS didn't select her, Helen decided to place herself in the 'select' line. The SS men caught her in the manoeuvre and put her in her designated place. As it turned out, she was chosen for the easiest line of work at the camp. In her own words: 'What seemed to be a misfortune was really a great fortune. . . . We don't know what we want, what's good for us.'

Aron clearly internalized the lessons of these pivotal moments in his mother's life. He lauds his parent's assertiveness and risk-taking, emphasizing the overall importance of actively choosing and shaping one's destiny. At the same time, he realizes that there are forces beyond one's control that affect life:

She [mother] couldn't sit there and let things happen, that she had nothing to lose by taking a chance. She figured—she realized that she was going to be dead anyway and so she had nothing to lose by taking these chances to try to survive. And yet I also learned that there were incredible elements of luck or fate or whatever, because one of the stories where she tried to do something and someone wouldn't let her and if that person had let her do what she wanted to do, she would have died.

His beliefs are predicated on his mother's pivotal memories and his own perception of their intrinsic messages and prescriptions for survival. From his point of view, both his mother's assertiveness and sheer luck colluded to secure her survival. Transposing these values onto his own life, he emulates his mother's intrepid nature:

It's a story of courage. It's a story of not being passive, and I guess it's something that shaped me, a determination to shape events rather than let them shape you, to—I mean, in groups that I'm involved with, I just need to get into a leadership role, whether it's chairing committees, being the head of an organization or club, a department head of whatever it is, in business and having sixteen employees at one time, and the main part is because I don't like to just sit back and let other people make decisions that are going to affect me. I get involved in it, and maybe that's one of the strongest things that I've taken from her, from those experiences, because if she had been passive she never would have survived.

Aron also draws a parallel between his parents' risk-taking during the Holocaust and his own choice to leave a secure job and start his own business. Here, as well as in other examples, the repeated rhetoric of 'a story' underscores how the experiences of his parents have been encapsulated and transformed by Aron into a narrative that is remembered and repeated with lessons for his own life. Later in the interview when Aron expounds upon his life philosophy, he invokes his mother's survival as well as his readings of Victor Frankl to affirm his belief in individual responsibility in life:

I really believe that we have a great deal of control over our destinies, over who we are, how we respond, and I'm a real believer in—from my mother and from what Frankl thought, that the ultimate freedom we have is how we choose to respond to situations and that we give meaning to events, that we find meaning, we give meaning, by what we do with it and so, you know, maybe if anything, if I've tried to give meaning to my mother's experiences, maybe that's reflected in that part of my personality, the way I try to bring up my daughters. To be assertive, to take control of situations, to know that they can make choices . . . that they don't have to be victims, that we take responsibility for ourselves.

Aron identifies not with the trauma in his mother's memory of life or death choices, but with the assertiveness that led to her survival. He uses examples from his life to prove his own self-reliance and causative approach to life. Additionally, he weaves several memories together to fashion a personal meaning system and philosophy regarding the roles of choice and fate in life. He is able to further develop his meaning systems through reading Victor Frankl's work and through testing his understanding against the demands of his reality. We conclude that what was transmitted to Aron was not an identification with victimization, but rather an identification with survivorship. His activist approach, gleaned from the parent generation, shapes his familial commitments as well as his penchant for organizational responsibility and leadership, including within the Jewish community.

In the interviews with brothers Isaac and Sidney, they interpret their parents' endurance and fortitude as a great triumph and success. Isaac believes that his father's ability to seize the opportunity to run away from the Germans was directly responsible for his survival:

My father was very close with one [brother] in particular, who he told stories about. How he and his brother were captured by the Germans, and I remember him telling me that people were going into this house but nobody was coming out. And they were taken in, and he said that they were taking everybody up to the second floor or something for interrogation of some sort or whatever. So he said to his brother, he said, 'Either we run away now, and take a shot at, a chance of getting out of here, or we're not getting out of here.' And my uncle, or his brother, was . . . didn't want to move, and he says, 'I'm going for it.' And he leaped through a window, my father, and ran with the Germans shooting after him. And was able to run into a forest and get away. And because of that he survived.

He shows great respect, almost awe, for his father's strength, saying 'he was always the rock', admiring the survivor's shrewdness that he purports to have inherited:

If they were going to survive, if there's a way that they were going to be able to survive, they were going to find a way to do it. As opposed to just saying, 'I can't do this' and giving up. And that is going to transcend itself into other functions of their life, other times of their life. And . . . at least for me, I think that has given me a . . . you know, I try to learn from their experiences without having to experience the whole thing, and say that, you know, not to let myself be rolled over type thing. Maybe that's why I said I'm a little militant in some way.

In Isaac's estimation, his father's survival as well as his business acumen emanated from the same intrinsic source of strength and stamina. He tries to be like his father by taking over the business and going on the business trips that his father took in the past. He has even adopted his father's political views, presenting himself as very right-wing: 'I'm my father's child. He was the same way. That . . . militant to the point where, I don't believe in . . . there are certain times that you stand up for what you believe in to a fault.' Echoing his own father's idealism and deep convictions, Isaac takes his child to work with him to instil in him the work ethic and appreciation for money that his father transmitted. He takes pride in his successes and in the fact that he can easily overcome obstacles, just as his father did. 'I think that's a great success'—he comments on his ability to revive his business after it burned down—'the fact that I was able to come through that and establish myself.' He lauds himself for the same traits that he associates with his father.

His brother, Sidney, also admires his father and replicates his courageous zeal. Inspired by his father's involvement with the Betar Zionist movement and his generally proactive and adventurous nature, Sidney decided to spend six months working on a kibbutz around the time of the Yom Kippur war.

I was sitting at the dinner table, and my father, as I said, spoke as being a hero. He was in Betar, he was a Zionist even before the war etc. And I had these feelings about should I get up, leave school, leave my cozy house and go volunteer to be on a kibbutz at least, because the able-bodied men, most of them, were on the front, and it was something that obviously was a scary feeling, because obviously there was a war going on, and it wasn't the kind of thing where my peers were getting up in droves and going to do it. And I think that my father's influence of him being the hero and doing the right thing had some influence on me.

These two cases are examples of identification with a hero mentality and with leadership. The sons see the father as an active agent in his survival and try to emulate his astute self-reliance. Their stories do not reverberate with the pain or angst of the past. Instead, they inherit a perhaps somewhat idealized notion of their father's prowess during the war, and boast of their resemblance to him. The family's pivotal narrative becomes itself a coping strategy, analysed by these two sons of survivors as an enactment towards an instrumental purpose that values heroism, success, and leadership. These brothers are leaders and supporters of many Jewish organizations in their local and metropolitan community. They have an impact on many lives in their various communal roles. It is interesting to note that they lead in different ways. The younger brother, who was the father's favourite, has a low profile and a generally easy personality as a leader. The older brother, who was often out of favour with his father, likes to have a very public persona and sometimes clashes with authority figures. One cannot avoid the ultimate drama of family-of-origin issues that are played out in adulthood.

From these examples, we see how the experience of trauma, and its memory and telling, must ultimately take us to the intersection of survival and identity. An integration of both the positive adaptation and the negative consequences of surviving extreme trauma is needed, and is made possible by looking at the survivor in the past and the survivor's family in the present. Individual differences emerge, while significant familial and group themes are illuminated. Without undermining or underestimating the tragedies and trials that individuals and communities experience, a legacy of resilience and resourcefulness becomes apparent when family units can be investigated, and when the social context is examined as well. As poignant narratives are shared on a deeper level, with oneself and with significant others, life themes emerge as representations of belief systems that are guided by human connection. The capacity for transforming trauma may depend on the capacity, ultimately, to negotiate memory, to recognize the personal teachings that are embedded in the process of sharing stories, whether or not the speaker or listener is consciously aware of the messages imparted, and to integrate these narratives through life-affirming belief systems.

New Perspectives, New Possibilities

If past and current literature has not garnered these kinds of transformative narratives, it may well be because of the circumstances under which the data were collected. A portion of existing Holocaust research is based on reparation interviews where, in order to receive payments, survivors had to prove damages to their physical and psychological well-being. Therefore, the emphasis was more on the recounting of details rather than the cultural transmission of narratives. Other writings are based on interviews conducted by mental health professionals treating survivors diagnosed with psychiatric symptomatology. Much of this previous scholarship categorizes Holocaust survivors on the basis of a constellation of psychiatric symptoms most often identified as 'survivor syndrome' (Chodoff 1963; Cohen 1953; Eitinger 1961, 1980; Krystal and Niederland 1971; Lifton 1980; Niederland 1961), and talks about standardized responses with little room for variability and diversity.

Distortion in the perception of the survivor population also derived from the unprecedented nature of the survivors' experiences. Mental health workers had little in their background or training to prepare them for understanding the enormity of the cultural transformations wrought by the Holocaust. The result was what Danieli has termed 'the long-term conspiracy of silence between Holocaust survivors and society' (Danieli 1988: 236). Neither survivor nor society could bear to directly confront the horrifying details of loss, dehumanization, torture, and murder. What followed were generalizations from a group of survivor psychiatric patients to the entire population of survivors, and subsequent generalizations from a group of children of survivors in treatment for personal and familial issues to the entire cohort of sons and daughters of survivors. Individual differences were ignored and models of coping, adaptation, and resilience had not yet established credibility. These generalized narratives themselves created an expectation that survivors and the children of survivors would manifest uniform responses of either devastation or superhuman strength in relation to the Holocaust and to life after the Holocaust. In fact, though, there is not only a variegated post-Holocaust experience for survivors, but also an integration into Jewish culture of a wide range of Holocaust narratives where both trauma and resilience play a role in the Jewish world-view.

In the 1980s the focus of Holocaust literature broadened to include more realistic assessments of survivors and their families. For example, Podietz et al. (1984) researched the role of closeness among family members. What had been clinically observed and referred to as 'enmeshment', with all its negative connotations, was empirically demonstrated to be 'engagement' with both positive and negative realities for Holocaust survivor families. Danieli (1985) contributed to the understanding of survivors and their families by formulating a typology of four characteristic family styles. These described the predominant coping strategies of survivor parents and the impact on the second generation. While Danieli's work helped to shift the emphasis away from individual pathology and towards intergenerational transmission and familial styles, the macroscopic focus that describes survivor families by means of four adaptational styles does not address the complexity of family systems. We have observed, for example, that a survivor with an adaptational style labelled 'hero' by Danieli could be married to a survivor with an adaptational style labelled 'victim'. While Danieli's typology allows for the discussion of a 'dominant' style, it does not address the impact of the 'secondary' style. Or, phrased somewhat differently, what, from a systemic perspective, is the impact of growing up in a family with two divergent adaptational styles?

The research of investigators engaging in a broader, integrated framework of enquiry (Halik, Rosenthal, and Pattison 1990; Helmreich 1992; Sigal and Weinfeld 1989) has shown that, despite the existence of a 'survivor syndrome', great variability characterizes the extent to which individuals manifest these post-traumatic characteristics. Some of these studies have involved large-scale, empirically based research with representative samples of survivors and comparable control groups (Kahana, Kahana, and Segal 1985; Kahana, Harel, et al. 1987). Others who concentrate on smaller samples also caution against defective research assumptions that ignore the complex dynamics of survivor adjustment (Hass 1990; Prince 1985). It is the consensus of every review of the trauma field that future research should focus on individual differences, the varying impact of specific traumas, and the role of contextual variables such as culture, belief system, family-of-origin dynamics, and current life events (Aldwin and Revenson 1987; Kahana, Kahana, Harel, and Rosner 1988; Kleber and Brom 1992; Krystal and Danieli 1994; Yehuda and Geller 1994).

There is no debate about whether trauma leaves long-lasting effects on its victims. It does. The questions that remain are the extent, nature, and intensity of the aftermath. Little effort has been made to incorporate what has elsewhere been called the 'salutogenic' orientation (see Antonovsky and Bernstein 1986), namely, investigating the positive adaptation that takes place after trauma has occurred where strength or renewal is derived from the experience. Individuals and communities who live through highly stressful, traumatic events continue to carry their pasts, as they change and adapt, coping with day to day life and anticipating the future. By analysing communication about trauma and adaptation in the private domains of family rituals and repertoires, the findings from this study will be of interest to those who can extrapolate patterns from this Jewish context for a broad range of trauma-ridden settings and situations.

The Transcending Trauma Project Research Methodology

Collecting the Data

Using a carefully designed questionnaire as a base, 275 qualitative in-depth interviews were conducted with survivors and, where possible, their spouses, children, and grandchildren. We taped and transcribed the interviews and developed a demographic profile of project participants and their family backgrounds, as well as other pre-war, wartime, and post-liberation experiences. In addition, we asked respondents to consider their views on Jewish identity, on Israel, and on the non-Jewish world. We also looked at the survivor parents' choices about conveying their past to their children, and at the ways in which the children learned about their parents' pre-war and war experiences, even when verbal communication was minimal.[1]

Each interview itself took up to an average of eight hours during approximately four visits to the respondent's home. Although there was an extensive schedule of questions, one set for survivors and one for children of survivors, plus a complementary set of questions for survivor and non-survivor spouses, the approach was to elicit data, encourage spontaneous associations, and deepen the level of personal sharing. All interviews attempted to track the information chronologically to whatever extent possible while flexibly responding to the interviewee's manner of answering the questions. Topics included: the current personal situation, the status of the nuclear family, the family of origin, the years before the war, wartime experiences, liberation, and post-war rebuilding. Attitude, belief, coping, and adaptation questions were crucial throughout the interviews. We encouraged the explication of what Bar-On and Gilad (1994) have distinguished as 'narrative truths', and not merely 'historical truths' in searching for ways in which memory is constructed, organized, and invoked.

The evaluation of the interviews addressed several possible entry points into the empirical data that were of concern to the Transcending Trauma Project, including: (a) the articulation of models of coping and adaptation; (b) the transmission of identity; (c) the deepened life history as a method by which (a) and (b) can be elicited; and (d) the analysis process as an evolution of understanding individual and cultural responses to trauma. We looked at the co-construction of narrative and meaning between interviewee and interviewer. This was part of our larger interest in the impact on interviewees and their interviewers of this different mode of summoning up and summarizing the 'facts', with its emphasis on internal experience as the mediating factor in understanding the impact of life events—and thereby the basis for personal belief systems, coping strategies, and life repertoires. Moreover, we were studying what it means to decode the text in order to understand the individual, and then recontextualize the text in order to understand the family. One way in which we accomplished this was by going beyond the limitations of a purely individual focus to see the influence of pivotal memories on the narratives of personal and group identity (Clandinin and Connelly 2000).

Our conclusion is that consequences and influences need to be identified and interpreted in terms of the specifics of the trauma experienced by the particular person, the personality of the individual and the personal resources available to them, and the social context of the event in the culture (Helmreich 1992; Kahana, Kahana, Harel, and Rosner 1988; Kleber and Brom 1992; Whiteman 1993). The development of a conceptual framework that facilitates an understanding of the heterogeneity of individual responses to trauma and stress comes with the challenge of finding a viable research methodology that accesses the scope and depth of human differences, as well as a viable theoretical framework that integrates diverse viewpoints. It is from the study of individual differences that we are better able to comprehend the mechanisms by which different coping strategies develop, as described in Lazarus (1993). An integrated systemic model views coping strategies as flexible processes that change with environmental demands and fluctuate over time as victims shift to the status of survivors.[2]

The methodological paradigms we employed in this study are rooted in the view that a trained interviewer and researcher can be a guide and facilitator of the articulation of a deepened life history. From this perspective, the self becomes part of the audience that hears the stories, and is in turn affected by them. 'Human communication', as Shotter summarizes, '. . . must be seen as ontologically formative, as a process by which people can . . . help to make each other

persons of this or that kind' (1989: 145). During our interviews, the survivors/
speakers and the researchers/listeners engaged in the emergence of deeper levels
of autobiographical accounts about the various modes of survivorship, conjuring
up the 'doorways to . . . [their] identities' (O'Hanlon 1994: 21).

For the survivors, their spouses, and their children, we examined and compared the early socialization of each individual, enquiring about the home environment, childrearing practices, the beliefs and values taught and internalized,
and the general communication of expectations. We asked interviewees about
their own personality traits, styles, and dispositions as well as descriptions of
their loved ones. Finally, we investigated the survivors' sense of Jewish affiliation,
or its absence, along with their religious faith before, during, and after the war.

The families we interviewed were introduced to the project through network-
ing with other survivors and their families, and through organizational contacts.
The areas of enquiry had a systemic framework that took into account not only the
individual subject but also the context and circumstances of the experiences
being reported. While the interviews covered the war years, the areas of enquiry
focused most heavily on pre- and post-liberation memories. We collected rem-
iniscences about family of origin, descriptions of family relationships and friend-
ships, and details of how the family of origin dealt with problem-solving and
conflict management, memories, dreams, loss, affection, discipline, religious
identity, life philosophy, and significant experiences before the war.

During the last meeting with each interviewee, when their deepened life history had been completed, each subject was given the COPE Scale, a multi-dimen-
sional coping inventory designed by Carver, Scheier, and Weintraub (1989) to
assess the different ways in which people respond to stress. This scale provides a
forum for comparing coping strategies as measured by psychometric testing and
coping strategies determined by qualitative ethnographic methods. Each subject
was also given the Transmission of Jewish Identity Survey, which covers basic
background information related to the subject's Jewish identity. This survey was
specifically developed for this study in order to track the impact of the Holocaust
on the Jewish identity of survivors and to track the process of transmission across
generations.[3]

Analysing the Data

The analysis took place in two stages. Stage I had two steps, the accumulation of
data involving seventy variables outlined on the analysis protocol guide for each
subject, and a thematic analysis that established consensus among the researchers about the role and relationship of the specific variables to each other in the
processes of coping and adaptation for each interviewee.

During Stage II of the analysis procedure, the interpretations of the data relevant to each variable and the interrelationships among variables for each subject
were compared to those for the other subjects in the sample. The aggregate out-

come of Stage I, which organized and interpreted the data for each individual subject and family, and Stage II, which compared the observations across subjects, constituted the validation of group trends and individual differences.

The methodology described above has been developed borrowing from the ethnographic tradition in qualitative research, whereby the understanding reached about people and their context develops by means of a collaborative effort, involving the investigator and the group members (Fabian 1990; Strauss and Corbin 1990; Tedlock 1983). In order to understand the multideterminism of post-trauma coping and adaptation, we employ a methodology that merges the traumatic event within the context of a life history that probes life pre-trauma as a root of life paths after tragedy.

Conclusions

There have been a number of studies of the testimonies of Holocaust survivors. What is distinctive about this study? In addition to the unique elements discussed above, we feel allied with the viewpoint expressed by one of the interviewees in the study of survivor testimonies by Langer (1991: 205): 'I think there are as many ways of surviving survival as there have been to survive.' This comment underlines what LaCapra (1994: 197) has suggested about 'the danger of homogenizing or overgeneralizing about the experience of victims or survivors'. By gathering the narratives of all generations, this study speaks to the complex process of surviving, as well as to the cultural integration of survivor experiences in the form of narratives transmitted through several generations.

The struggle to unravel the dilemma of having endured inhumanity in the past continues to preoccupy trauma victims as they seek to re-evaluate their survival, including Jews whose collective memory of trauma is ritualized with cultural narratives that link past and present. Every memory, Janet wrote over a century ago, is an act of creation, a fluid process that evolves continuously all the time as people adjust their internal schemes to external reality (Van der Kolk, McFarlane, and Weisaeth 1996). The lessons of the Holocaust are many, among them the capacity of individuals to use their memories to weave a narrative of survival that forms the foundation of meaning, and the foundation of self and of one's role in family and community.

Notes

1   The research project can be traced back to 1986, when the University of Pennsylvania's Marriage Council of Philadelphia, one of the country's leading centres for the study of the family and human relationships, now known as the Council for Relationships, sponsored a conference entitled 'Holocaust and Genocide', organized and chaired by one of the Marriage Council's senior staff members, Dr Bea Hollander-Goldfein. After the conference, a group of mental health practitioners and social scientists began to meet several

times a year as a study group to review the available scholarship on this issue. Out of their discussion of research and methodological concerns grew the Transcending Trauma Project and its unique interview and evaluation instruments. From 1991 until the formal onset of the project in August 1993, the original study group evolved into the nucleus of the project's research team, engaged primarily in conducting pilot interviews with selected survivors and their children. During this period, the team continued to refine the semi-structured questionnaire guides, the data-collection reports, and the consent forms. Currently, 275 transcripts are on file, and comprehensive protocols for analysing the data have been established. The research is conducted in accordance with the United States code of ethics mandatory for all studies involving human subjects.

2   Researching transformational processes is difficult. Longitudinal investigation would be the preferred method, but since this is often impossible it is critically important that trauma research incorporates a time frame that approaches the study of survival as a process. There are numerous constructs in the literature to describe, explain, and study the coping strategies of trauma victims. Carver, Scheier, and Weintraub (1989), Horowitz (1971), Horowitz, Wilner, and Alveraz (1979), Janoff-Bulman (1989), Lazarus and Folkman (1984), and Taylor (1983) are among those who have tried to move the field beyond the simplistic categorization and pathologization of trauma victims.

3   Items for this survey were derived from the Jewish Population Study conducted in 1990 by the Council of Jewish Federations, from the work of Cohen (1989), who assesses trends in the American Jewish community, and from the researchers' conceptualization of the transmission process.

References

AGGER, INGER, and SOREN BUUS JENSEN. 1990. 'Testimony as Ritual and Evidence in Psychotherapy for Political Refugees', *Journal of Traumatic Stress*, 3(1): 115–30.

ALDWIN, C., and T. A. REVENSON. 1987. 'Does Coping Help? A Reexamination of the Relationship between Coping and Mental Health', *Journal of Personality and Social Psychology*, 53: 337–48.

ANTONOVSKY, AARON, and JUDITH BERNSTEIN. 1986. 'Pathogenesis and Salutogenesis in War and Other Crises: Who Studies the Successful Coper?'. In Norman A. Milgram, ed., *Stress and Coping in Time of War: Generalizations from the Israel Experience*, 52–65. New York.

APPELFELD, AHARON. 1994. *Beyond Despair: Three Lectures and a Conversation with Philip Roth*. New York.

BAR-ON, DAN. 1999. *The Indescribable and the Undiscussable: Reconstructing Human Discourse After Trauma*. Budapest.

—— and NOGA GILAD. 1994. 'To Rebuild Life: A Narrative Analysis of Three Generations of an Israeli Holocaust Survivor's Family'. In Amia Lieblich and Ruthellen Josselson, eds, *Exploring Identity and Gender: The Narrative Study of Lives*, 83–112. Thousand Oaks, Calif.

BRENNER, IRA. 2004. *Psychic Trauma: Dynamics, Symptoms, and Treatment*. Lanham, Md.

CARUTH, CATHY. 1996. *Unclaimed Experience: Trauma, Narrative, and History*. Baltimore.

CARVER, C. S., M. F. SCHEIER, and J. K. WEINTRAUB. 1989. 'Assessing Coping Strategies: A Theoretically Based Approach', *Journal of Personality and Social Psychology*, 56: 267–83.

CHODOFF, P. 1963. 'Late Effects of the Concentration Camp Syndrome', *Archives of General Psychiatry*, 8: 323–33.

CLANDININ, D. JEAN, and F. MICHAEL CONNELLY. 2000. *Narrative Inquiry: Experience and Story in Qualitative Research*. San Francisco.

COHEN, E. A. 1953. *Human Behavior in the Concentration Camp*. New York.

COHEN, STEVEN. 1989. *The Dimensions of American Jewish Liberalism*, New York.

DANIELI, YAEL. 1985. 'The Treatment and Prevention of Longterm Effects and Intergenerational Transmission of Victimization: A Lesson from Holocaust Survivors and their Children'. In C. R. Figley, ed., *Trauma and its Wake*, vol. i: *The Study and Treatment of Post-Traumatic Stress Disorder*, 295–313. New York.

——1988. 'Confronting the Unimaginable: Psychotherapists' Reactions to Victims of the Nazi Holocaust'. In John P. Wilson, Zev Harel, and Boaz Kahana, eds, *Human Adaptation to Extreme Stress: From the Holocaust to Vietnam*, 219–38. New York.

DAVIDSON, SHAMAI. 1980. 'Transgenerational Transmission in the Families of Holocaust Survivors', *International Journal of Family Psychiatry*, 1(1): 95–112.

EITINGER, L. 1961. 'Pathology of the Concentration Camp Syndrome', *Archives of General Psychiatry*, 5: 371–80.

——1980. 'The Concentration Camp Syndrome and its Late Sequelae'. In J. E. Dimsdale, ed., *Survivors, Victims, and Perpetrators: Essays on the Nazi Holocaust*, 127–60. Washington, DC.

FABIAN, JOHANNES. 1990. *Power and Performance*. Madison, Wis.

FRIESEL, EVYATAR. 1994. 'The Holocaust as a Factor in Contemporary Jewish Consciousness'. In Jonathan Webber, ed., *Jewish Identities in the New Europe*, 228–34. London.

HALIK, V., D. A. ROSENTHAL, and P. E. PATTISON. 1990. 'Intergenerational Effects of the Holocaust: Patterns of Engagement in the Mother–Daughter Relationship', *Family Process*, 29 (Sept.), 325–39.

HASS, AARON. 1990. *In the Shadow of the Holocaust: The Second Generation*. Ithaca, NY.

HELMREICH, WILLIAM B. 1992. *Against All Odds: Holocaust Survivors and the Successful Lives they Made in America*. New York.

HOFFMAN, EVA. 1994. Review of Aharon Appelfeld, *Beyond Despair*, in *The New York Times Book Review* (23 Jan.), 5–6.

HOROWITZ, M. J., and S. S. BECKER. 1971. 'The Compulsion to Repeat Trauma', *Journal of Nervous and Mental Disease*, 153(1): 32–40.

——N. WILNER, and W. ALVERAZ. 1979. 'Impact of Event Scale: A Measure of Subjective Stress', *Psychosomatic Medicine*, 41: 209–18.

JANOFF-BULMAN, RONNIE. 1989. 'The Benefits of Illusions, the Threat of Disillusionment and the Limitations of Accuracy', *Journal of Social and Clinical Psychology*, 8(2): 158–75.

KAHANA, B., Z. HAREL, E. KAHANA, and M. SEGAL. 1987. 'The Victim as Helper—Prosocial Behavior During the Holocaust', *Humboldt Journal of Social Relations*, 13(1–2): 357–73.

—— E. KAHANA, and M. SEGAL. 1985. 'Finding Meaning in Adversity: Lessons from the Holocaust'. Presentation at a meeting of the Gerontological Society of America, Chicago.

KAHANA, E., B. KAHANA, Z. HAREL, and T. ROSNER. 1988. 'Coping with Extreme Trauma'. In J. P. Wilson, Z. Harel, and B. Kahana, eds, *Human Adaptation to Extreme Stress: From the Holocaust to Vietnam*, 55–79. New York.

KESTENBERG, JUDITH S., and EVA FOGELMAN. 1994. *Children During the Nazi Reign: Psychological Perspective on the Interview Process*. Westport.

KLEBER, ROLF J., and DANNY BROM. 1992. *Coping with Trauma: Theory, Prevention and Treatment*. Amsterdam.

KRYSTAL, H., and W. NIEDERLAND, eds. 1971. *Psychic Traumatization*. Boston.

—— and Y. DANIELI. 1994. 'Holocaust Survivor Studies in the Context of PTSD', *PTSD Research Quarterly*, 5(4): 1–5.

LACAPRA, DOMINICK. 1994. *Representing the Holocaust: History, Theory, Trauma*. New York.

LANGER, LAWRENCE L. 1991. *Holocaust Testimonies: The Ruins of Memory*. New Haven.

LAUB, DORI. 1992. 'Bearing Witness, or the Vicissitudes of Listening'. In Shoshana Felman and Dori Laub, *Testimony: Crises of Witnessing in Literature, Psychoanalysis, and History*, 57–74. New York.

LAZARUS. R. S. 1993. 'Coping Theory and Research: Past, Present, and Future', *Psychosomatic Medicine*, 55: 134–247.

—— and S. FOLKMAN. 1984. *Stress, Appraisal, and Coping*. New York.

LEYS, RUTH. 2000. *Trauma: A Genealogy*. Chicago.

LIFTON, ROBERT J. 1980. 'The Concept of the Survivor'. In J. E. Dimsdale, ed., *Survivors, Victims, and Perpetrators: Essays on the Nazi Holocaust*, 113–25. Washington, DC.

—— 1993. *The Protean Self: Human Resilience in an Age of Fragmentation*. New York.

MCNAMEE, SHEILA. 1992. 'Reconstructing Identity: The Communal Construction of Crisis'. In Sheila McNamee and Kenneth Gergen, eds, *Therapy as Social Construction*, 186–99. London.

NIEDERLAND, W. G. 1961. 'The Problem of the Survivor: The Psychiatric Evaluation of Emotional Disorders in the Survivors of Nazi Persecution', *Journal of the Hillside Hospital*, 10: 233–47; repr. in H. Krystal, ed., *Massive Psychic Trauma*, 8–22. New York, 1968.

O'HANLON, BILL. 1994. 'The Promise of Narrative: The Third Wave', *The Family Therapy Networker*, 18(6): 18–29.

PODIETZ, L. LENORE, ISRAEL ZWERLING, ILDA FICHER, HERMAN BELMONT, TALIA EISENSTEIN, MARION SHAPIRO, and MYRA LEVICK. 1984. 'Engagement in Families of Holocaust Survivors', *Journal of Marital and Family Therapy*, 10(1): 43–51.

PRINCE, ROBERT M. 1985. 'Second-Generation Effects of Historical Trauma', *The Psychoanalytic Review*, 72(1): 9–29.

ROSENMAN, STANLEY, and IRVING HANDELSMAN. 1990. 'The Collective Past, Group Psychology and Personal Narrative: Shaping Jewish Identity by Memoirs of the Holocaust', *The American Journal of Psychoanalysis*, 50(2): 151–70.

SHOTTER, JOHN. 1989. 'Social Accountability and the Social Construction of "You"'. In John Shotter and Kenneth J. Gergen, eds, *Texts of Identity*, 133–51. London.

SIGAL, J. J., and MORTON WEINFELD. 1989. *Trauma and Rebirth*. New York.

STRAUSS, ANSELM, and JULIET CORBIN. 1990. *Basics of Qualitative Research: Grounded Theory Procedures and Techniques*. Newbury Park, Calif.

TAYLOR, S. E. 1983. 'Adjustment to Threatening Events: A Theory of Cognitive Adaptation', *American Psychologist*, 38: 1161–73.

TEDLOCK, DENNIS. 1983. *The Spoken Word and the Work of Interpretation*. Philadelphia.

VAN DER KOLK, BESSEL A., ALEXANDER C. MCFARLANE, and LARS WEISAETH, eds. 1996. *Traumatic Stress: The Effects of Overwhelming Experience on Mind, Body, and Society*. New York.

VAN LANGENHOVE, LUK, and ROM HARRE. 1993. 'Positioning and Autobiography: Telling Your Life'. In Nikolas Coupland and Jon F. Nussbaum, eds, *Discourse and Lifespan Identity*, 81–99. Newbury Park, CA.

WHITEMAN, D. B. 1993. 'Holocaust Survivors and Escapees: Their Strengths', *Psychotherapy*, 30: 443–51.

YEHUDA, RACHEL, and EARL L. GELLER. 1994. 'Comments on the Lack of Integration between the Holocaust and PTSD Literatures', *PTSD Research Quarterly*, 5(4): 5–7.

Ambivalence and Identity in Russian Jewish Cinema

OLGA GERSHENSON

'The Jew is ambivalence incarnate.'
ZYGMUNT BAUMAN

HISTORICALLY, the representation of Jews in Soviet national cinema (when and where it has been allowed) has been a litmus test for the Jewish position in Russian culture. Jews have been variously, and paradoxically, stereotyped: they could simultaneously symbolize backwardness (as ignorant shtetl dwellers) or progressiveness (as the learned 'people of the book'); they could stand for emasculated weakness (as victims of pogroms and genocide) or virile leadership (as rabbis or commissars); they could be seen, in short, as heroes or anti-heroes (Bartov 2005). For scholars of contemporary Jewish cultures, film therefore provides eloquent material for research on identities and their construction and reconstruction. According to Stuart Hall (1990), cinema is a potent medium in which identities are produced. Rather than being a 'second-order mirror held up to reflect what already exists', it is 'a form of representation which is able to constitute us as new kinds of subjects, and thereby enable us to discover places from which to speak' (1990: 236–7). Moreover, because of their profound influence on society and culture, films constitute a source of the visual memory transmitted to future generations (Portuges 2005). Taking these formulations as a starting point, I will approach the subject of Russian Jewish identity by studying representations of Jews in Russian national cinema.

Russian Jews in the Soviet Union and After

The mass emigration of Russian Jews and the introduction of Western Jewish organizations to Russia have brought Russian Jews back into contact with world Jewry. This meeting revealed great cultural differences, and brought the issue of Russian Jewish identity to the fore. Russian Jews as a group are hardly homogeneous, and defining Russian Jewish identity can be a trying task, which is further complicated by the fact that most scholarship in the field has explored the history and culture of Jewish elites. With rare exceptions (such as Shternshis 2006), current studies of Russian Jewish identity focus mainly on 'Hodl's children'—descendants of Jewish migrants from the shtetls to the big urban centres in the early Soviet era who joined the ranks of the Soviet elite and the intelligentsia. The social and cultural profile of 'Tsaytl's children'—descendants of those Jews who remained in the shtetls in the east and south—remains largely unexplored.[1]

Defining Jewish identities is in general problematic, not only because they vary across different historical periods and geographical locations, but also because the very concept of Jewishness can be defined in so many ways: religious, ethnic, racial, or cultural. In addition, Jewish identities are influenced by both self-representations and representations by outsiders—and Jewish responses to these. Jewish identities therefore emerge as contradictory and ambivalent. This ambivalence, of both Jews themselves and the surrounding society, has been theorized in several historical and cultural contexts, including cinematic representations (Adorno and Horkheimer 1989; Bauman 1998; Biale 1986; Homberger 1996; Sutcliffe 2003). Here I will argue that the concept of ambivalence is useful in trying to understand how Russian Jewish identity, with all its ruptures and discontinuities, is constructed and reconstructed. Keeping in mind theories of identity as constantly in the making, I understand Russian Jewish identity not as a resting place but as a 'perpetual creative, diasporic tension' (Boyarin and Boyarin 1993: 714).

The concept of ambivalence (in psychoanalysis, a simultaneous attraction to and repulsion from a person or an object or a wanting of both a thing and its opposite) underscores the fluidity of identity and its resistance to essentialization. The usefulness of the concept of ambivalence here—and indeed its very meaning—is clear from the existing research on Russian Jewish identity. It has become a commonplace in the scholarly literature to see Jewishness in Russia as a matter of 'sentiment and biology' (Gitelman 2003: 55). Having roots in the racialized perception of Jews in imperial Russia, the notion of Jewishness as *natsional'nost'* (ethnicity) took a firm hold in the Soviet era. Even in post-Soviet times it remains completely disconnected from religion.[2] This means that Jewishness is understood as a primordial (rather than a constructed) category.[3] For Russian Jews, biology is destiny, and neither conversion to Christianity nor complete identification with Russian culture will change it. Jews are seen as fundamentally—i.e. biologically—different.

But in addition to biology Jewishness is also, in Zvi Gitelman's words, 'the subjective feeling of belonging to a group' (2003: 54)—an understanding in which Jewishness is constructed rather then primordial. This sense of one's Jewish identity can be either positive or negative. It can be forced on one as a result of an encounter with antisemitism or a memory of the Holocaust, or it can be experienced as a result of pride in Jewish culture and accomplishment, leading to an open awareness of one's Jewishness. Researchers vary in their evaluation and interpretation of this 'biological' and 'sentimental' identity. Gitelman (2003) concludes that in the absence of a 'thick culture' (language, religion, tradition), Russian Jewish identity is built on a 'thin culture' devoid of any real content, and as such is hardly viable.[4] This pessimistic position is supported by Rozalina Ryvkina, who announces a 'crisis of national self-identification' and a 'turning off of Jewish culture' (2005: 78), and quotes Leonid Radzikhovsky's expressive term *raz"evreivanie*, which may be translated as the 'unravelling of Jewish identity' (2005: 56). Building on earlier work by Gitelman (1991), Mikhail Chlenov (quoted in Ryvkina 2005: 84–5) expresses his concern that Russian Jewish identity is 'passive' (stemming from biology), in contrast to Western Jewish identity, which is 'active' (requiring actions from individuals).

Other scholars try to locate the characteristics of Russian Jewish identity without evaluating it or its future. Larissa Remennick reasons that the 'thinness' of the culture does not make it any less real for its carriers. She identifies several characteristics of Russian Jewish identity, all of them traced back to the traditional 'mercurian' (Slezkine's term, 2004) Jewish culture and lifestyle rather than religion. These characteristics are: 'cultivation of intellectualism, respect for hard effort and know-how in one's line of work, strength of family networks, in-group solidarity, moderation in . . . lifestyle, quiet negation or sheer manipulation of the Soviet system' (Remennick 2006: 31). Anna Shternshis (2006) builds an argument for the hybridity of Russian Jewish identity as both 'Soviet' and 'kosher'. She shows how this hybridity has evolved historically, in connection with such characteristics of Jewish identity as Jewish pride, solidarity, and the preference for cultural products with Jewish content. Alice Nakhimovsky (2003) sees in Russian Jews such cultural characteristics as a particular type of Jewish humour as well as a playful and verbose use of language. These characteristics have created cultural codes which have contributed to in-group Jewish identification. Simultaneously, these characteristics have been used by the surrounding society in negative stereotyping.[5]

In his discussion of Jewish identity as expressed in fiction, Mikhail Krutikov (2003) adds two major characteristics: the influence of a Jewish role model (usually an older male relative, who becomes a yardstick of Jewishness) and emigration (as the ability to emigrate was a singular prerogative of Jews in the USSR from the 1960s to the 1990s). The prospect of emigration, whether real or theoretical, opened up questions of national loyalty and belonging, and also separated Jews into a distinct group, for better and for worse.

Another important dimension of Russian Jewish identity has been the adoption of what Slezkine (2004) coins as 'Pushkin faith'—admiration of and adherence to great Russian culture and literature. This led Russian Jews to identify with the Russian intelligentsia (the words 'Jew' and 'intelligent' were virtually synonymous in Russian) and as a result, despite the Soviet-era barriers and tacit quotas, Jews were markedly successful in the sphere of Russian high and popular culture, including film-making. As in the United States, the 'people of the book' became what I would call the 'people of the media'.[6]

Other characteristics that have had a profound effect on Russian Jewish identity have not yet been theorized: the Jewish body, Jewish names, and Jewish communicative performance.[7] There are multiple references to these characteristics in Russian Jewish literature, folklore, and art, suggesting that they play an important role for both in-group identification and solidarity, as well as for negative stereotyping by outsiders, internalized at times as Jewish self-hatred.

All these characteristics combine into an uneven and contradictory picture which is constantly in flux and eludes definition. They reflect the ambivalent position of Russian Jews as—in the words of an old Soviet joke—'either kikes or the pride of the Russian people' (*ili zhidy ili gordost' russkogo naroda*).[8] Indeed, in the Soviet era Jews occupied a paradoxical position as what Larissa Remennick calls 'discriminated elites' (2006: 31). Though subject to discrimination, Jews were also capable of achieving incredible social success—they were simultaneously deprived and privileged. In turn, they were ambivalent about themselves: they were proud to be Jews yet embarrassed by it; they looked back on their shtetl past with nostalgia but also with repulsion. As Mariya Yelenevskaya and Larisa Fialkova have noticed: 'Jewish self-stereotypes . . . are polar, and either idealize Jews, or humiliate them' (2005: 80). Ryvkina notes that Russian Jews today combine the 'unravelling of Jewish identity' (2005: 107) with pro-Jewish positions. At the same time, Jews were also conflicted in their attitudes toward Russianness. In Ryvkina's terms, their identity is 'a Russian Jewish hybrid: a combination of Jewish sensibility and Russian-language culture' (2005: 113). And so, despite Pushkin faith, Jews remained proud of their *yiddishe kop*, and looked down on people whom they perceived as 'the sluggish and drunk Russian bears'. As the Russian Jewish writer Efraim Sevela notes, 'earlier on, Jews were kicked around'; now they 'demonstrate their superiority' (quoted in Ryvkina 2005: 110).

Another locus of Jewish ambivalence is in gender expression and representation, which, as Bryan Cheyette and Laura Marcus note, 'is in constant dialogue and conflict with "racial" and cultural identity and difference' (1998: 7). Jewish gendered expressions have been theorized as ranging from 'sissy', with its historic variations of *yeshiva-bochur* and *mensch*—'the East-European Jewish ideal of a gentle, timid, and studious male' (Boyarin 1997: 2)—to 'tough Jews' (Breines 1990), with its variation 'Muscle-Jew' (Nordau 1980), and, later, 'sabra' (Almog 2000). Jewish women can be perceived as materialistic, independent 'princesses' or selfless and overbearing 'Jewish mothers' (Prell 1996), 'beautiful Jewesses' or 'ugly old kikes'. All these ambivalent images both challenge and reinforce gendered ethnic stereotypes within the context of Russian–Jewish relations.

In conjunction with gender, the theme of intermarriage, with its threat and lure, has been at the centre of the cultural imagination, reflecting relationships between Jews and non-Jews at least since the Middle Ages. The representation of

Russian–Jewish intermarriage is equally important for understanding the cultural positioning of the Jew as a desirable partner or as a forbidden one. This is still a work in progress, but demographic data hint at some trends: the fact that in Russia many more Jewish men than women intermarry (73 per cent of men and 62 per cent of women: Tolts 2004) may suggest that Jewish men are more desirable as partners (or have a more positive image) than Jewish women. Russian polls confirm these attitudes (Kreiz 2005: 17–18). With such a high rate of intermarriage among Russian Jews, the vast majority have mixed backgrounds. As Elena Nosenko's (2004) pioneering research indicates, these Jews (conversationally known as 'halves' and 'quarters') are even more ambivalent about their Jewishness than their parents.

In sum, the concept of ambivalence is needed to theorize the multiple ruptures and discontinuities of Russian Jewish identity, and this ambivalence arises at multiple points for Russian Jews, including national identification, intermarriage, and gender. For the purposes of my analysis, I will consider three expressions of this Russian Jewish ambivalent identity as they are represented on screen. First, there is the issue of national identification: do the Jewish characters feel Russian or Jewish? Are they at home in Russia? Second, there is the issue of intermarriage (or inter-ethnic romance), attitudes towards which serve as an important indicator of Jewish identity in the cinema. Is intermarriage desirable? Is it a viable option, and for whom? The third and final expression of Jewish ambivalence occurs in connection with the gendered construction of the characters. What are the gendered expressions of Russian Jewish identity, and how is this identity constructed through gender?

Love and *Daddy*: A Cinematic Context

I will look at two representative films, *Love* (*Lyubov'*) directed by Valery Todorovsky (1991), and *Daddy* (*Papa*), directed by Vladimir Mashkov (2004), to identify and discuss the ambivalent points of Jewish identification outlined above. Like any complex texts, these films are open to multiple interpretations, but my project here is to focus on the image of the Jew as these films create and circulate it. As Omer Bartov argues, if Jewish stereotypes were once produced and disseminated through other genres, today it is in film that 'one encounters the formation of stereotype and the impregnation of viewers' minds by those stereotypes' (2005: 311).[9]

Both *Love* and *Daddy* emerged in the cinematic context of post-Soviet Russia. The new openness of perestroika brought both Jewish culture and popular anti-semitism out into the public sphere. After decades during which Jewish topics in art had been silenced, bans were lifted, and films on Jewish issues started pouring onto the screens. This Jewish cinematic renaissance encompassed a wide range of subjects, genres, and authors,[10] reflecting and shaping the ambivalent portrayal of Jews. Whatever the topic, Jewish characters are always portrayed at one polar extreme or the other, either as victims or heroes, as miserable, persecuted women and elderly folk or as noble warriors. These films combine a view of Jews as members of refined Russian intelligentsia with stereotypical ethnic schmaltz, evoking feelings ranging from philosemitism to antisemitism. Other media, such as newspapers and fiction, featured similarly complex images of Jews (Elias and Bernstein 2006; Kreiz 2005).

Love and *Daddy* are among the more significant of the post-perestroika Jewish films in terms of critical success, audience popularity, and the celebrity of the film-makers and actors. *Love* was a winner of awards at the international festivals in Montpellier, Chicago, and Geneva, as well as at the national Russian festivals, Kinotavr and Sozvezdie. It also won the Russian film critics' annual award and was popular with audiences. *Daddy* won the audience popularity award at the Moscow International Film Festival and several awards at the national film festivals. It received a positive critical reception at home and was distributed abroad. Both films were clearly interpreted by critics and audiences as Jewish. Given their cultural significance, they provide excellent sites for studying the pervasive cultural ideas about Jewish identity that they both reflect and help shape.

Valery Todorovsky (b. 1962) and Vladimir Mashkov (b. 1963) are among the most popular and critically acclaimed Russian film-makers of the young generation. Todorovsky, who is ethnically Jewish, is the son of the famous film-makers Petr and Mira Todorovsky. His films have all been major hits, including *Katya Izmailova* (1994), *The Country of the Deaf* (1998), *Lover* (2002), and *My Stepbrother Frankenstein* (2004). In many cases he has also acted as screenwriter and producer (*Love* was both written and directed by him). The influential Russian daily *Nezavisimaya gazeta* called him 'the most successful director of the young generation' (Salnikova 2001).

Vladimir Mashkov, originally trained as an actor, became internationally famous for his portrayal of extremely masculine gangsters in *Thief* (1997), *Quickie* (2001), and *Tycoon* (2002). He is tagged as a sex symbol in Russia. *Daddy* is the second film which Mashkov has directed (the first, in 1998, was a comedy, *Sympathy Seeker*). He also co-wrote *Daddy* (with Ilya Rubinstein). Mashkov is ethnically Russian, but has a long history of representing Jewish characters. He played the handsome communist Aaron in *I Am Ivan, You Are Abraham* (1993), directed by Yolande Zauberman, for which he allegedly learned Yiddish (Mashkov 2005). In *Tycoon*, he played a character loosely based on Boris Berezovsky, a Russian Jewish businessman. Finally, he cast himself as Abram Schwarz, one of the main characters of *Daddy*.[11]

Todorovsky's *Love* and Mashkov's *Daddy* have much in common: both focus on the Jewish theme, and both combine the genres of Bildungsroman, family drama, and romance. Both have Jewish and non-Jewish casting and crew, and thus combine Jewish and non-Jewish points of view.[12] Both films highlight critical moments in Russian Jewish history—the Holocaust and emigration. Both present a generally sympathetic picture of Jews. But even this sympathetic representation is deeply ambivalent.

Love/Hate Relationship

Love, as its title promises, is a love story of two inter-ethnic couples: one Russian and Tatar (Vadim and Marina), the other Russian and Jewish (Sasha and Masha). The courting of the first couple, although not ideal, ends with a wedding, and they are comfortably settled. The story of the second couple, which occupies most of the screen time, is more complex. Throughout the film, Sasha (Evgeny Mironov) and Masha (Natalya Petrova) grow, moving from an awkward start, through a violent row, to true intimacy and trust. Yet theirs is a story of disrupted love, of life together undone by antisemitism. Ultimately, it is a story about the impossibility of Russian–Jewish romance (in a sense Vadim and Marina function as a 'control group', demonstrating successful inter-ethnic romance). At the end of the film, Masha and her family are pushed out of their Russian life by persistent and omnipresent antisemitism. They have no choice but to go to Israel.

Love is thus also a film about emigration. Naturally, this is a recurrent theme in Jewish films, which often deal with the issues of displacement and otherness. Yet the focus of *Love* is not so much the Jewish experience as the Russian–Jewish relationship. Speaking more broadly, it is the story of both the potential for and the failure of love between different, or rather divided, people. This is why emigration is an end point in its plot, rather than a point of departure.

Filmed in a discomfiting tone typical of the post-perestroika era (Lawton 2002: 321), much of the *mise en scène* is set among cold, grey apartment blocks completely devoid of Moscow charm, or in cramped, dark interiors. The atmosphere of alienation and impending danger is emphasized by documentary footage of wars and catastrophes, introduced into the narrative through the depiction of Marina's grandmother watching the television news. These images of violence and destruction hover over the entire movie.

Masha's actions, including emigration, are merely a response to events that have been forced on her—literally. In one of the most visually haunting scenes, she recounts her experience of being victimized on two levels: as a woman and as a Jew. First she was gang-raped; then, when her mother tried to prosecute the offenders in a Soviet court the antisemitic judge sneered: 'Go to Israel, demand your rights there.' Masha's story of rape and failed litigation is told through a montage of disjointed medium shots depicting her and Sasha doing chores around his house. The scene is shot without diegetic sound and is held together by Masha's whispered voiceover. As if to express their alienation and the incommensurability of their experiences, the camera pans at high and low angles, with Sasha and Masha in the same frame, but in different corners, or upside down in relation to each other. The characters finally make eye contact, but their mouths are conspicuously stuffed with food. Only at the end of the scene do they appear facing each other in close-up, filmed in grey, cold tones. The barrier is broken, and they both cry. Masha's voice trails off as she says: 'They call you a kike once . . .' and, presumably, your life is changed. As Mikhail Krutikov has said, 'Jewish identity is completely arbitrary, but once a person is marked as Jew it becomes his fate' (2003: 270).

Symbolically, there are no men in the family, as her mother has thrown out Masha's father for his inability to stand up for them (signalling his emasculation). Masha's family's femininity stands for weakness, passivity, and an inability to defend oneself. The stereotype of a Jewish sissy here is taken to the extreme— when male Jews do appear on the screen it is only as little boys or fragile old men. At the end, Jews are feminized to such a degree that they are not just 'Jewish male femme[s]' (Boyarin's term, 1997), they are actual women. In Masha's female household, Sasha—the man, the proletarian, the Russian—comes to help the weak, feminine, and incompetent Jews. His masculinity is brought out cinematically, as in the shot/reverse shots of him facing Masha, her mother, and her grandmother, lined up and smoking in an identical fashion, as if reproducing different versions of the same image.

Sasha helps the family in minor practical ways, but cannot protect them from antisemitic harassment. Antisemitic slurs are scattered throughout the film (for example a policeman near a synagogue asks Sasha, 'Looking for a kike bride?'), yet the audience's most direct diegetic exposure to antisemitism is through the anonymous voice of a telephone harasser, who persistently rings Masha at home. Antisemitism does not have a face; it is everywhere, like the air. Sasha's attempts to confront this antisemite and meet him face to face fail: when he rushes to the deserted phone booth, he sees only his own reflection in the glass. Everybody is an antisemite. This antisemitism robs Masha of her sexuality, and she can have sexual relations only once she escapes it, on the brink of her departure. The silent scene of final intimacy between the lovers is the only poetic episode in the movie. Filmed in a series of beatific close-ups, awash in warm cream and yellow tones, it stands out from the gloomy colours of other scenes. The only sound is the noise of airplanes, emphasizing Masha's impending departure.

At the end of the film, Masha's family is gone. Sasha comes into their empty apartment. He brings a phone with him, and plugs it in, perhaps hoping to deal with the antisemitic caller, or perhaps, symbolically taking the Jews' place. The Jews are gone, and only Russians are left. Sasha, the good Russian, comes to settle the score with the bad, antisemitic Russian. But Jewish absence is as conspicuous as Jewish presence. As Krutikov sadly comments, 'Antisemitism is a core element of the Russian collective identity, but at the same time, life without Jews is unimaginable to the Russian mentality' (2003: 270). Historically Jews have played a special role in the Russian national imagination, as paradigmatic internal others whose 'otherness' served as a touchstone for Russian 'sameness'. Thus Russian national identity evolved in reflexive connection with perceptions of Jewishness: stereotypical Russian soulfulness, generosity, and rootedness in the Russian soil emerge in juxtaposition to stereotypical Jewish intellectualism, calculated pragmatism, and rootlessness or double loyalty.

In *Love*, Masha has to leave because she is Jewish. Yet 'Jew' appears to be an empty signifier. Masha's Jewishness is residual at best. Her dark hair and slightly hooked nose mark her as non-Russian. Her mother is a dentist, perceived as a Jewish profession. Her grandmother's voice has shtetl-like intonations, and she has hopes for a Jewish match for Masha. The family's religious observance amounts to serving matzo with tea, instead of cookies (rather than as a part of Passover celebrations). But what really makes Masha Jewish is antisemitism. In fact, according to Todorovsky's film, Jews are not intrinsically different from Russians; they are othered through antisemitism and hatred. The key to understanding Jewishness as *Love* presents it is victimhood.

Here is the parting message of *Love* on the place of Jews in Russia. As to national loyalty, the Jews have left for Israel. As to Jewish–Russian romance, it is impossible. As to gender, the Jews are portrayed as feminized, confirming antisemitic stereotypes of them as weak, disempowered, and unmasculine. That is why the bad Russians can rape or torture them, and even the good, strong Russians like Sasha cannot save them. The Russian Jewish stereotypes are polar— they are either 'kikes' or 'the pride of the Russian people'. In *Love*, Jewish representation is located at the pole of victimhood. Even though the sympathies of the film-makers are clearly with the Jews, they emerge as displaced, effeminate, and powerless. The film thus represents one extreme of the Jewish ambivalent position.

Daddy and the Motherland

Daddy is based on Aleksandr Galich's play *Sailors' Rest*, written between 1945 and 1958, and banned from performance for over thirty years. In 1993 Oleg Tabakov (the famous director, who played a minor role in the original banned production in 1958) directed the play, with 24-year-old Mashkov cast as the elderly Abram. The production was so successful that it ran for over 400 performances. In 2004 the script was turned into a $4 million feature, produced by Jewish producer Igor Tolstunov and financed by the Russian Ministry of Culture. Even though the narrative is set in the first half of the twentieth century, the film begs to be read within a contemporary context.

The entire form of the film is different from that of *Love*. Gone is the post-perestroika gloominess: the film is shot in a socialist realism-meets-Hollywood style; the colours are bright and vivid, and the shots are long and deep, letting the

Figure 1 *Daddy*: Egor Beroev as David Schwarz

viewer fully enjoy the perspective (metaphorically, a promising future). And even as the internal spaces remain dark and cramped, the outside shots are full of air and often flooded with sunlight. The editing is Hollywood-smooth.

Daddy is a Bildungsroman—the coming-of-age story of David Schwarz. As is characteristic of such films, the narrative is structured as a triptych—childhood, youth, and young adulthood. The childhood segment takes place in 1929 in Tulchin,[13] where the young David (Andrey Rozendent) is growing up. The opening scene at a railway station introduces the leitmotifs of trains and railway tracks. For the Jewish imagination operative in the transnational media circuits (including post-Soviet Russia), trains symbolize both the Holocaust and social/geographical mobility. Low-angled close-ups of rotating wheels and pumping pistons (repeated throughout the film) also echo the visual aesthetics of the avant-garde Russian Jewish film-maker Dziga Vertov.

This segment sets the stage for future drama, namely David's conflict with his father Abram (Vladimir Mashkov). Abram is portrayed with sympathy but stereotypically. He is a shtetl Jew—grimy, scheming, worried, but deeply invested in his son's musical education. David, despite his 'Jewish' violin, is strong and proud; he is a 'new Jew', as tough as his Russian friends. (He makes a bet with a gang of rough local boys over who will stay on the tracks longer in front of an oncoming train—and wins.) Abram collects postcards of European cities (symbols of his unrealized dreams); David cherishes only one picture, a photograph of Moscow (a symbol of his future)—hinting at his national loyalty.

Yet David inherits Abram's dream. As Abram puts it: 'A big hall, beautiful men and women look at the stage, and they hear: David Schwarz. You come out, start playing, and they cry "Bravo!" and applaud, send you flowers and ask you to play again.' Abram's dream is a paradigmatic Jewish success story, yet David is hardly another one of those musical prodigies whom Isaac Babel described as 'Jewish dwarfs . . . with swollen blue heads' (2002: 628). Neither is he a descendant of the folksy 'fiddler on the roof' reminiscent of Sholem Aleichem's Stempenyu or Chekhov's pathetic Rothschild. David (had he been real) would have belonged to the elite group of Jewish musicians, along with David Oistrakh, Elizaveta Gilels, Boris Goldstein, and Mikhail Fikhtengolts, who conquered both local and international stages in the Soviet era (Svet 1968).

The scenes of David's adventures are interspersed with those of another Jewish character, Meyer Wolf (Sergey Dontsov-Dreiden), who returns from Palestine. It is the meeting with Meyer that sets up another theme in the movie—that of a national home. In an extraordinary monologue, Meyer tells David that his return is a true homecoming: 'When I was young and travelled with my father, in every shtetl there was a wise man who said, go to the Wailing Wall . . . But the Wailing Wall proved to be just some old lousy wall, and when I came to Jerusalem, it turned out that I had come not home, but to a foreign country, where one can only weep and die, and where people are strangers to me.' As the camera pans from the startled and confused David to Meyer, who is turning to leave, the long pause indicates the importance of Meyer's words for David. Perhaps this moment poses to David (and the audience) the question of his loyalty, and asks him to locate his own Wailing Wall. This is the first point in the film where the loyalty of Jews to their Russian motherland is stated directly (in Meyer's words). Later on this loyalty will also be expressed through narrative. But beyond the diegetic importance, this moment has particular resonance for contemporary Russian Jewish audiences. In Galich's play, Meyer's words might have reflected the experiences of early Jewish settlers in Palestine, but in the 2004 movie they refer more immediately to recent Russian immigrants to Israel, some of whom, like Meyer, returned to Russia.[14]

The second segment takes place in 1939 in Moscow. The Jewish dream has come true: a grown-up David (Egor Beroev) is playing solo at a May Day concert at the Great Hall of the Conservatory. Moreover, he has a beautiful Russian girlfriend, Tanya (Olga Krasko).[15] The scenes of David's triumph are visually contrasted with the shots of Abram, who has come for an unannounced visit. He is portrayed as a pathetic shtetl Jew in the big city. In a conspicuously comic sequence the camera follows Abram's awkward walk through bright red and white Moscow, as he juggles his meagre luggage and bags of garlic (a markedly Jewish flavouring). Although Mashkov's ethnic acting style was probably supposed to echo Solomon Michoels's charming *luftmentsh* in the classic 1925 Soviet Yiddish film *Jewish Luck*, it fails to do so. Instead, his portrayal of Abram in these scenes reproduces the crudest stereotypes of the Jewish body (Gilman 1996), including the shaking hands and 'clumsy, heavy-footed gait' (Muscat 1909, quoted in Gilman 1992: 228). Predictably, the visit results in a falling out—David rejects Abram, with his scheming, his garlic, and his worries. In this way, David rejects the 'old Jewishness'.

The third segment of *Daddy* takes place in 1944. Relying on a flashback structure, it intercuts David's fighting in the Second World War with his delirious visions as he lies injured in a hospital train. Two scenes are particularly significant here. In the first, one of the nurses who happens to be a friend from the past tells David about her last meeting with Tanya, now David's wife. She describes how the women were listening to the news on the street radio, read by the legendary Soviet announcer Yury Levitan, followed by a broadcast of David himself performing a piece by Tchaikovsky. This scene encapsulates the place of the Jews in Russian culture: the official voice of the motherland throughout the war is the voice of a Jew, Levitan; the music of the national composer which follows this voice is performed by another Jew. Importantly, in Galich's play, David plays a mazurka by Wieniawski, a Polish Jewish composer, not a concerto by Tchaikovsky, a composer who is a symbol of Russian national music. In this way, the movie deliberately places emphasis on David's embrace of Russianness, while at the same time giving him (and by extension other Jews) a more central place in Russian culture. In the second key scene, David has a vision of Abram, who tells David the story of his execution in the Tulchin ghetto. His words come to life on screen, presenting the now iconic image of Jews with yellow stars, walking towards their death; Abram walks next to Meyer. Here *Daddy* also departs from Galich's original story. In the play, Abram does not die passively: provoked by the antisemitic insults of a local Nazi collaborator, he hits him with David's childhood violin, and is shot. The presence of a Russian Nazi collaborator and Abram's active resistance did not fit *Daddy*'s narrative.

Intercut with Abram's story is David's story of fighting for Tulchin, told in voiceover as the camera surveys the desolate landscape with anti-tank barriers. Finally the camera finds the wall next to the railway station, where young David used to play. Echoing an earlier scene, David's voice continues, 'Meyer went to Jerusalem to see the Wailing Wall, and I saw it in our town—a simple stone wall.' As David asks Abram for forgiveness, Abram reassures him: 'This is your motherland for which you are fighting.' The statement is clear: the true Wailing Wall is in Tulchin, and the real motherland is Russia. Both Abram and David made their choice.

How is Jewishness expressed in *Daddy*? David is portrayed as an *über*-Jew. He is typed as both Jewish-looking (with wavy dark hair and large expressive eyes) and conventionally attractive. Rejecting centuries-long stereotypes of Jews as unfit for military service, he is a fighter (his wounds make him even more of a battle hero). But he is not only a man of the sword, he is also a man of culture—a talented violinist, recognized nationally. He is not only the son of a shtetl Jew, he is the husband of a beautiful Russian woman, and (as the script hints) the father of a Russian Jewish son. So, in all respects David embodies the heroic (as opposed to the victimized) pole of Russian Jewish ambivalence. David's Jewishness is less arbitrary then Masha's—he is connected to his roots more directly—through a shtetl childhood, through losing his father in the Holocaust, and even through a reference, however negative, to the larger picture of Jewish history and culture (the Wailing Wall, Palestine). Moreover, the very negotiation between the 'old Jew' and the 'new Jew' is typical of modern Jewish histories, since, as Joseph Roth noted, 'Attacking the tradition is an old Jewish tradition' (quoted in Hoberman 1998: 281). But what emerges in this negotiation is a rejection of victimhood. David, the new Jew, is a proud, strong, and dignified Jew, and he is fighting on the same side of the barricades as the Russians.

The film also marks a change in the content of Jewish identity, which becomes positive (or active) in a particularly Russian way. This new content emerges from a combination of 'Pushkin faith' and professional excellence. And so, paradoxically, the positive active Jewish content comes from the leading Jewish position in Russian culture. Jews are not only staying with the Russians, they are becoming the best of them. This Jewish drive for excellence becomes a source of assimilation. Jews become Russians because they are so good at being Jewish.

So what is the message of *Daddy* on the place of Jews in Russia? As to national loyalty, the Jews in *Daddy*, from Meyer to David, choose Russia. The Jews are staying, and these Jews are men who are marrying and impregnating Russian women. And if the old generation were led 'as sheep to the slaughter', the new generation have fought for their motherland and reasserted their masculinity.

Significantly, there are no positive characters of charismatic Jewish women in *Daddy*: the film's only Jewish women are sad, needy Hanna and her fat, overbearing mother. They are portrayed sympathetically, but they are hardly charismatic. In order to give a positive portrayal of Jews, the film needed to depict them as men. The impossibility of creating a positive Jewish female character confirms an unfortunate stereotype of the undesirability of Jewish women (Berger 1996: 102).

Ambivalence and Identity

Jews appear in *Daddy* and *Love* at opposite ends of the spectrum. If in *Love* they were portrayed as victims, in *Daddy* a different image emerges—a rooted, masculine, and powerful Jew, 'the pride of the Russian people'. *Love* and *Daddy* capture different moments in Russian Jewish history. *Love* is a film about emigration, yet it is an unusual film in this genre. Emigration films are often made from the vantage point of the émigrés themselves, reflecting their experiences of leaving the old home and coming to terms with a new one. *Love* is a story of emigration filmed from the vantage point of those who stayed. Therefore the journey taken by Sasha from his own antisemitism to outright advocacy, and from indifference to deep sympathy, is more important than Masha's trip from Russia to Israel. This is indeed reflected in Todorovsky's autobiographical comment: 'When I shot *Love* in 1990, the country was going through a very unpleasant moment: mass emigration, empty shelves in the stores, and an atmosphere of impending civil war in the air . . . And I remember how I argued, sitting in a kitchen with my friends, tried to convince them: wait, don't leave, it will get better . . .' (Salnikova 2001).

As a snapshot of the mass exodus of Russian Jews, *Love* presents a grim picture. The Jews are forced out of Russia. Their decision to go to Israel is influenced by the direct experience of antisemitism. Historically, these reasons are not typical. Persecution and antisemitism were not the main 'push' factors of the Russian Jewish exodus of the 1990s. People left for a variety of reasons, mainly economic difficulties and political instability, but also the hope of improving their quality of life. Antisemitism contributed to the decision to emigrate mainly on the level of latent fear.[16] Neo-fascist organizations such as Pamyat never implemented their threats, and the majority of Soviet Jews did not take them seriously. But this is the story that Todorovsky chose to present in 1991, when antisemitism was a newly permissible subject in cinema. Indeed, film critics in Russia hailed *Love* as an honest look at antisemitism. However, the portrayal of Russians as antisemites also entails the portrayal of Jews as victims.

In contrast, Mashkov captures a different historic moment. The enormous wave of emigration is over. The Jewish population in Russia has diminished dramatically (recent estimates range from 230,000 to 500,000: Aviv and Shneer 2005). At the same time, there has been a great surge in the establishment and rebuilding of Jewish communities, including cultural centres and educational and political organizations (Aviv and Shneer 2005). Some Jews have joined new Russian professional and business elites, and even though their numbers are small they have achieved a strong public presence. All this has led to a resurgence of the old antisemitic suspicions of Jewish political, economical, and cultural dominance, and foreign loyalties.

Daddy can be read as a response to these attitudes: without underplaying Jewish membership of elite circles, the film gives it a highly positive framing, simultaneously alleviating anxieties over Jewish 'double loyalty'. The Jews in *Daddy* have not only stayed in Russia, but they have also integrated into Russian culture and intermarried. They have chosen to live in Russia, to fight for it, and to call it their motherland—by implication, like real-life Russian Jews today. Indeed, as Slezkine writes, based on the 2002 census, 'More and more Russian Jews (the absolute majority) marry non-Jews, strongly identify with Russia as a country, and show no interest in perpetuating their Jewishness in any sense whatever' (2004: 361).

Paradoxically, along with a resurgence of antisemitic attitudes in post-Soviet Russia, there is also a greater acceptance of Jews as a result of the emergence of new cultural others. These include Muslims from the Caucasus and central Asia, perceived as terrorists, enemies, and in general racially and culturally inferior people. In contrast to these new others Jews appear as more acceptable members of the Russian nation. The question about the future of Russian Jews remains open. But it is clear that contemporary Russia emerges as a site of Jewish expressions of identity that were not possible before. It is in this context that *Daddy* represents Jews positively.

The fluid concept of ambivalence provides insight into Russian Jewish identity as it is constructed in both films. Here I have considered three expressions of this ambivalence: national loyalty, intermarriage, and gender. In *Love*, Jews are forced out of Russia by pervasive antisemitism, and must find their home elsewhere, in their true home, Israel.[17] Their Jewishness is mainly a result of the antisemitism, rather than any authentic or identifiably Jewish culture. In *Daddy*, Jews are not only staying in Russia, they are becoming the elite of its citizens. In the paradoxical affirmation of their Jewishness in its Russian incarnation (professional excellence), they take a leading role in Russian culture and history. It is through being Jewish that they become exemplary Russians, or through being Russians that they become exemplary Jews.

In *Love*, intermarriage is impossible. In *Daddy*, it is not only possible, it is a viable and productive option (at least for Jewish men), one which is even preferable to in-group marriage. Indeed, recent polls show that the majority of non-Jews in Russia are neutral or positive about marrying Jews (Slezkine 2004: 361).

The representation of gender in *Love* feeds into long-standing stereotypes: Jews are not just metaphorical 'sissies'—they are actual women. Passive, powerless, and weak, Jews are in need of defence and advocacy. In *Daddy*, Jews are male. Even as *Daddy* represents both 'old Jew' and 'new Jew', the identification is with the winning image of the 'new Jew'. However, the conspicuous absence of positive images of Jewish women is also a perpetuation of Russian gender and ethnic stereotypes.

Today, when post-Soviet Russia is struggling with the creation of a new collective identity, film (and other media) are using images of others to draw and redraw symbolic borders between 'us' and 'them'. Both *Love* and *Daddy* reflect this struggle. Both films aim to resolve the tension of hybrid Russian Jewish identity by forcing it to one side or the other. *Love* ends by choosing Jewish identity (and Israeli nationality), *Daddy* chooses Russia and the Russians. Through the delicate shifts of inclusions and exclusions, both films reveal ambivalence about Jewishness. On the one hand, 'the Jew' becomes a stockpile of negative images—a symbolic trashcan of unwanted meanings and polluting influences. But at the same time 'the Jew' is also a projection of the desirable qualities and character that a Russian collective identity aspires to. The Jew is ambivalence incarnate.

Notes

I would like to thank Mikel Koven and Simon J. Bronner for their insightful suggestions. Thanks also to Mark Leyderman (Lipovetsky), Julia Lerner, and Larissa Remennick for their comments on earlier drafts of this essay, to Galina Aksenova for first drawing my attention to the film *Daddy*, and to Susan Shapiro for helpful discussions of gender. Every effort has been made to contact the copyright holder and to obtain their permission to reproduce the image from *Daddy*.

1   The term 'Hodl's children' is from Slezkine 2004, and refers to Tevye's second daughter in Sholem Aleichem's *Tevye's Daughters* (dramatized as *Fiddler on the Roof*). Hodl is the first to leave the shtetl, to follow her revolutionary husband. 'Tsaytl's children' is also from Slezkine 2004, and refers to Tevye's eldest daughter, who marries a tailor from the shtetl.

2   This disconnection is even expressed linguistically. In contemporary Russian, two different words are used to mean 'an ethnic Jew' (*evrei*) and 'a religious Jew' (*iudaist*); see e.g. Chkhartishvili 2006.

3   For more background on primordialist and constructivist approaches to ethnicity see Comaroff (1994), Scott (1990), Smith (1998), and the special issue of *Theory and Society*, 20 (1991), on ethnicity in the USSR.

4   Many scholars of culture would disagree with Gitelman's argument. Starting from Edward T. Hall's now classic study (1966), the established view is that the most profound and resilient cultural differences are found in the invisible, 'tacit' understandings that cultures share, rather than in the visible, tangible differences of language, custom, dress, food, etc. But this issue is beyond the scope of the present discussion.

5   These characteristics are transnational and resonate with east European Jewish traditions elsewhere, for instance in the US. For characteristics of Jewish American humour and culture, see Desser and Friedman 2003: 1–34.

6   For an excellent analysis of a similar process in the United States, see Gabler 1988.

7   For research on the issues of the Jewish body and communication in other cultural contexts, see e.g. Gilman (1996) and Tannen (1981). As to Jewish names, there is an extensive literature that covers history and etymology (Singerman 2001), including Russian Jewish names (Feldblyum 1998), but not their social and cultural function.

8   I am grateful to Gennady Estraikh for reminding me about this joke.

9   A similar argument is made for Asian Americans, whose stereotypes range from 'yellow peril' to 'model minority', and are expressed cinematically, as well as in other genres of popular culture (Lee 1999).

10 For the study of the Jewish representational tradition in Soviet cinema, see Chernenko 2006 and Hoberman 1994. The phenomenon of Jewish film in the post-Soviet era was so prevalent that in 1992 the foremost Russian film journal *Iskusstvo kino* published a special 'Jewish' issue (vol. 5). The topics of these Jewish films ranged from literary classics (several adaptations of Babel, Sholem Aleichem, and Kuprin's *Gambrinus*) to the topics of the Holocaust (*Lady's Tailor*, dir. L. Gorovets, 1990; *The Parrot Who Spoke Yiddish*, dir. E. Sevela, 1991; *Get Thee Out!*, dir. D. Astrakhan, 1991), antisemitism (*To See Paris and Die*, dir. A. Proshkin, 1993), emigration (*Nice Weather on Deribasovskaya, Rain on Brighton Beach*, dir. L. Gaiday, 1992), and the history of Soviet Jews (*...and the Wind Returns*, dir. M.

Kalik, 1990; *Chekist*, dir. A. Rogozhkin, 1991). There were also several co-productions, among them *Passport* (dir. G. Daneliya, 1990, USSR/Austria/France/Israel); *Jewish Vendetta* (dir. A. Shabataev, 1999, Russia/Israel); and four Russian/French films by P. Lungin: *Taxi Blues* (1990), *Luna Park* (1992), *Tycoon* (2002, Russia/France/Germany), and *Roots* (2006).

11   Unsurprisingly, the paths of Mashkov and Todorovsky crossed. Todorovsky directed and Mashkov acted in *Katya Izmailova* (1994). Further, Mashkov's acting partner in Tabakov's production of *Sailors' Rest* was Evgeny Mironov, who played the main role in *Love*.

12   They also had the same producer, Igor Tolstunov.

13   Tulchin is the town where Babel's Baska grows up, in the story 'Father'. This is potentially also a reference to Tulczyn as a site of Jewish martyrdom in 1648 (Fram 1998). The story of this martyrdom was widely circulated and available in Russian, but there is no way of knowing whether Galich was exposed to the story.

14   For more background on Jewish emigration from Palestine see Alroey 2003. For contemporary emigration from Israel to Russia, see Ryvkina 2005.

15   *Daddy*'s cast had celebrity status in Russia: the actors playing David and Tanya (Egor Beroev and Olga Krasko) went on to star in *Turkish Gambit* (dir. D. Faiziev, 2005), a Russian blockbuster based on the cult novel by Boris Akunin. Beroev plays the leading male role of the charismatic officer Fandorin, and Krasko plays the leading female role.

16   For an overview of the motivation to emigration, see the empirical studies by Al-Haj and Leshem (2000: 11–13) and Yelenevskaya and Fialkova (2005: 47–63). Although their data differ slightly, both report that the majority of immigrants were motivated by economic and social concerns. Antisemitism was not a defining factor.

17   This conclusion echoes the message of earlier international films on Jewish topics, such as the acclaimed *Europa, Europa* (dir. Agnieszka Holland, 1990), in which the protagonist negotiates his three different identities—German, Jewish, and Russian. But in the end he chooses his Jewish identity in Israel.

References

ADORNO, THEODOR, and MAX HORKHEIMER. 1989 [1944]. *Dialectic of Enlightenment*. New York.

AL-HAJ, MAJID, and ELAZAR LESHEM. 2000. *Immigrants from the Former Soviet Union in Israel: Ten Years Later. A Research Report*. Haifa.

ALMOG, OZ. 2000. *The Sabra: The Creation of the New Jew*. Berkeley, Calif.

ALROEY, GUR. 2003. 'The Jewish Emigration from Palestine in the Early Twentieth Century', *Journals of Modern Jewish Studies*, 2(2): 111–31.

AVIV, CARYN, and DAVID SHNEER. 2005. *New Jews*. New York.

BABEL, ISAAC. 2002. *The Complete Works of Isaac Babel*, trans P. Constantine, ed. N. Babel. New York.

BARTOV, OMER. 2005. *The 'Jew' in Cinema: From The Golem to Don't Touch My Holocaust*. Bloomington, Ind.

BAUMAN, ZYGMUNT. 1998. 'Allosemitism: Premodern, Modern, Postmodern'. In B. Cheyette and L. Marcus, eds, *Modernity, Culture and 'the Jew'*, 143–57. Stanford, Calif.

BERGER, MAURICE. 1996. 'The Mouse that Never Roars: Jewish Masculinity on American Television'. In N. L. Kleeblatt, ed., *Too Jewish? Challenging Traditional Identities*, 93–108. New York and New Brunswick, NJ.

BIALE, DAVID. 1986. *Power and Powerlessness in Jewish History*. New York.

BOYARIN, DANIEL. 1997. *Unheroic Conduct: The Rise of Heterosexuality and the Invention of the Jewish Man*. Berkeley, Calif.

—— and JONATHAN BOYARIN. 1993. 'Diaspora: Generation and the Ground of Jewish Identity', *Critical Inquiry*, 19: 693–725.

BREINES, PAUL. 1990. *Tough Jews: Political Fantasies and the Moral Dilemma of American Jewry*. New York.

CHERNENKO, MIRON. 2006. *Krasnaya zvezda, zheltaya zvezda: Kinematograficheskaya istoriya evreistva v Rossii 1919–1999*. Moscow.

CHEYETTE, BRYAN, and LAURA MARCUS. 1998. 'Introduction: Some Methodological Anxieties'. In B. Cheyette and L. Marcus, eds, *Modernity, Culture and 'the Jew'*, 1–23. Stanford, Calif.

CHKHARTISHVILI, GRIGORY. 2006. *Pisatel'i samoubiistvo*, 2nd edn. Moscow.

COMAROFF, JOHN. 1994. 'Natsionalnost', etnichnost', sovremennost': Politika samoosoznaniya v kontse XX veka'. In V. Tishkov, ed., *Etnichnost'i vlast'v polietnichnykh gosudarstvakh*. Moscow.

DESSER, DAVID, and LESTER FRIEDMAN. 2003. *American Jewish Filmmakers*, 2nd edn. Champaign, Ill.

ELIAS, NELLY, and JULIA BERNSTEIN. 2006. 'Wandering Jews, Wandering Stereotypes: Media Representation of Russian-Speaking Jews in Russia, Israel and Germany'. Paper presented at the international conference, 'Russian-Speaking Jewry in Global Perspective: Power, Politics and Community', Bar-Ilan University, 18 Oct.

FELDBLYUM, BORIS. 1998. *Russian-Jewish Given Names*. Bergenfield, NJ.

FRAM, EDWARD. 1998. 'Creating a Tale of Martyrdom in Tulczyn, 1648'. In E. Carlebach, J. M. Efron, and D. N. Myers, eds, *Jewish History and Jewish Memory*, 89–113. Hanover, NH.

GABLER, NEAL. 1988. *An Empire of their Own: How the Jews Invented Hollywood*. New York.

GILMAN, SANDER. 1992. 'The Jewish Body: A Foot-note'. In H. Eilberg-Schwartz, ed., *People of the Body: Jews and Judaism from an Embodied Perspective*, 223–43. Albany, NY.

—— 1996. 'The Jew's Body: Thoughts on Jewish Physical Difference'. In N. L. Kleeblatt, ed., *Too Jewish? Challenging Traditional Identities*, 60–74. New York and New Brunswick, NJ.

GITELMAN, ZVI. 1991. 'The Evolution of Jewish Culture and Identity in the Soviet Union'. In Yaacov Ro'i and Avi Beker, eds, *Jewish Culture and Identity in the Soviet Union*, 3–27. New York.

—— 2003. 'Thinking about Being Jewish in Russia and Ukraine'. In Zvi Gitelman, M. Glants, and M. I. Goldman, eds, *Jewish Life after the USSR*, 49–61. Bloomington, Ind.

HALL, EDWARD T. 1966. *The Hidden Dimension*. Garden City, NY.

HALL, STUART. 1990. 'Cultural Identity and Diaspora'. In J. Rutherford, ed., *Identity: Community, Culture, Difference*. London.

HOBERMAN, J. 1994. 'A Face to the Shtetl: Soviet Yiddish Cinema'. In R. Taylor and I. Christie, eds, *Inside the Film Factory: New Approaches to Russian and Soviet Cinema*, 124–51. London.

—— 1998. *The Red Atlantis: Communist Culture in the Absence of Communism*. Philadelphia.

HOMBERGER, ERIC. 1996. 'Some Uses for Jewish Ambivalence: Abraham Cahan and Michael Gold'. In B. Cheyette, ed., *Between 'Race' and Culture: Representations of 'the Jew' in English and American Literature*. Stanford, Calif.

KREIZ, SHIMON. 2005. 'Stereotypes of Jews and Israel in Russian Detective Fiction', *Analysis of Current Trends in Antisemitism*, 26: 1–54.

KRUTIKOV, MIKHAIL. 2003. 'Constructing Jewish Identity in Contemporary Russian Fiction'. In Z. Gitelman, M. Glants, and M. I. Goldman, eds, *Jewish Life after the USSR*, 252–75. Bloomington, Ind.

LAWTON, ANNA. 2002. *Before the Fall: Soviet Cinema in the Gorbachev Years*, 2nd edn. Philadelphia.

LEE, ROBERT. 1999. *Orientals: Asian Americans in Popular Culture*. Philadelphia.

MASHKOV, VLADIMIR. 2005. Website, <www.vladimirmashkov.webcentral.com.au>, accessed 7 Mar. 2005.

NAKHIMOVSKY, ALICE. 2003. 'Mikhail Zhvanetskii: The Last Russian-Jewish Joker'. In M. Berkowitz, S. L. Tananbaum, and S. W. Bloom, eds, *Forging Modern Jewish Identities*. London.

NORDAU, MAX. 1980 [1903]. Jewry of Muscle. In P. R. Mendes-Flohr and J. Reinharz, eds, *The Jew in the Modern World: A Documentary History*. New York.

NOSENKO, ELENA. 2004. *Byt' ili chuvstvovat'? Osnovnye aspekty formirovaniya evreiskoi samoidentifikatsii u potomkov smeshannykh brakov v sovremennoi Rossii*. Moscow.

PORTUGES, CATHERINE. 2005. 'Traumatic Memory, Jewish Identity: Remapping the Past in Hungarian Cinema'. In A. Imre, ed., *East European Cinemas*. New York.

PRELL, RIV-ELLEN. 1996. 'Why Jewish Princesses Don't Sweat: Desire and Consumption in Postwar American Jewish Culture'. In N. L. Kleeblatt, ed., *Too Jewish? Challenging Traditional Identities*, 74–93. New York and New Brunswick, NJ.

REMENNICK, LARISSA. 2006. *Russian Jews on Three Continents: Identity, Integration, and Conflict*. New Brunswick, NJ.

RYVKINA, ROZALINA. 2005. *Kak zhivut evrei v Rossii? Sotsiologicheskii analiz peremen*. Moscow.

SALNIKOVA, ELENA. 2001. 'V yubilei "Lyubvi" snimaetsya "Lyubovnik"', *Nezavisimaya gazeta*, 8 Dec.

SCOTT, GEORGE M. 1990. 'A Resynthesis of the Primordial and Circumstantial Approaches to Ethnic Group Solidarity: Towards an Explanatory Model', *Ethnic and Racial Studies*, 13(2): 147–71.

SHTERNSHIS, ANNA. 2006. *Soviet and Kosher: Jewish Popular Culture in the Soviet Union, 1923–1939*. Bloomington, Ind.

SINGERMAN, ROBERT. 2001. *Jewish Given Names and Family Names: A New Bibliography*. Leiden.

SLEZKINE, YURI. 2004. *The Jewish Century*. Princeton, NJ.

SMITH, ANTHONY D. 1998. *Nationalism and Modernism: A Critical Survey of Recent Theories of Nations and Nationalism*. London.

SUTCLIFFE, ADAM. 2003. *Judaism and Enlightenment*. New York.

SVET, GERSHON. 1968. 'Evrei v russkoi muzykal'noi kul'ture v sovetskii period'. In Y. G. Frumkin, G. Y. Aronson, and A. A. Goldenveizer, eds, *Kniga o russkom evreistve*, 248–65. New York.

TANNEN, DEBORAH. 1981. 'New York Jewish Conversational Style', *International Journal of the Sociology of Language*, 30: 133–49.

TOLTS, MARK. 2004. 'The Post-Soviet Jewish Population in Russia and the World', *Jews in Russia and Eastern Europe*, 1(52): 37–63.

YELENEVSKAYA, MARIYA, and LARISA FIALKOVA. 2005. *Russkaya ulitsa v evreiskoi strane: Issledovanie fol'klora emigrantov 1990-kh v Izraile*. Moscow.

EIGHT

The Delicatessen as an Icon of Secular Jewishness

TED MERWIN

Most of the big, old-school Jewish delis in New York are old—Katz's, Second Avenue, Carnegie. Artie's, by comparison, is new. Erected in 1999, Artie's doesn't drip with the same kvetching immigrant history, but it does drip with the same kvetching immigrant pickled brine. In the heart of Upper West Side schmooze, the low-key deli aims to please its core contingency while not alienating a contemporary secular crowd unfamiliar with abstract concepts like kugel, knish, and lox. The menu is made up of the classics—try the pastrami and corned beef Reuben with sauerkraut, flanken in a pot with mushroom barley, and a big tuna salad platter. The Hebrew National hot dogs and burgers are biblically big, and one of the latter even boasts strips of pastrami sunbathing on top of its patty. By the time you get to dessert (home-made ruggelach, apple strudel, more pastrami), the only thing you'll wish was history are your clogged, kvetching arteries.[1]

Is there a more instantly recognizable symbol of American Jewish culture than the Jewish deli? For many, Jews and non-Jews, the very words 'Jewish delicatessen', with their overtones of the fatty, salty dishes of east European cuisine, make the mouth water. Anyone who lived in a Jewish neighbourhood in New York City in the first half of the twentieth century will tell you that there was a Jewish deli on every block. Today the deli has become so identified with Jews that it has become a symbol for Jewish life in general, a shorthand for American Jewish culture. Jews and delis are inextricably linked in the American popular imagination. Furthermore, as the above review of Artie's, a 'kosher-style' delicatessen in New York, written by Yon Motskin in the *AOL City Guide*, suggests, Jewish food lies at the heart of contemporary 'secular' Jewish identity.

This essay will draw on historical research, images and representations of the deli in pop culture, and postmodern theory to demonstrate the functional relations between the deli as a central ritual space of secular Jewishness and the ways in which deli food is both commodified and nostalgicized to make the deli a Jewish cultural signpost. Indeed, this symbolic role is increasing as actual delis close, at least in the New York area, where they once were a central feature of the urban landscape and a crucial repository of Jewish culture.

That the deli could be a potentially 'sacred' space for secular Jews is nothing new. As Hasia Diner (2000) and Jenna Weissman Joselit (1996) have pointed out in their work on the construction of the Lower East Side in American Jewish culture, the immigrant ghetto became invested with an almost religious aura; it became a place of pilgrimage for later generations of American Jews. On the other hand, Artie's location in the heart of the Upper West Side, a ritzy neighbourhood where many secular, upwardly mobile Jews live, ideally situates it to appeal to the ambivalence that many Jews feel about their own tradition by providing non-kosher Jewish food in a modern setting. As Artie's website boasts, while the food signals the 'comeback of a heritage almost lost', the overall restaurant is quite up to date. Indeed, 'the wine list is contemporary; the service staff is young and knowledgeable and the music up-beat and hip'.[2]

Motskin seems attentive to this paradox; he warns the reader that Artie's is a new-fangled, 'low-key' Jewish deli that walks a thin line between giving its presumably Jewish customer base the dishes that they remember from their youth and also satisfying the 'contemporary secular crowd' whose tastebuds still need to be educated. Interestingly, he seems to ignore the possibility that the 'secular crowd' could—and almost definitely would—include Jews, and he implies that even Jews might not be conversant with some of their own traditional foods. At the same time, he undermines his own distinction between those who are knowledgeable about Jewish culture and those who are not by his frequent use of Yiddishisms ('kvetching', 'schmooze'), which he seems to take for granted will be understood by every reader. With his offhand invocation of religion—summed up in his comment that the frankfurters and hamburgers are of 'biblical' proportions—his description of the pastrami as 'sunbathing' on top of a burger, his joke that Artie's patrons eat pastrami even for dessert, and his waving away of history as a kind of irrelevancy, Motskin himself seems to speak for a stereotypical postmodern secular Jew, whose nostalgia is constantly undercut by irony, whose lack of religious faith is far from a source of angst, and whose Jewishness is mostly inseparable from bodily pleasure.

Are you what you eat, or rather what your parents and grandparents ate? We may inherit our ethnic identity, but it is given meaning partly by the ethnic food that we are fed, and by the sense that we are eating the same foods that our forebears did. The old joke that all Jewish holidays can be summed up in one line— 'They tried to kill us. We won. Let's eat!'—emphasizes the extent to which many Jews, impatient with lengthy remembrances and rituals, see food as emblematic of Jewish tradition. As communications scholar Wendy Leeds-Hurwitz asks, 'Why are foods among the last identity markers to be abandoned?' despite the fact, as she rightly points out, that food often divides the generations as much as it unites them, causing conflict between different ways of relating to tradition (Leeds-Hurwitz 1993: 97–8).

Nevertheless, the chain of our existence is reinforced most palpably at mealtimes, especially in the company of those eating the same food. If, for sociologist Emile Durkheim, eating a communal meal makes us all one, in that the very substance of our bodies is altered by the food that we share, does eating in a crowded

Jewish deli make us all Jewish, at least temporarily? Even take-out can create ethnicity; as Kate Simon wrote in her lyrical memoir of her childhood during the interwar period, the Sunday evening 'company' meal in her secular Jewish family included 'slices of salami and corned beef, a mound of rye bread, pickles sliced lengthwise, and the mild mustard dripped into slender paper cones from a huge bottle, gratis with each order. The drinks were celery tonic or cream soda, nectars we were allowed only on state occasions, in small glasses' (Simon 1982: 117–18).

According to cookbook author Joan Nathan, 'More than anything else the delicatessen became *the* "Jewish eating experience" in this country' (Nathan 1998: 185). Indeed, eating deli became as important a part of many Jews' lives as Jewish rituals and religious observances. The eating of deli food was, in many ways, an invented tradition; Jews living in an east European shtetl almost never ate meat of any kind, save perhaps for chicken on the sabbath; beef was consumed only on special occasions. It was only on the Lower East Side of New York that pickled and smoked cuts of beef became incorporated into the Jewish diet.

For the poor, delicatessen fare represented both sustenance and long-denied pleasure. In *Bread Givers*, Anzia Yezierska's semi-autobiographical novel of poverty on the Lower East Side, she describes her frantic desire for meat when she is starving from working in a sweatshop, so that 'whenever I passed a restaurant or a delicatessen store, I couldn't tear my eyes away from the food in the window. Something wild in me wanted to break through the glass, snatch some of that sausage and corned-beef, and gorge myself just once' (Yezierska 1999: 165). In Sholem Aleichem's story 'Tevye Strikes It Rich' the dairyman is rewarded for conveying two rich ladies home to their dacha; the feast that is spread before him includes foods that he can never afford for his own family, including 'soup brimming with fat, roast meats, [and] a whole goose'. Tevye is stunned: 'I stood a ways off and thought, so, this, God bless them, is how these Yehupetz tycoons eat and drink . . . The crumbs that fell from that table alone would have been enough to feed my kids for a week, with enough left over for the Sabbath' (Aleichem 1996: 13).

Eating meat connoted upward mobility, as in the story that Morris Raphael Cohen, the Jewish philosopher and legal scholar, told about his immigrant uncle, who used to go around with a toothpick wiggling in his mouth to show off that he had just eaten meat (Diner 2003: 164). Meat was such a luxury, and was so highly taxed, that only the wealthy could afford to eat it on a regular basis. In America, to be able to eat meat represented nothing less than the attainment of the American Dream.

The Growth of the Deli

Delicatessens (derived from the German word for 'delicacies') emerged in the aftermath of late eighteenth- and early nineteenth-century wars and revolutions

Figure 1 Many Jews who grew up in New York recall that there was a kosher deli 'on every corner' in interwar Brooklyn neighbourhoods like the one shown in this photo, and that 'eating deli' was a Sunday-night ritual. *Photo from the collection of Ted Merwin*

in Europe. Gourmet stores, featuring imported foodstuffs, were first opened in west European capitals by former chefs to royalty. They spread to the major cities of eastern Europe by the nineteenth century, where they served an affluent clientele that included few Jews.

While history books tend to skip over the phenomenon of the Jewish delicatessen, aficionados recite the names of vanished delis as if they are summoning up the spirits of the departed. From Grabstein's in Canarsie to Cousin's on Kings Highway; from Mother's on the Grand Concourse to Zeimar's in Brighton Beach; from Aaron's in Coney Island to Benny's in the garment district; from Weitzman's on Delancey Street to Schmulke Bernstein's on Essex Street—these delis were landmarks in their New York neighbourhoods. Like Jo Goldenberg's on the Rue des Rosiers in Paris or Bloom's of Golders Green in London, they served generations of Jews for whom no celebration—wedding, bar mitzvah, *bris* (circumcision), or *shiva* (the gathering after a funeral)—was complete without fresh deli food.

Beginning as *schlacht* (provisions) stores with deli meats, canned beans, and ketchup for sale, Jewish 'delicatessen stores' developed into sandwich shops with grills for heating hot dogs and knishes, and then into full-fledged restaurants with take-out counters. They spread throughout the country and became indispensable symbols not just of Jewishness but also of New York in general. Indeed, film-maker Orson Welles famously quipped that 'without pastrami sandwiches, there could be no picture making' (*Commentary* 1946).

Jewish deli food carried a host of connotative and symbolic meanings, connected to nurture, tradition, and community. The Jewish deli was always about much more than food; it was a linchpin of communal life in Jewish neighbourhoods where business deals were made, gossip was retailed, and political campaigns were launched. Delis were places where politicians wanted to press the flesh and be photographed eating down-to-earth Jewish food, where Jewish comedians gathered to practise their jokes on each other, where young Jews could go out on dates or meet potential mates. They were, in short, where the life of the Jewish community was carried on.

As Joselit has pointed out, the kosher delicatessen in particular served as a communal meeting ground, where Jews of all religious and political persuasions could break bread—inevitably rye with caraway seeds—together. She calls it a 'neutral Jewish place', that 'signaled Jewishness in the public square, transcending traditional divisions between different types of Jews'.[3] It was a place where Jews who came from different countries in eastern Europe began to form a more unitary Ashkenazi American Jewish identity. It was a place where non-Jews could sample Jewish culture in a comfortable environment—unlike, for example, the Yiddish theatre, which few outsiders could enjoy.

While the hole-in-the-wall delis on the Lower East Side in the late nineteenth and early twentieth centuries were cramped and unprepossessing, they had not yet spawned their rebellious offspring. This changed in the interwar era, when the over-stuffed sandwiches named after stage stars that Jews ate with cheesecake in the theatre district delis such as Reuben's and Lindy's (or in Junior's in Brooklyn) gave off an aura of fame and celebrity. It was no accident that both the gangster Arnold Rothstein and, later, the radio personality Walter Winchell used deli tables as their offices, doing all their business while munching on corned beef sandwiches and pickles. During the Second World War, with meat rations firmly in place, deli food overcame suspicions connected to its Germanic roots by creating patriotic associations summed up in the slogan of Katz's delicatessen, 'Send a Salami to Your Boy in the Army'.

By the 1960s, the deli was firmly entrenched in popular culture, through the comedy routines of Jewish entertainers ranging from Sid Caesar to Mickey Katz. But during this and the following decade a growing preoccupation with healthy eating led deli food to be demonized as high in fat and cholesterol, not to mention being too low-class to grease the wheels of either business or romance. Candle-lit kosher gourmet restaurants like La Kasbah, Levana's, and Benjamin of Tudela (named after the legendary medieval Spanish explorer) catered to the growing yuppie crowd that preferred kosher versions of French, Moroccan, and north

Italian specialities to plebeian deli soups and sandwiches. Observant Jews appeared to seek 'lighter alternatives to the gastronomic barbells of dairies and delicatessens', in the words of Bryan Miller (1986), then food critic of the *New York Times*.

Perhaps the eating of Jewish deli food became a civil religion in its own right, even though many Jews had begun to gravitate towards Chinese food on Sunday nights. As food writer Mimi Sheraton wrote in the *New York Times*, 'One of the few hard and fast rules of thumb in the otherwise mercurial restaurant business is that a Chinese restaurant will have the best chance of success if it opens in a Jewish neighborhood' (Sheraton 1980: 44). As Gaye Tuchman and Harry Gene Levine (1993) have speculated, Jews were drawn to Chinese food because it seemed exotic and cosmopolitan, had similar flavours and methods of preparation to Jewish food, and was so diced up that Jews could enjoy forbidden foods like pork without thinking too much about what they were eating. Chinese restaurants—always open on Christmas Eve, when Jews needed to find their own way of celebrating the season—were also relatively non-threatening: the Chinese were generally viewed as being of even lower social status than the Jews.

One can therefore trace the steep decline in the number of Jewish delis to a host of factors, including the suburbanization of the Jewish population, the rise of health consciousness, the unwillingness of the younger generation of Jews to work in a low-status occupation, the turn by Jews towards Chinese food and other 'cosmopolitan' ethnic cuisines, and the overall globalization of the American palate.

By the early years of the twenty-first century, most delis, especially the kosher ones (which, since they flouted Jewish law by remaining open on Saturdays and Jewish holidays, were not kosher enough for the growing Orthodox population), had closed. The shuttering of the half-century-old Second Avenue deli in January 2006 was viewed as the end of an era; as one downcast blogger put it, 'sic transit gloria matzoh balls'.[4]

The Creation of Group Identity

But what do Jews mean when they talk about Jewish food? Jews have lived in diasporic conditions for millennia, and have absorbed the foodways of each civilization that they have inhabited. What constitutes Jewish food for a Jewish immigrant from Israel, or from Yemen, or from Russia for that matter, may bear little or no relationship to anything that an American Jew would recognize: when most American-born Jews think of Jewish food, they tend to think of foods that are actually Russian, Polish, Romanian, or Hungarian in origin. Claudia Roden calls Jewish food 'the cooking of a nation within a nation, of a culture within a culture, the result of the interweaving of two or more cultures. The almost complete dispersion of the old communities has radiated their styles of cooking in different parts of the world.' (Roden 1998: 11)

The foodways of an ethnic group accomplish many different functions in the constitution of that group's identity. Jews apply the concept of kosher and non-kosher to many aspects of life beyond food: a 'kosher yid' is a good Jew, and non-Jews were traditionally seen as *trayfe* when it came to their eligibility as marital partners. In like manner, some non-Jewish Europeans associated Jews with noxious odours, especially garlic; the foods that Jews ate made them seem unfit for participation in polite society. As Linda Keller Brown and Kay Mussell have written, 'Foodways bind individuals together, define the limits of the group's outreach and identity, distinguish in-group from out-group, serve as a medium of inter-group communication, celebrate cultural cohesion, and provide a context for performance of group ritual' (Brown and Mussell 1984: 5). The consumption of ethnic food does not just reinforce ethnic identity; it actively helps to create it, and for American Jews eating deli food continues to be a way of 'performing' their ethnicity, both for themselves and for others. As sociologists Shun Lu and Gary Alan Fine have written in an article on the presentation of Chinese food, 'In contemporary American society, ethnicity is revealed as much by symbolism through public display as by any other factor' (Lu and Fine 1995: 535).

Indeed, the deli is a place where Jews go to 'see and be seen'. In a recent episode of the television series *Curb Your Enthusiasm* (first broadcast in 2000), actor Larry David has a sandwich named after him in a fictitious Los Angeles deli, which is depicted as a hangout for Hollywood stars who battle over who gets their name attached to which sandwich. Even during High Holiday services at the local synagogue, the characters squabble over these sandwich-naming rights, their minds more set on physical cravings than spiritual transcendence. As in Woody Allen's film *Broadway Danny Rose* (1984), in which a group of ageing comedians trade jokes in a back room in the Carnegie deli in New York, the deli is shown as the site of socio-cultural transactions in which not only is Jewishness publicly affirmed but the meaning of Jewish identity is contested and redefined.

A recent survey found that the number of Jews defining themselves as Jewish by religion or ancestry fell from 80 per cent in 1990 to just 68 per cent in 2001, while those defining their Jewishness in secular terms rose from 20 to 32 per cent during that same period (Mayer, Kosmin, and Keysar 2001: 20). Samuel Heilman (1995) and Samuel Freedman (2001) have both described the growing divisions between different types of American Jews, with Heilman in particular pointing to a bifurcated Jewish populace, with increasing numbers of Jews gravitating either to the secular or the religious extreme.

But when Jews are asked what it means to affirm a Jewish identity in the absence of religious commitment, they tend, overwhelmingly, to profess a predilection for Jewish food. If, for Frederic Jameson, the Bonaventure Hotel in San Francisco was the perfect symbol of the postmodern age in its 'milling confusion', perhaps the chaotic Jewish deli is, for the secular Jew, the ideal symbol of his postmodern secular Jewishness. De-affiliated from religion, mostly illiterate in his own tradition, and given over to nostalgia, the secular Jew is yet drawn to a type of eating establishment that, if it doesn't 'drip' with history, at least drips with a kind of simulacrum of it. Is this so different from the type of nostalgia that advertisers in other fields frequently try to tap into? Take Ralph Lauren's 'Safari' fashion and perfume line, which theorist Linda Hutcheon calls a 'combination of commercial nostalgia—that teaches us to miss things we have never lost—and "armchair nostalgia"—that exists without any lived experience of the yearned-for time'.[5]

That Jewish food should be an object of nostalgia is perhaps nothing new. Nevertheless, one looks in vain in the writings of secular Jewish European intellectuals such as Chaim Zhitlovsky, Simon Dubnow, or Ahad Ha'am for a sense that a non-religious, often Zionist, form of Jewish belonging should be based on foodways. By dedicating themselves to the emancipation of Jews from discriminatory treatment, and thus to gaining full citizenship for Jews in the European societies in which they dwelled, supporters of the Haskalah saw it as necessary to cast off sentimental attachments to Jewish foodways in the interests of building a more rational, less superstitious foundation for Jewish life.

The maskilim's modern-day, university-educated counterparts in America have become 'more American than the Americans', as the phrase goes, in terms of their success in American society. What came naturally to many of their Yiddish-speaking parents and grandparents—a Jewish identity based on socialism or anarchism, a Jewish culture that reinvented Jewish ritual as a tool of resistance against a society that insisted that Jews were second-class citizens—no longer speaks to the comfortably acculturated Jews of today. Perhaps it is no wonder, then, that food has become the one remaining link that many secular Jews have to their heritage.

American Jews also no longer tend to fit the residential and social patterns that marked earlier generations. Many no longer live in neighbourhoods with dense Jewish populations, in which they tended to socialize and conduct business mostly with other Jews. The intermarriage rate is now close to 50 per cent, and two-thirds of the children of these intermarriages are not raised as Jews.[6] Secular Jews are not, in the main, linked by a shared sense of oppression, a common framework of belief based on the Torah, or an overriding commitment to Jewish peoplehood. Judaism's emphasis on this-worldly pleasure and its many food-centred holidays (including the sabbath, viewed traditionally as the greatest of all the holidays in the Jewish calendar, despite its weekly recurrence) have contributed to the placement of food as a cornerstone of contemporary American Jewish culture.

Some secular Jews, who tend to describe themselves as 'humanistic', even have their own movement within American Judaism. While this movement used to be considered a fringe phenomenon, it is rapidly gaining visibility. Rabbi Peter

Schweitzer, spiritual leader of the City Congregation for Humanistic Judaism in New York, regularly contributes his views on controversial religious topics in Judaism (for example life after death) to the feature in *Moment Magazine* in which rabbis from across the denominational spectrum are represented. Rabbi Schweitzer's wife, Myrna Baron, directs the Center for Cultural Judaism in New York, an organization that channels money from a Swiss foundation established by British philanthropist Felix Posen to a variety of secular Jewish causes, including funding college and university courses on secular Judaism on dozens of campuses (including my own).

But when Rabbi Schweitzer recently gave away his entire collection of American Judaica (comprising more than ten thousand items) to the American Museum of Jewish History in Philadelphia, the first exhibit mounted by the museum dealt with—what else?—Jewish food. As Schweitzer told the Jewish weekly newspaper *Forward*, 'for many the delicatessen is just as sacred a place as the *shul* [synagogue]' (Yaffa 2006: 18;). At a time when delis are disappearing from the New York landscape—there are now only a few dozen in the entire metropolitan area—one does actually need to make a pilgrimage of sorts to eat in one.

Many observers from across the Jewish spectrum are offended by the notion that food can serve as a durable basis for Jewish identity. Even the late founder of the Humanist Movement, Rabbi Sherwin Wine, expressed dismay at the idea. Trying to dispel the common assumption that Jewish food and Jewish humour are virtually all that is left to secular Jews, Wine said that 'a life of courage is not about food; it is filled with Jewish memories, Jewish inspiration and philosophy' (the idea that the Jewish memories might be memories of eating Jewish food did not seem to occur to him).[7]

More observant Jews also often look down on their bagel-eating counterparts, although an enjoyment of Jewish food is hardly limited to Jews who disclaim religious observance. 'We do not know', a Conservative synagogue in Princeton, New Jersey, pointed out in a statement on the importance of outreach to intermarried families, 'which Bar or Bat Mitzvah child will go on to be a rabbi, the president of Hadassah, an active congregant, a bagels-and-lox Jew or an adherent to another faith, but that doesn't stop us from investing heavily in religious school year after year.'[8] In the minds of the lay leaders of the congregation, resources needed to be expended on those who seemed to be on the verge of leaving the fold. This included the marginal, 'bagels and lox' Jew, who occupied a position on the communal ladder just one rung above the Jew who converts to another religion.

The Semiotics of the Jewish Deli

In America, the names of the kosher food companies were carefully chosen to appeal to Jews whose Jewishness was more a matter of ethnic pride than religious commitment. Almost all Jews were expected to identify with the notion of Jewish

peoplehood and solidarity with other Jews. Thus, even before the modern State of
Israel was established in 1948, companies chose names like Hebrew National
and Zion Kosher to suggest that a sense of Jewish peoplehood could be reinforced
through consumption of pastrami and corned beef.

Hebrew National's famous slogan, 'We Answer to a Higher Authority',
invented in 1965, implies fidelity to the sacred while implicitly claiming that their
products are of higher quality than non-kosher foods. The company's television
commercials, featuring Uncle Sam gazing upwards, emphasized, in a joking
manner, that eating kosher products was not incompatible with being fully American and up to date. As food writer Matthew Goodman has noted, 'This prodi-
gious bit of marketing jiujitsu took the kosher laws, which never had mattered to
more than a very small segment of the population, and made them a selling point
for the population at large' (Goodman 2004). The idea of kosher supervision was
presented in a jocular way, which worked equally well for both observant and secular Jews. (Ironically, most Orthodox Jews nowadays refuse to eat Hebrew
National products, because they no longer trust the organization that certifies the
products as kosher.)

Figure 2 The towering meat
sandwiches consumed in non-kosher
delis like the Carnegie (pictured here)
and the Stage represented the bounty
of America that Jews incorporated into
their foodways. *Photo: Kenneth Chen*

Even before entering the deli, the secular Jew could be reinvested with the grandeur of his tradition simply by seeing the neon window sign advertising the kosher meat companies. Whether the Hebrew National or Zion Kosher sign in New York or the Sinai 48 sign in Chicago, the mystical glowing letters, connected with tubes carrying the fantasmically coloured gas, had a kabbalistic fascination all their own. Just as the Zohar, the primary book of Jewish mysticism, says that the letters of the Torah were inscribed in 'black fire written on white fire', the lighted letters of the kosher deli signs hung in the air with the dazzling radiance of supernal energy.

For a secular Jew such as Alfred Kazin, the most vivid memory of Jewishness was when, at the magical moment of dusk on Saturday night, he would wait for the deli sign to be illuminated. 'At Saturday twilight, as soon as the delicatessen store reopened after the Sabbath rest, we raced into it panting for the hot dogs sizzling on the gas plate just inside the window. The look of that blackened empty gas plate had driven us wild all through the wearisome Sabbath day. And now, as the electric sign blazed up again, lighting up the words JEWISH NATIONAL DELICATESSEN, it was as if we had entered into our rightful heritage' (Kazin 1951: 34). It was those three words, Kazin recalls, that were the means of his deliverance. Not Hebrew words, not words from the Torah, but words from an advertising sign, that reunited him and his peers with their people. The signifier (sufficient, even before the signified was tasted or even seen) was able to reinstall—even as the electricity in the sign completed its own circuit—an overwhelming feeling of connection with Jewish tradition.

According to Baudrillard, consumer culture can be seen to be composed of a proliferation of signs, which have become free floating to the point that they are detached from their signifiers. Theorists of the Frankfurt School of neo-Marxist theory have been criticized, however, for their presentation of an undifferentiated mass culture, in which all consumers respond to advertising signs in the same way. This makes little sense in the case of the kosher deli sign, which was undoubtedly read differently by observant Jews (who ate only kosher food, and thus looked for kosher symbols on all food-related advertising and packaging), secular Jews (many of whom viewed kosher food as a special treat), and non-Jews (for whom kosher food represented something alien, even if pleasurably so).

Mike Featherstone has written that consumer goods can become 'de-commodified and receive a symbolic charge (over and above that intended by advertisers) which makes them sacred to their users' (1991: 121). In sharp contrast to other scholars, Featherstone concludes that consumerism, far from destroying the sacred, has co-opted it for its own purposes. By investing commercial goods with sacred qualities, advertisers are able to create an aura about their products that lifts them above the everyday.

Following Baudrillard's notion of the 'commodity sign' as a combination of the material and the symbolic, Davide Girardelli argues that contemporary Italian

American food should be theorized as a 'food package', a synthesis of the actual food and the ways in which it is commodified. His investigation of the 'Italian-icity' of a Fazoli's Italian restaurant franchise in a large city in the Midwest reveals that an array of both verbal and non-verbal marketing strategies combine to stoke feelings of nostalgia and yearning, promote the idea of Italian food as both healthy and 'rustic', and create the myth that eating Italian food makes 'everyone Italian', as one commercial for the chain suggests—an ethnic identity associated with romance, family, togetherness, and expressiveness. By promoting such asso-ciations, the restaurant chain implicitly claims a kind of 'authenticity' for the food that it serves, even as it offers such menu items as a 'traditional' Alfredo sauce, which in fact cannot be found anywhere in Italy (Girardelli 2004).

What works for an Italian restaurant, however, may not work for a Jewish deli. Fazoli's has little need to promote nostalgia for the Italian restaurant—with its red and white-checked tablecloths, its heavy sauces, and its wine bottles on the table—in America: Italy is a country that many Americans originate from or long to visit (or have already visited), and its food long ago joined the American diet. But Jewish deli food? How many Americans, whether Jewish or not, are inter-ested in either a real or nostalgic connection to eastern Europe, where millions were massacred in the Holocaust? Jewish culture may be pleasurably 'expressive' but every non-WASP culture is viewed as 'expressive' by contrast—just think of the films *Moonstruck* and *My Big Fat Greek Wedding*.

Recent Hollywood films about ethnic groups tend to showcase ethnic food as a symbol of family and ethnic cohesion. In these films, Diane Negra writes, food is a pleasurable symbol of bonds, both those between family members and those between members of an ethnic group. Food becomes an antidote to the anomie and instability of late capitalist society. In fact, as Negra perceptively notes, food is often referenced and displayed at moments in the films when commercial inter-ests become subsidiary to the claims of familial affection. While Negra does not use any Jewish films as examples, her discussion of comfort food is illuminating: she sees ethnic food as fetishized, as seeming to promise a kind of pleasurable infantile regression, an 'imagined return' to the bosom of the family and commu-nity. Yet she points out that this desire inevitably gives rise to a sense of ambiva-lence, since the fantasized return is in tension with the need to move forward and not be weighed down by the past (Negra 2002: 69).

Girardelli's case of the 'construction and commodification of the Italian ethnic identity' does have parallels to the case of the Jewish deli. The Second Avenue deli had an office above the restaurant where three women spent all day taking tele-phone orders from customers across the country who were dying for an authentic matzoh ball soup, a plate of pastrami, a loaf of rye bread, and some rugelach. The prices were more than twice the usual restaurant prices—with overnight ship-ping charges included, it was hard to get a meal for less than a hundred bucks. Even nowadays, in any Jewish deli in New York, a soup and sandwich can easily

Figure 3 Meat companies such as Hebrew National, Zion Kosher and 999 (pictured here) distributed neon signs, clocks, and other advertising paraphernalia to delis that sold their kosher products. *Photo courtesy of the National Museum of American Jewish History*

run upwards of $20, and that's before adding the tax and tip. Jewish deli food is so pricey that one would be unlikely to eat it more than once a week even if it weren't so artery-clogging and gassy.

Jewish delis 'construct' Jewish identity in different ways. While Katz's still maintains a grungy, cafeteria-style decor in keeping with the unpretentiousness of the neighbourhood, the Ben's chain of delis on Long Island (in addition to a large restaurant in the garment district in Manhattan and another one in Boca Raton) depends on a glamorous art deco aesthetic to flatter Jewish baby boomers' self-image, their self-congratulation on their economic success; it links them to the period in which Jews were just beginning to convince themselves that they had an inalienable right to a hefty cheesecake-like slice of American society. Meanwhile the most successful of all Jewish delis, the Carnegie, has its walls plastered with photos of entertainers, politicians, and other celebrities who have eaten there—suggesting, implicitly, that Jews are 'kosher' in the minds of the movers and shakers in America.

It has often been remarked that Jews are a people who, while perpetually seeming to be on the verge of disappearing, have perennially managed yet one more astonishing come-back. Perhaps the Jewish deli is itself awaiting such a miraculous resurrection. But postmodern Jewish culture has a built-in quality of impermanence: it takes new forms in every generation.

When Jews were outsiders in American society, it was difficult for their Jewishness not to be at the core of their identity. But the identity of postmodern Jews seems to lack a centre: doing what has been described as a kind of iPod shuffle, each of its many components comes to the fore only temporarily and sporadically. For young Jews, in particular, Jewishness is not their primary identification; it is only one of many different ways in which they understand themselves and their place in the world.

Deli food consumed in other settings may taste the same, but the experience of eating it is quite different. It may still provide nurture, but it is not linked in the same way to participation in the community; the public dimension is missing. The only way that most Jews now get to see the inside of a deli is on film or television, as for example the VH1 documentary *So Jewtastic* (2005) about the rise of Jewish celebrities (including heavy metal rockers, wrestlers, and porn stars), which included a segment in which comedian Elon Gold interviewed patrons of Canter's deli in Los Angeles, showing them a piece of gefilte fish to see if they could identify it, and asking why bagels have a hole.

Eating take-away deli food permits Jews to do other things at the same time, such as watch television, so that they are only partly occupied with Jewish associations as they eat. This makes sense in an era in which declining numbers of Jews organize their identity around their Jewishness. As Jennifer Bleyer has written, many young Jews see Judaism as only one item on their personal menu:

For some, I began to think, being Jewish was the big honking main-course brisket on their identity dinner tables. Everything they do, everyone they know is Jewish, everything they see is through a Jewish lens. Maybe they have a couple of side-dish identities—being a woman, a litigation attorney, from St. Louis—but by and large, they are big Jewey Jews. But then, there were people for whom identity itself is more of a dim sum, and their Jewish part like one small, tasty (mock) ham dumpling amid a variety of other yummy treats. I was a dim sum Jew, and so were most of my friends. (Bleyer 2005: 31)

There may be secular Jews who still view their Jewishness as at the core of their identity, but their number is diminishing with the general decline of *Yiddishkeit* —all those aspects of east European Jewish culture that, while they were transformed in an American context, still served as a powerful glue not just for immigrants but for their children and grandchildren. Deli food is only one aspect of Jewish culture that is beginning to lose its salience as a symbol of Jewish identity. Jews may have been one of the first ethnic groups to discover Chinese food, and even made its consumption part of their identity, but even Chinese food has been relentlessly mainstreamed. Indeed, the kosher Chinese restaurant has replaced the deli as the *sine qua non* of any self-respecting Jewish community with a sizeable percentage of Orthodox Jews. Many of these Chinese restaurants also serve sushi, mirroring overall trends towards 'pan-Asian' and 'fusion' cuisine.

Nor is deli food found only in delis; bagels have become assimilated into the American diet and deli meats have been widely available in supermarkets since the 1950s. With sandwich nationwide franchises like Subway and Quiznos now offering pastrami sandwiches, most consumers feel little need to soak up the Jewish atmosphere in a deli when they can eat the same food at home. Most Jews live in suburbs, disconnected from strong networks of Jewish activity, and where 'mom and pop' stores of all kinds, not just delis, are closing in the face of competition from Walmart and other huge chain stores.

Perhaps the delicatessen as a communal meeting ground is being replaced by other forms of Jewish culture. Jewish book, music, and film festivals continue to proliferate, new Jewish websites spring up every day, and no top university is without a programme in Judaic studies. Yet these provide mostly intellectualized, disembodied forms of Jewish cultural consumption. With every bite and crunch in a Jewish deli, previous generations of Jews connected to their Jewish identity, which they associated with comfort and nurture. In the absence of the deli, can anything nourish secular Jewish identity in quite the same way?

Notes

1   <www.cityguide.aol.com/newyork/restaurants/arties-new-york-delicatessen/v-106973475>.

2   <www.arties.com>, accessed 20 Nov. 2006.

3   Interview with the author, 8 Jan. 2006,

4   <www.roadfood.com/Forums/topic.asp?TOPIC_ID=11018>.

5   <www.library.utoronto.ca/utel/criticism/hutchinp.html>.

6   See the *National Jewish Population Survey 2000–2001*, and the *United Jewish Communities Report*, Sept. 2003 (updated Jan. 2004): <www.ujc.org/local_includes/downloads/temp/njps2000-01_revised_1.06.04.pdf>.

7   <www.jewishsightseeing.com/usa/california/san_diego/cong_beth_israel/reform_humanist.htm>.

8   <www.thejewishcenter.org/InclusionRpt.htm>.

References

ALEICHEM, SHOLEM. 1996. *Tevye the Dairyman and the Railroad Stories*, trans. Hillel Halkin. New York.

BLEYER, JENNIFER. 2005. 'Among the Holy Schleppers'. In Ruth Andrew Ellenson, ed., *The Modern Jewish Girl's Guide to Guilt*. New York.

BROWN, LINDA KELLER, and KAY MUSSELL. 1984. *Ethnic and Regional Foodways in the United States: The Performance of Group Identity*. Knoxville, Tenn.

Commentary. 1946. 'From the American Scene: One Touch of Delicatessen', *Commentary*, 2(1) (July): 67–72.

DINER, HASIA. 2000. *Lower East Side Memories*. Princeton.

—— 2003. *Hungering for America: Italian, Irish, and Jewish Foodways in the Age of Migration*. Cambridge, Mass.

FEATHERSTONE, MIKE. 1991. *Consumer Culture and Postmodernism*. London.

FREEDMAN, SAMUEL. 2001. *Jew vs. Jew: The Struggle for the Soul of American Jewry*. New York.

GIRARDELLI, DAVIDE. 2004. 'Commodified Identities: The Myth of Italian Food in the United States', *Journal of Communication Inquiry*, 28(4): 307–24.

GOODMAN, MATTHEW. 2004. 'Good Dog! A Summer Taste Treat', *Forward* (23 July).

HEILMAN, SAMUEL. 1995. *Portrait of American Jews: The Last Half of the Twentieth Century*. Seattle, Wash.

JOSELIT, JENNA WEISSMAN. 1996. 'Telling Tales, or How a Slum Became a Shrine', *Jewish Social Studies*, 2(2): 54–63.

KAPLAN, MORDECHAI. 1994. *Judaism as a Civilization*. New York.

KAZIN, ALFRED. 1951. *A Walker in the City*. New York.

LEEDS-HURWITZ, WENDY. 1997. *Semiotics and Communication: Signs, Codes, Cultures*. Hillsdale, NJ.

LU, SHUN, and GARY ALAN FINE. 1995. 'The Presentation of Ethnic Authenticity: Chinese Food as Social Accomplishment', *The Sociological Quarterly*, 36(3): 535–53.

MAYER, EGON, BARRY KOSMIN, and ARIELA KEYSAR. 2001. *American Jewish Identity Survey*. New York; available at <www.culturaljudaism.org/pdf/ajisbook.pdf>.

MERWIN, TED. 2006. 'Hold Your Tongue', *New York Jewish Week*, 13 Jan.

MILLER, BRYAN. 'Kosher Dining Out: The Options Grow', *New York Times*, 8 Oct. 1986: C1.

NATHAN, JOAN. 1998. *Jewish Cooking in America*. New York.

NEGRA, DIANE. 2002. 'Ethnic Food Fetishism, Whiteness, and Nostalgia in Recent Films and Television', *The Velvet Light Trap*, 50: 62–76.

RODEN, CLAUDIA. 1998. *The Book of Jewish Food: An Odyssey from Samarkand to New York*. New York.

SHERATON, MIMI. 1980. 'Moo Goo Gai Pan and Strictly Kosher', *New York Times*, 27 Dec.

SIMON, KATE. 1982. *Bronx Primitive*. New York.

TUCHMAN, GAYE, and HARRY GENE LEVINE. 1993. 'New York Jews and Chinese Food: The Social Construction of an Ethnic Pattern', *Journal of Contemporary Ethnography*, 22(3): 382–407.

YAFFA, JOSHUA. 2006. 'Historic Bites', *Forward*, 16 June.

YEZIERSKA, ANZIA. 1999. *Bread Givers*. New York.

PART III

Representation

NINE

Hasidism versus Zionism as Remembered by Carpatho-Russian Jews between the Two World Wars

ILANA ROSEN

PEOPLE broach disturbing topics in story that they may hesitate to bring up in conversation or writing. Frequently, the significance of the lore that people share orally is that it reflects the unity of the world-view of the culture about which it is told, and also reveals its conflicts. Such is the case with the oral personal narratives of present-day secular Israelis who come from the Carpatho-Russian diaspora.[1] These Israelis endorsed Zionism and underwent a process of moderating their national, cultural, and personal identity during the 1920s and 1930s.

Before the First World War most of Carpatho-Russian Jewry opposed the Zionist movement and excoriated families and youths who joined it. After the war, the Zionists, a minority group of never more than a few thousand divided into several ideological streams, founded the Hebrew academic high schools in the towns of Munkács and Ungvár,[2] organized groups of potential emigrants to Erets Yisra'el, prepared them for pioneering and agricultural life in a training process called *hakhsharah*, and, where possible, sent them on *aliyah* (literally 'ascent', but idiomatically meaning emigration) to Palestine. Until they emigrated, the newly recruited Zionists were often a cause of social and cultural upheaval in their home towns and villages, as they challenged the long-standing reign of hasidism by presenting an alternative new ethos.

Here I will deal with three kinds of conflict brought about by the rise of Zionism in Carpatho-Russia, as reflected in the personal narratives of people who came to Israel from that region as Zionists. One is the ideological, verbal, and physical battle between members of the two movements.[3] The second is the inner struggle of the region's Zionist youth while they were in transition between hasidism and Zionism. Thirdly, I will look at family relations and the conflicts that were the inevitable result of the first two clashes.

The Jews of Carpatho-Russia: A Historical and Cultural Survey

Jewish life in Carpatho-Russia began in the Middle Ages. However, historians cite three events which prompted large waves of Jewish emigration from the east westwards to Carpatho-Russia. These are the pogroms of 1648–9, the divisions of Poland in 1772, 1793, and 1795, and the emancipation of the Jews of the Austro-Hungarian empire in the 1860s (Dinur 1983; Stransky 1968). Each influx brought with it Jews striving to better their lives and, if possible, move further westwards or southwards to the more developed parts of the empire. In addition, there were also smaller waves of immigration to this region from the west, but the movement from the east outnumbered these by far. In the short period between the defeat of the empire at the end of the First World War and that of the Third Reich at the end of the Second World War, the region went through many changes of regime. But even before this period, it was known for its pluralism of nations, languages, and cultures, including Hungarian, Czech, Slovak, Ruthenian, German, and Hebrew/Yiddish.

The Jewish population of Carpatho-Russia, numbering about 100,000,[4] was roughly divided into two major geographic, demographic, and cultural areas: east and west. The eastern area, consisting mainly of the county of Máramaros,[5] was largely hasidic (encompassing the courts of Vizhnitz, Spinka, Belz, and some smaller groups), Yiddish-speaking, agricultural, and poor; the western area, which included the counties of Ugocsa, Bereg, and Ung, was less hasidic (notwithstanding the influential Munkács court), as it was influenced by the Hatam Sofer dynasty of Pressburg in the west.[6] The western counties were more Hungarian than Yiddish in terms of language and culture, less poor (although not affluent), and closer to industry because of the economic influence of Czecho-slovakia. Notwithstanding these distinctions, the region as a whole was con-sidered poor and undeveloped in comparison to both the south-east (Hungary) and the west (Czechoslovakia).

As for other trends and influences existing in neighbouring Jewish communi-ties in this period, such as the Haskalah or Jewish Enlightenment, secularism (as an influence separate from that of Zionism, as described in Arye Amikam's nar-rative below), communism, and conversion to Christianity, it is important to note the negligible influence of these movements in Carpatho-Russia in general. In fact, they are scarcely mentioned in the few authoritative academic studies of the region (such as Jelinek 1995, 1998, 2003[7]) or in the semi-historical writings of educated ex-Carpatho-Russians or the strictly personal accounts of Holocaust survivors from the region.

These writings on Zionism make little mention of the movement's formal activities, such as congresses, conventions, and fundraising, of the deeply felt differences between the various factions, or of the famous speeches by renowned Zionist figures, except when, like Berl Katznelson and Zeev (Vladimir) Jabotin-sky, they actually visited the region. Apparently, these formal organizational aspects were too remote from local young people, whose own accounts or reports (not necessarily written) are in fact more preoccupied with their own activities and identity. These revolved to a great extent around educational issues, such as learning Hebrew and using it in everyday conversation, studying in the Hebrew schools of Munkács and Ungvár, changing the content, form, and meaning of traditional holidays such as Hanukah and Tu Bishevat (the Jewish new year for trees), joining *hakhsharah* groups and camps, and the gradual change that was taking place in their ideology and lifestyle.

As for the relative support for hasidism and Zionism, the two major forces in the region, hasidism nominally outnumbered Zionism by ten to one, in terms of both the number of its adherents and its financial, social, and cultural resources. Nevertheless, as we will see in the narratives below, Zionism gradually deepened its roots in the region, to the extent that many households were divided or influenced by it, from those with a formal affiliation with the most rigorous hasidic court of Munkács to those who simply pursued a generally orthodox Jewish lifestyle. Moreover, although Zionism usually prided itself on its appeal to young people, who were more obvious candidates for *hakhsharah* and *aliyah*,[8] the narratives below reveal that the actions of sons and daughters were dependent on the support, or at least the silent acceptance, of parents and, at times, grandparents (the latter being a significant factor in these clan-like, middle-class extended families, whose members often co-operated in running a business or small-scale industry). Because these were intra-familial divisions, it is difficult to make any objective assessment of the extent of people's tacit support for Zionism in the region in the interwar years. Here I have worked on the assumption that, as the saying goes, behind (almost) every Zionist youngster there was a supportive older generation. In fact, Zionism was stronger than it appeared, and narratives such as those below thus become an important source of qualitative evidence of social attitudes, power relations, and ethnic sensitivities between Jews and their non-Jewish environment.

In the interwar period Jews throughout Carpatho-Russia enjoyed relative cultural prosperity as the Czechoslovak regime acknowledged the diversity of the region's various ethnic groups and encouraged them to use and develop their own language, culture, and education system (Sole 1968: i. 134; 1986). The Zionist movement took this permission a step further in the direction of the explicit formation of a Zionist national identity so that, when war broke out in 1939, the Zionists were organizationally and psychologically ready to uproot, as they were either already preparing to leave for Palestine (albeit this route was soon blocked for most of them) or better prepared to face rejection and exclusion, since they in any case conceived of themselves as not belonging to Carpatho-Russian society.[9] This does not mean that they actually survived the Holocaust in significantly greater numbers than non-Zionists, but rather that in their narratives they express a stronger sense of control of events than their non-Zionist brethren. In other words, these people perceived the war as a temporary delay in their plan to make *aliyah* rather than as the final demise of their home in the Diaspora.[10] Whatever their ideological disposition, the Jews of Carpatho-Russia as a whole were largely murdered in the Holocaust, and after the war the survivors re-established their lives[11] mostly in the newly created state of Israel and in North America (Gutman 1990: iv. 1472–3). To this day, the former hasidim and Zionists of Carpatho-Russia, wherever they are, argue bitterly, and mostly within their separate circles rather than with each other, about what would have happened had they not undermined each other, and—from the Zionist perspective—had hasidism not prevented thousands of potential emigrants from leaving for Palestine before the Holocaust.

The Oral Lore of the Jews of Carpatho-Russia

The narratives of the Jews of Carpatho-Russia presented here were gathered as part of a research project carried out in the 1990s by the Diaspora Research Institute of Tel Aviv University.[12] The project also included a historical study covering the period between 1848 and 1948.[13] It was supported by the World Union of the Jews of Carpatho-Russia and former students of the Hebrew schools. This in itself points to a significant development among present-day Israeli ethnic groups of central and east European origin, who have come to realize that to commemorate their past communities and traditions they first have to acknowledge their ethnicity apart from and in addition to their proud, Israeli identity. This is a new departure for them, as hitherto it was mainly the Jews from Islamic countries who perpetuated and took pride in their ethnic origins while acknowledging their new nationality.[14]

The fieldwork with the Carpatho-Russian community in Israel included interviews with fifty people, thirty-one men and nineteen women, who came from all over the region and who were mostly living in Israel at the time of the interview.[15] As can be seen from the narratives below, these people were from homes that were to some extent traditional, but most of them were now either less religiously observant or completely secular. Still, although none of the fifty was a 'practising' hasid, most were not as preoccupied with Zionist ideology and its past struggles as they were with present-day issues. Mostly retirees at the time of interview, most of them had acquired professions and held jobs throughout their lifetime. Many were now the parents and grandparents of accomplished sabras—born in Israel, and with a decidedly Israeli identity. In this, too, they differed from Israelis with roots in Islamic countries, many of whom still complain about their acceptance into their new country and about the attitudes of the Israeli authorities towards them despite the fact that they are long-established residents.

The folkloristic material of the interviews consists of 450 items,[16] divided into personal narratives, jokes, anecdotes, proverbs, riddles, ditties, curses, legends of every possible sub-genre, and oral history accounts, as well as static, non-narrative descriptions of customs, individuals, and groups. The characters in all these various categories are the narrators themselves; members of their extended families and communities; rabbis, teachers, and other religious functionaries; and fools and beggars. In terms of scope, the corpus reflects a wide range of experience and knowledge related to the religious and folk life of the Jewish communities of Carpatho-Russia. Among these are many stories involving conflict: conflict between Jews and non-Jews, between Jews of different persuasions, and between adults and children or women and men within the family circle, bearing out Yeshayahu Jelinek's description of the region's Jewish communities as being constantly preoccupied with conflicts and divisions concerning almost every area of their life, great and small (Jelinek 2003: 144–9).

Notwithstanding the richness of the material in all the categories, the personal narratives turned out to be the most rewarding in terms of their number and length, the degree of personal expression and exposure they contained, and their relevance to central communal and ideological issues. They were particularly used to broach painful topics. In addition to analysing the sensitivity to conflict in personal narrative, in keeping with William Labov's dramatic-linguistic model for the narrative analysis of personal experience I also looked at non-dramatic elements of the narrative, or elements which were external to the plot, which Labov terms 'evaluation' (Labov 1972; Labov and Waletzki 1967).[17] This kind of analysis offered in turn the possibility of viewing the personal narrative as predominantly 'expository discourse', following folklorist Gillian Bennett's term (Bennett 1986: 415–34), albeit not in the sense of justifying belief in unnatural events, as in her work, but in the sense of exposing and explaining one's inner world.

Hasidism versus Zionism

Even though Carpatho-Russian Jewish society historically had a number of socio-political divisions (including socialist and communist youth groups), it is significant in understanding the collective memory that the split between hasidic and Zionist groups dominated the narratives collected in Israel. The conflict between hasidism and Zionism occupies a central position in the oral tradition of Jews from Carpatho-Russia. Out of the 450 items in the entire narrative corpus, fifteen deal directly with this conflict and some of these are repeated with slight variations by several of the narrators. Fifteen other items, mainly personal narratives, relate to Zionist activity and lifestyle irrespective of the hasidic view of, or reaction to, it, or to the presumed attitude of hasidism towards Zionism. Eleven of these describe how the narrators became Zionists, the visits of famous Zionist figures to the region, the Zionist-national aspect of holidays, and the military-style glamour of Zionist educational or youth movement activities such as sports, trips, parades, and camps. As for the presumed hasidic view of all this, four of the fifteen depict the hasidim's objections to Zionism as part and parcel of hasidism's own backwardness, tendency towards superstition, and stereotypical thinking. It is important to note here that the preoccupation of these narratives with the tellers' lives and heritage as pioneering Zionists in an extremely hostile environment reverberates in many memoirs, semi-professional or amateurish histories, and strictly professional histories of the region dealing with this issue.[18]

As for the fifteen items devoted to direct conflict between the two movements, these can be divided into three thematic categories: (1) stories or the brief quotation of curses, witty sayings, bans, and other forms of hasidic attack on Zionism, including one report of a brother's funny imitation of the speech of the rabbi of Munkács (six items); (2) stories about struggles between the two movements concerning education, language, and identity (seven items); and (3) stories or claims blaming the hasidic rabbis for the outcome of the Holocaust (two items). In all three categories, two trends are prevalent. The first is the centrality of the figure of Rabbi Haim Eleazar Shapiro, the rabbi of Munkács (known as the Munkácser Rebbe), who figures prominently in nine of the fifteen items. The second trend is the apparently total passivity of the Zionists in the face of the hasidic offensive, which in many cases is carried out by means of curses and swear words of all kinds.[19] As for Rabbi Shapiro, he is characterized as ideologically extreme even in comparison to other hasidic leaders, such as the rabbis of Belz and Spinka, and also as merciless.[20] Moreover, the rabbi was not complaisant in words or gestures. Informants report that he would spit at rivals or even in the direction of an ex-rival's funeral procession. In his curses, he used—or rather abused—the Holy Scriptures to voice criticism of his enemies. Coming from the rabbi's mouth, these curses were not mere swear words, but speech which had an actual physical effect in the external world. They were live and contextualized illocutionary acts in terms of both speech act theory (see Austin 1965; Ohmann 1972; Searle 1969[21]) and magical psycho-anthropology.[22] Both these theories would suggest that it is very likely that people feared him and the possibility of his words coming true and hurting their addressees.

This fear led in turn to an almost complete lack of criticism of, or direct response to, the rabbi and his inept and heavy-handed ways, beyond describing his crude behaviour or quoting his offensive sayings and witticisms. This remained so even over half a century later in the accounts of many of the living narrators. They might cite what the rabbi said about the Zionists and his other opponents, but not what they said in return, to and about him (except for light mockery), or else they avoided the subject altogether. No one in the narratives openly contested the rabbi's negative stance regarding Zionism or his opposition to Zionist-related activities and events, such as his condemnation of the mixed-sex *hakhsharah* groups (Benedek, no. 25), or his vilification of a Zionist Hanukah play (Biggelman, no. 1). Narrators also reported that when an epidemic caused the death of two daughters in one family, the rabbi blamed it on the family for sending the girls to the Hebrew school (Hoffman, no. 2), but none of them challenged the rabbi's verdict either at the time or in their retrospective narratives. In this regard, therefore, Zionism remains remarkably mute.

The only time the Zionists come close to some sort of response to the rabbi's assault is in a seemingly bureaucratic but in fact highly symbolic struggle concerning the names of the streets where Jews resided in Munkács (Heruti, no. 9), which ended with the Czechoslovakian regime's imposition of a compromise. Finally, looking back at this period, the Zionists accuse the overall hasidic leadership, for which the rabbi stands, of indirectly causing the death of many young people who wanted to leave for Palestine before the Holocaust, but were intimidated from doing so by the hasidic leadership, and thus lost their lives (Benedek, no. 25; Erlich, no. 8).

Nevertheless, and notwithstanding its apparent passivity, Zionism did fight hasidism by virtue of its very existence and the ideological alternative it offered. Zionism introduced an entirely new and different 'language' to that of traditional Judaism in this region, as it did in neighbouring areas in that period and earlier. It is therefore little wonder that the enormous gap created between these two movements has meant that they could not then, and hardly can today, speak or negotiate with each other. It is small wonder too that all this left in the souls and memories of the pioneering Zionists of Carpatho-Russia imprints not only of pride but also of fear, insecurity, and remorse.

A memorable experience in my fieldwork with the ex-Carpatho-Russians was meeting groups of people (a few married couples or close friends) at their request. In relating their collective memories, the groups consistently raised the central issues of the rise of Zionist consciousness in the region, the Holocaust, and the relation between the two events or processes. As for the process of recounting these events, it often turned out that the members of these groups relied on each other's support, or argued with one another in the telling, and were thus better able to cope with—and at times be relieved of—the burden of painful issues brought up in these shared storytelling events.[23]

At one such meeting that took place at the home of Zipora Nemesh in Haifa in the spring of 1995, four people participated: Zipora Nemesh and Dvora Gross, both retired elementary school teachers, Arye Amikam, a retired commanding officer in the police, and myself. Nemesh and Gross grew up in Munkács, whereas Amikam grew up in Ungvár. All three went to the Hebrew school in their home town. This fact, combined with their Zionist pride, their occasional use of high or archaic Hebrew, and their drawing on the Tanakh or Bible, as opposed to the Talmud, constitute a 'dominant' (Jakobson 1978) in the texts of the three and influence their form, content, and, most of all, the messages they convey. It turned out that the issue of studying at the Hebrew school, as opposed to the traditional *ḥeder* (mainly for young boys, but also for girls from progressive and/or well-off families) or any non-Jewish school, was a major area of conflict between hasidism and Zionism and is remembered as such by those who were young Zionists at the time. This may simply be a way of compensating for the absence of any memory of the other issues that preoccupied pioneering Zionists in nearby communities, such as congresses, factions, fundraising, and so on. Or it may be that educational issues were more conspicuous and long-lasting and were therefore more controversial for hasidic society. At any rate, the clash between the two ideologies stands out in the collective memory of the present narrators as well as supplying the material for a fruitful narrative creation.

Personal Narratives

The following are translations from the Hebrew of personal narratives concerning education and its meeting points with the struggle between hasidism and Zionism as experienced, remembered, and told by the narrators. For the sake of the present discussion I shall quote and analyse the narratives of only two of the three participants in that shared interview and storytelling event in Zipora Nemesh's house—those that have a direct bearing on the issues of education and Zionism versus hasidism. In addition, I shall present and analyse the narratives of two other participants in the same research project, Peretz Litman from Munkács and Avraham Perri from nearby Muzsoj. Both were interviewed in their homes in Haifa a few months after the storytelling event described above, by Zipora Nemesh, the hostess of that event, who was also one of five community members acting as volunteering interviewers for the research project.[24] These two narrators also attended the Hebrew school at Munkács and both had careers in high technology and management until their retirement. The four excerpts are presented below to create a narrative succession that moves from the decision to send the child-narrator to Hebrew school to specific events that the child experienced as it grew up in this system.

Peretz Litman

My studies at the Hebrew school caused trouble at home, because the Munkácser Rebbe banned [from attending synagogue] all those who went to the Zionist school, which was [considered] impure for Orthodox Jews. My grandfather suffered from it, because we lived next to the synagogue, by the railway station, and he was usually invited to pray by the holy *amud* [as cantor]. But now that I went to the Hebrew school, they did not let him pray there any more, because his grandson had defied the *rebbe*'s command and gone to the impure Hebrew school. But it did not help him [the *rebbe*]. Beforehand, at the age of 6, I had to start school, so my parents thought of enrolling me in the Czechoslovak school. I went there with my mother, and my mother told the principal of the Czechoslovak school, my son does not write on *shabat*. The principal looked at her angrily and said, We need no Saturday Jews. Upon hearing this remark, at the age of 6, I was so insulted, that I told my mother, Mummy, I will never go to a gentile school. I will only go to a Jewish school. All the requests of my father and grandfather did not help, and I enrolled at the Hebrew school. This also shaped my character and made me a devoted Jew, made me remain Jewish all my life. Life brought me, through concentration camps, to Israel. I refused to go to America or anywhere else after the war. I could not give up my Jewishness and that has been my commitment from my childhood to this day. To this day, I can say I am well off and I do not envy my friends, whom I visit [in the States], and see they have swimming pools in their yards. It does not attract me. I do not envy them but am happy with my choice. (Litman, no. 2)

Avraham Perri

Father enrolled me at the Hebrew high school, because he had seen what had happened with my brother's studies at a yeshiva. So, when they heard that I would go to Hebrew school, [they said] No, no, don't send him there. And they said, If you put him in this high school, we will ban you. Father said, I pray on my own on weekdays anyway, so I'll pray by myself on *shabat* too. But you forget that I am *hatan bereshit* [the person accorded the honour of reading aloud the first *haftara*, or portion from the prophets attached to each *parasha*, or portion of the Torah], that I receive this honour every year, and that I give you wood for heating, or else you could not cover this cost. They said, Oh well, someone else will give us [wood]. But no one did. So they came to talk with father. They said, there is a Hungarian high school in Beregszász, there is a Czechoslovak high school in Munkács, just don't let him go to the Hebrew high school, because it will corrupt him. So father knew a bit, and said, in the Hebrew school they don't study on *shabat*, and in the Christian schools he will have to. They thought about it and then said, the Torah says *zakhor* ['Remember the sabbath day to keep it holy', Exod. 20: 8] and *shamor* ['Observe the sabbath day to keep it holy', Deut. 5: 12]. So, he cannot maintain *shamor*, but *zakhor* he can, because [on the sabbath] he will write with his left hand and that will remind him that it is Saturday. Father laughed at them and enrolled me in the Hebrew school. They never banned him and he went on giving them wood. (Perri, no. 4)

Arye Amikam

There were four families in our building: my uncles and us upstairs, a gentile woman, and a very religious Jew, our neighbours. Once in four or five years the rabbi of Belz came to visit. He had a big court. They built a giant tent and all the town's Jews came to greet him and receive a *berakhah* [blessing]. For *shabat* they made a challah [sabbath bread] as long as three-quarters of the length of the table, three such challahs. To get to [see] him, entry was not simple. Myself, I was from a Zionist home. The neighbours knew we were going to Hebrew school. Still, for some reason, mother wanted us to be blessed. So she did it in a somewhat convoluted way, with the help of this Habadnic [a Jew belonging to Habad, a major hasidic group] who was our night guard. He took us and we entered the rabbi's chambers. He, however, did not want to be dishonest, so he told the rabbi that we were orphans with no one in charge of us, and that he should bless us. I remember, it was as though he hesitated a bit, the hand hesitated in rising, but he blessed us nevertheless. I do not recall exactly what he said and did. We wore *kipot* [the traditional head covering for males] and had *peot* [ear-locks], and in addition to attending the Hebrew school we also studied in the *ḥeder*. Not all did. Many [pupils] came from semi-assimilated or even secular homes. They were secular Jews, not religious. He blessed us, and it was considered a very important achievement. (Nemesh, no. 25)

Dvora Gross

There were eight of us at home and we all went to the Hebrew school, all. Opposite us was the ḥeder, where some of the pupils of the Hebrew school studied, some of them in the afternoon and some in the morning. In the same yard as us lived a rebbe [in this context, a teacher in the ḥeder]. We called him, der royter rebbe [Yiddish: the red rabbi], for he had a red beard. He was a very, very weird man. Even the children in the ḥeder feared him. He had a b'helfer [Yiddish: an assistant], who held a kantshik [Yiddish: a whip]. The rebbe would beckon and the assistant would beat a certain boy. Usually, this royter rebbe would build a separate sukah [booth erected for the festival of Sukkot] every year. Now, when hard times began in Munkács, each family could not build a separate sukah anymore, so they built a shared sukah with the neighbours. The children would decorate the sukah. I always liked to watch father cut the ornaments at night. We would glue, prepare all kinds of decorations for the sukah, mostly us girls. When we had finished, I once wanted to study in the sukah. It was a big thing, to be able to study. I learned the 'Song of Dvora' by heart, aloud. I sang, 'So sang Dvora and Barak, the son of Abinoam' [Jud. 5: 1], exactly when the royter rebbe stepped into the sukah. When he heard me reciting the 'Song of Dvora' in Hebrew, he cried out loudly, oy vey, di sukkah iz trayf [Yiddish: the sukah isn't kosher]. He ran out of the sukah, did not enter it again. Later, he caught my father and complained to him, How could he let his daughters learn Hebrew and the 'Song of Dvora' by heart in the sukah, when even boys should not? But we spoke Hebrew aloud in the street. So the Munkácsers would not let father enter the synagogue. He became a Spinker hasid, but then they also told him that they would bar him from the synagogue, unless he took me out of Hebrew school. I was the last of eight children, and he asked father to take me out. Father refused, but at home he said to me, 'Why don't you leave the Hebrew school?' I said to him, 'If you take me out of school, I will commit suicide, I am ready to die.' Then father agreed to pray at home and said, Vos is zu Got is zu Got un' vos is zu leit is zu leit [Yiddish: What is for God is for God and what is for people is for people], meaning that he could talk to God anywhere. He did not go to synagogue and prayed at home, three times a day. (Nemesh, no. 16)

Peretz Litman states at the outset of his narrative that his studies at the Hebrew school of Munkács caused trouble at home, because of the Munkácser Rebbe's objection to the school. The trouble or conflict with the rebbe, however, doesn't so much concern the child-narrator or his parents as much as it does his grandfather. In his other narratives, Peretz Litman dwells a great deal on the family's supposedly problematic roots as Polish Jews in Carpatho-Russia, since his grandparents had moved to the region in the 1890s. It took the Litmans almost fifty years to become accustomed to and accepted by the rather closed hasidic middle-class world of Munkács (Rosen 2004: 29–31). In other words, it took Grandfather Litman a long time to attain his honorary status in the Munkács community in general and at its hasidic court in particular. As for the Munkács hasidic court and its leader, we might guess that their price for such high status was absolute loyalty. In the context of the narration of the rebbe as an authority figure, the stories elaborate on how severely he would treat anyone who dared to defy his

authority. Therefore, the punishment of ostracizing the otherwise venerable eld-erly grandfather was a severe measure taken in response to the rebellious act of his offspring.

All this serves as but a preface to another episode that took place early on, and which led the grandson to insist on studying in the Hebrew school and to his grandfather's humiliation. The connecting element between the two scenes is the clause: 'But it [the ostracism] did not help him [the *rebbe*].' In this scene, the narrator learns a lesson about what it means to belong to a minority group whose rules and way of life are criticized and looked down on by the majority. In fact, such events often function as major 'revelation' scenes in the narratives of many Diaspora Jews concerning their experience of antisemitism. Needless to say, the headmaster's remark echoes popular antisemitic libels about Jews as being non-conformist and non-productive.

In most cases, Jewish youngsters had no choice but to swallow the initial insult and the ensuing humiliation of belonging to a system that was hostile to their faith and culture. But for Litman, as he well understands in retrospect (or as he retrospectively reads this understanding into his narrative, a possibility dis-cussed in my summary of all four analyses below), it is exactly the option of the Zionist Hebrew school that offers him escape from the offences of the non-Jew-ish system. From a contemporary perspective, with a Jewish state having existed for some sixty years, all this seems natural and rational. But in the eyes of pre-war Diaspora Jews, who did not conceive of themselves as primarily a nation but rather as an ethnos with a unique ethos, and who maintained a stressful tension between sameness and difference with regard to their host nation,[25] the option of living as a nation within a nation seemed intimidating because it threatened not only the traditional religious hegemony[26] but also the overall relationship between the country's Jews and their social environment. Seen thus, the *rebbe*'s treatment of the Litmans is not just an aggressive act in a battle for control but also an attempt to maintain inter-communal order and status, which are never-theless shaken at this point in the region as elsewhere because of the rise of Zionism.

To return to Peretz Litman and his earlier experience with a non-Jewish school, the dismissive remark of the school headmaster about 'Saturday Jews' became a major force in Litman's later life, including his Holocaust experience and his conception of his life in general. In the final section of his narrative he turns to open ideological discourse, as opposed to his more descriptive narration beforehand, to state his beliefs and affirm his position as an established Israeli whose origins go back through the Holocaust to the interwar strictly hasidic Munkács community Surprisingly, he does not use the label 'Israeli' although this is clear from both the context and the contrast drawn between himself and his American Jewish friends at present. Instead, he invariably defines himself as a 'devoted Jew', 'Jewish', committed to his 'Jewishness', and happy with his 'choice'. This shows that, despite his otherwise clear Zionist ideology, when it comes to personal identity he perceives himself as primarily Jewish, a term which stands for a non-hierarchical complex of ethnicity, religion, and nationality, rather than as Zionist or Israeli, which attributes priority to nationality over ethnicity and religion. The repetition of this self-identification makes it clear that it is not an incidental matter but a deeply rooted part of his inclusive conceptualization of identity. In that sense, his Jewish ideological discourse deconstructs his Zionist narrative. In addition, the brief mention of his Holocaust experience, which regularly receives much more attention in narratives of survivors, further erodes the exclusiveness of his Zionist identity/consciousness, although in this instance he is more in control, as is suggested by his lack of elaboration of the point. At any rate, this is the only place in which Litman lets even the smallest sign of doubt or ambivalence into his narrative, which is otherwise decisive in its Zionist message.

This is not the case concerning his family, at least not the two older generations of it, who suffer from the sanction inflicted on them by the community after years of doing their best to become part of it. As for the family's attitude to Peretz's insistence, we are told that 'all the requests of [his] father and grandfather did not help'. This means that they at least tried to change his mind but failed. Moreover it shows either that he had great influence at home, which is unlikely for a child of that time and place, or that his family were not that adamantly opposed to his choice even though they were afraid of the Jewish community's reaction to it. So they preferred to look helpless,[27] suffer the expected sanction, and still let Peretz have his way. Given the circumstances, this is probably the most they could do by way of silently supporting his choice, or the least by way of accepting their community's norms. In the discussion below we shall encounter a variety of other combinations among the choices of young Zionists, the reactions of their families to both their action and the community's criticism of it (the one recurrent element in all these narratives), and the manner and tone in which it is all recounted decades afterwards.

In contrast to Peretz Litman's narrative, the narrator in Avraham Perri's story plays a much smaller role, though it describes a similar conflict. Instead, it is Perri's father who is involved in a lengthy talmudic-style debate with what appear to be several hasidic authority figures—referred to as 'they'—over the question of the right school for Avraham. In addition, the narrator tells us that all this happened after his family had a previous bad experience with another son's studies at a yeshiva, although the exact nature of this experience is not specified beyond its generally negative connotations. In this fight, after the family's initial decision to send Avraham to Hebrew school, each side makes three moves. The community's authorities repeatedly complain about the Hebrew school, and Avraham's father repeatedly refutes their arguments. This continues until the narrative's ending, in which Avraham is finally enrolled in the school, and the community nevertheless refrains from banning the family as it first threatened.

At first, the controversy revolves around the status of Avraham's father, similar to the experience of Peretz's grandfather and of Dvora Gross's father (Arye Amikam is spared all this, as his father has already died, and his mother leans towards compromise, as we shall soon see). The community threatens to ban the father, but the father reminds them that he is not only an honoured member (like Peretz's grandfather) but also a generous donor. At first, the community belittles the importance of the father's donation of wood for heating the community institutions, but as soon as the gift is missed, since no one else is willing or able to assume the donor's role, they 'came to talk with father', and a process of negotiation, as opposed to one-sided imposition, begins. This is also the point in which the narrative begins to sound like a pastiche of a debate among sages, or like a popular version of such debates.

The community authorities now offer the father a variety of possible educational options for his son, a typical situation in this multinational and multicultural region, as reflected in other narratives in the research project. For a family living in the county of Bereg, either the Hungarian high school in Beregszász or the Czechoslovak high school in Munkács are reasonable choices in the eyes of the Jewish hasidic authorities, but the Hebrew school of Munkács is out of the question. This rejection of the Hebrew school stems from the traditional hasidic world-view in which there is a strict division between Jewish and non-Jewish practice. The hasidic authorities considered the Hebrew school disturbingly ambiguous in its religious commitment and expression of Jewishness. Apparently, they were mostly bothered by the fact that, unlike other current revolutionary movements, and especially communism, Zionism did not dismiss Jewish tradition altogether, but instead offered new ways of relating to and living by some parts of it. The principle of defining a group's centre by contrasting it to what it is not is well demonstrated in books such as Mary Douglas's *Purity and Danger* (2002) and Marvin Harris's *Cows, Pigs, Wars, and Witches* (1974), which show that in the eyes of traditional societies danger derives from situations in which the border between the allowed and the forbidden is unclear, and not—or much less—from the knowledge or closeness of the forbidden entity. The forbidden is not a threat as long as it is over the border in all senses. But once the border is not clear-cut and the forbidden is at least partly legitimate or esteemed, its danger grows. In other words, anxiety derives from the loss of a clear boundary rather than from the nature of the entity on the other side. Thus, in all four narratives, Hebrew school is seen as more dangerous than a Christian school: Hebrew school subverts the authority of the ages-old Jewish traditional system while still offering a meaningful way to live as a Jew. Here again, then, as in Peretz Litman's narrative, there is a shift of emphasis from the ethnic-religious to the national principle, and here, too, the story concerns not only the Jewish systems in question but also their overall relationship with the surrounding non-Jewish society.

While the issue of which school to choose is cardinal here, the issue of fulfilling a specific Jewish dictate, a *mitsvah*, is of much less importance, although the *mitsvah* in question concerns the holiness of the sabbath, or *shabat*, which is usually considered paramount in Judaism. It turns out that for the Munkács hasidic court, as central as *shabat* can be, it is still negotiable when there is a bigger issue at stake, or, to put it another way, at times of danger it is better to give up a part in order to still keep the whole. According to this principle, as the hasidic authorities explain to Avraham's father, in a non-Jewish school, although Avraham will not be able to observe *shabat* (thus contravening the biblical precept of *shamor*) since he will have to write on the sabbath, he will still be able to *remember* it (and thus maintain the precept of *zakhor*), through the strategy of writing with his left hand. In fact, they offer an option which prevents him from fulfilling his religious obligations when the possibility of avoiding this is both literally and figuratively right across the street, in the Hebrew school. This makes their solution artificial and absurd, which is why Avraham's father responds to it with laughter and fearlessly enrols Avraham in the Hebrew school.

In this narrative, which is told from the viewpoint of a detached narrator, the narrator himself is spared the burden of doubt, hesitation, or remorse, unlike the other three narrators discussed here. Moreover, even the father, who basically belongs to the system he confronts, seems free of these sensations as he engages in debate with the hasidic authorities with atypical self-confidence. The father first states his willingness to pray alone at home if necessary, but never has to, unlike Dvora Gross's father, who is forced to do it even though it is painful for him to do so. Avraham's father then brings up the argument of his donation and is proven right when no one else takes his place. Last, when the authorities come to talk with him and raise the absurd possibility of his son's writing on the sabbath as this still allows him to remember the restriction against it, he rightly laughs in their face and finally enrols his son in Hebrew school, where both *zakhor* and *shamor* are observed as there is no school at all on *shabat*. In all these respects, this narrative stands out because of its light tone, the deep commitment of the Zionist participants (with Avraham included as both omniscient narrator and object of the debate), and the aggressively clear-cut Zionist message.

In Arye Amikam's narrative, there is vacillation between the worlds of hasidism and Zionism and their respective sets of values. The family's children attend the Hebrew school in Ungvár, but they also study in the traditional *ḥeder*, where they go early in the morning and continue later in the day. Moreover, with *kipot* and *peot* they look like their hasidic neighbours. No less important than the children's actions and appearance is how these are perceived in their community, or the narrative's handling of point of view. In this regard, it is important to point out the role of the authorities and the neighbours. They do not play much of a role in Amikam's narrative, yet they function as critical watchdogs who scrutinize the deeds of the narrator and his family. In fact, because there are so many onlookers in the narrative, it sometimes seems as if the story is told from several viewpoints simultaneously, although the only actual voice in it is that of the narrator recalling his childhood. In addition, this voice maintains a double perspective: that of the adult speaking, and that of the child he used to be. At any rate, the over-emphasis on public opinion reflects the narrator's own vacillation and uncertainty—the same stance attributed to the Belzer Rebbe in the narrative—and is a projection of the narrator's own mixed feelings about the process he underwent, both at the time of the narrated event and that of the narration itself.

As for the central action in this story, we might wonder why the Zionist boys come for the rabbi's blessing in the first place. The narrator himself wonders about his mother's motives for sending her sons to the famous rabbi, as the vague phrase 'for some reason', without specifying the reason, discloses. What is indicated, however, is the generational split in the family, which probably joins the ideological disagreement between mother and sons. In this specific incident, though, the boys obey their mother and go to the rabbi with a mediating figure, the Habadnic night guard, who acts here as an ad hoc father-figure. This guard sees fit, for fear of the rabbi's possible wrath, to express his reservations. He points out that they are orphans (as their father is dead) and therefore uncontrollable and tending towards Zionism, which in this context is likened to delinquency. Thus the guard exonerates himself from any possible blame for misleading the rabbi. In addition, he hints that the rabbi should act *davka* or *dafka*, which idiomatically means 'exactly to the contrary', and bless the so-called degenerate boys, thus perhaps leading them back to the right path. The rabbi hesitates, perhaps weighing in his mind whether his blessing might strengthen the boys' hasidism or their Zionism, but eventually he gives them his blessing.

The narrator points out that the blessing—both the act and the content—was considered an important achievement, but he does not specify for whom: is it for the boys, whose course of life in fact led them away from the influence of the rabbi and the principles he represented? Is it for their mother, who insisted on the blessing in the first place? Or is it for the hasidic neighbours, who sense the novelty of Zionism and its attraction to the community's youth in general? In fact, the blessing is significant for all. The boys, whose consciousness and education are twofold and in conflict, win at least a temporary détente regarding the criticism of their hasidic social environment, which, as shown above, could be very fierce. Their mother also temporarily regains her peace of mind. As for the neighbours, the rabbi's act suspends their criticism for a while. This suspension is significant in a delicate familial and communal situation, in which this fatherless family is regularly scrutinized by the community, since orphanhood means more freedom both for the orphans and for the authorities and meddlers of all sorts.[28]

This in turn means that, in Amikam's case, both external and internal conflicts are more present and more clearly felt than in the other three narratives.

As for the inner conflict between hasidism and Zionism, Amikam's narrative sounds strongly apologetic as he attempts to downplay the rupture caused in his community, his family, and his own consciousness as a result of his turning to Zionism. Here he digresses from his narrative line, employing what linguist William Labov calls the evaluative device of comparison (Labov 1972), to make the point that—unlike others who had a 'secular Jewish' consciousness, a very disturbing phenomenon in Orthodox eyes even sixty years later—he and his family were 'religious *and* Zionist' at the same time. This shows that he still cares a great deal about how his decisions and actions are regarded, although in the Israel of the 1990s, the time of the narration, both options are widespread and acceptable, though the second one is obviously more charged ideologically. But in the Ungvár of the 1930s people who supported Zionism were criticized and intimidated exactly because of the blurring of divisions they caused between the legitimate and the forbidden. Therefore, even—or especially—the 'religious *and* Zionist' need the rabbi's blessing in order to cope with their social environment and mollify their neighbours, even if only for a while.

The narrative of Dvora Gross about the 'Song of Dvora' relates to the core of the ideological conflict between hasidim and Zionism. Gross opens her narrative by a declaration of identity concerning herself and her seven siblings: they all studied in the Hebrew school of Munkács. Some of the pupils at this school also studied in the traditional *ḥeder*, just like Amikam and his brother in Ungvár. Therefore for them the passage or movement from *ḥeder* to Hebrew school, Yiddish to Hebrew, Talmud to Tanakh, and from single-gender (and mainly male) studies to mixed-gender classes is not a black and white change but a process with many in-between stages and shades. The in-between phase is also a marker of the difficulties of the so-called revolutionists when breaking with tradition. By contrast, the traditional world is much more decisive and rigid in its rejection of those disloyal to its values, of novelty in general, and of liminal or borderless situations.

The *royter rebbe*, the red-haired and bearded teacher, jealously maintains his strict rules as long as possible, in the relatively good times before the Second World War. Still, in hard times, when several families are forced to share one *sukah*, he is exposed against his will to new trends, to which he vehemently objects. For him, a girl studying holy matters in the holy language aloud in a *sukah* is utter blasphemy,[29] *trayf*. However, in the present context, as in the two previous narratives, the term alludes to a more specific form of non-kosherness, namely, to the non-permissible mixing of entities, such as milk and meat or kosher and non-kosher food.[30] In this context, the *royter rebbe*'s reaction to Dvora's performance labels as *trayf* all the following combinations: girls and boys, silence (or chanting, or murmur) and loud speech, house and *sukah*, secular studies and holy studies,

Yiddish and Hebrew, and hasidic and Zionist Jews and their respective world-views.

The unacceptable mixing of these categories is perceived as an attack not only on the teacher and the ethos he represents but also on the entire community. In that regard, the response of the *ḥeder* teacher, a lower-level religious leader, is just as fierce and authoritative as that of the eminent hasidic *rebbe*. At any rate, such an attack on the reign of hasidism necessarily calls for quick sanction and restoration of order, as described in Victor Turner's model of social drama.[31] The sanction or counter-attack takes the form of pressuring the narrator's father to take his daughter out of the Hebrew school, thus figuratively restoring the purity or kosherness of his home and the communal *sukah*, or else be banned from the Munkács community. The father resists the sanction and becomes a member of another hasidic court, but is expelled from there too. At some point he tries to persuade his daughter to give in, but she turns it all into a matter of life and death, life meaning Hebrew school and all that goes with it, and death meaning giving it all up, as she threatens to commit suicide if forced to leave school. Faced with his daughter's adamant objection, the father gives up membership of the hasidic community altogether, thus challenging the very authority of the community and its ritual specialists to act as mediators between God and himself, and ends up praying at home alone, just like Avraham Perri's father (who already prayed at home on weekdays). As for the community, not only do they not win this specific battle—which is surely not the first of its kind in this family of eight children with the narrator being the youngest—but they lose the obedience of the father as well as the souls of his children for good.

As for inner conflict, in this narrative it seems to be found more in the experience of the narrator's father than in that of the narrator, who does not express any hesitation or second thoughts. The reason for this might be the child's focus, which governs Gross's entire narrative and does not leave much room for other themes. This distinguishes her narrative from those of Arye Amikam, which presents the combined focus of the child and the adult, and Peretz Litman, in which the two remain separate and represented by the narrator and his grandfather respectively, and from Avraham Perri's narrative, which is exclusively governed by one and the same focus of the pro-Zionist father and son. Dvora's ideological response concerns not just the conflict between hasidism and Zionism, but also the exclusion of women from ritual practices by the *royter rebbe* and the patriarchal order he represents. For her Zionist community by contrast, gender is much less important in determining communal and cultural practices. Although it is significant for expressing external conflict, Dvora's femininity is less germane to the context of inner conflict. In her narrative content and performance, she is just as self-assured as the male narrators, if not more so than some of them.

On the thematic plane, the function of the Bible and the way in which it is drawn on as a central model or paradigm call for special attention. Gross consciously describes several of the characters in her other narratives (herself included, if we consider the ties between her Hebrew name and that of the biblical prophetess Dvora) as avatars of biblical figures. 'Samson the Hero', the virile shoemaker who is brutally murdered on the way to deportation in the Holocaust, is an example of this (Nemesh, no. 13), and so is the milkman who gives the narrator occasional rides in his carriage and seems to her like an undefined 'biblical hero' (Nemesh, no. 18). These characters set up a comparison with the figures of the local rabbis and other religious figures, who are either absent or criticized in all four narratives. Seen thus, the Bible, with its mythical figures, ancient landscape (Seir, Edom, earth, mountains, and the highways and byways of 'Dvora's Song'), Hebrew language, and emphasis on the Jewish people's physical superiority in terms of their land and armies, stands in sharp contrast to the Talmud as taught and lived by the hasidic communities of Carpatho-Russia and virtually all other traditional Jewish diaspora communities of the period. The principle of the Bible in this context fulfils the function of challenging traditional leadership with a return to *the* original text and reading it in a new and redemptive manner. This manner defies the traditional reading of the Bible, or more accurately, its hitherto systematic and deliberate disregard, as hinted in the *rebbe*'s warning that 'even boys' should not read the Bible the way Dvora did. In fact, the majority of traditional Jewish studies to this day are devoted to exegesis of the Bible, for example in the Mishnah (a compendium of moral-jurisdictional instruction based on the Torah) and Talmud, and to ritual reading of biblical passages as part of the performance of prayer, rather than to the Bible as a text or narrative. Against this established background, a girl's reading of 'Dvora's Song' aloud from the Bible in the Munkács of the early 1940s was indeed a revolutionary act. No wonder that it made the traditional hasidic authorities of the period object so vigorously.

In sum, in all four narratives the childhood education of the narrators is a major source of tension in the community, although the specific incident in the last two narratives appears to revolve around a different matter. But even in these two narratives, Zionist education is the source of trouble—otherwise Arye would not need his neighbour's tedious apologies in order to receive the Belzer Rebbe's blessing, and Dvora would never have given a performance of the song of her biblical namesake in a communal *sukah*. Considering Zionist education, then, in all four cases the narrators ultimately received their childhood education in their local Hebrew school. In Labov's terms, therefore, the Hebrew school is always either the initial problem or the final solution (Labov 1972), but in any case it is always at the heart of the plot.

As for the child-narrators' stance in the face of the trouble caused by their choice of school, Avraham Perri is protected by his father's figure and force and is therefore very sure of himself, but all the other narrators are painfully aware of the suffering they have caused their dear ones by their choice. Peretz Litman delineates his grandfather's via dolorosa since his immigration to the region, slow absorption into the Munkács hasidic community, and rejection on the grounds of his grandson's 'corrupt' education. Likewise, Arye Amikam identifies with his widowed mother's concerns while raising two boys in a changing and challenging world. As for Dvora Gross, although she adamantly sticks to her choice just like her siblings before her, she still sees the agony of her father as the one who pays for it all, much like Peretz Litman's grandfather.

The parents' acceptance of their children's choice of education and their ability to face communal sanction is related to the child's stance, and at times the parents' stance determines the child's choice. This is probably the case with Avraham Perri, who does not say a word of his own about choosing the Hebrew school. Similarly, the response of the other parents also depends on their social and communal status, although in all three narratives this works against the parents and families. The Litmans are forever suspect because of their Polish origins; Arye Amikam's mother is weakened by widowhood into both accepting her sons' choice and letting the community interfere in it; and Dvora Gross's father, who sent all his eight children to the Hebrew school, still wishes to belong to any hasidic community that will accept him, and that in itself weakens him in his struggle over Dvora's studies.

The hasidic objection to any breaching of the community's norms and values is the one constant factor in all these narratives, as it is in others told or written by past members of Carpatho-Russian communities. This objection could be fierce (as in the narratives of Litman and Gross), or it could allow for compromise (as with Amikam), or entail diplomacy (as in Perri's narrative), but the goal is always the same: to remain in power and delegitimize all opponents and other options.

As for the tone in which these events are recounted in our four representative narratives, here, too, there are shades and variations. All end with the narrator's victory, in the sense that he or she starts or continues to study in the Hebrew school despite objections from within the hasidic community. Still, in some of the narratives, either the narrator or his or her family pays a high price and is aware of it. In Litman's account the victims are his grandfather and probably also his parents, and helplessness is a dominant theme of the narrative. This is the sense in which the phrase 'but it did not help him' may refer not only to the *rebbe* but also to the grandfather and the family he heads.

In Amikam's story, the victims are his brother and himself in addition to their mother, since all three are too weak to face criticism and delegitimization in the absence of the family's father. In Gross's narrative, the victim is the father but not the children, who are a strong team of eight with each strengthening the others (regarding studies in Hebrew school), although even Dvora on her own seems well able to manage the conflict and win. In the narrative of Avraham Perri, the tone of amusement derives both from the narrator's party's clear victory and the shameful characterization of the hasidim as willing to compromise values normally held to be sacred in order to retain control. In the context of the overall relations between the two movements and ideologies, this narrative can be seen as a compensation for the otherwise utter weakness of Zionism in the face of hasidism, and the act of telling it in this way, decades after the event, is a form of *tikun*, or mending, of the Zionist experience of this relationship. In fact, these four narratives present a rare example of the clear victory of Zionism over hasidism, both dramatically and ideologically.

How does our own historical distance affect the way we read these four stories? They would have been told entirely differently had there not been a Zionist Jewish state, in which the values fought for in these narratives are appreciated within a pluralistic system that includes hasidism as one of many persuasions. In other words, historical facts and processes and their implications serve here as socio-cultural context to these narratives and in fact both textualize and contextualize them, in that they determine their content, messages, and the ways in which they are understood. From the Zionist point of view, too, history has supplied some justification for these individual narrators, who fought for Zionism in a hostile world, against tradition and hostile leaders, and eventually won, although mostly because of forces beyond their agency.

Often what emerges from the analysis of personal narrative is the contradictory quality of the narrative structure, its 'vacillation' (or 'hesitation', to use Amikam's word), reluctance, or inability to embrace absolutes. Surprisingly, though, this tendency does not weaken the status of these narratives as ideological discourse, a status supported by the identities of the narrators and the consensual atmosphere of the shared storytelling event in which two narrators participated at one time. Rather, the hesitant stance is shown to be a sign of maturity and a marker of the understanding that all gains entail losses and vice versa, and that opinions can and should change with time and historical developments.

As for the relations between genre and group, the personal narrative depicting collective memory well expresses this group in general and the four narrators specifically. These narrators have now reached the point at which, although loyal to their lifetime creeds, they are ready to challenge them from within, express what might or should have bothered them, feel remorse, face their old fears, and—most importantly—talk about it openly. The sensitivity of the content of personal narrative means that its study can shed light, at times from unexpected angles, on historical, sociological, cultural, and psychological processes.

Any narrative of personal experience is not only a recapitulation of the past but must also be a reflection of the narrator's present world-view. To the narrators in this project, however, the risks entailed by remoteness and reframing seemed preferable to remaining silent, leaving on record only the account of the other party (which at the time in question had in any case practically silenced its opponents). As a form of expression that allows researchers to understand motives and strategies in their social context as well as the individual story they tell, the personal narrative would repay closer scrutiny in Jewish cultural studies. In modern (and postmodern) societies, the personal is the medium of communication and the lens through which experience is interpreted; in traditional societies, by contrast, the personal is seen as a threat to the communal, and is closely controlled in the interests of the wider community.

Notes

1   Carpatho-Russia (formerly called Sub-Carpathian Ruthenia) is an area in western Ukraine covering about 13,000 km², which today has no significant Jewish population. Apart from Holocaust-related studies, and excluding the works of Yeshayahu A. Jelinek, most Jewish and/or Israeli sources are only semi-professional, coming mostly from Jewish immigrants from Carpatho-Russia, and should be perceived as such, notwithstanding their significant contribution to the understanding of the region's Jewry. For non-Jewish sources, readers should consult the wide range of writings by Paul Robert Magocsi, which include historical, geographical, and linguistic studies of the region and its population, with a stress on Slavic culture. For readers of Carpatho-Russia's native languages, the literary writings of Ivan Olbracht on the region and its Jewry may be of interest.

2   The language of instruction in these schools was Hebrew, which meant, in the period discussed here, that they were Zionist. At first there were only high schools, but later on elementary schools were also established. The schools were officially acknowledged by the Czechoslovakian authorities.

3   See Aviezer Ravitzky's interpretation of R. Haim Eleazar Shapiro's objection to physical *aliyah* to the Holy Land in Ravitzky 1996: ch. 2.

4   See the relevant table in Jelinek 2003: 25.

5   This is according to the historical division of the Austro-Hungarian empire. In the period in question it was no longer the official division, but its social and cultural implications still existed.

6   Bratislava in Slovak; Pressburg in Yiddish. In his teaching Rabbi Moses Sofer (1762–1839) stressed learning and exegesis and deprecated the veneration of holy figures; he strongly opposed the teachings of the Haskalah, claiming that this and similar departures from tradition were forbidden by the Torah. See *EJ*, xv. 77–9.

7   Carried out in the mid-1990s, Jelinek's study was able to benefit from the reopening of the region's archives (mainly in Ungvár and Beregszász) after the collapse of the communist regimes in the area around 1990. Concerning communist movements in the interwar period in the region, Jelinek points out that, although local Jews were attracted to them, they were strongly divided on the question of nationality, and this put communism in a weaker position than Zionism. Despite the richness of archive materials, little has therefore been written about these movements, while other persuasions and factions are not referred to in the archives at all. See Jelinek 2003: 159–69 ('The Political Stage').

8   In her essay about the development of cultural and political awareness in east European shtetls at the turn of the 19th century, Alina Cała enumerates Zionism as one of the options attracting young people rather than the older generation. See Cała 2004: 139.

9   Jelinek (2003: 185) stresses the devotion of Zionists to *aliyah* and their consequent readiness to leave in as great numbers as the available emigration certificates allowed.

10   The narrative of Peretz Litman, with its significant lack of reference to the effect of the Holocaust on his life, is a clear example of this.

11   Jelinek (2003: 288) cites an estimate of between 12,000 and 25,000 survivors out of a total Jewish population of about 100,000.

12   This study is summed up in Rosen 1999, which contains several in-depth analyses of groups of narratives relating to central issues for this community, such as the development of Zionism in the area, the Holocaust, and the memory and narration of a destroyed world. In addition, it presents the process of working with ex-members of this community and thus outlines the methodological aspects of the study, such as past and present personal and communal portrayals, detailed lists of places of origin and oral materials recorded in the project, and a representative selection of these materials, divided into several thematic sections.

13   This part of the project is presented in Jelinek 2003.

14   The large number of Israeli Folklore Archives publications containing stories by Jews of Middle Eastern origin supports this claim, as well as pointing to a similar attitude in Israeli folklore scholarship that existed until recently. Haya Bar-Itzhak's *Jewish Poland* (2001) marks a change in this attitude, as does my own work on central and east European Jewish communities.

15   There are two exceptions to this: one woman, Oli (Olga) Klein, was a Hungarian citizen presently living in Budapest, who was visiting her friends when she met me; Ludwig Weiss divides his time between Israel and Austria.

16   All the project's recorded materials are stored in its archives at Tel Aviv University, and are in the process of being archived at the Dov Noy Israeli Folktale Archives at Haifa University as well. References below are to the Tel Aviv archives, and give the name of the interviewee (or host/hostess of a shared interview event) and the file name and number of the item (all in Hebrew in the original).

17   In his writings Labov creates a threefold narrative syntax accounting for the levels of action, action description (or performance), and reasoning, the last of which is predominant in his work. In the analysis of personal narrative, a relatively new genre of oral folklore, this level turned out to be crucial for analysing both the text and its socio-cultural contexts.

18   See Dinur 1983; Jelinek 2003; Ravitzky 1996; Reinhartz 1980; Sole 1968, 1986; Stransky 1968, as well as the following representative personal memoirs, all in Hebrew: Friedman 1999; Gross n.d.; Hoffman n.d.; Litman 1996; Meizlish and Shefi n.d.; Moshkovitz 1997; Tsahor 1997; Yakobi n.d.

19   The following are a few examples of the rabbi's typical comments on Zionism and other movements to which he was opposed: 'Utterly detest it and loathe it, for it is doomed' (Deut. 7: 26), file Weiss, no. 9; 'Zionists and communists—may they all rot', file Nemesh, no. 37; '"All who are thirsty, go to the water" [Isa. 55: 1]. "Thirsty" [in Hebrew: *tsame—tsadi, mem, alef*] stands for *tsiyonim* [Zionists, understood as secular Zionists], *mizraḥim* [supporters of the Mizrahi religious Zionist movement], and *agudistim* [supporters of Agudas Yisrael, an Orthodox Ashkenazi movement]. All those should be thrown into the water', file Dinur, no. 4.

20   File Friedman, M., no. 5; on this see Ben-David 1996: 56, and Jelinek 2003: 130, who also shows that R. Shapiro's court management was corrupt—failing to pay salaries, for example.

21   The socio-linguistic speech act theory explicates the ways in which, under the right conditions, significant utterances—such as verdicts, declarations, agreements—are in fact actions. These conditions are fulfilled in many traditional societies such as that of the Munkács hasidic court, where there was a powerful leader, a restrictive social order, and obedient followers. A person cursed by the *rebbe* actually believes that he is doomed and is so regarded by others; someone who is ostracized is literally banned from entering the community's institutions, and so on.

22   Although there is no evidence that the rabbi actually engaged in such activities, the general hasidic environment did conceive of his curses and similar acts as carrying magical power. In this sense these people, like other traditional societies world-wide, tended towards a form of thinking in line with the general principles outlined by James Frazer in *The Golden Bough* (see Frazer 1993: 11–60). Of these, sympathetic, or metonymic, magical thinking is the most relevant here. Considering, for example, the rabbi's sayings quoted in n. 19 above and the lack of response to them, we might infer that his followers actually 'detested and loathed' the cursed opponents enough to ostracize or physically beat them, and that these opponents were intimidated enough to suppress their natural response. See Middleton 1987: 82–9, which offers a general review of the writings of key 20th-century anthropologists such as Mircea Eliade, E. E. Evans-Pritchard, Lucien Lévy-Bruhl, Émile Durkheim, Claude Lévi-Strauss, and Mary Douglas on this subject. For an example in a nearby Carpatho-Russian community, see Rosen 2006.

23   In my first study of Carpatho-Russian Jewish lore I devoted a whole chapter to three shared storytelling events and the unique texts and dynamics they yielded. Portions of one section in that chapter appear in the present essay (see Rosen 1999: 62–70). My second book on the subject (Rosen 2004) is wholly devoted to the Holocaust experience of the same community.

24   It may be that Mrs Nemesh was influenced by her own interview when interviewing these two men, each on his own, but in the main she was following a general interviewer guide covering sixteen potential topics which I formulated and which appears in the appendix to Rosen 1999.

25   In her essay on the borders between Jewish and non-Jewish societies in the east European shtetls, Annamaria Orla-Bukowska (2004) emphasizes the difference between present-day critical views of segregation and attitudes in the shtetls themselves, where maintaining distinctions and divisions was welcomed by all sides. This was so even though they had close relations in almost every aspect of their otherwise necessarily shared lives.

26   In his essay about the rise and decline of Zionism in Congress Poland, Joseph Goldstein enumerates this fear of hasidic circles together with their objection to secularism and fear of postponing the coming of the messiah. See Goldstein 1990: 115, 119.

27   In the original Hebrew text Mr Litman uses the plural noun *haftsarot* deriving from the verb *lehaftsir*, 'to beseech', whose sense is close to 'begging' and which reinforces the weakness of the father and grandfather in this narrative. This usage has been slightly changed in the English translation in order to retain the sentence's structure, as there is no noun to this verb in English.

28　　As illustrated in Sholem Aleichem's *Adventures of Mottel the Cantor's Son* (1953).

29　　On the halakhic and aggadic attitude towards learned women see Boyarin 1993: 186–8.

30　　The term *terefah* originally refers to the forbidden flesh of an animal that had not been ritually slaughtered but had died or been killed by another animal (Exod. 22: 30). It has since
been used for all non-kosher food, as well as to the mixing of dairy foods and meat
(*EJ* 1971: xv. 1016–17).

31　　For the stages of 'social drama' see Turner 1982. For an implementation of Turner's
model, see Meyerhoff 1979: 31–2, 149.

References

ALEICHEM, SHOLEM. 1953. *Adventures of Mottel the Cantor's Son*, trans. Tamara Kahana.
New York.

AUSTIN, J. L. 1965. *How To Do Things with Words*. New York.

BAR-ITZHAK, HAYA. 2001. *Jewish Poland: Legends of Origin, Ethnopoetics, and Legendary
Chronicles*. Detroit.

BEN-DAVID, DAVID. 1996. *Bridge Over Abysses: A Biography* [Gesher altehomot: biyo-
grafiah]. Nir Etzion.

BENNETT, GILLIAN. 1986. 'Narrative as Expository Discourse', *Journal of American Folklore*, 99: 415–34.

BOYARIN, DANIEL 1993. *Carnal Israel: Reading Sex in Talmudic Culture*. Berkeley, Calif.

CAŁA, ALINA. 2004. 'The Shtetl: Cultural Evolution in Small Jewish Towns', *Polin*, 17:
130–41.

DINUR, DOV. 1983. *Chapters in the History of the Jews of Sub-Carpathian Ruthenia (from the
Beginning of Settlement to the Holocaust, 1493–1943)* [Perakim betoledot yehudei
rusiyah hakarpatit (mithilat hahityashvut adhashoah, 1493–1943)]. Jerusalem and
Tel Aviv.

DOUGLAS, MARY. 2002. *Purity and Danger: An Analysis of Concepts of Pollution and Taboo*.
New York.

EJ 1971. *Encyclopaedia Judaica*, 22 vols. Jerusalem.

FRAZER, JAMES. 1993 [1890–1915]. *The Golden Bough*. Edition cited: Wordsworth.

FRIEDMAN, RACHEL BERNHEIM. 1999. *Earrings in the Cellar: To Grow Up in Ruined
Worlds* [Agilim bamartef: litsemoah me'olamot neheravim: sipur ishi]. Tel Aviv; 2nd
edn 2004.

GOLDSTEIN, JOSEPH. 1990. 'The Beginning of the Zionist Movement in Congress
Poland: The Victory of the Hasidim over the Zionists?', *Polin*, 5: 114–30.

GROSS, DVORA. n.d. 'Life Story' [Sipur hayim]. Manuscript, archives of the Research
Project.

GUTMAN, ISRAEL, ed. 1990. *Encyclopedia of the Holocaust*, 4 vols. New York.

HARRIS, MARVIN. 1974. *Cows, Pigs, Wars, and Witches: The Riddles of Culture*. New York.

HOFFMAN, MOSHE. n.d. 'Stories' [Sipurim]. Manuscript, archives of the Research
Project.

JAKOBSON, ROMAN. 1978. 'The Dominant'. In Ladislav Matejka and Kristina Pomorska, eds, *Readings in Russian Poetics: Formalist and Structuralist Views*, 82–7. Michigan.

JELINEK, YESHAYAHU A. 1995. 'Carpatho-Rus' Jewry: The Last Czechoslovakian Chapter, 1944–1949', *Shvut—Studies in Russian and East European Jewish History and Culture*, 1–2(17–18): 265–95.

—— 1998. 'Jewish Youth in Carpatho-Rus': Between Hope and Despair (1920–1938)', *Shvut*, 7(23): 147–65.

—— 2003. *Exile in the Foothills of the Carpathians: The Jews of Carpatho-Rus' and Mukachevo, 1848–1948* [Hagolah leragle hakarpatim: yehudei karpato-rus' umukatsavo, 1848–1948]. Tel Aviv.

LABOV, WILLIAM. 1972. *Language in the Inner City: Studies in the Black English Vernacular*. Philadelphia.

—— and JOSHUA WALETZKI. 1967. 'Narrative Analysis: Verbal Versions of Personal Experience'. In June Helm, ed., *Essays on the Verbal and Visual Arts: Proceedings of the 1966 Annual Spring Meeting of the American Ethnological Society*, 12–44. Seattle, Wash.

LITMAN, PERETZ. 1996. *A Boy from Munkács: The Story of a Survivor* [Hana'ar mimunkats: sipuro shel nitzol]. Haifa. Also available in manuscript at the archives of the Research Project.

MEIZLISH, SHAUL, and YAAKOV SHEFI, eds. n.d. *Song of David: Life Chapters of David Shmerler, Blessed Be his Memory* [Shirat dovid: pirkei hayim shel dovid shmerler, zikhrono leberakhah]. Petah Tikva.

MEYERHOFF, BARBARA. 1979. *Number Our Days*. New York.

MIDDLETON, JOHN. 1987. 'Theories of Magic'. In Mircea Eliade, ed., *The Encyclopedia of Religion*, 82–9. New York.

MOSHKOVITZ, MOSHE. 1997. *Jews of a Different Kind: From a Small Village in Carpatho-Russia to Israel* [Yahadut aheret: mikfar katan bekarpato-rusiyah leyisra'el]. Lehavot Hafakot.

OHMANN, RICHARD M. 1972. 'Speech Acts and the Definition of Literature', *Philosophy and Rhetoric*, 4: 1–19.

ORLA-BUKOWSKA, ANNAMARIA. 2004. 'Maintaining Borders, Crossing Borders: Social Relationships in the Shtetl', *Polin*, 17: 171–95.

RAVITZKY, AVIEZER. 1996. *Messianism, Zionism, and Jewish Religious Radicalism*. Chicago.

REINHARTZ, JEHUDA. 1980. 'Zionists and Jewish Liberals in Germany, Austro-Hungary, and Bohemia'. In Haim Avni and Gideon Shimoni, eds, *Zionism and its Opponents in the Jewish Nation* [Hatsiyonut umitnagedeha ba'am hayehudi: kovets ma'amarim], 89–100. Jerusalem.

ROSEN, ILANA. 1999. *There Once Was...: The Oral Lore of the Jews of Carpatho-Russia* [Ma'asei shehaya...: hasiporet ha'amamit shel yehudei karpatorus]. Tel Aviv.

—— 2004. *'In Auschwitz We Blew the Shofar': Carpatho-Russian Jews Remember the Holocaust* (Heb.). Jerusalem.

—— 2006. 'Saintly and Sympathetic Magic in the Lore of the Jews of Carpatho-Russia between the Two World Wars', in Gábor Klaniczay and Éva Pócs, eds, *Demons, Spirits, Witches*, vol. ii: *Christian Demonology and Popular Mythology*. Budapest and New York.

SEARLE, JOHN. 1969. *Speech Acts: An Essay in the Philosophy of Language*. Cambridge.

SHPIEGEL, YEHUDA. n.d. *A History of the Jews and the Development of Hasidism in Sub-Carpathian Ruthenia* [Toledot yisra'el vehitpathut haḥasidut berusiyah hakarpatit]. Tel Aviv.

SOLE, ARYE. 1968. 'Sub-Carpathian Ruthenia: 1918–1938'. In *The Jews of Czechoslovakia*, vol. i, pp. 125–54. Philadelphia.

—— 1986. *Lights on the Mountains: Zionist Hebrew Education in Carpatho-Russia in the Years 1920–1944* [Orot beharim: haḥinukh ha'vri hatsiyoni bekarpatorus bashanim 1920–1944]. Tel Aviv.

STRANSKY, HUGO. 1968. 'The Religious Life in Slovakia and Sub-Carpathian Ruthenia'. In *The Jews of Czechoslovakia*, vol. i, pp. 347–92. Philadelphia.

TSAHOR, BARUCH. 1997. *I Was No Hero* [Lo hayiti gibor]. Maarechet.

TURNER, VICTOR. 1982. 'Social Dramas and Stories about Them'. In Victor Turner, *From Ritual to Theatre: The Human Seriousness of Play*, 61–88. New York.

YAKOBI, ITZHAK. n.d. *My Life History* [Toledot hayai]. Manuscript, archives of the Research Project.

The Sublimity of the Jewish Type: Balzac's *Belle Juive* as Virgin Magdalene *aux Camélias*

J U D I T H   L E W I N

STUDIES OF JEWISH WOMEN in literature have generally been a mere footnote under studies of 'the Jew in Western literature'—the appellation 'Jew' assuming a study of the Jewish man as representative of the Jewish community.[1] Even in groundbreaking work on the representation and construction of the Jew as symbol such as that of Sander Gilman there remains the same frustrating tendency: in his words, '(The category of the female Jew all but vanishes)'.[2] Here I want to break open the parenthetical phrase to which Gilman relegates Jewish women while discussing the feminization of the Jewish male by rendering visible the 'female Jew' and examining her representation.

Ann Pelligrini deplores the separation of race and gender into incommensurable analytical structures with the striking phrase: '*All Jews are womanly but no women are Jews.*'[3] While the Jewish woman is in a different category to the male Jew by virtue of her gender, she is also set apart from the general category of Woman by virtue of her status as a Jew. These two categories of investigation demand a model to examine their formerly invisible intersection. While critics have had difficulty imagining (or imaging) the Jewish woman, this difficulty reflects the ambiguity discernible in her literary representations. That is to say, the complex identity of Jewish women makes literature, as a place where cultural fantasies may be worked through, a good place to look. The complexity of the Jewish woman's image in literature cannot be captured in the formula 'Jew + Woman', for she is somehow more than, less than, and beyond this summation. Conventional depictions of Jewish women rely on stereotypical codes that apply to each of the separate groups. It is where these codes overlap that complexity is created.

The literary and cultural image of the Jewish woman is exempt from some of the economic antisemitism levelled against the Jewish man (for example his stereotypical depiction as a usurer), yet, as a woman, she participates in the economic sphere through the circulation of her body. As a woman, she is subject to literary codes that characterize most women in fiction: object of desire or threat; candidate for marriage or candidate for sacrifice. Her Jewishness, however, mediates her eligibility for certain plots or actions: for example, though her desirability as a lover may be expressed in an orientalist idiom, she is largely ineligible for the marriage plot without conversion. If the Jewish man is subject not only to economic prejudice but also to antisemitism, as Freud—and Gilman after him—have argued, because fear of his circumcised status may lead to fear of castration, perhaps displaced onto other physical markers, such as the nose, how do Jewish women, not subject to circumcision, make out? One reaction is to treat the Jewish woman with less prejudice, thinking of her as more accessible to conversion; other reactions, however, consider her perceived lack of bodily 'marking' as more dangerous (she may be an irresistible, castrating *femme fatale*), or as misleading so that, as I have argued elsewhere, for the sake of categorical stability Jewish male circumcision may be displaced onto the Jewish female body (for example in the form of turbans, earrings, or earring-holes) in order to render her difference legible, indelible, and incontrovertible (see Lewin 2006; Metzger 1998: 59–60).

The Jewish woman's difference from feminized Jewish men and marriageable Christian women is not, however, enough to delineate her specificity and hence her function as a fictional character. She also is seen through the lens of orientalism, because of the constructed image of her roots in the Middle East as a member of the 'Hebraic' or 'Israelite' race. In addition, she is othered by the common literary depiction of her dark-haired, dark-eyed physiognomy, though she is frequently differentiated from the orientalized Jewish man by being seen as closer to Western sensibilities. The French Romantic writer Chateaubriand suggested that the treatment of Jews by Christian society varied according to their gender and physical appeal: only Jewish men were to be held responsible for the crucifixion, and this guilt was revealed in their distinctive physical traits. He argued that Jewish women were exempted from perpetual misery and persecution by the grace Jesus accorded to Mary Magdalene, and that this was the root of Christian men's attraction to and sexual associations with Jewish women.[4] Chateaubriand's musings fully participate in the rhetoric of orientalism: where do the 'borders' lie between orientalized women, set up in opposition to the Christian majority women of 'home', and orientalized Jewish women? Theories of orientalism(s), derived from (and defined against) Edward Said's *Orientalism* (1979), rely on spatial difference, based on a geographical opposition between Europe and the rest of the world, or north/south, east/west (using a binary opposition that Homi Bhabha's notion of 'hybridity' (Bhabha 1994) has helped to break down). Jonathan Boyarin has suggested, however, that concentrating strictly on the spatial axis marginalizes the 'othering' of Jews, which he calls 'temporal othering' (Boyarin 1994: 429). The reification of biblical models of Jewishness removes the Jews from the present, from history, as 'eternal and unchanging', terms that crop up to describe the specifically 'Jewish' character of someone's features or actions. This neutralization of Jewish difference through temporal segregation remained in effect at least until a modern Jewish Other was recognized and admitted into view, which became inevitable as the Enlightenment raised the question of Jewish emancipation and religious and cultural tolerance. The device of temporal othering, however, continues to inflect and interfere with literary attempts to represent a modern Jewish female figure.[5]

I do not offer here an all-encompassing account of representations of Jewish women. My goal is, rather, to offer specific examples from a limited place and time: in this case the Jewish woman in Paris of the 1830s and 1840s as she appears in Balzac, one of the nineteenth century's most popular and influential European writers.[6] The Jewish woman as represented in Balzac's *Comédie humaine*, and in French society in general, has been relatively neglected in the face of burgeoning work on British and east European literary models and German and American historical ones. This examination of the figures found in Balzac may contribute to a larger comparative project to test ideas about a universal Jewish female 'type'. Below, I place Balzac's characters in the context of other Jewish female literary characters with which he would have been familiar, and other Jewish female characters drawn by his French contemporaries. While Balzac had limited contact with actual Jewish women in Paris, I would suggest that the figures he created had a tremendous influence on the rhetoric of representing what has come to be known as *la belle Juive*.

Cultural and Historical Paris, 1830

In 1830, after the July Revolution, the 'citizen king' Louis-Philippe assumed the throne of France and inaugurated a liberal phase in French politics, heralded for the Jews by the 1830 charter that declared Catholicism no longer the state religion but rather the religion of the majority.[7] France was populated by 60,000 Jews, 8,500 of whom lived in Paris. French Jews had been declared citizens in 1791; despite the fall of Napoleon, this status remained in force.[8]

Scott Lerner summarizes the three schools of thought, which he calls discourses, about the 'Jewish question' in this period. The first discourse advocated 'integration and unconditional rights' for the Jews as a step towards 'regeneration' which would ultimately lead, it was thought, to conversion. The second discourse held that Jews were absolutely foreign to Frenchmen and should be neither integrated nor tolerated. The third discourse 'fought for rights and promoted reforms, but also respected the substance of Jewish life and aimed to preserve it in a modern form' (Lerner 2004: 256–7).

Since it was the first discourse, under the Abbé Grégoire, that prevailed politically in 1791, the latent pressure to assimilate and ultimately to convert was the dominant influence. Historians differ, however, over whether conversion was truly a frequent occurrence (it was much more so in Germany, for example) or, rather, whether this perception derived from the apostasy of some extremely visible Jews.[9] Many accounts of the period refer to the case of Simon Deutz, the son of the Grand Rabbi of France and a convert to Catholicism, who was responsible for the arrest in 1832 of the Duchesse de Berry for conspiring to overthrow the government of Louis-Philippe. Deutz became a symbol for the second discourse, for, though a convert to Catholicism, he was portrayed as retaining his Jewishness 'in the flesh': popular songs depicted him as a Judas, and in a poem by Hugo ('To the Man who Delivered up a Woman') he is seen as without honour, a quality to which Jews were denied access. 'Although he was no longer necessarily identifiable as a Jew . . . this [lack of identifiability] seemed to be his most telling characteristic' (Kalman 2003: 673). The Deutz case attested to the fact that for French conservatives, and possibly for the French in general in this period, Judaism had an 'immutable' quality: 'even apostasy was not a guarantee of respectability, and one could revert to one's inherent "Judaism" simply by one's acts' (Kalman 2003: 677–86; see also Ezdinli 1993: 28).

As I shall show, the mixture of conversionist fervour, toleration, and the sense of absolute foreignness makes its way into the depictions of Jewish women in this period, as do the concepts of Jewishness as immutable yet at the same time hidden and not identifiable. Despite the absence of Jewish women in the public sphere and a complete lack of familiarity with the Jewish world, the fantasies of non-Jewish authors about Jewish women resonate as archetypes—'a greedy courtesan', 'an instrument of her father's will' (Landau 2004: 13)—that describe a society in the midst of change. As even this brief overview of the situation of Jews in France in the 1830s and 1840s demonstrates, Balzac's *belle Juive* both responded to his cultural context and exerted an influence on later cultural representations and rhetoric. Balzac recognized the usefulness of the Jewess as a character, and added her to his stock of anti-figures that reinforce the conservative centre of his novels. He made much of the contradictions at the character's core—sacred yet sensual, spiritual yet secular—not to mention of her *beauté sublime*.

Biblical as well as early modern literary images of Jewish women (Shakespeare's Jessica, Racine's Esther) influenced Balzac's characterization, alongside the wave of enthusiasm that swept Europe for the character of Rebecca in Walter Scott's historical novel of 1820, *Ivanhoe*.[10] The biblical matriarchs and lesser figures such as Dinah, Yael, Esther, and Judith present nurturingly maternal and vividly sexual, if not explicitly threatening, images. Where Shakespeare's Jessica gives birth to the expectation of Jewish female conversion, Scott's Rebecca is significant for her refusal to convert—and therefore for the sublimation of her own desires to her duty to her father and people. Rebecca established a tradition of English Jewesses as sexy celibates—in contrast to the French *belle Juive*, who, according to *fin-de-siècle* writer J.-K. Huysmans, was 'indispensable' to every self-respecting brothel.[11] As Pelligrini points out, stereotypes of the 'Jewess' that join a '"positive" image of moral virtue to a "negative" image of sensuality and deceit' are a familiar fusion of the virgin and the whore 'inflected by a racialized difference'.[12]

Scott's Rebecca was immediately appreciated as a breakthrough character. Scott's literary influence, especially his technique of historical ekphrasis, a mode that describes people, objects, and landscapes in a pictorial idiom, imitating the visual, became fundamental to the rise of, in Georg Lukács's words, the '*present as history*' of realism (1983: 83). Close on the bard's heels was Scott's great admirer, Honoré de Balzac. If Scott was thoroughly saturated by his immersion in Shakespeare, Balzac began his writing career at the time of *walterscottomanie* (Walter Scott mania).[13] He took the historical novel, which reinvigorates the remote past, and transposed it to present-day Paris. Though the relationship between Scott and Balzac is well known and Scott's influence on the Frenchman easily recognized, a closer look at the cultural and literary history surrounding the genesis of Balzac's *belles Juives* suggests that Balzac himself contributed to a wave of Jewish female cultural representations in 1830s France. Alfred de Vigny, for example, in addition to the biblical figures appearing in his collection *Poèmes antiques et modernes* (1826), translated *The Merchant of Venice* in 1828 as *Shylock*, bringing a French adaptation of Jessica to the stage. Victor Hugo offered his own collection, *Les Orientales*, in 1829, and Edgar Quinet revisited the legend of the Wandering Jew with *Ahasvérus* in 1833 (Ezdinli 1993: 39 n. 13). Several writers, however, focused specifically on the Jewish woman, frequently in isolation.

Eugénie Foa, born Rebecca Eugénie Rodrigues Henriques to a wealthy Bordeaux Jewish family in 1796, began her career as a novelist, journal contributor, and children's author with a series of novels on Jewish themes in 1830.[14] *Le Kidouschim* appeared in 1830, according to a review in the *Journal des débats* on 27 May, where the novel is described as 'translated from the Hebrew by Mme Foy [Mrs Faith]' (Ezdinli 1993: 39 n. 21), though no copies of it appear to have survived. In 1833 Foa published a collection of short stories called *Rachel* that opened with 'Rachel ou l'héritage', the tragic story of a contemporary Jewish woman writer. It is framed as the posthumously discovered memoirs of a Jewish woman whose marriage to her Christian lover is forbidden and who is subsequently abandoned by her Jewish husband (as was the case with Foa).[15] This story is one of three in the collection of nine that clearly targeted a non-Jewish readership, given that it is studded with notes explaining customs and rites and identified as 'scenes of Jewish manners'.[16] Also in 1833, George Sand published a short story, 'Lavinia', about a Sephardi woman courted by both English and French gentry, who in the end chooses a life of travel rather than marriage to either suitor.[17] In 1835 Foa published *La Juive*, a historical fiction set in the eighteenth century, that told the tragic tale of a Jewish woman, her Christian lover, and her blocking, authoritarian father, and which included set pieces of Jewish ceremonies in order to satisfy the public's curiosity about Jewish cultural exoticism. This 1835 novel appeared shortly after the first performance of Eugène Scribe and Fromental

Halévy's opera, also called *La Juive*, featuring a heroine also called Rachel, who is cast into a cauldron of boiling oil at the very moment when she is declared the daughter of her Christian inquisitor rather than a Jewess.[18] Foa's sister Léonie, a sculptor, was in fact married to Fromental Halévy (Muelsch 1997: 69 n. 10; Landau 2004: 106). The opera and novel unleashed a wave of 'faddish interest in Jewish themes', which every writer with 'sound commercial instincts' could cash in on. 'Piano redactions of the major arias from *La Juive* were in almost every parlor when Foa's novel appeared, and a favorite masquerade costume for the Carnival Ball that season was an oriental Jewess (perhaps because it permitted women to wear pants)' (Stuhlman 1997: 45).[19]

Balzac's short story 'La Torpille' (The Torpedo/Sting Ray), in which his Jewish courtesan Esther first appears, was planned in 1835 and intended for subsequent serial publication in the journal *La Presse*, but ultimately did not appear there. It was published independently in 1838, and only later became the first section of the novel *Splendeurs et misères des courtisanes*, which is the main focus of my discussion below. In 1838 the Jewish actress Elisa Félix debuted at the Comédie-Française, adopting what may have been her middle name, Rachel, apparently as a response to the public's continuing enthusiasm for Halévy's Jewess.[20] Mademoiselle Rachel was known for her performances of classical tragedy, especially Racine and Corneille, and she appeared early in her career (with a turban) as the oriental despot Roxane in *Bajazet*, as the Christian convert Pauline in *Polyeucte*, and—ironically with less success—in *Esther* (first performed in 1839) and in *Judith*, a play written especially for her by Delphine de Girardin in 1843.[21] A clear double for Rachel may be found in Josépha, an irresistible but rapacious Jewish courtesan, in one of Balzac's late novels, *La Cousine Bette* (1846) (see Brownstein 2004; Spitzer 1939: 16). Rachel and Balzac both frequented Delphine de Girardin's salon, where they were known to compete for attention. In an apocryphal story, found in Léger's biography, *Balzac mis à nu*, Balzac insisted on one occasion on performing alongside Rachel when she was called on to recite from *Bajazet*. Not only did Balzac swear that he knew all of Racine by heart, but after losing his way and demanding a copy of the play to be brought to him, he turned out to be a deplorable actor, and emitted an ill-timed burp that discountenanced Rachel, who, by commenting under her breath, inadvertently mortified the novelist (Spitzer 1939: 16–17). If this story is true, it goes far towards explaining the bitterness that inspired the singular late depiction of the avaricious, self-serving, and sexually savvy Jewess, Josépha.

Balzac's *Belles Juives*

The fates of two of Balzac's *filles perdues*, Coralie and Esther, are immortally connected in Esther's final message to Lucien de Rubempré, protagonist of *Illusions perdues* (1836–43) and *Splendeurs et misères des courtisanes* (1837–47).[22] Lucien falls in love twice in his two-novel lifetime—both times with *une belle Juive*. In each of these liaisons he forms a love triangle with a married, well-off, older business-man and would-be suitor, whom the young lovers fleece in order to fund Lucien's ascent into high society.[23] As Esther reminds him in her suicide note, each of these *belles Juives* sacrifices her life on his behalf: 'Say to yourself now and then: there were two good-natured harlots, both of them beautiful, who both died for me, without bearing me any grudge, who both worshipped me; raise up in your heart a monument to Coralie, to Esther, and go on your way!' (*HHL* 369).[24] Esther is the exemplary courtesan in *Splendeurs et misères*, but in their discussion of the novel critics have by and large overlooked the noteworthy issue of her Jewishness. Coralie, the actress from *Illusions perdues*, plays a supporting role in the discussion that follows, helping to establish recurring patterns associated with Balzac's *belle Juive*. In addition, I will also look at another of Balzac's women, Paquita, the exotic oriental *fille aux yeux d'or* in the novella of that name, whose character provides a means of distinguishing between the function of the Jewish woman and that of generalized oriental exoticism in Balzac's stories.

It is hard to imagine a male fantasy that Esther could not satisfy. She is at once a prostitute and a penitent, a virgin and a magdalen, a Jew and a Christian, and an emblematic incarnation of *la belle Juive*. What makes her death a narrative necessity and her survival simply impossible? Balzac's *belle Juive,* embodied in Esther, is invited into the narrative as an Other for her exotic effect, only to be domesticated, converted, and ultimately sacrificed to the needs of her lover, her (authorial) creator, and to the narrative paradox she comes to incarnate. What is the threat that she somehow poses? I would suggest that it has to do with anxiety about the (in)visibility and convertibility of Jewish women: a Jewish conversion may never be a true conversion without the absolute sacrifice of the body for the sake of the soul. Balzac's *belle Juive* is, first, a paradoxical figure: the epitome of female currency and circulation is reserved for one man; the epitome of the fallen woman is re-created as a virgin; and the epitome of the biblical, Jewish 'eternal type' ('Queen Esther') is reincarnated as the ultimate Christian penitent harlot, Mary Magdalene.[25] Each of these incarnations is more transcendent, and ultimately more untenable, than the last. Second, *la belle Juive* is indispensable specifically in her contradictions. This is because in his depiction of her Balzac raises the issue of conversion, which hangs on a contradiction between the stated aim of total assimilation (Jewishness as religion) and the implicit belief in a 'blood taint' (Jewishness as race). Balzac's *belle Juive* resolves this paradox through a 'sanctified' suicide-sacrifice.

Gold and Pleasure

La belle Juive conventionally describes a young, nubile, orientalized, and seductive Jewess—a figure of (sexual) fantasy. Esther comes to be read as the epitome of this type, a process theorized by Lukács through the concept of character type, which he defines as 'a peculiar synthesis which organically binds together the general and the particular' (1964: 6). Literature relies on the use of accredited models, whether or not they are recognized as such, but recognition makes the difference between a 'naturalized model' that the reader accepts as 'real' and therefore 'true', and a 'prefabricated mould' rejected as excessive, codified, or distorted, and thus 'fake' (Amossy 1984: 689; see also Brinker 1982–3, 1985). Recognition, however, is based on previous cultural knowledge: depending on the reader's familiarity with similar cultural models, a character may be perceived as either 'real' (or in Ruth Amossy's phrase an 'eternal type') or caricature. Homi Bhabha (1994) has referred to this reading through recognition as the cultural 'baggage' readers bring to the text. Here I will look at the type of *la belle Juive* in the context of this theoretical framework.

In terms of ideology one must note that, in Esther, mythic descriptions jarringly combine with other, more familiar, Balzacian concerns: social aspirations, commerce, and corrupted and corrupting capitalism. Balzac presents a reified, idealized model of the Jewish woman by isolating her in time and space, first completely removing her from social circulation in a convent, and then imprisoning her with her lover in a hideaway, where they pass '[a] boring chapter, since it describes four years of happiness'. As Balzac puts it, 'Happiness is without history' (HHL 76, 80).[26] For Balzac, the figure of *la belle Juive* must have been a useful one as she could be considered exempt from occidental Christian codes of behaviour. She appears nonetheless to have been most useful to him as an isolated figure: orphaned, and removed from the Jewish community. On the one hand, placing her in Paris complicates Balzac's project, obscuring the boundaries between characteristics produced by heredity and those produced by environment; on the other hand, in Balzac's Paris, with its crucial emphasis on social mobility, the Jewish woman becomes the ideal social mover. As a courtesan she can climb from the bottom to the top of the social pyramid—and frequently slide back down again: 'At eighteen, this girl had already known the highest wealth, total destitution, men at all levels' (HHL 29).[27]

Balzac's views on the forces motivating society are summed up in an unequivocal narratorial pronouncement in the opening pages of 'La Fille aux yeux d'or' (1834–5): the dynamic driving society is created by the desire for 'l'or et le plaisir'. This dual passion becomes a refrain during the lyrical discussion of the morals of Paris during the opening twenty or so pages of the story, culminating in the final explicit statement (added to the implicit one in the title, which is continually repeated), phrased as a maxim: 'All passion in Paris is resolved into two terms: gold and pleasure' ('Girl' 322).[28] The main object of desire in this story, Paquita, the 'girl with the golden eyes' as she is generally known—or more aptly the harlot (*fille*) with eyes of (for?) gold—incarnates the fusion of the two desires, money and pleasure, into one unstable, exotic object. Though the focus here is on figures that exemplify the point of convergence of these two axes, it is important to note that the two objects of desire are conventionally separated between the male and female Jew.[29] Jean-Paul Sartre, using a problematic, ironically fascist vocabulary, is nevertheless revelatory in his description of the term *la belle Juive*, a term to which he ascribes exploitative connotations:

There is in the words 'a beautiful Jewess' a very special sexual signification . . . This phrase carries an aura of rape and massacre. The 'beautiful Jewess' is she whom the Cossacks under the czars dragged by her hair through the streets of her burning village. And the special works which are given over to accounts of flagellation reserve a place of honor for the Jewess. But it is not necessary to look into esoteric literature . . . the Jewess has a well-defined function even in the most serious novels. Frequently violated or beaten, she sometimes succeeds in escaping dishonor by means of death, but that is a form of justice; and those who keep their virtue are docile servants or humiliated women in love with indifferent Christians who marry Aryan women.[30]

Though Balzac may not have imagined Cossacks per se, there is certainly a despotic aspect to his oriental fantasies. Consider, for example, the submissive Paquita, her murderous lover, the marquise de San-Réal, and her other lover, the marquise's half-brother Henri de Marsay ('une main de fer' and a 'despote oriental'). The parallel between Paquita—a Spanish woman of Georgian descent imprisoned by her lesbian lover—and Esther—a Jewish courtesan kept in secret by her lover and his (bisexual) protector—becomes clearer when one recognizes that Balzac's imaginary Orient includes Spain and parts of Russia as well as the six other non-European continents (see Citron 1968: 306–7). The hideous serving-women appointed as Esther's gatekeepers make this opposition—as well as Esther's liminality, situated between the continents, as it were—explicit. Called 'Europe' one servant is 'the nicest little lady's maid . . . pretty as a weasel', while the other, called 'Asia', is described in terms of apes, tigers, dogs, and cats, as well as 'Hindu idols' and figures on 'Chinese screens', the end result being an Asiatic monster (*HHL* 72–3; Pléiade 484). Esther is neither of these—European nor Asian—or she is both. At stake in this discussion are not just the conventions of orientalist depiction, but rather the serious repercussions of conflating 'l'or et le plaisir' into a lone figure. The Jewish courtesan epitomizes the locus where two primal desires can meet and be exchanged: pleasure for gold, gold for pleasure.

If, according to Sartre, Jews are located by French society as 'outside History', they nonetheless form a presence within the history of literature, as an ever-evolving eternal type: 'The Jew is not yet *historical* and yet he is the most ancient of peoples, or nearly so. That is what gives him the air of being perpetually aged and yet always young: he has wisdom and no history' (1948: 84; 1954: 102, emphasis original). Sartre's 'Jew' corresponds, then, to Balzac's 'Happiness': neither has a history. What does it take for a Jew to enter into history and become part of the story?

In Chateaubriand's comments on the rift between perceptions of Jewish men and Jewish women, he offers a memorable explanation based on his own observations in an Italian ghetto:

The Jewish quarter [La Giudecca] where we stopped on our return trip still contains a few poor Jewish families: one can recognize them by their traits. *In this race the women are far more handsome than the men; they seem to have escaped the malediction with which their fathers, their husbands and their sons have been cursed.* One cannot find a single Jewess mixed into the crowd of priests and people who insulted the Son of Man, whipped him, crowned him with thorns, made him suffer ignominies and the pains of the cross. The women of Judea believed in the Saviour, loved him, followed him, helped him by their own means, assuaged his afflictions . . . the sinner-woman poured perfumed oil on his feet and wiped them with her hair. Christ, in turn, extended his mercy and grace to Jewish women . . . His first apparition after his glorious resurrection was to the Magdalene; she did not recognize him, but he said to her, 'Mary'. At the sound of his voice the eyes of the Magdalene opened and she answered, 'My Master'. *The reflection of some beautiful ray of light must have remained on the faces of Jewish women.* (Chateaubriand 1964: 389; my translation, emphasis added)

Exempt from eternal punishment for the crime of crucifying Jesus, the Jewish woman was considered with indulgence in some traditional Christian representations, as a *victime pathétique* (Klein 1970: 11–33). Inherited from the Middle Ages was the perception of the Jewish woman as more accessible to a missionary Christianity (a premise of Chateaubriand's argument above) and hence more easily baptized. In addition, she was available to the Christian gaze almost solely through indistinct, frozen, yet generally positive literary representations, for in the social sphere she was virtually invisible. It is precisely this which allows the figure of the Jewish woman to lend itself to literary representation: in her invisibility she is infinitely creatable; representation of her as an 'eternal type' ensures its own reality and constitutes its own Truth, and her inaccessibility fuels her exotic, idealized attraction. What it takes, then, to enter 'History', or the story, is the notice of a Christian man.[31]

For Balzac, Romantic, Jewish, orientalized female figures become symbols of the natural and the irrational, the slave and the dominatrix (Bitton 1973b; Bitton-Jackson 1982; Klein 1970: 38–49). In *La Comédie humaine* it is clear that there exists no absolute Good or Evil, no pure Mary or sinful Eve. *Splendeurs et misères* serves as a prime example of this fact, portraying a world where criminals and police are on an equal footing and where the spheres of prison and prostitution blend with the worlds of the law, finance, and the aristocracy.[32] Jews represent a mixture of both the Orient and the Occident, a bewildering fusion of what could be the quintessence of both hemispheres defined in opposition.[33] In some cases the tension of this perception resolves into a re-simplified, divided image of the Jews: biblical Jews versus contemporary Jews; *la belle Juive* in opposition to *le Juif maléfique*. But Balzac's Jewish actress-courtesan offers a recombined refusal of dualisms: in her, business meets pleasure and biblical beauty extracts a capitalist fee. The courtesan becomes the idealized figure of an exemplary soul, of a life without rules lived to excess (positive vitality in Balzac's system of values), and of someone who shatters all of the *cadres sociaux*.

Finally, as Charles Bernheimer has shown, the courtesan is a figure of extreme instability, the meeting-point of luxury and misery, that lends itself admirably to literary creation (Bernheimer 1989; see also Heathcote 2004). The setting in which Esther is found the day after she is discovered at the masked ball that opens the book is symptomatic of this fusion: 'here and there a card of dirty thread, white, scented gloves, a delicious hat propped on a water jug, a Ternaux shawl stuffing a crack in the window, an elegant dress hanging on a nail . . . such was the array of joyous and dismal, wretched and expensive objects which met the eye' (*HHL* 37–8).[34] The juxtapositions emphasize confusion, a mixing of luxuriousness and poverty, elegance and tastelessness, and purity coexisting with decay. An exotic shawl is used to fill gaps in the window when Esther tries to kill herself through carbon monoxide poisoning, but having forgotten to close a door she runs out of coal before she dies, and is left in a death-like faint instead. If the false start of a failed suicide jump-starts the events of the novel, this non-death foretells the story's inevitable ending in successful self-sacrifice. The discovery of Esther's half-dead body in these jumbled surroundings by the sham priest sets the stage for Balzac's set piece in bewilderment: the fusion of a dark, exotic Jewess with the icon of a fair, Christian saint.

The Magdalene

In the failed suicide attempt examined above, Esther appears with the following description: 'A handkerchief soaked with tears proved the sincerity of this Mary Magdalene, whose classic pose was that of the harlot without religion. This final repentance made the priest smile' (*HHL* 37).[35] Balzac's orientalist model of fusion has been redoubled by combining the courtesan and the *Juive*. To this constructed image, he layers on another character type, that of *la fille repentie*, a recurring trope so forceful that Esther passes at once through the stages of sinner, penitent, and saint: 'Her admirable fair hair hung to the ground and made a carpet beneath the feet of this messenger from heaven . . . "I have heard tell of a woman like me who poured aromatic ointment upon the feet of Jesus Christ. Alas, virtue has made me so poor that I have only tears to offer"' (*HHL* 49).[36] Some editors attribute Esther's blonde hair to a gaffe by Balzac, who was putting together a novel composed over many years, and preserve what they take to be his error.[37] A later plot point, however, turns on the very opposition between blonde and brunette (Jacques Collin tries to trick Nucingen by replacing Esther with an English woman): 'He was stupefied to see a woman totally the opposite of Esther: fair indeed where she had been dark, weakness where he had admired strength! A soft night in Brittany where the sun of Arabia had blazed' (*HHL* 145).[38]

One explanation of Esther's sudden blondeness is that in the original story, 'La Torpille', her character was to be called Olympe and had blonde hair like Balzac's mistress at the time, Mme Guidoboni-Visconti, but she later became a brunette like his last mistress, Mme Hanska.[39] Translator Rayner Heppenstall adopts this view when explaining his choice of translating Esther's nickname 'la Torpille' (electric ray or floating mine) as 'the Torpedo', despite the anachronism: 'I have allowed Esther to be referred to as "the Torpedo", fully aware that this lends her associations we might nowadays think more characteristic of some blonde bombshell, Esther being neither a bombshell nor (except on an early page, through Balzac's forgetfulness) blonde' (HHL xiii).

A contrasting view that takes into account the iconography of character types would suggest that, just as the epithet 'Torpedo' still gets at the subaqueous, hidden threat of coming into contact with one such as Esther (though it replaces the serpentine, stinging, organic shock with a more mechanical and mortal one), the retention of 'blonde' in this instance is no error at all, but, rather, contains associative layers that beg to be unearthed. 'Daughter', says the priest Herrera to Esther, 'your mother was a Jewess, and you were not baptized, but neither were you taken to the synagogue: your place is in the religious Limbo to which little children go' (HHL 48).[40] The depiction of Esther is that of the emblematic holy sinner: 'no longer a harlot, but a fallen angel getting up again', learning by innocent baby-steps, 'a girl of eighteen who could neither read nor write, to whom all knowledge, all instruction were new' (HHL 51, 54).[41] To reinforce this identification, Balzac leans on the iconic association of fairness with purity rather than the dark exoticism he uses elsewhere.

The chapter title itself is more than explicit: 'The Rat Becomes a Mary Magdalene' (HHL 48).[42] Susan Haskins explains that Mary Magdalene is a 'composite character'. In the eleventh century, details such as the long golden hair that grew to cover the nakedness she had assumed as a penitent in the desert were added to her mythology. Thirteenth- to fifteenth-century images depict her as the 'hairclad penitent' (Haskins 1993: 120, 232). Katherine Jansen adds, 'It is significant that at the moment of her conversion her hair—the symbol of her sexual sin—became the emblem of her penitence' (2000: 130–2). Hair, therefore, is an essential element in the description of the Magdalene, though, as Haskins points out, it does not exclude other important markers. The fact that beauty, 'the devil's instrument', tempts men through 'the female glories, her *mouth, eyes, and hair*' is a constant refrain in medieval writings:

It is through these organs, so abhorred by the men of the Church, that Mary Magdalen [sic] alternately seduces and repents . . . the eyes which had been used to lure men now *wept*, that glorious hair which she had bedecked with gold to entice young men she now used in humility to *dry Christ's feet*, the mouth which had so delighted her seducers now in sorrow *kissed the soles of his feet*, and the body which had lain prostrate with many men now *lay at Christ's feet*. (Haskins 1993: 153, emphasis added)

That Esther so clearly enacts the iconic Magdalene in the description of the 'admirable fair hair' that 'hung to the ground and made a carpet' is all the more evident in the full description that precedes it: 'She fell on her knees again, she kissed the priest's shoes, made them wet with her tears' (*HHL* 49).[43] This reading would suggest that the fair (or blonde) hair is no error, nor does it reflect a shift in Balzac's personal life, but is meant, rather, to establish an overt iconographic allusion.

In point of fact, the emblems of the tearful, penitent Magdalene are well in place pages before, when the priest first discovers Esther's prostrate body and 'the handkerchief soaked with tears'. Esther's conversion seems to be as spontaneous as it is heartfelt, which lends it credibility and wins the reader's sympathy. She is called 'this Mary Magdalene'—a member of a category of reformed women— even as she is elevated to the incarnation of *the* Mary Magdalene, having assumed the 'classic pose . . . of the harlot without religion'.

How should readers imagine this 'classic pose'? The phrase clearly signals an activation of shared cultural currency. In the mid-sixteenth century Titian painted what is arguably the best-known portrayal of the weeping Magdalene. Along with tearful, upraised eyes, she has 'magnificent red-gold tresses which she gathers to her. Her hair is no longer a mantle but an adornment . . . [that] emphasizes her sensuousness.' Titian portrayed this saintly sinner in 'the pose of an antique statue, the classical Venus Pudica, or "Venus of Modesty", which was described as expressing the "dual nature of love both sensuous and chaste"' (Haskins 1993: 239–40). If readers have not yet got the point from the repeated references to 'this Mary Magdalene' and 'a Mary Magdalene' (*HHL* 37, 48), fair hair, tears, and penitent poses drive it home. What is more, the description of Esther, a set piece of ekphrasis, is announced under the herald, '*A Portrait Titian Would Have Liked To Paint* (*HHL* 51).[44]

Haskins makes one final point regarding the signification of hair:

long hair in the Renaissance served as an erotic cipher . . . The ideal colour of a woman's hair shows remarkable consistency down through the ages . . . the crowning glories . . . have always been blonde or golden. Loose hair had been a moral indicator in the Middle Ages, symbolizing the *innocence of the virgin* . . . in an adult woman, however, it alluded to *moral laxity* . . . fair hair was a symbol of purity [however] the thickness of a woman's hair also implied her degree of wantonness. (1993: 246, emphasis added)

We can thus trace the idealization in blondeness, the allegory of the 'holy sinner', and the ultimate, underlying sexual availability of the courtesan character from whom Esther derives all layered together in Balzac's compressed description. The paradoxical 'dual nature' of the Titian Magdalene is evinced again in the following description of Esther's hair: 'She had . . . hair no hairdresser's hand could hold, so abundant was it, and so long, that falling to the ground it coiled there' (*HHL* 52).[45] Considered in the context of Haskins's comments, the combined features of Esther's hair reflect her complexity. Despite her spontaneous conversion to chastity associated with her blondeness, her body, as represented by her hair, none the less asserts itself by signalling eroticism, moral laxity, and wantonness. So long, so loose, so uncontrollable is this hair (read body, read woman) that nature will assert itself in the end. As we will see, however, the complex sexual symbolism of Balzac's Jewish courtesan manifests itself in more ways than through her hair.

The Sublime Type

Though the courtesan Esther was likely in Balzac's mind before he created her counterpart Coralie in *Lost Illusions*, there is little doubt that they are doubles.[46] Although Coralie, in her deathbed scene, is not quite as soulful as Esther, she also incarnates *la fille repentie*, converting at the last minute: 'By a strange reversion, Coralie insisted that Lucien should bring a priest to her. She wished to be reconciled with the Church and die in peace. Her repentance was sincere and she made a Christian end' (*LI* 470).[47] Both women are a mixture of soul and body, their 'sublime beauty' standing for a divine heart. But ultimately their vocation is not religion—as in Christian self-sacrifice for God—but, rather, love—as in a woman's self-sacrifice for a man.

Lucien's first vision of Coralie specifies that 'hers was the *sublime type* of Jewish face'.[48] Esther, in a similar narrator's description, takes on a similar value as a 'pure strain': 'Esther came from this cradle of the human species, the homeland of beauty: her mother was Jewish. The Jews, even though so often debased by their contact with other peoples, yet present among their numerous tribes strains in which the *sublimest type* of Asiatic beauty is preserved' (*HHL* 51).[49] The expression 'a sublime type', especially of beauty, is a Balzacian favourite. In the history of aesthetics the two concepts of the sublime and the beautiful are opposed (Mitchell 1986: 125–49). Is 'sublime beauty' fearsome, awesome, ancient, or incomprehensible? A sublime type of beauty (Asiatic, Jewish, or otherwise exotic) would seem to indicate a place where taste meets sentiment, or where rational pleasure meets irrational fear.[50]

The ambivalence of Esther's identification with both the sacred and the worldly reflects Balzac's own ambivalence towards the cultural inheritance of eighteenth-century spiritual Illuminists and Occultists and the more scientific physiognomists and physiologists of his own time. Consider for a moment the conflation of categories of thought present in the two sentences quoted above: the vocabulary ranges from ethnology to history to genetics and eugenics.[51] Terms such as 'debasement' and 'strains' derive from the theories of hygiene, the infection of gene pools, and the corruption of minors through prostitution that were promulgated from 1836 onwards by Alexandre Parent-Duchâtelet, of whom Balzac was an avid reader, and which anticipate the racial virulence and degeneration theories of later generations (Parent-Duchâtelet 1836, 1838; Corbin 1986). Purely natural, pre-civilized, pre-self-aware, non-reflexive femininity is of course a dominant Romantic and orientalist trope. Esther's description runs the gamut from flora to fauna to physiology: 'That abundant health, that animal perfection of the creature in whom voluptuousness takes the place of thought must be a salient fact in the eyes of physiologists' (*HHL* 51).[52] In a mystical-zoological triumph, Balzac poses the following questions:

In the eyes of the desert races alone may be seen the *power to fascinate everybody*, for a woman may always fascinate one or two. No doubt their eyes retain something of the infinitude they have contemplated. Can it be that nature, in her prescience, has provided their retinas with some capacity for reflecting back and thus enduring the mirage of the sands, the torrents of sunlight, the burning cobalt of the ether? or that human beings, like others, derive some quality from the surroundings among which they have been developed, and that its attributes stay with them over centuries! (*HHL* 52–3)[53]

At some point long, long ago, in this Balzacian mythology, environmental conditioning unalterably conquered nature, and the effects of this immutable mutation are still to be discerned. Mixed in with this primary message is that of Esther's absolute alterity ('the power to fascinate [be the Other for] everybody [read 'man']'). In a tour de force, the third sentence presents a personified Nature as Providence, juxtaposes scientific vocabulary ('retinas') with vivid metaphors ('tapis réflecteur') and moves through 'mirage', 'sands', 'sunlight', 'cobalt', and 'ether' to effect a shift from Western science to the flying carpets of Eastern exoticism. Somehow Balzac comes to an answer that satisfies him:

The instincts are living facts whose cause resides in some necessity endured . . . To be convinced of this truth so greatly sought, it is enough to extend to the human herd an observation recently made on flocks of Spanish and British sheep . . . The acquired and transmitted instinct is barely modified after several generations. At a hundred years' distance, the mountain spirit reappears in the refractory lamb, as, *after eighteen hundred years of exile, the East shone through the eyes and in the visage of Esther.* (*HHL* 52–3)[54]

Consider the final image here. The basic, secular-scientific, meaning is that Esther will continue to act like the sheep that she is (in Balzac's example, the lone sheep of the Spanish mountains is the exotic type and the gregarious British sheep the more civilized). This may be taken as a reflection of conventional scepticism about Jews' conversion and fears of their reversion. On a symbolic level of course, the lamb and the eighteen hundred years are both messianic references, especially in combination with 'refractory'—as in heretical—and 'spirit'—associated with the Trinity: in Balzac's play with science, religion, and irony, Esther thus becomes a Christ figure, embodying the return of a messianic age, heralded, it is said, by the conversion of the Jews. Finally, eighteen hundred years of exile cannot help but suggest the popular myth of the Wandering Jew or, in this case, Jewess. In 1833 Edgar Quinet invented Rachel, the Wandering Jewess who became the companion to the previously solitary Wandering Jew, Ahasvérus, in his novel of that name. She came to typify 'the transcendent power of human love which is capable of any sacrifice' (Anderson 1965: 414). Eugène Sue, Balzac's arch-rival in *feuilleton* publications, resuscitated this figure (now Ahasvérus's sister, not his wife) in his ultimately ten-volume serial publication *Le Juif errant* of 1845. Esther, incarnation of the 'prostitute with the heart of gold', is not at all far from these models of sacrifice.[55] The question remains: why is it that marginal figures such as the Jewess, the prostitute, or the Jewish prostitute adapt so well to 'sublime figures' of the absolute—in this case, absolute love and absolute sacrifice? Is it not possible to see them as ordinary human beings, or must they always be abstract, obstructive figures employed by authors simply to set their plots in motion?

The Virgin *aux Camélias*

The mixing of spheres of influence, divine and vulgar, is all too evident in the last words of both sacrificed women. As Lucien contemplates Coralie's corpse on her deathbed, 'it seemed at moments that those two purple lips were about to open and murmur "Lucien!", whose name, together with the name of God, she had murmured with her dying breath' (*LI* 472).[56] In turn, Esther's suicide note ends: 'I've only got five minutes left, I give them to God; don't be jealous of him, my angel, I only want to talk to him about you, ask him to make you happy in return for my death, and my punishment in another world. I wish I weren't going to Hell, I should have liked to see the angels and find out whether they are at all like you' (*HHL* 370).[57]

Here it would appear that Balzac is following conventional models of *la fille repentie*, but he then deliberately subverts them by celebrating the 'divine passion', which he calls 'le vrai amour'. This leads to an even more paradoxical discovery. Balzac not only returns his repentant sinner-turned-saint to her previous situation (now cleansed, having realized her true vocation and renounced all carnal love or love for profit in favour of a 'sanctified love'), but he also presents her as somehow sanctified by sex. True love must be innocent, therefore Balzac would have readers believe that a fallen woman who sleeps with her true lover returns to a state of virginity. This state is emphatically not the same as chastity—playing upon immaculate conception itself; it is strangely and significantly a 'sexual virginity'—the creation of a fusion, a new state of purity, an anomalous third term between the virginal and the sexual, and, of course, a paradox.[58]

Balzac embeds a symbol in the descriptions of Coralie and Esther that makes this conversion/reversion to virginity clear: a flower called the camellia. It is associated with the vocabulary of innocence, purity, and virginity that pervades Lucien's thoughts and visions as he wakes up after a night of love in Coralie's boudoir:

By five o'clock the poet was again asleep, sunk deep in voluptuous pleasure. He had caught a glimpse of the actress's bedroom, a ravishingly luxurious creation in white and pink, a wonderland . . . [Coralie] had been enthralled and could never be sated with this *noble love* which united heart and senses and enraptured both. The *deification* which makes it possible to feel as two separate people on earth and to love as one single person in heaven was like a priest's *absolution* to her . . . As she knelt by the bed, happy to love for love's sake, the actress felt a sort of *sanctification* . . . In the light . . . Lucien was dazzled and indeed fancied he was in a fairy palace . . . the richest stuffs . . . a carpet fit for royalty . . . the white marble mantelpiece . . . a silk-draped ceiling. All around were wonderful jardinières filled with choice flowers, pretty white heather and *scentless camellias. The whole room was a picture of innocence.* How could one imagine an actress and the morals of the theatre in such a setting? (*HHL* 320–4)[59]

For Esther, the symbolic return to innocence and virginity occurs just before she takes her life, on the eve of the 'sacrifice' of her purity to Nucingen, whom she has been keeping at bay. The scene is that of her second debut in *le monde parisien*, clearly depicted as a 'white wedding', and again it is completed with the sign of the camellia:

At five o'clock that evening, Esther dressed herself like a bride. She put on her lace gown over a skirt of white satin, with a waistband also white and white satin slippers, a shawl of English point about her beautiful shoulders. In her hair she put *white camellias, so that she appeared garlanded like a young virgin.* . . . When the doomed woman appeared in the drawing-room, there was a cry of admiration. Esther's eyes gave off a light of infinity in which the soul lost itself as it saw them. *The blue-black of her splendid hair showed off the camellias.* (*HHL* 286–8)[60]

Collections of flower poems and the use of flowers as a symbolic language between lovers were tremendously popular in the eighteenth to mid-nineteenth centuries. Of course, the symbolic meanings of flowers are culturally dependent. Many come from a common interest and 'knowledge of plants, their habits, their uses, their histories, and their appearance' (Seaton 1982–3: 70). A flower book dedicated to the cultivation specifically of the camellia by a French clergyman and amateur botanist of this period reads as follows:

The elegance of form, the perfect symmetrical arrangement of the petals, the *immaculate purity* of the white . . . The CAMELLIA was certainly cultivated in Europe as early as the year 1730 . . . For the next 60 or 70 years it remained a scarce plant and was so little known that its usual appellation was simply *Japonica* . . . Every civilized nation immediately adopted the *Japanese adventurer*, with emulous admiration and now *the Camellia has become a cosmopolite.* But in consequence of the eagerness which everyone has evinced to welcome this *beautiful stranger* into their conservatories . . . it [was] produced [in] several varieties, rivalling each other in elegance and splendour . . . (Berlèse 1838: 1–2, 9, 95, emphasis added)

From Berlèse we confirm the camellia's symbolic meanings of purity and virginity, but also learn of its popularity, its foreign associations, and its sudden ubiquity.

Jack Goody points out that the notion that a language of flowers existed and could be used as a lovers' code was introduced by Lady Mary Wortley Montagu's *Turkish Letters* and by Goethe in his *West-Oestlicher Divan*. This language was considered a 'language of harems' and had a strong orientalist connotation. In France, the most influential codifier of flower language was Charlotte de Latour, who published her *Langage des fleurs* in 1819. Goody writes that 'Balzac was clearly making a reference to the current vogue' when the the hero in his *Le Lys dans la vallée* (The Lily of the Valley, 1834–5) composes bouquets as secret messages to his love interest. Balzac describes the floral code as 'a knowledge lost to Europe where flowers on the desk replace the written words of the East with fragrant colours' (Goody 1993: 237, 250; see also Comfort 1998; Schuerewegen 1983).

I have detailed this background to clarify the now forgotten orientalist subtext of flower coding and the particularly foreign and parvenu associations of the camellia (in Berlèse's terms the Japanese adventurer, cosmopolite, and beautiful stranger).[61] This adds to an understanding of the symbolic meaning of the camellia internal to Balzac's oeuvre—what it means as a lover's message from Coralie and Esther to Lucien.

Lucien establishes his personal interpretation of flower codes in a poem called 'Camellia' from his collection of flower poems, *Les Marguerites* (Daisies), written but unpublished during the course of *Lost Illusions*:

> *The Camellia*
> Each flower's a word in Nature's book to read.
> On love and beauty is the rose intent;
> Sweet modesty the violets represent
> And simple candour is the lily's screed.
> But the Camellia, *not of Nature's breed*,
> *Unstately* lily, rosebud *void* of scent,
> To bloom in *frigid* seasons seems content
> And *chilly virgin's coquetry* to feed.
> Yet, in the theatre, when fair women lean
> Over the balconies to view the scene,
> Its *alabaster* petals give delight:
> *Snow*-garlands, setting off the raven hair
> Of love-inspiring ladies gathered there.
> No Phidias *marble* is more *chastely white*.[62]

The same poetry collection reappears as the publication that launches Lucien's career in the opening pages of *Splendeurs et misères*. Balzac's intention to set up a code is explicit in the first line of Lucien's poem: 'Each flower's a word in Nature's book to read.' The association with virginity here is clear (alabaster, snow, chastely white), albeit combined with an ambivalent pose that the somewhat jaded poetic voice expresses towards virginity per se (not of Nature's breed, unstately, void of scent, coquetry, chilly, marble). As evinced by both deathbed scenes examined above, and as terms such as 'deification', 'absolution', and 'sanctification' show, true love must be innocent, and therefore true sex—especially with a partner one believes is godly—transforms the courtesan into a virgin.

The sanctification of true love, at least on the part of the woman, leads to an ambiguous mixture of exoticism and innocence, and ultimately plays upon the idea of erotic virginity, tied to a fusion between the Virgin Mary and Mary Magdalene. Initiated as children into perverse sexual exploitation, with the advent of true love, Esther the courtesan and Coralie the actress both 'retrieve' virginity. Sexually active virginity is a paradoxical resolution to the virgin/whore dichotomy, a fantasy that demands faith not reason, based on appeals to mythical characters at a remove from conventions and experience which would cast doubt on their functioning.

Infinity

In an earlier section I identified the uncanny suitability of the term 'sublime' for the figure of *la belle Juive*. It is to this question that I now return. In several of the passages examined above, references recur to 'infinity' or *l'infini*. The evocation of *l'infini* in relation to Esther suggests that she attains spiritual heights that go beyond the possibilities of Western description: 'Esther's eyes gave off a light of infinity in which the soul lost itself as it saw them'; 'No doubt their eyes retain something of the infinitude they have contemplated' (*HHL* 288, 52).[63]

In my introductory remarks I began to distinguish between type and stereotype, and historical, conventional, and allegorical models in a way that can now be fruitfully followed up. Whereas Lukács believed that Balzac's social and psychological types were in good faith and therefore character types, others have maintained that they are stereotypes overlaid with the conservatism he wished to promote—the support of monarchy over capitalism (Prendergast 1995). Esther represents a locus of this conflict and of the anti-capitalist argument behind *l'or et le plaisir*. Boyarin's term 'temporal othering' describes the distancing effect, through both time and space, of both the orientalist and the messianic terms highlighted above: the sands of Arabia, eighteen hundred years. When Balzac recurs to idealization he treats Esther as an exemplar, an allegory, an archetype, or an 'eternal type'. Esther is idealized as 'Queen Esther', her namesake after all. She is idealized in her comparison to Mary Magdalene, the Virgin Mary, the *type sublime*, and *l'infini*. In fact, the last two instances reveal the function of Esther and *la belle Juive* as an idea: she incarnates the paradoxical, combined idea of true love, sacrifice, circulation, corruption, sublimity, and infinity.

In the figure of *la Juive* an author may express a messianic hope for the future conversion of the Jews. It is significant, however, that Balzac's converted *Juives* die. They *must* die, it seems. Repenting their worldly sins, they can achieve the salvation of true Christians, but paradoxically, in their eternal Jewishness, true salvation is unachievable (Jews do not go to a Christian heaven). What is unclear, however, in the layers of Balzac's irony, is whether he embraces the conversionist discourse of his period while pointing to its limits, or whether, by making clear the contradictions, he sends up the entire conversion project.

Both Coralie's and Esther's ultimate sacrifice involves a return to sexual availability and circulation and an abdication of their 'exclusive sexual virginity' to serve again as a conduit for money extorted from the inflamed old patron and needed by the young, penniless lover. Thus they again fall. The attachment of the Jew/ess is to this life. In Balzac's mixed incarnations, the Jewish body is at war with a nascent spirituality made possible by a turn to Christianity, creating a dual image, a divided self. Conflict between soul and body, spiritual and carnal, is the essence of the Jew as a symbol of those who have not yet reached the 'full development' implied by Christians who see the Christian faith as a 'completion' of potential that remains stunted in Judaism.

The Jewish woman who tries to exist between two religions and cultures cannot, for she is both Jewish and female. The Jewish courtesan enters Christian society by leaving an invisible role and putting her body into circulation. If, however, contact with the Christian world takes its desired course and she wants to convert, a true conversion can never be effected without her body being removed from circulation again. Virtue is only regained in an illusory way, while the Jewish essence in her blood is instinctive, indestructible, and corrosive (as Balzac illustrated in the example of sheep). Hence the only true conversion is one in which the body is completely sacrificed for the sake of the soul's salvation—conversion and death are equivalent. This purified, Christian death is one of transformation or even transubstantiation ('This is my blood . . .') but not one that allows for a (Jewish) past, a (Jewish) body, desire, or lived and accepted conversion. This non-solution uncovers the incoherence or contradiction underlying Balzac's depiction of Jewish women: *déjudéisation* and isolation *enhance* Jewish identification; in a sense they serve as a catalyst for creating a precipitate of pure 'Jewish essence'. A projected, impending, total assimilation is in direct conflict with a genetic theory of racial integrity and virulence.[64] Assimilation is impossible, for the only acceptance is one of corpses.

Anxieties and Temptations

If one of the aims of literature is to serve as an outlet for a culture's anxieties (or fantasies), does literature broach anxieties only to purge them, or do they remain in place? *La belle Juive* elicits the fear of sexual corruption, and yet the penitential deaths of both Coralie and Esther purge the novels of temptation. Still, the hero whose life they touch dies as well. And, in a sense, one *belle Juive* replaces another in series, suggesting that there may be no limit to this temptation's potential to replicate itself.

The Abbé Herrera (Vautrin) suggests at the end of *Splendeurs et misères* that Lucien's lack of success in society can be directly attributed to his affairs with Coralie and Esther. Without the Jewess, therefore, there would be no story (or at least no tragedy). Conversely, her function in the story is to start the plot by creating the first obstacle. Balzac's *belle Juive* possesses conventional oriental features combined to create a 'sublime beauty' that exercises an inescapable, magical, chemical attraction or temptation (like a sorceress, or an electric ray—*la Torpille*). In her native environment she remains an abstract idea; heredity and surroundings are totally fused. It is in isolation from her origins that the character realizes a dynamic function; she is inserted into present society but somehow exempt from its codes, as a figure that is young but wise, age-old but fresh, outside History but a necessary force of the storyline (*l'histoire*). In Paris, the Jewish woman is fashioned into *la belle Juive*, an object of sexual desire and exploitation, a mixture of Orient and Occident, a locus of misery and luxury, of *or et plaisir*. At the apex of a love triangle the exchange of these two forces becomes apparent, the gold she receives from one lover creates pleasure for the other. But once this mystical triangle is in place another significant, paradoxical transformation occurs: the courtesan becomes a virgin and the triangle is no longer viable, unless the exploited protector takes on a fatherly role. Coralie fends off her patron by calling him 'papa Camusot'; in the case of Baron Nucingen, Esther perpetuates this unstable, triangulated state a mystical, biblical, forty days.[65] The Jewish woman experiences true love as an absolute combination of the spiritual and the physical, revealing her vocation to love, her devotion to one (Christian) man and his deification. Through the idealization of one man, who cannot, for the sake of his ambitions, marry a former *fille perdue*, her life is sacrificed.

The specific use of *la belle Juive* reveals ideas that underlie Balzac's project in *La Comédie humaine*. First, society operates on the basis of motivation by two forces, gold and pleasure, and these two forces are in opposition. One must be exchanged for the other, hence their meeting point in the Jewish woman creates an explosive tension that pushes inexorably towards resolution. Second, the Occident projects a vague and fantastic idea of the Orient, and the Jewish woman who incarnates the meeting and mixing of these two spheres again underscores their incommensurability. If the Christian world claims the soul then the Orient is the body, and the Jewish woman represents the impossibility of dissociating the soul from the body through conversion. Third, the Jewish woman as a figure of the infinite reveals an infinite composed both of woman's multiplicity and her substitutability. Her infinitude is self-negating because it is a form of transcendence, whereas the essence of woman is immanence: she can only contemplate infinity; in aspiring to be it, she must perish.

La belle Juive combines the biblical register not only of Esther but also of the Virgin Mary and Mary Magdalene with secular, exploitative realities, rewriting the myth according to contemporary issues and values. Balzac draws on the persecution and forced conversions of medieval Spain in the character of Herrera, along with the popular *feuilleton* and the *roman noir* of Sue and Quinet's Wandering Jewesses. Mysticism confronts racial theory and the double image of the Jew as divided between good and evil, female and male. Former myths of incestuous relations between Jewish father and daughter metamorphose into myths of orphans with interiorized, redoubled personalities: dominatrix-slave, virgin-courtesan. Mythic models and 'eternal types', enveloped in an appearance of 'realism', make for characters that are more layered, vital, and palatable than are flatly symbolic or stereotypical ones. These mythic, typological characters crucially and unconsciously resonate with readers and are hence accepted as a faithful reproduction of reality.

Notes

1   Classic studies include Debré 1970; Gilman 1986; Gross 1992; Marks 1996; Modder 1939; Spitzer 1939. Subsequent to the writing of this article I learned of a new book with the same title as Spitzer's—*Les Juifs de Balzac* by Ketty Kupfer (2001). Exceptions to the rule include Bitton-Jackson 1982; Klein 1970; Ockman 1995; and Lathers 2001.

2   Gilman 1991a: 22. Likewise, Adam Bresnick remarked, though only in a footnote, that the 'fascination with Jewish women is a topic that deserves further study in its own right' (1998: 843 n. 23). Matthew Bibermann calls for a periodization and offers a revision of the 'critical commonplace' of the feminized image of the Jewish man (Bibermann 2004: 1).

3   Pelligrini 1997: 28; emphasis original. See also the provocative statement, 'East is to West as phallic women are to angels in the house'—or becoming (performing, passing as) a proper, mature, and passive woman is structurally analogous to the 'Westernization' of eastern Jews (1997: 29).

4   Chateaubriand 1964: 389. On this text see Poliakov 2003: 326–7.

5   More recently, Ivan Davidson Kalmar and Derek Penslar have suggested that even Said's geographical orientalism 'has always been not only about the Muslims but also about the Jews' in so far as orientalism combines not just a fervour to 'civilize' (colonize) but also to convert the Other (Kalmar and Penslar 2005: p. xiii). See also the special issue of *Shofar* on Orientalism and the Jews (Omer-Sherman 2006).

6   This study is part of a larger project on representations of Jewish women across Europe in the early 19th century, where I discuss literary figures such as Rebecca of *Ivanhoe* and Mirah of *Daniel Deronda*, in addition to the historical Jewish women Rahel Levin Varnhagen, Rebecca Gratz, and Rachel Félix.

7   The standard reference texts for the history of French Jewish society in this period are Graetz, *The Jews in Nineteenth-Century France* (1996) and Berkovitz, *The Shaping of Jewish Identity in Nineteenth-Century France* (1989).

8   The Alsatian Jewish population was subject to special legislation, called the 'infamous decree', which targeted Jews as perceived usurers, prohibited them from leaving Alsace (or from settling there), and forbade them to nominate substitutes for military service, a right accorded to non-Jews. The decree was in force from 1808 to 1818. See Kalman 2003: 666–7 n. 22.

9   Ezdinli 1993: 28. According to Philippe Landau, in Paris between 1830 and 1848, 74 Jews converted, 44 of whom were women (Landau 2004: 109).

10   Edgar Rosenberg has amply sketched the literary history of the English Jewess through Marlowe, Shakespeare, Scott, Balzac, and George Eliot: 'It became customary after Marlowe to invest the Jew with a daughter, a girl sufficiently good and beautiful to serve as a foil to the wicked father. Where the Jew had been all along an object of hate, the Jewess, within the context of the myth, became an object of lust, who could be stolen from under her father's nose all the more readily because her seduction by the Gentile automatically conferred upon her the patent of salvation. The type, which reaches its apotheosis in Jessica and, with some significant historic hindsight, in Scott's Rebecca, may be literally prostituted: at a fairly early stage in the history of the myth she reappears ... as the type of *la belle juive*, the exotic (or patriotic) whore, a stock-figure in the stories of Balzac, Maupassant, Huysmans, Zola, and Proust' (Rosenberg 1960: 33–4). Klein (1970) and Lehrmann (1971) list the same French authors but add Vigny (*Shylock*, 1828), Hugo (*Les Orientales*, 1829), Quinet (*Ahasvérus*, 1833), Sand, Scribe, and Delphine de Girardin (whose works will be discussed below). Jewish characters appear in nine of Balzac's novels: *Gobseck* (1830), *Le Curé de Tours* (1832), *Louis Lambert* (1832–3), *Le Médecin de campagne* (1833), *Illusions perdues* (1837–43), *La Maison Nucingen* (1838), *Splendeurs et misères des courtisanes* (1839–47), *La Cousine Bette* (1847), and *Le Cousin Pons* (1847).

11   A brunette with 'prominent eyes and a hook nose' holds 'the indispensable position of the handsome Jewess', clearly a sexual type with a concrete iconology. See Huysmans 2003: 66.

12   Along with Pelligrini, we should add 'even if it is sometimes difficult to tell the difference between stereotypes of the *belle juive* and stereotypes of "generic" femininity' (1997: 33).

13   Of the top seven writers cited by Balzac in his entire oeuvre, Scott is second only to Molière, and, along with Byron, is one of only two non-Frenchman. See Robb 1994: 62, 469 n. 67. On the relationship between Scott and Balzac see Conner 1980; Guise 1972; Haggis 1974, 1985; Massie 1983; Samuels 2004; and Smith 1999.

14   Rachel Stuhlman declares that she is 'today one of the most forgotten of women authors, but in her lifetime she sustained a modest reputation as a writer of fiction' (Stuhlman 1997: 44). For corrected biographical information I have relied on Muelsh 1997 and Ezdinli 1993.

15   I cannot help but notice the coincidence of the publication of *Rahel*, the posthumous collection of Rahel Levin Varnhagen's letters, in Germany in the same year.

16   'scènes de mœurs hébraïques'; for a reading of this text see Ezdinli 1993.

17   Sand 1900–2. On 'Lavinia' see Ezdinli 1993 and Rosner 1999.

18   See Lessing's Recha in *Nathan der Weise* and Edgeworth's Berenice Montero in *Harrington* for parallel stories of 'Christianity *ex machina*'. On Halévy's *La Juive* see Bara 2004; Hallman 2002; Lerner 2004; Newark 2001; and Stuhlman 1997: 44–5.

19   In a watercolour of the costume designs by de Faget, Rachel's costume includes a yellow 'Asiatic turban and scarves' (Hallman 2002: 219 n. 26), as does a subsequent portrait by Grevedon in 1837 of the actress Cornélie Falcon, who portrayed Rachel (Newark 2001: 157). According to Lerner, Falcon was 'known to be Jewish herself and "le type même de la beauté hébraïque"' (2004: 268 n. 39). In the Pléïade edition of *Splendeurs et misères* (p. 1342 n. 3), Pierre Citron notes that the Balzacian portraits of Coralie and Esther

(examined below) remind one of the descriptive portraits of Falcon written by Gautier and published in *Le Figaro* in 1837 and 1838. Hallman (2002: 220) makes the connection between the 'symbolic yellow fabric' of Rebecca's turban in *Ivanhoe* and Delacroix's 1832 watercolour of a Jewish woman, *Jeune femme juive assise*. On the oriental representation of *la belle Juive* in general see Lathers 2001 and Ockman 1995. On the turban in general see M.-J. Hoog 1988 and Jirousek 1995; on the yellow turban in particular see Matar 1996, esp. 44, and Lewin 2005 and 2006.

20   Lerner 2004: 275; Brownstein 2004; Falk 1936: 38. Of the abundance of material on Rachel the most relevant and reliable are Brownstein 1993; Chevalley 1989; A. H. Hoog 2004; and Musée d'Art et d'Histoire du Judaïsme 2004. Sarah Bernhardt was apparently born Rosine, but adopted the more Jewish name Sarah due to the long-standing association between Jewish women and theatrical talent.

21   Alyce Jordan points out that both Judith and Esther were 'identified typologically as Old Testament prefigurations of the Virgin and the Church' (1999: 340–1). They are distinguished by the fact that one is militant, bold, and direct, the other is courtly, and uses deference and indirection.

22   Reference to Balzac's works is to the following editions and translations, using the abbreviations given in square brackets. 'La Fille aux yeux d'or', in *Histoire des Treize: La Duchesse de Langeais*, ed. Pierre Barbéris, Livres de Poche (Paris: Librairie Générale Française, 1983) ['Fille']; 'The Girl with the Golden Eyes', in *History of the Thirteen*, trans. Herbert Hunt (New York, 1974) ['Girl']. *Illusions perdues*, ed. Philippe Berthier (Paris, 1990) [*IP*]; *Lost Illusions*, trans. Herbert J. Hunt (New York, 1971) [*LI*]. *Splendeurs et misères des courtisanes*, ed. Pierre Barbéris, 1835–47 (Paris: Gallimard, 1973) [*S&M*]; *Splendeurs et misères des courtisanes*, vol. vi of *La Comédie humaine*, ed. Pierre-Georges Castex, Pléiade edn (Paris: Gallimard, 1976) [Pléiade]; *A Harlot High and Low*, trans. R. Heppenstall (London: Penguin, 1970) [*HHL*].

23   Coralie's patron is a rich bourgeois judge named Camusot, and Esther's is a comically accented Jewish banker called the Baron de Nucingen (who also figures in *La Maison Nucingen*).

24   'Dis-toi souvent: il y a eu deux bonnes filles, deux belles créatures, qui toutes deux sont mortes pour moi, sans m'en vouloir, qui m'adoraient; élève dans ton cœur un souvenir à Coralie, à Esther, et va ton train!' (Pléiade, 761).

25   Ironically, in June 2004 Madonna reversed this movement from 'Old' to 'New' Testament by relinquishing the name Madonna (the Virgin Mary) in favour of Esther, saying that 'her identification with the Biblical queen . . . stems in part from her adherence to the study of . . . Kabbalah' (Reuters 2004); see also Jordan 1999.

26   This quotation is from a chapter title omitted by the Pléiade edition (Pléiade, 491).

27   'À dix-huit ans, cette fille a déjà connu la plus haute opulence, la plus basse misère, les hommes à tous les étages' (Pléiade, 442).

28   'Toute passion à Paris se résout par deux termes: or et plaisir' ('Fille', 370).

29   Jean Forest's reflections on the whole of *La Comédie humaine* confirm this schema: 'Balzac's Jews and Jewesses. In the females, a lot of the mother; in the males, a lot of the child. The women give . . . Giving is infinite; the mother dies of having nothing left to give: the child protests that this abundance is too little for him, stamps his foot, hangs himself by his tie. Jewesses of pleasure, Jews of gold. What do these furiously thirsting people

want? Gold and pleasure? To die of, and more . . . It is the desire of the locked casket [*coffre-fort*]' (Forest, 1984: 215; my translation). 'Coffre-fort' may also be translated as 'safe' but here I have tried to bring out the implicit reference to antecedents such as Jessica in *The Merchant of Venice* and her relation to locked and stolen 'caskets' or treasure chests. Also, 'hang[ing] himself by his tie' points towards the method of Lucien's suicide at the end of *Splendeurs*.

30 Sartre 1948: 48–9; 1954: 57. Naomi Schor is the latest in a series of commentators (Michael Walzer, Pierre Birnbaum) to critique Sartre for 'the ethno- or Francocentrism of his view of the Jew's situation . . . [that] gives his text its dated, not to say outdated, quality' (Schor 1999: 107). See also Suleiman 1995.

31 See Aizenberg 1984. Interestingly, however, in *Splendeurs et misères* the four unnarratable years of happiness for Esther and Lucien begin when she is 'seen' at the Opera ball and end when she is 'noticed' by the Baron de Nucingen, the old *Jewish* banker. As the figure of the old Jew, he conventionally serves as the father-obstacle (Shylock, Barabas, even Isaac of York), thwarting the marriage of his daughter to the Christian hero. In this instance, he serves rather as a Jephthah-like figure—Esther sacrifices herself to him to fulfil her vow (made to gain money for Lucien's sake) which precipitates her suicide. The same set of circumstances—self-sacrifice for Lucien's sake to her former patron Camusot (rich, but not Jewish)—is what causes Coralie to die of heartbreak. At the start of the novel there is a direct reference to the plight of Jephthah's daughter when Esther, on arriving at the convent, learns that she will wear white for her baptism: 'It was the opposite of the scene of Jephthah's daughter upon the mountain' (*HHL* 54). Jephthah's daughter went for two months with her female companions to the mountain 'to mourn her virginity'; the opposite, it would seem, is mourning an enforced virginity (Esther has no hope of seeing Lucien again at this point). The white baptism should be recalled when we examine the final, bridal 'sacrifice' scene that precedes Esther's suicide. By the end of the novel, she has become stoically prepared for sacrifice, like Jephthah's daughter.

32 Jacques Collin—alias Herrera, alias Vautrin, the arch-criminal—doubles the Baron Nucingen just as he doubles Corentin the policeman. See Miller 1984; Prendergast 1973.

33 At least from the Western perspective. See Said 1979, esp. 2–7, 12.

34 'une pelote salie, des gants blancs et parfumés, un délicieux chapeau jeté sur le pot à l'eau, un châle de Ternaux qui bouchait la fenêtre, une robe élégante pendue à un clou . . . tel était l'ensemble de choses lugubres et joyeuses, misérables et riches, qui frappait le regard' (Pléïade, 450).

35 'Un mouchoir trempé de larmes prouvait la sincérité de ce désespoir de Madeleine, dont la pose classique était celle de la courtisane irréligieuse. Ce repentir absolu fit sourire le prêtre' (*S&M* 72).

36 'Ses beaux et admirables cheveux blonds ruisselèrent et firent comme un tapis sous les pieds de ce messager céleste [Herrera] . . . "J'ai entendu parler d'une femme comme moi qui avait lavé de parfums les pieds de Jésus-Christ. Hélas! ma vertu m'a faite si pauvre que je n'ai plus que mes larmes à vous offrir"' (*S&M* 85).

37 Pierre Citron comments that the portraits of Esther were subject to extensive rewriting (in the three drafts), which resulted in repetitions and errors (Pléïade, 1342 n. 1); he also observes that both Esther and Paquita experience 'curious mutations: here blonde there brunette. Europe and Asia are present' (Pléïade, 405).

38   'Il resta stupide en voyant une femme absolument le contraire d'Esther: du blond là où il avait vu du noir, de la faiblesse où il admirait la force! une douce nuit de Bretagne là où scintillait le soleil d'Arabie' (S&M 188).

39   Mme Guidoboni-Visconti (née Frances Sarah Lovell) was a tall, blonde English countess with whom Balzac had an affair (and possibly a son born around the time this story was conceived). 'Olympe' refers to the courtesan Olympe de Pelissier, a dark-haired, dark-eyed lover of Balzac's from 1830 to 1831, who, according to Graham Robb, inspired the 'curious sympathy' Balzac expresses for his courtesan-heroines (Robb 1994: 182). See also Maury 1975.

40   'Mon enfant... votre mère était juive, et vous n'avez pas été baptisée, mais vous n'avez pas non plus été menée à la synagogue: vous êtes dans les limbes religieuses où sont les petits enfants' (S&M 72).

41   'Ce n'était plus une courtisane, mais un ange qui se relevait d'une chute' (S&M 76); 'une fille de dix-huit ans qui ne savait ni lire ni écrire, à qui toute science, toute instruction était nouvelle' (S&M 79).

42   'Le Rat devient une Madeleine' (S&M 72, emphasis original).

43   'Elle retomba sur ses genoux, elle baisa les souliers du prêtre, elle y fondit en larmes et les mouilla' (S&M 74). The transformation of a contemporary Jewish prostitute into the Magdalene is fully ironized by the 'messenger from heaven' who appears to Esther in the guise of Abbé Herrera. He is Vautrin, a recurring character from Père Goriot, the devil's double and always in disguise. On one level, Esther's transformation is perceived to be innocent and 'real'; on another, the appearance of Balzac's recurring, death-defying character known as 'Trompe-la-mort' as heaven's messenger undermines the possibility of, as well as one's faith in, discovering the truth of any character. See Rifelj 2003–4: 90.

44   'Un portrait que Titien eût voulu peindre' (S&M 76, emphasis original). In terms of Esther's influence on future depictions of the Jewish woman, especially in painting, Willi Hirdt claims that Théodore Chassériau's 1841 painting La Toilette d'Esther derives directly from Balzac's Esther (Hirdt 2004).

45   'Elle avait ... des cheveux qu'aucune main de coiffeur ne pouvait tenir, tant ils étaient abondants, et si longs, qu'en tombant à terre ils y formaient des anneaux' (S&M 77). In this sentence her hair is compared to that of the duchesse de Berri, who, if she is the same duchess who instigated a failed attempt to overthow Louis-Philippe in 1832, is a model of threat and political instability, but also strangely associated with uncontainable, invisible Jewishness, since, as noted above, the converted Jew Simon Deutz was castigated in the press as being dishonourable for arresting her.

46   'La Torpille', planned in 1835, was intended for serial publication in La Presse but was pulled in 1837 and first published in 1838. Splendeurs et misères was not completed, however, until 1847; by contrast, the first part of Illusions perdues appeared in 1836 and was completed in 1843.

47   'Par un retour étrange, Coralie exigea que Lucien lui amenât un prêtre. L'actrice voulut se reconcilier avec l'Église, et mourir en paix. Elle fit une fin chrétienne, son repentir fut sincère' (IP 450).

48   'offrait le type sublime de la figure juive' (IP 304; translation and emphasis my own). Hunt officially translates this as 'Her face was of the perfect Jewish type' (LI 295) rather than the 'sublime Jewish type'. Was it perfect, was it perfectly Jewish, was she Jewish at all, or just of

'that type'? I believe it reductive to call sublimity perfection, though perhaps there is something horrible about being perfect.

49 'Esther venait de ce berceau du genre humain, la patrie de la beauté: sa mère était Juive. Les Juifs, quoique si souvent dégradés par leur contact avec les autres peuples, offrent parmi leurs ... tribus des filons où s'est conservé *le type sublime* des beautés asiatiques' (*S&M* 87, emphasis added).

50 Adam Bresnick confirms this premise: 'Coralie is one in a long series of Balzac's exotically alluring Jewesses ... "Coralie montrait le type sublime de la figure juive" ... It is of course significant that Coralie should be described as being sublime as opposed to merely beautiful, for ... the Jewish woman works as a kind of obsessive index of seductive feminine alterity in Balzac's fictions' (Bresnick 1998: 850 n. 23).

51 The ethnology and theory of the influence of environment on human beings and history may also indicate a reading of Herder's *Ideen zur Philosophie der Geschichte der Menschheit* in a French translation by Edgar Quinet (Herder 1834).

52 'Cette richesse de santé, cette perfection de l'animal chez une créature à qui la volupté tenait lieu de la pensée doit être un fait éminent aux yeux des physiologistes' (*S&M* 88).

53 'Il n'y a que des races venues des déserts qui possèdent dans l'œil *le pouvoir de la fascination sur tous*, car une femme fascine toujours quelqu'un. Leurs yeux retiennent sans doute quelque chose de l'infini qu'ils ont contemplé. La nature, dans sa prévoyance, a-t-elle donc armé leurs rétines de quelque tapis réflecteur, pour leur permettre de soutenir le mirage des sables, les torrents de soleil et l'ardent cobalt de l'éther? ou les êtres humaines prennent-ils, comme les autres, quelque chose aux milieux dans lesquels ils se développent, et gardent-ils pendant des siècles les qualités qu'ils en tirent?' (Pléiade, 434–5, emphasis added). According to Pierre Citron (Pléiade, 1342–3 n. 4), Balzac replicates this portrait of Esther in the preface to *Une fille d'Eve* (1839) with the comment that such a phrase might cost a whole night of work, the reading of several volumes, and pose important scientific questions.

54 '*Les instincts sont des faits vivants* dont la cause gît dans une nécessité subie ... Pour se convaincre de cette vérité tant cherchée, il suffit d'étendre aux troupeaux d'hommes l'observation récemment faite sur les troupeaux de moutons espagnols et anglais ... Plusieurs générations réforment à peine les instincts acquis et transmis. À cent ans de distance, l'esprit de montagne reparaît dans un agneau réfractaire, comme, *après dix-huit cents ans de bannissement, l'Orient brillait dans les yeux et dans la figure d'Esther*' (*S&M* 88–9, emphasis added).

55 According to Bitton, in contrast to the name Judith ('archetypal for Jewish literary *femmes fatales*'), the name Esther, meaning 'star', 'is devoid of dark implications of tragedy and psychological complexities. It evokes a picture of wholesome simplicity, bright warmth, kindness, unassuming yet magnetic charm and innocence bordering on naiveté' (1973a: 103, 104–5).

56 'il semblait par moments que ces deux lèvres violettes allaient s'ouvrir et murmurer le nom de Lucien, ce mot qui, mêlé à celui de Dieu, avait précédé son dernier soupir' (*IP* 452).

57 'je n'ai plus que cinq minutes, je les donne à Dieu; n'en sois pas jaloux, mon cher ange, je veux lui parler de toi, lui demander ton bonheur pour prix de ma mort, et de mes puni-

tions dans l'autre monde. Ça m'ennuie bien d'aller dans l'enfer, j'aurais voulu voir les anges pour savoir s'ils te ressemblent' (*S&M* 429).

58   Mireille Labouret would concur with this assessment since she also writes, 'Love decidedly "re-establishes the virginity" of these fallen angels' (Labouret 2002: 189).

59   'À cinq heures, le poète dormait bercé par des voluptés divines, il avait entrevu la chambre de l'actrice, une ravissante création du luxe, toute blanche et rose, un monde de merveilles . . . [Coralie] s'était enivrée sans pouvoir se repaître de ce *noble amour*, qui réunissait les sens au cœur et le cœur aux sens pour les exalter ensemble. Cette *divinisation* qui permet d'être deux ici-bas pour sentir, un seul dans le ciel pour aimer, était son *absolution* . . . Age-nouillée à ce lit, heureuse de l'amour en lui-même, l'actrice se sentait *sanctifiée* . . . Aux lumières, Lucien étourdi se crut en effet dans un palais du Cabinet des fées. Les plus riches étoffes . . . un tapis royal . . . la cheminée en marbre blanc . . . plafond tendu de soie. Partout des jardinières merveilleuses montraient des fleurs choisies, de jolies bruyères blanches, *des camélias sans parfum. Partout vivaient les images de l'innocence.* Comment imaginer là une actrice et les mœurs du théâtre?' (*IP* 325–8, emphasis added).

60   'À cinq heures du soir, Esther fit une toilette de mariée. Elle mit sa robe de dentelle sur une jupe de satin blanc, elle eut une ceinture blanche, des souliers de satin blanc, et sur des belles épaules une écharpe en point d'Angleterre. Elle se coiffa en *camélias blancs naturels, en imitant une coiffure de jeune vierge. . . .* Quand la mourante parut dans le salon, il se fit un cri d'admiration. Les yeux d'Esther renvoyaient l'infini dans lequel l'âme se perdait en les voyant. *Le noir bleu de sa chevelure fine faisait valoir les camélias*' (*S&M* 330–1, emphasis added).

61   In this context one cannot neglect to mention the famous novel by Alexandre Dumas *fils*, *La Dame aux camélias* (1848). The story appeared one year after *Splendeurs et misères*; its reincarnation as a play in 1852 and as an opera in 1853 (*La Traviata*, by Verdi) gave endless renown to the main character, Marguerite Gautier, and a star turn to every actress who took on the part (especially Sarah Bernhardt). The story is the same conventional, mythic *histoire de cœur* that ends in death, that, Dumas once said, will be 'replayed throughout the world wherever there are courtesans and young men', based on an actual affair between Dumas and Marie Duplessis, who in 1840, at the age of 16, became the queen of Parisian courtesans, but who was already dead at 23 (1847). The similarities between this story and Balzac's emphasize their participation in 'a popular myth . . . at the centre of the collective unconscious', according to David Coward's introduction to Dumas's novel (p. xix). Falling into the tradition of *Manon Lescaut, Paul et Virginie*, and *Werther*, Dumas turns a famously unfaithful courtesan into an 'ideal of submissive, self-sacrificing womanhood' and insists that she 'remains "virginal" in the midst of vice', depicting her as a saint and a martyr (p. xvii). Marie Duplessis was in fact known for buying herself camellias, though, unlike Marguerite, no one in her lifetime had 'taken to calling her the Lady of the Camellias' (see Dumas 1848: 8–9). Dumas's portrait could be of Esther's twin, though with one marked difference: Marguerite surrounds herself habitually and continually with camellias whereas in Balzac they are used on specific occasions to highlight a particular effect of sexual sanctification. David Coward suggests that Dumas's title derives from a reading of George Sand's *Isidora* (1846), whose heroine is 'a courtesan with horticultural interests' referred to as 'la dame aux camélias'. 'Dumas admitted that he had written "camélia" (and not "camélia")', Coward adds, 'not because he wished to contest the accepted spelling but . . . "since Madame Sand spells the word as I do, I prefer to be incorrect with her than cor-

rect with others"' (Dumas 1848: 207 n. 9). Balzac appears to have insisted on spelling the flower name incorrectly, along with both Dumas and Sand, and uses the same flower language in order to achieve the same effect. The standard spelling's still being in flux re-emphasizes the flower's exoticism, cost, and its *effet recherché* as the 'beautiful stranger'.

62 *LI* 242. 'Chaque fleur dit un mot du livre de nature: | La rose est l'amour et fête la beauté, | La violette exhale une âme aimante et pure, | Et le lys resplendit de sa simplicité. | Mais le camélia, *monstre de la culture*, | Rose *sans* ambroisie et lys *sans majesté*, | Semble s'épanouir, aux saisons de *froidure*, | Pour *les ennuis coquets de la virginité*. | Cependant, au rebord des loges de théâtre, | J'aime à voir, évasant leur pétales *d'albâtre*, | *Couronne de pudeur, de blancs camélias* | Parmi les cheveux noirs de belles jeunes femmes | Qui savent inspirer un *amour pur* aux âmes | Comme les *marbres grecs* du sculpteur Phidias' (*IP* 260, emphasis added).

63 'Les yeux d'Esther renvoyaient l'infini dans lequel l'âme se perdait'; 'Leurs yeux retiennent sans doute quelque chose de l'infini qu'ils ont contemplé' (*S&M* 331, 89).

64 The vocabulary is that of Parent-Duchâtelet on prostitution picked up by the proponents of racial degeneration that followed. See Gilman 1991b: 174–6.

65 The three men in the biblical story of Queen Esther—Ahasverus the lover, Haman the villain, and Mordecai the old Jewish uncle—are transposed onto Lucien, Vautrin, and Nucingen. After Esther's suicide her heritage becomes clearer: she is a descendant of a Jewish courtesan, Sara (van) Gobseck, or 'La Belle Hollandaise', who is the niece of Jean-Esther Gobseck, a banker born of a Jewish mother and Dutch father (who stars in his own Balzac novel of that name). Gobseck, as one of my reviewers kindly pointed out, combines a biblical reference to 'Gob' (the location of the battle between Israelites and Philistines in 2 Sam. 21: 18–19) and the modern French *sec*, which means dry. This name therefore also mixes registers, suggesting the same tension between biblical and modern (or perhaps Jewish and Dutch) identities. (*Gob* in modern French can mean mouth—in slang *gueule*—or sailor, but there is no record of this word in the 1835 *Dictionnaire de l'Académie française*. Dry-mouth or dry-sailor are also suggestive but apparently anachronistic readings.)

References

AIZENBERG, EDNA. 1984. '"Una Judía muy fermosa": The Jewess as Sex Object in Medieval Spanish Literature and Lore', *La Corónica*, 12(2): 187–94.

AMOSSY, RUTH. 1984. 'Stereotypes and Representation in Fiction', trans. Therese Heidingsfeld, *Poetics Today*, 5(4): 689–700.

ANDERSON, GEORGE. 1965. *The Legend of the Wandering Jew*. Providence, RI.

BARA, OLIVIER. 2004. '*La Juive* de Scribe et Halévy (1835): Un opéra juif?', *Romantisme*, 125: 75–89.

BERKOVITZ, JAY. 1989. *The Shaping of Jewish Identity in Nineteenth-Century France*. Detroit.

BERLÈSE, LORENZO [Abbé]. 1838. *Monography of the Genus Camellia, or an Essay on its Culture, Description, and Classification*, trans. Henry A. S. Dearborn. Boston.

BERNHEIMER, CHARLES. 1989. *Figures of Ill Repute: Representing Prostitution in Nineteenth-Century France*. Cambridge.

BHABHA, HOMI. 1994. *The Location of Culture*. London.

BIBERMANN, MATTHEW. 2004. *Masculinity, Anti-Semitism and Early Modern English Literature: From the Satanic to the Effeminate Jew.* Burlington, Vt.

BIRNBAUM, PIERRE. 1988. *Un mythe politique: La 'République juive'.* Paris.

BITTON, LIVIA E. 1973a. 'Biblical Names of Literary Jewesses', *Names*, 21: 103–9.

—— 1973b. 'The Jewess as a Fictional Sex Symbol', *Bucknell Review*, 21(1): 63–86.

BITTON-JACKSON, LIVIA. 1982. *Madonna or Courtesan? The Jewish Woman in Christian Literature.* New York.

BOYARIN, JONATHAN. 1994. 'The Other Within and the Other Without'. In Lawrence Silberstein and Robert Cohn, eds, *The Other in Jewish Thought and History: Constructions of Jewish Culture and Identity*, 424–52. New York.

BRESNICK, ADAM. 1998. 'The Paradox of *Bildung*: Balzac's *Illusions perdues*', *Modern Language Notes*, 113(4): 823–50.

BRINKER, MENACHEM. 1982–3. 'Verisimilitude, Conventions, and Beliefs', *New Literary History*, 13: 253–67.

—— 1985. 'Le "Naturel" et le "conventionnel" dans la critique et la théorie', *Littérature*, 57: 17–30.

BROWNSTEIN, RACHEL. 1993. *Tragic Muse: Rachel of the Comédie-Française.* New York.

—— 2004. 'Rachel au cœur des lettres'. In *Rachel: Une vie pour le théâtre.* Paris.

CHATEAUBRIAND, FRANÇOIS-RENÉ, VICOMTE DE. 1964 [1848]. *Mémoires d'outre-tombe*, pt IV. Paris.

CHEVALLEY, SYLVIE. 1989. *Rachel: 'J'ai porté mon nom aussi loin que j'ai pu...'.* Paris.

CITRON, PIERRE, 1968. 'Le Rêve asiatique de Balzac', *L'Année balzacienne*, 303–36.

COMFORT, KATHLEEN. 1998. 'Floral Emblems of Health in Balzac's *Le Lys dans la vallée*', *Dalhousie French Studies*, 44: 31–8.

CONNER, WAYNE. 1980. 'Scott and Balzac', *Scottish Literary Journal*, 7(1): 65–72.

CORBIN, ALAIN. 1986. 'Commercial Sexuality in Nineteenth-Century France: A System of Images and Regulations', *Representations*, 14: 209–19.

DEBRÉ, MOSES. 1970. *The Image of the Jew in French Literature from 1800 to 1908*, trans. Gertrude Hirschler. New York.

DUMAS, ALEXANDRE *fils*. 1848. *La Dame aux camélias*, trans. David Coward. World's Classics. Oxford, 1986.

EZDINLI, LEYLA. 1993. 'Altérité juive, altérité romanesque', *Romantisme*, 81: 27–40.

FALK, BERNARD. 1936. *Rachel the Immortal.* New York.

FOREST, JEAN. 1984. *Des femmes de Balzac.* Montreal.

GILMAN, SANDER. 1986. *Jewish Self-Hatred: Anti-Semitism and the Hidden Language of the Jews.* Baltimore.

—— 1991a. *Inscribing the Other.* Lincoln, Nebr.

—— 1991b. *The Jew's Body.* New York.

GOODY, JACK. 1993. 'The Secret Language of Flowers in France: Specialist Knowledge or Fictive Ethnography?'. In Jack Goody, *The Culture of Flowers*, 232–53. Cambridge.

GRAETZ, MICHAEL. 1996. *The Jews in Nineteenth-Century France*, trans. Jane Marie Todd. Stanford, Calif.

GROSS, JOHN. 1992. *Shylock: A Legend and its Legacy*. New York.

GUISE, RENÉ. 1972. 'Le Problème de "Falthurne": Pour une nouvelle lecture du premier essai romanesque de Balzac', *L'Année balzacienne*, 3–42.

HAGGIS, D. R. 1974. 'Clotilde de Lusignan, *Ivanhoe*, and the Development of Scott's Influence on Balzac', *French Studies*, 28: 159–68.

—— 1985. 'The Popularity of Scott's Novels in France and Balzac's *Illusions perdues*', *Journal of European Studies*, 15(1): 21–9.

HALLMAN, DIANA. 2002. *Opera, Liberalism, and Antisemitism in Nineteenth-Century France: The Politics of Halévy's* La Juive. Cambridge.

HASKINS, SUSAN. 1993. *Mary Magdalen: Myth and Metaphor*. New York.

HEATHCOTE, OWEN. 2004. 'Negative Equity? The Representation of Prostitution and the Prostitution of Representation in Balzac', *Forum for Modern Language Studies*, 40(3): 279–90.

HERDER, JOHANN GOTTFRIED. 1834. *Idées sur la philosophie de l'histoire de l'humanité*, trans. Edgar Quinet. Paris.

HIRDT, WILLI. 2004. 'L'Image d'Esther', *L'Année balzacienne*, 3rd ser., 5: 203–9.

HOOG, ANNE HÉLÈNE. 2004. 'La Marge, l'exemple et l'exception: Le Parcours d'Elisa Félix dite Mademoiselle Rachel', *Romantisme*, 125: 91–101.

HOOG, MARIE-JACQUES. 1988. 'Ces femmes en turban'. In Michael Guggenheim, ed., *Women in French Literature*, 117–23. Saratoga, Calif.

HUYSMANS, J.-K. 2003 [1884]. *Against Nature [A rebours]*, trans. Robert Baldick. New York.

JANSEN, KATHERINE LUDWIG. 2000. *The Making of the Magdalen*. Princeton.

JIROUSEK, CHARLOTTE. 1995. 'More than Oriental Splendour: European and Ottoman Headgear, 1380–1580', *Dress*, 22: 22–33.

JORDAN, ALYCE. 1999. 'Material Girls: Judith, Esther, Narrative Modes and Models of Queenship in the Windows of the Ste. Chapelle in Paris', *Word & Image*, 15(4): 337–50.

KALMAN, JULIE. 2003. 'The Unyeilding Wall: Jews and Catholics in Restoration and July Monarchy France', *French Historical Studies*, 26(4): 261–86.

KALMAR, IVAN DAVIDSON, and DEREK J. PENSLAR. 2005. 'Orientalism and the Jews: An Introduction'. In Kalmar and Penslar, eds, *Orientalism and the Jews*, pp. xiii–xl. Waltham, Mass.

KLEIN, LUCE. 1970. *Portrait de la Juive dans la littérature française*. Paris.

KUPFER, KETTY. 2002. *Les Juifs de Balzac*. Paris.

LABOURET, MIREILLE. 2002. '"Fabriquer le temps" à rebours: Problèmes romanesques et mécanismes reparaissants dans "La Torpille"', *L'Année balzacienne*, 3rd ser., 3: 181–203.

LANDAU, PHILIPPE. 2004. 'Les Débuts de l'émancipation des femmes juives sous la Monarchie de Juillet'. In Musée d'Art et d'Histoire du Judaïsme, *Rachel: Une vie pour le théâtre*, 104–13. Paris.

LATHERS, MARIE. 2001. *Bodies of Art: French Literary Realism and the Artist's Model*. Lincoln, Nebr.

LEHRMANN, CHARLES. 1971. *The Jewish Element in French Literature*, trans. George Klin. Cranbury, NJ.

LERNER, L. SCOTT. 2004. 'Jewish Identity and French Opera, Stage and Politics, 1831–1860', *Historical Reflections/Réflexions historiques*, 30(2): 255–81.

LEWIN, JUDITH. 2005. 'Legends of Rebecca: *Ivanhoe*, Dynamic Identification and the Portraits of Rebecca Gratz', *Nashim: A Journal of Jewish Women's Studies and Gender Issues*, 10 (Fall): 178–212.

—— 2006. 'The "Distinction of the Beautiful Jewess": Rebecca of *Ivanhoe* and Scott's Marking of the Jewish Woman', *Jewish Culture and History*, 8(1): 29–48.

LUKÁCS, GEORG. 1964. *Studies in European Realism*, trans. Edith Bone. New York.

—— 1983. *The Historical Novel*, trans. Hannah Mitchell and Stanley Mitchell. Lincoln, Nebr.

MARKS, ELAINE. 1996. *Marrano as Metaphor: The Jewish Presence in French Writing*. New York.

MASSIE, ALLAN. 1983. 'Scott and the European Novel'. In Alan Bold, ed., *Sir Walter Scott: The Long-Forgotten Melody*, 91–106. London.

MATAR, NABIL. 1996. 'Renaissance England and the Turban'. In David Blanks, ed., *Images of the Other: Europe and the Muslim World before 1700*, 39–54. Cairo.

MAURY, CHANTAL. 1975. 'Balzac, Olympe Pélissier, et les courtisanes de *la Comédie humaine*', *L'Année balzacienne*, 199–215.

METZGER, MARY-JANELL. 1998. '"Now by my hood, a gentle and no Jew": Jessica, *The Merchant of Venice*, and the Discourse of Early Modern Jewish Identity', *PMLA* 113(1): 52–63.

MILLER, D. A. 1984. 'Balzac's Illusions Lost and Found', *Yale French Studies*, 67: 164–81.

MITCHELL, W. J. T. 1986. *Iconology: Image, Text, Ideology*. Chicago.

MODDER, MONTAGU FRANK. 1939. *The Jew in the Literature of England*. New York and Philadelphia.

MUELSH, ELISABETH-CHRISTINE. 1997. 'Creativity, Childhood, and Children's Literature, or How to Become a Woman Writer: The Case of Eugénie Foa', *RLA: Romance Languages Annual*, 8: 66–73.

MUSÉE D'ART ET D'HISTOIRE DU JUDAÏSME. 2004. *Rachel: Une vie pour le théâtre*, exhibition catalogue. Paris.

NEWARK, CORMAC. 2001. 'Ceremony, Celebration, and Spectacle in *La Juive*'. In Roger Parker and Mary Ann Smart, eds, *Reading Critics Reading: Opera and Ballet Criticism in France from the Revolution to 1848*, 155–87. Oxford.

OCKMAN, CAROL. 1995. *Ingres's Eroticized Bodies: Retracing the Serpentine Line*. New Haven.

OMER-SHERMAN, RANEN, ed. 2006. *Shofar*, 24(2): special issue on Orientalism and the Jews.

PARENT-DUCHÂTELET, ALEXANDRE JEAN BAPTISTE. 1836. *Hygiène publique*, 2 vols. Paris.

—— 1838. *De la prostitution dans la ville de Paris*, 2 vols. Paris.

PELLIGRINI, ANN. 1997. *Performance Anxieties: Staging Psychoanalysis, Staging Race.* New York.

POLIAKOV, LÉON. 2003. *The History of Anti-Semitism*, vol. iii, trans. Miriam Kochan. Philadelphia.

PRENDERGAST, CHRISTOPHER. 1973. 'Melodrama and Totality in *Splendeurs et misères des courtisanes*', *Novel*, 6: 154–62.

—— 1995. 'Introduction: Realism, God's Secret, and the Body'. In Margaret Cohen and Christopher Prendergast, eds, *Spectacles of Realism: Gender, Body, Genre*, 1–10. Minneapolis.

QUINET, EDGAR. 1833. *Ahasvérus*. Paris.

REUTERS. 2004. 'Material Girl goes from Madonna to Esther', 18 June. <http://www.msnbc.msn.com/id/5234922/>, accessed 9 Aug. 2006.

RIFELJ, CAROLE. 2003–4. 'The Language of Hair in the Nineteenth-Century Novel', *Nineteenth-Century French Studies*, 32(1–2): 83–103.

ROBB, GRAHAM. 1994. *Balzac*. New York.

ROSENBERG, EDGAR. 1960. *From Shylock to Svengali: Jewish Stereotypes in English Fiction*. Stanford, Calif.

ROSNER, ANNA. 1999. 'Clôture et ouverture: Le Refus de mariage dans *La Princesse de Clèves* de Mme de Lafayette et "Lavinia" de George Sand'. In Chantal Bertrand-Jennings, ed., *Masculin/féminin: Le XIXe siècle à l'épreuve du genre*, 105–20. Toronto.

SAID, EDWARD. 1979. *Orientalism*. New York.

SAMUELS, MAURICE. 2004. *The Spectacular Past: Popular History and the Novel in Nineteenth-Century France*. Ithaca, NY.

SAND, GEORGE. 1900–2. *Lavinia*, vol. xx of *Novels by George Sand*, trans. unknown. Boston.

SARTRE, JEAN-PAUL. 1948. *Anti-Semite and Jew*, trans. George Becker. New York.

—— 1954. *Réflexions sur la question juive*, repr. of 1946 edn. Paris.

SCHOR, NAOMI. 1999. 'Anti-Semitism, Jews and the Universal', *October*, 87: 107–16.

SCHUEREWEGEN, FRANC. 1983. 'Pour effleurer le sexe: A propos d'*Honorine* de Balzac', *Studia Neophilologica*, 55(2): 193–7.

SEATON, BEVERLY. 1982–3. 'French Flower Books of the Early Nineteenth Century', *Nineteenth-Century French Studies*, 11(1–2): 60–71.

SMITH, EDWARD C. 1999. 'Honoré de Balzac and the "Genius" of Walter Scott: Debt and Denial', *Comparative Literature Studies*, 36(3): 209–25.

SPITZER, MARTHE. 1939. *Les Juifs de Balzac*. Budapest.

STUHLMAN RACHEL. 1997. 'Luxury, Novelty, Fidelity: Madame Foa's Daguerreian Tale', *Image*, 40(1–4): 2–61.

SUE, EUGÈNE. 1845. *Le Juif errant*, 10 vols. Paris.

SULEIMAN, SUSAN RUBIN. 1995. 'The Jew in Sartre's *Réflexions sur la question juive*: An Exercise in Historical Reading'. In Linda Nochlin and Tamar Garb, eds, *The Jew in the Text*, 201–18. London.

ELEVEN

As *Goyish* as Lime Jell-O?
Jack Benny and the American Construction of Jewishness

HOLLY A. PEARSE

IF SOMEONE IS JEWISH, how is that Jewishness communicated to others? The question of whether Jack Benny, who in a career spanning from 1932 to 1965 was internationally renowned as a star in the classic radio period and, later, the 'golden age' of television, was a Jewish comic or not is hard to answer.[1] The belief among popular culture critics that his screen and radio persona had no ethnicity and was part of a more universal strain of comedy as radio sought popularity outside urban centres[2] has been expressed in many summaries of his life and career. However, scholars looking to Jewish cultural studies more than to media studies for analytical perspectives have argued that celebrities play a role in the construction of American Jewishness, even those ethnic performers who appropriate apparently non-ethnic stage personas (see Altman 1971; Hoberman and Shandler 2003). Performance can encode so-called 'Jewish sensibilities', though in a highly commodified form largely produced by generations of media portrayals of Jewishness. This essay examines this thesis by giving special attention to Jack Benny in performance on the radio at a formative time for mass culture.[3]

Whether or not we accurately identify a performer as Jewish will depend, first, on our knowledge of their biographical details. Naturally, performers who, through public relations information or fan journalism, are known to be Jewish are more likely to be identified as Jewish performers, but not in every case. Although biography and perception feed off one another incessantly, biographical details may in fact contradict the communication of Jewishness if audiences' understanding is based on either incorrect stereotypes of 'authentic Jewish behaviour' or cultural chauvinism. Charlie Chaplin, for example, was often identified as a Jew, but was not Jewish by birth or faith (see Hoberman 2003), while Sammy Davis Jr., was Jewish, but as an African American convert to Judaism he poses significant problems for the scholar in terms of how to use him to elucidate the popular image of the Jew in American entertainment.

But birth and biography alone do not supply scholars with enough justification to deem someone a 'Jewish public figure'. While they might be enough in some cases—such as that of the overtly Jewish Mel Brooks or the self-styled secular universalist Woody Allen, one would not be inclined to include, for example, the Three Stooges in a study of Jewish public figures, despite the fact that these stars were ethnically Jewish. Thus, we must conclude that there is more to the identification of a Jewish author or performer than the publicized details of their upbringing. This 'more' resides in persona-performance elements, as well as in popular recognition.

The identification of Jewish sensibility depends on several key factors. The first is the element of 'performing Jewishness', or how a star acts and sounds Jewish according to socially defined modes of Jewish behaviour. The second is that people involved in the identification of Jewish performers, including scholars and interested lay audiences, are (or feel themselves to be) trained to identify certain strains of 'Jewish humour' or narratives or character aspects, thereby 'reading' the performance of Jewishness. The third factor is that these performances and readings depend upon the Jewishness of the audience as well as that of the star, or at least upon the audience's sensitivity to such things. This means that a star may be seen as Jewish by a Jewish audience member, while appearing universal to a non-Jewish one: this has the effect of ensuring that the performance will not alienate the 'mainstream' consumer. This communication, the so-called double-coded performance of ethnicity (Bial 2005: 3; see also Murray 2002: 105–6), works on something close to the 'secret language' of ethnic and religious minorities.

The process of identifying a performer's Jewishness is part of the decoding that audiences sensitive to Jewish content undertake. They frequently understand and comment on the category as an ethnic 'other', but since what they accept as authentically Jewish will vary depending on their own personal knowledge and experience, they will use their own behaviours and beliefs as a yardstick by which Jewishness is judged (Bial 2005: 146). Public Jewish figures also have a role in the creation of Jewish identity (and have themselves been affected by such processes), so learning from them (how they are labelled, and how they communicate) remains a major way of understanding not only how Jewish content in the media reflects societal norms, but also how it constructs Jewishness. This is particularly true of the formative period of the American broadcast media, which many Jews participated in.

Because he is so often described as 'non-ethnic',[4] Jack Benny provides an exemplary case of possible conflicting readings of a performer's 'mass appeal'. Was he a Jewish comic, or a comic who was Jewish? The line of nuance that separates these two options may be fine, but it is still important in the understanding of artistic performance as both a subject of appreciation and, for cultural studies, evidence of the performer's tradition and identity. As film scholar Lester Freidman wondered (1982: 66), is every star who was born Jewish a Jewish performer, even though he or she was not aware of it?

A famous and insightful definition of Jewishness, which highlights the illogical dimension of ethnic construction, comes from Jewish comic Lenny Bruce. For him, the world of American popular culture was not defined along religious lines distinguishing Jew from non-Jew, but by the distinction between 'Jewish'—that which is edgy, ethnic, urban, and subversive—and *goyish*—the Yiddish term for all things non-Jewish, here denoting anything popular, safe, and associated with the sterility of the suburbs. To Bruce, Eddie Cantor (Jewish by birth) was *goyish*, while African American musician Count Basie was in this sense Jewish. Bruce even categorized inanimate materials along these lines: Kool-Aid was *goyish* but chocolate was Jewish, and lime Jell-O (one of the 'six delicious flavours' flogged by Benny weekly for years) was definitely *goyish*.[5] Thus, for Bruce, Jewishness was not defined by religion or birth, but by a feeling of 'cool' or a counter-cultural subversion of mainstream norms that in his estimation resonated with African American culture. Jewish people and things are those which have flavour and which speak to the passionate rather than the bland side of human life in America. Al Jolson in *The Jazz Singer* (1927), the first talking film, exemplifies the style, rather than content, of Jewish sensibility: he performs the popular song 'Blue Skies' for his mother in the family's living room, singing it as Broadway knew it, then showing her how he plans to jazz it up for his audition for a big production. The scene represents how an 'outsider' plans to succeed in mass culture: the Jewish performer, through the conduit of new and innovative African American cultural styles, subverts mainstream norms to gain entry to the American dream. It is this flavour of ambition, in the form of work located in the entertainment industry, that makes this character and story so Jewish, recognizable to Jewish audiences longing for the dream themselves, but feeling perpetually alienated by the 'polite' norms of mainstream society.

A 'Jewish' Reading of Jack Benny's Work

So how is Jack Benny Jewish *and* not-Jewish? Is he Jewish or *goyish*?

I will try to answer these questions by investigating aspects of the Benny persona, such as his vanity and self-absorption, his stinginess, and his demasculinized performance. Born Benjamin Kubelsky on St Valentine's Day 1894, in Chicago, he was the son of Meyer and Emma, Jewish immigrants from a Russian town near the Polish border. The family was part of the early Jewish community in Waukegan, Illinois, a small town that their son would later make famous. His father first owned a saloon, but later sold it to enter haberdashery. Benny displayed talent as a violin student, but showed little promise elsewhere. He dropped out of school and felt the pull of the vaudeville stage. His father, who had hopes of him being a future violin virtuoso (or at least a haberdasher), was outraged, but his mother defended the boy's choice.[6]

This story is almost a legend. It contains within it many stereotypically Jewish elements familiar from *The Jazz Singer*, and fits with what is almost a trope of

Figure 1 14-year-old violin student Benjamin Kubelsky (later changed to the stage name Jack Benny), 1908. *Photo courtesy of the Jack Benny estate*

Jewish entertainer biographies. A second-generation Jewish American born to an Orthodox, east European family (yet himself leaning away from Old World traditions), he is weighed down by the expectations of parents wishing only that he should have a better life than they had (and repay the debt they owe to America), and faces a choice of three archetypal Jewish paths: high art or religious piety (in the form of the violin or serving as cantor), a life in business, or vaudeville and popular theatre, one of the most iconic American Jewish experiences of the late nineteenth and early twentieth centuries. The only major idiosyncrasies in Benjamin's story are his lack of interest in school, which runs against 'type', and the fact that his story takes place in Waukegan, Illinois, instead of the Lower East Side of New York City. In her article 'Ethnic Masculinity and Early Television's Vaudeo Star' (2002), Susan Murray identifies a common pattern in the stories of such ex-vaudeville stars as Groucho Marx and Milton Berle. Such stories often include a particular emphasis on immigrant hardships and uncertainty, which are overcome by the young comedian's entrance into vaudeville with the help of a compassionate and understanding mother, and a move towards secularization in the hope of American success. While the Benny story does not over-emphasize poverty, and while he did not enter vaudeville at as young an age as Groucho (and certainly not as young as 5-year-old Miltie), it is more or less what one would expect of a 'Jewish star' of his generation. Though it is essentially true, it has possibly been moulded to fit the archetype, emphasizing certain elements because they seem more 'real' and downplaying those that collide with the myth. Certainly the parallels serve to show how easily, given some knowledge of his background, one can read Benny as a Jewish performer.

However, it is problematic that he grew up not in urban New York but in Waukegan. New York, with its accompanying accent (see Appel 1957) and neighbourhoods once strictly defined by ethnic make-up, was the early 'vaudeo' star's main method of self-identification. If a star made a reference to his childhood on, say, Hester Street, the Jewish audience would likely be able to pin him as having a Yiddish Jewish background, while non-Jews in the Midwest unfamiliar with Jewish and New York lore would understand it as a joke about New York, but would not get the hidden significance of the geographical location (Murray 2002: 105). Clearly, however, this was not an option for a comic from Waukegan, though Benny had other 'Jewish resources' on hand.

But although he is no longer a household name, Benny's stage image is still widely remembered: impeccable suit, odd walk and stance, elbow cradled in one hand, the other hand on the cheek, with possibly a cigar or a violin as a prop. This is the Jack Benny that even generations born after his death may well call to mind, and the construction of a persona so well calibrated and consistent is remarkable. Nearly ranking with the Chaplin tramp and the Woody Allen *nebish*, the Benny miser is as sound a façade as there has ever been, complete with its own form of distinctive Benny comedy.[7]

The performance of Jewish humour[8] is often characterized by the use of dialect parody, such as a Yiddish accent (Hoberman and Shandler 2003: 112). The jokes themselves are frequently marked by the use of verbal acrobatics in which chaos and surrealism upset the logic of a conversation through punning or double-talk[9] (as in the humour of Groucho Marx[10]), perhaps reflecting the discombobulating immigrant experience in combination with a cultural appreciation of argumentation, rhetoric, and discussion. These common aspects are mostly lacking in Benny's work, however. His humour, though clever, is not consistent with the quick wit of the typical Jewish vaudeville comedian. In fact, his slow and deliberate pacing made him unique. Perhaps this 'lack' indicates why he is so often overlooked as a creator and performer of 'Jewish humour'. Nevertheless, despite the fact that his verbal style does not follow the norm, there are major elements in Benny's performance of comedy that may be read as Jewish.

In addition to its distinctive vocal performance, Jewish humour is highly character-driven, and contains what could be called the 'shnook' element (from the Yiddish *shnuk*, or snout). In his detailed and entertaining biography of Benny, his long-time friend Milt Josefsberg describes the shnook as 'a sad sack, a patsy, an ineffectual type' (Josefsberg 1977: 317), and the character is usually a male dupe who cannot win, who is consistently oppressed by a world against him, but who can also exude a bratty and vain innocence. This can perhaps be traced back to Fanny Brice's Baby Snooks character in the 1930s, which she played with a nasal ('snouty') voice, and whom she described as a 'good kid' despite the character's shenanigans. When Benny participated in the creation of his radio show persona he had several choices. He could, for example, have made his supporting players—Mary, Dennis, and Rochester—his stooges, conning or belittling them as Groucho does in the Marx Brothers' films. However, anyone who is a fan of Benny knows this was hardly ever the case. His real-life wife Sadye Marks (1905–83) played Mary Livingstone, Jack's platonic friend who seemed determined to cut him off at the knees at every turn. Wisecracking and hardly deferential, she defied the usual fictional image of the submissive white Protestant suburban housewife. The juvenile, overtly Irish American singer Dennis Day, though portrayed as a shallow character, was rarely bested by Jack. Valet-chauffeur Rochester van Jones, an African American figure, was clearly the brightest member of the Benny household, aside, possibly, from Polly the parrot.[11] Beyond all of these, announcer Don Wilson's constant ability to flummox Jack with his knowledge of trivia clearly illustrates that the Jack Benny persona was one of a man who tried to dominate the situation as the boss, but for whom luck and power never seemed to coincide. In short, he was a shnook. And, aside from blustering, what was Jack's only defence against such outrages? An ignominious 'Well!' or a shrill 'Now cut that out!'

One might ask why, aside from the word's Yiddish origins, this trope is so Jewish. Why is it not simply American?[12] It would seem that mass audiences associate the shnook persona with a Jewish sensibility—for example, this is reportedly the reason that Chaplin was seen as Jewish (Hoberman 2003). Attacked by cops, dogs, fellow tramps, a Murphy bed . . . the tramp was a shnook to end all shnooks; he was a modern version of the Yiddish *luftmensch* ('man of air') of folklore and literature, who always managed to survive on slender means, but only through much hardship (Ausubel 1951: 2–5). Granted, Benny had not one degree of the tramp's hope, but therein may rest the reason why his persona was a more thoroughly Jewish American shnook than Chaplin's. The tramp's was a character of faith; Benny's was a character of practicality, but one who never ultimately triumphed even on his own show. The shnook element in Benny's character is so ingrained and so complementary to several other 'Jewish characteristics' that it is hard to ignore its importance. Take for example the way the character's elements are combined with a distinct form of (good-natured) self-deprecating humour.[13] Benny was an attractive man by most standards, with blue, heavily lidded eyes, youthful skin, and a kind smile, along with good taste in clothing and, at 5' 8", average height. Yet in his radio broadcasts he is often described as old, short, vain, bald, and weak: it seems that, as it becomes a subject of description for Diaspora Jews, the Jew's body is more likely to become an object of humour or ridicule than one of admiration. His romantic failures are noted by everyone from Mary's maid to the telephone operators at CBS, and his lack of personal charm is heavily emphasized (see McFadden 1993). He is helpless, childish, and temperamental a

'Jewish American princess' in a business suit, if you will. Further, though he may not have been the violin virtuoso that his father had dreamed of, he was certainly no failure at music or in the entertainment field in general. Yet his programme gave him a violin coach who longs for death, and included repeated memorials to 'the worst movie he ever made', his *The Horn Blows at Midnight* (1945), making little mention of his greatest screen work, in Ernst Lubitsch's *To Be or Not To Be* (1942), which ranks second only to Chaplin's *The Great Dictator* (1940) as a famous early anti-Nazi comedy.[14]

A primary device in his self-deprecating humour was his stinginess, which developed on stage in his vaudeville act and continued into his film, television, radio, and advertising roles. On the radio show, Jack is audited by the IRS because they cannot believe he has only spent $17 on entertainment expenses in the past year. He saves cab fares by taking the free Chamber of Commerce bus tour of Beverly Hills to get to and from work. One successful storyline on the show is when Jack hits his head while taking an inventory of his pantry (during which he allows Rochester to estimate the number of plain toothpicks, but demands an exact count of the decorative ones), and the resulting amnesia causes him to forget his cheap ways. Upon recovery, he almost has a breakdown when he discovers how much money his transformed self has wasted. There is no doubt that Jack's penny-pinching ways were a major source of humour on the show, and he doesn't just believe in saving money but in making it as well. For example, when he buys a former cab for his personal car, he decides not to repaint it so that he can pick up fares on the way to work; this is not so bad though, he claims, because he gives discounts to his friends.

It is no secret that part of the stereotype of Jewish behaviour is money-grubbing and miserliness, and one might be tempted to connect these character traits to Benny's 'Jewish humour'. However, Mr Kitzle, the true vaudeville-style, dialect-driven Jewish character on the show (voiced by Artie Auerbach), was never cast as a money-obsessed man. Rather, his concerns are fairly common ones: work and marriage foibles, problematic in-laws, and raising a family. Therefore, while Jews might read Benny's own stinginess as an affectionate rib of a Jewish stereotype, it is not likely that he meant it in an antisemitic way. There is evidence that in real life Benny was concerned about how his actions would be perceived by a non-Jewish audience and how they might reflect poorly on Jews: for example, one year he worried that people on the east coast would notice that his show was being broadcast after sundown local time on Yom Kippur, the Day of Atonement, as it was also being broadcast local time on the west coast, and he wanted to add a reference to the sun setting later in California than in New York. His writer Milt Josefsberg notes that Benny realized Jews in New York would not notice, as they would be in synagogue, but he did not want 'the Gentiles to think I [don't] respect my religion' (Josefberg 1977: 281–2). Moreover, it is difficult to suggest that he portrayed stinginess as specifically Jewish when in the radio show it relates to issues such as the price of bacon and eggs for breakfast or the cost of Christmas presents; the Benny stinginess rarely, if ever, resulted in attacks on the show from antisemites (Josefberg 1977: 313). As I turn my attention to the 'universal Benny humour theory' below, one might applaud the fact that Benny was able to make parsimony a universal comic value, and thereby subvert the negative Jewish stereotype (Hoberman and Shandler 2003: 200).

This self-deprecating and defenceless quality in Benny meshes with another aspect of his character that may assist in a Jewish reading of his comedy and persona. The voice, activities, dress, and body posture he exhibited on stage were all designed to place him, comically, outside norms of manliness as established by non-Jewish society (see Garber 1992: 224–33; Goldberg 1979; Boyarin 1997; Murray 2002: 110). A high and nasal voice (Garber 1992: 226), limp wrists in publicity photos and screen appearances, and typically delicate, effeminate posture were all hallmarks of Benny's characterization. Further, while most men would hide their vanity, on the programme Jack boldly acted it out, right down to dyeing his roots. One of the show's running storylines had him reading pulp novels, lounging in bed as one imagines a soap-opera dowager doing. Jack's radio persona had feminine, middle-class associations, and this is clearly carried over to his gestures and walk on camera. Of course, this image, combined with Benny's naturally mincing walk and his often submissive attitude towards women, led to persistent off-screen rumours that he was 'a bit gay' (Josefsberg 1977: 351–6). I will not labour the point, but Milton Berle's famous love of comedic transvestism illustrates the subversive qualities of American Jewish (and vaudevillian) humour and its effects on gender norms. While Benny never appeared on stage dressed as Little Bo Peep, he made a fairly fetching lead in *Charley's Aunt* (1941), and he also played quite a fine Gracie Allen at Friar's Club festivities, where he did it well enough to shock people with his shapely, nylon-clad legs.[15] Susan Murray elaborates on this trend of Jewish gender subversion by concluding that it was, in fact, because these men were known to be Jewish that they were able to toy with sexuality to such a perilous degree. The audience, recognizing them as outside the white Protestant norm, acknowledged that their ambiguous sexuality had no bearing on mainstream values (Murray 2002: 102). The (circumcised) Jewish male seems to suggest an ambiguous sexuality, and Benny is one of the clearest examples of non-traditional virility in early television and radio.[16]

The practical level of this humiliating and/or self-deprecating humour is that it is funnier to belittle someone than it is to praise them. This is a comedy writer's maxim. However, when you consider the shnook's failure even once to catch a lucky break, along with the self-deprecation inherent in Jack's comedy, you get a form of the *shlemiel* character from Yiddish folklore and literature (less of a victim than the shnook but more stupid), later solidified by Woody Allen.[17]

Jack Benny's Lived Jewishness and the Public Eye

Perhaps the most significant reason to study Jack Benny as a Jewish American entertainment figure is that his Jewishness was never a secret, and, regardless of how his upbringing was made manifest in his work, the way he was perceived should be of importance to people who study Jewishness and its construction. His humour can be said to contain some elements linked to European Jewish culture, so his firm identification as a universal (read 'non-ethnic') comic is not as sound as it may appear. Further, there is no evidence that, although he was not Orthodox as an adult, he ever rejected Judaism. In fact, he remained a synagogue member all his life, raised money for many Jewish charities, felt hurt as a Jew at the reports coming out of Europe during the Second World War, worried about antisemitism, and openly spoke of his Jewishness in daily life. He was familiar with Yiddish, and used it, though not often on air, and he was clearly not interested in hiding his roots, as we can see from his public affiliation with such organizations as B'nai B'rith.[18] Further, contrary to the views of some critics (e.g. Altman 1971: 191), I do not believe that he used greenhorn immigrant characters such as Kitzle and Schlepperman in order to make fun of Jews or to establish himself as universal or non-Jewish. Rather, I would suggest that the presence of these immigrant stock figures shows that he was unconcerned about the possibility that people might make a connection between them and their Jewish host.

One of the *Jack Benny Show*'s most famous and longest-running gags demonstrates that Benny made no bones about his public Jewishness. It centred on Manischewitz, the kosher wine, which had hardly been heard of by non-Jews in the 1940s and 1950s (Josefsberg 1977: 121), and on the idea of musicians as lushes.[19] Bing Crosby's brother, Bob, played one of Benny's band leaders on the show, and, in a gag that was constructed to play upon Bob's clear status as a non-Jew and a drunk, Jack asked Bob what he was drinking, whereupon he replied, 'Manischewitz on the rocks.' However, 'Manischewitz' not being a word Bob often pronounced, it came out as 'Many-schva-va-va-va-va-va-vitz'. Benny, who enjoyed laughing and was easily amused, could not control himself in the face of this absurdity, and broke up on air. This became a recurring joke on the show, and led to a popular series of ads for Manischewitz in 1954. The joke rested on the audience's appreciation of the situation: a non-Jew becomes an outsider for once, and is presented with something so Jewish, and so outside his realm of experience, that it becomes one of the best on-air mistakes in the history of radio. Benny's knowledge of Manischewitz (and, by association, Jewish ritual and holidays) placed him inside Jewish culture, allowing him to teach Bob how to pronounce the difficult brand name.[20] For once, the insider/outsider roles were reversed as the non-Jew became the butt of the joke. By accessing the 'hidden language', Benny placed himself as a Jew in a way that had no need of a specific accent (Gilman 1991: 32).

Figure 2 64-year-old Benny, still clinging to 39, shows his vain persona, 1958. *Photo courtesy of the Jack Benny estate*

Finally, one cannot analyse the impact of Benny and his long career without including the contribution of his wife and co-star, Sadye Marks. Young Sadye was a teenager living in Vancouver when Zeppo Marx, a family friend, brought Jack along to dinner for Passover. Jack paid no heed to the skinny girl; to him, the dinner was a mere splash of traditional domestic comfort in a career spent on the road. However, they met again a few years later after he had been through a disastrous engagement to Mary Kelly, an Irish Catholic, which had been dissolved due to her family's objections to a Jewish son-in-law. Sadye had grown up sufficiently to catch his eye, and in 1927 the two married. Soon after, in an attempt to save money on the less lucrative touring routes, Jack persuaded Sadye, who by now had adopted the stage name Mary Livingstone, to replace his female co-star in the act. Despite major stage fright and a certainty that she was no actress, Mary consented, and became a significant stage partner to Jack until her retirement in 1954. Refusing co-star billing such as their friends George Burns and Gracie Allen shared, Mary was content to take part in the show and avoid the stress of a star position. However, if she was not his co-star in name, she certainly was in practice, and her character was a major part of the show.[21]

In the show-within-the-show plot, Mary was not Jack's wife, but a smart-aleck actress who played opposite him, and whom he adored from afar, with little success. In real life, Mary seems to have fluctuated between supportive wife and insult comic (Josefsberg 1977: 255), the latter of which was fully seen in her radio character. Brash, opinionated, smart, and strangely likeable, with a distinctive, uncontrolled laugh and brassy voice, Mary displayed several key elements of what one might describe as 'stereotypical Jewish behaviour' of the self-assured woman, though female Jews were hardly dominant in the public imagination at that period. However, by the time of the classic radio era of the 1930s and 1940s (decades after the start of the film industry and on the cusp of the television revolution), the American imagination had begun to create several archetypal Jewish female tropes. The first of these, naturally, was the long-suffering (and often long suffered) Jewish mother, as seen in the melodramatic *Jazz Singer*, and in the milestone radio soap opera (later a television drama), *The Goldbergs*. The second major female trope was not, as one might assume, the indulged, materialistic Jewish American princess, which did not become prevalent in American folklore until the late 1960s (for example in Philip Roth's *Goodbye Columbus*, 1969), but rather a feminized version of the vaudevillian motor-mouth,[22] consistent with later well-known Jewish American television characters such as Rhoda (CBS, 1974–8) and *The Nanny*'s Miss Fine (Fran Drescher; CBS, 1993–9).

Comparing Mary Livingstone to one of the only comedic and overtly female Jewish characters of the time, Hannah from Chaplin's *The Great Dictator* (1940), played by Chaplin's then wife Paulette Goddard (born Paula Levy), one finds some provocative parallels. Both speak with an accent similar to the stage 'New York' voice (despite the fact that Hannah was a Jew living in a European ghetto), which includes the high and nasal pitch that has become part of later stereotypes of Jewish women. Both are prone to streams of meandering conversation, both are opinionated and self-assured, and both enjoy the ability to laugh without restraint. Both approach the men in their lives as equals. These women are fast-talking, funny, and charming (in an urban sort of way), and both represent challenges to the demure norm of female gentility in circulation at the time. Further, both are clearly distinct from the other strong female character type of the time, the dominant, white, Protestant, upper-crust female as played by Katharine Hepburn. Mary Livingstone may thus have contributed to the creation of Jack Benny's Jewishness, though she later changed her image by bleaching her hair and having a nose job. The Jewish man is feminized (with Benny almost a Jewish American princess himself), while the female object of his interest is afforded extra masculinity in compensation (Garber 1992: 229). What could be more shnook-like than to be derided even by one's own wife?[23]

Jack Benny and the 'Universal' Theory: An Assessment

In *The Encyclopedia of Ethnic Groups in Hollywood*, Jack Benny has an entry in the Jewish section, but it appears to be included only so that the authors can tell us he was a non-ethnic humorist (Parish 2003: 411). Why then, one may ask, is he in the book at all? The most widely used description of Benny is 'universal', and most analysis of his humour seems bent on convincing the reader that this universality eclipses any Jewish traits apparent in his persona (see for example Altman 1971: 185). However, such assertions only serve to highlight his Jewishness, as behind all of them there is the implication of 'hiddenness', and either admiration for a man who has escaped his own 'Jewishness' or reprimand for having downplayed it, whether for profit or out of self-hatred. But whatever the spin, it seems that Benny has been widely accepted as a universal comic as opposed to a Jewish one.

The major flaw in this analysis is that, like most assertions of Benny's Jewishness, it stems from a stereotypical view of Jewish nature. His accent, with its flat, Midwestern tones, should not be seen as hiding Jewishness just because it does not sound like Groucho Marx. The fact remains that, having been raised outside New York, Benny did not exhibit the stereotypical trappings of vaudevillian Jews (Hoberman 2003: 200). But there is no reason why this should be labelled as a deliberate attempt to hide his Jewishness.

To say that there is a particular and exclusive nature to Jewish humour, and to go even further and say that it communicates primarily to Jews, is faulty. The truth may be that Jewish humour, growing out of a history of oppression and the experience of immigration, is representative of that of many similar groups. Perhaps there is no exclusively Jewish humour, only a form of humour that expresses experiences that are most commonly connected in American popular culture with Jewish comics. In short, Jewish humour *is* universal humour, just with a different flavour . . . like chocolate instead of lime.[24]

In the introduction to J. Hoberman and Jeffrey Shandler's important work, *Entertaining America: Jews, Movies and Broadcasting*, the authors point to a significant social-psychological phenomenon—the drive in Jewish people (and sadly also in antisemites) to engage in the identification process of Jewish celebrities (Hoberman and Shandler 2003). That is, people with an interest in Jewish culture and Judaism are inspired to go over the question of Jewishness repeatedly. 'I didn't know that person was Jewish!' or 'Of course, so-and-so is Jewish!' The first criterion by which Jews are identified is very likely based on how they identify themselves—if a person says they are Jewish, they are Jewish. However, such a direct affirmation is seldom offered or needed, and sometimes it is not actually believed by the public. Jewishness is therefore not merely a biographical fact about some entertainment heroes; it is also a subjective mystery in which the viewer participates. As I have said, the determination of a celebrity's Jewishness is made on the basis of the audience's feelings and beliefs about their own Jewishness, as well as on the question of which characteristics warrant membership status, and the investigation of how and why a celebrity is labelled 'Jewish' thus reveals cultural assumptions about how Jews see themselves. Jewish audiences also 'intuit' Jewishness, though this impression is often subconscious (Bial 2005); they may therefore 'feel' Jewishness in a performance without being able to describe their criteria in any logical way. There is 'something' about a performer's material, attitude, screen persona, look, accent, and activities that makes them Jewish. Sometimes this identification is accurate and undisputed, as is the case with Milton Berle and Groucho Marx, and sometimes, as with Charlie Chaplin, it is just plain wrong. Further, the image of so-called 'Jewish performers' contributes to the ways in which the community is seen by non-Jews as well.

Therefore, when critics and fans speak of Jack Benny as 'Jewish' (meaning a performer who communicates his Jewishness at least to his Jewish audience) or as 'universal' (meaning that his humour has no particular ethnic character), they are speaking of more than the fact that young Benny Kubelsky was the child of Jews and was educated in Judaism. The question of Benny's Jewishness for his audience is certainly affected by his birth, but the larger question is one of persona, not of intimate spirituality. The Jewishness of Jack Benny becomes a question of *how* Jewish was that magnificent 39-year-old fiddler and skinflint who was welcomed into American homes every Sunday through the airwaves.

So, we come back to our main question. Is Jack Benny a Jewish comic? Benny did have a humour that was easily accessed by a large number of people, and this was the key to his success. Nevertheless, his persona, humour, and legend all have elements that may encourage one to identify him as Jewish through his performance, even though he was not, as vaudeville would have understood the term, an 'ethnic comedian' (Gilbert 1968: 287–92; Murray 2002: 102). However, the Jewish elements observable in his work should not be overlooked as much as they have been by proponents of the 'universal comic' theory. That he is named as a Jewish entertainer and then dismissed as 'non-ethnic' is unhelpful, and, I think, too abrupt. Rather, the possibility remains that exploring Benny's 'Jewish performance' helps to dethrone the New York vaudevillian stereotype so prevalent in nostalgic waltzes down the Sullivan and Considine music-hall circuit, and allows us to see the wide range of Jewish American experience.

Jack Benny, therefore, becomes an important focus for study because he raises key questions about the Jewish need for visibility and distinctiveness. One should ask to what extent the study of Jewish popular culture has been a quest for how Jews are visibly (and audibly) different from the mainstream, rather than a search for the variety of Jewish identity constructions and performative 'incorporations' to be found in cases like Benny's. Is it that, as Bial notes, Jews fear that invisibility equals disappearance (Bial 2005: 18)? Benny was, in some ways, a model 'modern Jew', a template of post-war American Jewishness. His name, speech, and dress had no traces of the shtetl, but he was not ashamed of his heritage. A forerunner of the religiously Jewish suburban Jews of the 1950s, he was not Jewish in the second-generation New York manner; his Jewishness was expressed by affiliation rather than by an all-encompassing Jewish world-view and cultural identity. He was friendly with presidents and vaudeville regulars alike; he entertained American troops, supported the USO, and donated to charities benefiting the State of Israel with equal vigour. Jack Benny is interesting to scholars precisely *because* he inhabits this borderland: American *and* Jewish, Jewish *and* universal. It is through comics like him that Jewish culture has gained entrance to American mainstream consciousness. He was universal enough to be appreciated in Kansas, but resisted whitewashing just enough to be able to transmit Jewish American words and meanings beyond the urban centres, and even beyond the United States.

The Legacy of Jack Benny and the Jewish TV Male

The practice of performing Jewishness on television covertly, as opposed to the more overt and unsubtle ethnic performances of early vaudeville, is certainly not unique to Jack Benny. Jewishness, as I have argued, was something which was often communicated only to those who could appreciate the 'insider jokes', and was generally downplayed in order to prevent alienating mainstream audiences. While this was a general trend in pre-1960s television and radio comedies, one can see how, in the post-civil rights era, the American media have changed their practice in the area of overt Jewishness. This is not to say that Jewish characters commonly display their religious traditions or perform Jewishness without regard for the need of universal appeal but, rather, that there seems to have been a door opened to Jewish self-disclosure among Jewish television personas.[25] Are there many viewers, for example, be it in New York or Kansas (or even in London or Kyoto), who do not know that Jerry Seinfeld is Jewish? Jerry's name, appearance, and status as a New Yorker are all means by which most audience members would 'get' the Jewishness at play, even without the rare shows when Jerry is actually identified as Jewish. For someone familiar with Jewish literature, this 'show about nothing' may strike many chords in terms of its consistent rhetorical examination of minute detail when it comes to ethics, behaviour, and meanings. In short, if one wishes to read *Seinfeld* as Jewish, one can simply call it talmudic.

Seinfeld was, in many ways, something of a watershed show for the performance of Jewishness. Working on many of the same 'shroud of secrecy' network pretensions to universality when it came to Jerry Seinfeld's Jewish heritage, it had very few episodes that really relied on his Jewish background as a plot point. Nevertheless, many of its jokes had extra depth for those in the audience who understood the Jewishness at work in the sitcom. For example, when Jerry makes out with his girlfriend at *Schindler's List*, we know that anyone doing so would be frowned upon; but it is left up to audience awareness to know that it is extra offensive here because Jerry is Jewish, and should therefore be more sensitive to the picture and its meaning.

It was the way in which this popular series carried a brand of secular, urban (read New York), and non-political (i.e. non-threatening) Jewishness into American homes every week that made the casual Jewish performance of the post-ethnic *Seinfeld* the borderland between the hidden Jewishness of Jack Benny and the robustly Jewish character of some post-*Seinfeld* television. After *Seinfeld*, everyone who watched network television in America was 'in on' the coded Jewishness to some extent, and it was now rendered so common and familiar that audiences could choose to play along or ignore it, according to whatever comfort level they had with Jewish identity, or the degree to which they cared about the ethnic identity of the star. The Jewish male, albeit in a sanitized and standardized New York form, was now 'out of the closet' in the American media. Post-*Seinfeld* comedies such as *Seinfeld*'s co-creator Larry David's *Curb Your Enthusiasm* (HBO) now work on a new overt level of Jewishness, such as when the 'hero' of the series, Larry David, beseeches his non-Jewish wife to invite some Jews to their next dinner party ('Some Goldbergs, a few Schwartzes, anything in that family . . .'), or is boldly referred to as 'Jew face'.

Nonetheless, *Seinfeld* did not definitively mark the end of Benny's form of coded television Jewishness. However open the performance of Jewishness is, there is also present another, deeper, layer of Jewishness conveyed to audience members sensitive to such modes of coded communication, embedded in characterizations and narrative devices familiar from the Jewish comics of Benny's era. In comparing the Jack Benny persona and the Larry David persona of *Curb Your Enthusiasm*, the similarities can appear striking on even a cursory examination, despite the overtly ethnic presence in the latter. David follows Benny in his portrayal of a perfect shnook. If we take 'the ineffectual type' as our working definition, David is a modern descendant of Benny's patsy. Vain, aggressive, insensitive, and often annoying, David is no saint, but neither does he really deserve the immense amounts of suffering he receives at the hands of everyone from bodybuilders to sweet little old ladies and parking attendants. His money is extorted from him by neighbours, and he is continually victimized by long strings of freak annoyances that build upon one another to ruin his goals and plans. David would have us believe that we all have such setbacks in life, though he has exaggerated them for comedic purposes. Nevertheless, only a perfect shnook could have such runs of bad luck, aggravated so heavily by his own weak and irritating nature. Like Benny, David has a regular stable of available patsies, and, like Benny, he is never, ever allowed to best any of them; no one in *Curb Your Enthusiasm* is a bigger or more perfect patsy than David himself. It is in this performance of ineffectualness that David shows us how the shnook elements of the Benny character are still alive and well in contemporary American television portrayals of the Jewish male.

The similarities go further than the nature of their personas, however, into the basic situation of the sitcoms themselves. Larry David, Jack Benny, and Jerry Seinfeld all share the plot device of a show within a show. All three comics play fictionalized versions of themselves, presenting false views of their own 'real' lives, down to the most insignificant detail. Benny played himself preparing his weekly radio programme. Larry David, co-creator of *Seinfeld* and a writer, plays the co-creator of *Seinfeld* and a writer. Jerry Seinfeld, a stand-up comedian, played, again, a stand-up comedian. All three are presented as versions of their 'true selves', complete with the use of their real names as screen names. In so doing, these performers are creating a subversive image of reality (part of which is a seemingly true account of Jewish masculinity) through fiction. All three shows are presented as critical commentaries, in a way, of how these men see their own situations and experiences. One could argue that *The Jack Benny Show, Curb Your Enthusiasm*, and *Seinfeld* all represent critiques on the Jewish place in a hostile and alienating world that their 'heroes', often weak and frustrated onlookers rather than participants, did not create. All three experience harassment from all corners, despite having obtained success in the American Dream, possibly expressing an ineffable something about the Jewish experience in America. To live as a Jew is to suffer. To suffer, at least as a Jew on television, is to *kvetch* (moan and whine) in a comedic way. Therein lies the legacy of Jack Benny—the shnook element resonates still.

Even without the explicit references to Jewish culture that now seem commonplace in such sitcoms, a Jewish audience could thus very well place such characters within a Jewish context without needing the Jewish heritage to be made explicit. This communication works because some norms of ethnic communication, such as the shnook persona, have been so well established by comics like Jack Benny. Though silenced on the subject of ethnicity by the requirements of the network entertainment marketplace, Benny and his generation of comics spoke volumes about the place of the Jew in American culture. By understanding the ways in which Jewishness was constructed by and around Benny's persona, we can further elucidate some trends in the Jewish understanding of self, as well as the public image of the Jew in American popular culture today.

The construction of Jewish identity is often covert and, even beyond references to bar mitzvahs and Schwartzes, there appear to be subtle ideological expectations of Jewish masculinity that can be seen in greater relief when we compare modern Jewish portrayals to that of Jack Benny, who was both brought into being by and helped to create modern ideas of Jewishness in the American media.

Notes

1   This essay focuses primarily on the weekly radio sitcom *The Jack Benny Show*, which ran on NBC, first for General Mills Foods, specifically Jell-O and then Grape Nuts cereal, from 1934 to 1944, then for Lucky Strikes cigarettes from 1944 to 1949, after which Benny switched to CBS from 1949 to 1955. As a television sitcom it ran from 1950 to 1965, and featured much the same style, characters, and situations as on radio. A strange meta-comedy, the basic situation of the Jack Benny show(s) has Jack playing himself as a star of a weekly show, and the plots revolve around him and his cast, including his real-life wife Mary Livingstone and his long-time partner Eddie Anderson (Rochester the Valet), preparing for the show.

2 McFadden 1993: 114. However, radio seems not to have been as heavily subjected to white-washing as was film in the 1930s/1940s and early television.

3 The case of Benny is further complicated by the facts that his screen character, including some of his film roles, was a fictionalized version of himself, and that, although he was credited as editor or story manager of his shows, and had the final say on scripts, he did not write them, but had a series of dedicated and talented (and nearly all Jewish) comedy writers.

4 Clearly a problematic term, as one must ask if it is even possible to be completely without ethnicity of some kind.

5 Found in Novak and Waldoks 1981: 60; quoted in Bial 2005: 19 and Altman 1971: 190.

6 Biographical information on Jack Benny was found in Livingston and Marks 1978; Josefsberg 1977; Fein 1976.

7 For a solid exploration of Jack Benny within the social context of the Depression, and a look at the Benny persona, see McFadden 1993. Unfortunately, McFadden includes only African Americans in her exploration of race (not ethnicity), and does not handle Benny (or even the outrageous greenhorn hot-dog vender Kitzle) as Jewish figures.

8 This is a very loosely defined and problematic term; see Ben-Amos 1991: 36. Here I mean it in terms of European Jewish humour as conceived by audiences and observers of trends, not as a reified and concrete object.

9 See Telushkin 1992 and the introduction to Ausubel 1951.

10 For example, the excellent line from *Animal Crackers* (1930), 'If you took cranberries and stewed them like prunes, they would taste much more like strawberries than rhubarb would. Now you tell me what you know.' The transmutational rhetoric, combined with a fast delivery, turns this line into a refutation of both sense and reality. The end line, urging the stuffy art dealer to whom he is speaking (who later turns out to be a Jewish fish peddler 'passing' in disguise) to 'tell what he knows' leaves the dealer, and the audience, dumbfounded, for there is simply no response to such a non sequitur.

11 For an interesting interpretation of Rochester as Benny's wife-character, as well as the portrayal of African Americans in *The Jack Benny Show*, see McFadden 1993.

12 As Novak and Waldoks note in the introduction to their lively *Big Book of Jewish Humour* (1981: p. xiv), the very success of Jewish humour is possibly what makes it so hard to distinguish in North America. Jewish humour has permeated 'American' humour, and vice versa.

13 Caution should be exercised when assuming the myth of masochistic Jewish self-depreciation; however, self-criticism and the reversal of jokes against oneself can certainly be said to be a common element in Jewish American humour; see Novak and Waldoks 1981: p. xv.

14 Jack does not play a Jew in this film, but, rather, a Pole, who, indecently, is a vain (would-be) cuckold, in keeping with his established stage persona.

15 For instances of implied homosexuality in Benny's humour, see McFadden 1993. McFadden concludes that Benny's effeminate and homosexual character elements were linked to the emasculating effects of unemployment during the Great Depression of the 1930s. However, it is unclear to what extent this aspect of the Benny persona had already been settled on stage, well before the Depression: in 1929, when he played himself as master of ceremonies in MGM's early talkie *The Hollywood Revue of 1929*, released in August of that year, much of the later effeminate Benny style is largely already present.

16 This is not to say, of course, that the Benny persona was created out of conscious anti-semitism. Benny and his Jewish writers cannot be assumed to have held anti-Jewish views; however, one must admit the possibility of internalized antisemitic images. It is more likely, however, that these concepts were not seen as antisemitic, but rather as mere comedic actions and gags. Further, though less likely, as Garber (1992: 233) suggests, such uses of Jewish/gender issues may have been meant to empower Jewish men against attacks upon their sexuality.

17 For an excellent discussion of the Woody Allen persona as *schlemiel* see Bial 2005: 86–106.

18 For details and impressions of Jack Benny's personal Jewishness, read Milt Josefsberg's Jewish-infused biography.

19 Likewise, these band leaders tended to be hyper-male, especially in the case of Phil, the band leader who preceded Bob. These men provided a clear contrast to Jack, who was effeminate and could not drink. See McFadden 1993: 128.

20 Although it is unsettling that, in a subsequent ad, Bob's mispronunciation eventually rubs off on Benny.

21 For an account of Mary's life with Jack, see Livingston and Marks 1978.

22 While the 'errant daughter' trope seems to pre-date this tougher image of Jewish femininity, such as the childlike and suggestible girl in *The Golem* (1920) who is led astray into an inter-faith tryst against the wishes of her family, such characters do not seem to be clearly differentiated as specifically Jewish. However, more research into this category of female Jewish imagery would be welcome. See Riv-Ellen Prell's discussion of gender tropes in Prell 1999: 10–14.

23 This trend is mirrored in a way by the vaudevillian myth itself, in terms of the high numbers of ineffectual fathers who are unable to fully support their families and tales of crafty and strong mothers who make ends meet through their own supra-feminine powers and strength (see Murray 2002: 108). McFadden (1993: 126) refers to Mary as a 'little man' adrift in an all-male fantasy family within the show, and this does express some of her role.

24 Of course, it should also be pointed out that the Jewish approach to universalism has its own causes and matrices within Jewish communities, and thus may be seen as part of Jewishness itself. Cf. Bial 2005: 26.

25 Of course, there are still hazy cases, such as the Midwestern character of Roseanne Barr, who, perhaps due to the same lack of NYC accent and urban mannerisms as Jack Benny himself, is hardly ever identified as Jewish, but when it comes to Jewish characters set in the geographical location of New York, Jewishness has apparently been relieved of its gag order on television.

References

ALTMAN, SIG. 1971. *The Comic Image of the Jew: Explorations of a Pop Culture Phenomenon*. Madison, NJ.

APPEL, JOHN J. 1957. 'Jewish Literary Dialect', *American Speech*, 32/4: 313–14.

AUSUBEL, NATHAN, ed. 1951. *A Treasury of Jewish Humor*. New York.

BEN-AMOS, DAN. 1991. 'Jewish Folklore Studies', *Modern Judaism*, 11/1: 17–66.

BIAL, HENRY. 2005. *Acting Jewish: Negotiating Ethnicity on the American Stage and Screen.* Ann Arbor.

BOYARIN, DANIEL. 1997. *Unheroic Conduct: The Rise of Heterosexuality and the Invention of the Jewish Man.* Berkeley, Calif.

FEIN, IRVING A. 1976. *Jack Benny: An Intimate Biography.* New York.

FREIDMAN, LESTER D. 1982. *Hollywood's Image of the Jew.* New York.

GARBER, MARJORIE. 1992. *Vested Interests: Cross-Dressing and Cultural Anxiety.* New York.

GILBERT, DOUGLAS. 1968. *American Vaudeville: Its Life and Times.* New York.

GILMAN, SANDER. 1991. *The Jew's Body.* New York.

GOLDBERG, M. HIRSH. 1979. 'Praise the Lord and Pass the Baseballs, Footballs, and Basketballs, Too: More Jews where You'd Least Expect Them'. In M. Hirsh Goldberg, *Just Because They're Jewish*, 131–51. New York.

HOBERMAN J. 2003. 'The First "Jewish" Superstar: Charlie Chaplin', in J. Hoberman and Jeffrey Shandler, *Entertaining America: Jews, Movies and Broadcasting*, 34–9. Princeton.

——and JEFFREY SHANDLER. 2003. *Entertaining America: Jews, Movies and Broadcasting.* New York.

JOSEFSBERG, MILT. 1977. *The Jack Benny Show.* New Rochelle, NY.

LIVINGSTON, MARY, and HILLIARD MARKS, with Marcia Borie. 1978. *Jack Benny.* New York.

MCFADDEN, MARGARET T. 1993. '"America's boy friend who can't get a date": Gender, Race, and the Cultural Work of the Jack Benny Program', *Journal of American History*, 80/1: 113–34.

MURRAY, SUSAN. 2002. 'Ethnic Masculinity and Early Television's Vaudeo Star', *Cinema Journal*, 42/1: 97–119.

NOVAK, WILLIAM, and MOSHE WALDOKS, eds. 1981. *The Big Book of Jewish Humor.* New York.

PARISH, JAMES ROBERT, ed. 2003. *The Encyclopedia of Ethnic Groups in Hollywood.* New York.

PRELL, RIV-ELLEN. 1999. *Fighting to Become Americans: Jews, Gender, and the Anxiety of Assimilation.* Boston.

TELUSHKIN, JOSEPH. 1992. 'What Is Jewish about Jewish Humor?'. In Joseph Telushkin, *Jewish Humor: What the Best Jewish Jokes Say about the Jews*, 15–26. New York.

TWELVE

Jewish Coding: Cultural Studies and Jewish American Cinema

MIKEL J. KOVEN

THERE IS A MOMENT in *Exodus* (Otto Preminger, 1960), where young Dov Landau (Sal Mineo) is being initiated into the Israeli terrorist organization, the Irgun. Akiva (David Opatoshu), the fictional leader of the Irgun, holds a Bible (one assumes an Old Testament) with a pistol. He takes Dov's left hand and places it on top, and with his right hand he picks up a six-stemmed menorah and gets Dov to swear an oath of allegiance. Here we have the crux of *Exodus*'s use of Jewish iconography in its narrative: it in no way attempts cultural verisimilitude, but instead utilizes iconography which non-Jews are likely to identify as Jewish.

Although the icons in the sequence are recognizably Jewish—the Old Testament, the menorah—the swearing of an oath on them appropriates the standard (Christian) American practice of 'swearing on a Bible', and the inclusion of the menorah is apparently to add 'Jewish colour'. The gun is symbolic, on a narrative level, of the Irgun's commitment to the violent overthrow of the British-controlled mandate in Palestine. Perhaps it would have been more 'culturally accurate' to have Dov swear on a *sefer torah*, but to avoid potentially confusing the non-Jewish world with that visual icon, Jewish director Otto Preminger substitutes the Westernized standard of a 'black book', a Bible.

Joan Radner and Susan Lanser have noted that 'appropriation' is a legitimate technique of implicit coding. The appropriation of the legal 'swearing on the Bible' for an emerging Israeli loyalty oath, and the requisite replacement of iconography is, it could be argued, intentionally drawing attention to its own absurdity for the Jewish audience. Seen in terms of Luce Irigaray's concept of 'ironic mimicry' within feminist studies, wherein the 'feminine position' is purposefully exaggerated in order to highlight itself (self-reflexively) as a patriarchal construct (Radner and Lanser 1993: 10), this sequence from *Exodus* reveals the fatuity of the way in which Jewish identity is expressed through Jewish 'mimicry' of the Christian hegemony's perception of the culture; although the icons themselves are not fatuous—they have an independent existence within Jewish culture—their use in *Exodus* is likewise self-reflexively exaggerated. If this analysis is correct, then Dov's initiation into the Irgun is an intentionally absurd moment for the Jewish audience, and its absurdity is implicitly encoded. It can therefore be argued that the sequence is designed to self-consciously call attention to a Christian society's perceptions of Jewish ritual icons.

In *Schindler's List* (Steven Spielberg, 1993), we see a bourgeois family being forced out of their luxury apartment in a Nazi appropriation of Jewish property. As they pass the doorway, the man stops and removes the mezuzah from the doorpost, kisses it, and places it in his pocket. The action of taking this artefact with him as he leaves works at a deeper level for the Jewish spectator than for non-Jewish members of the audience. At the narrative level, the man leaving his home is just taking this last personal effect with him. However, the cultural knowledge of the insider—known to folklorists as 'esoteric' to distinguish knowledge shared by members of a group about themselves from 'exoteric' lore about the group by non-members—leads those conversant with the culture of Judaism to a broader and more emotionally effective act of decoding. For them, the removal of the mezuzah from the door signifies that the next owner of the apartment will not be Jewish as Jewish law requires that if someone moving house knows that the next owner will be Jewish, the mezuzah must be left in place, a knowledge that has even deeper resonance in the context of a film about the Holocaust. Under-standing the mezuzah icon and the cultural meaning of removing it is en-coded as 'complicit', since anyone familiar with the symbol will understand its significance.

We can take this issue even further. The family vacating their apartment have not sold it to the Nazis; the Nazis have 'repatriated' it for a non-Jewish German. Foreknowledge of what is likely to befall the family in question signifies not only that a non-Jewish family will be moving into that apartment, but also that no Jewish family will ever live in that apartment again, since there will be no more Jews. The use and meaning of specific icons within Jewish traditions, as noted in these two examples from *Exodus* and *Schindler's List*, may not be identifiable or accessible to non-Jews. Some of these icons are obvious, some are not.

This essay uses the concepts developed in folklore studies and cultural studies to examine such coding within Jewish American cinema (whose roots are within the Ashkenazi Jewish tradition) as a way of facilitating intra-group communica-tion. While I have situated the essay firmly within these discourses, my readings are informed by my own 'esoteric' knowledge of Ashkenazi Jewish culture as an insider.[1] I will explore how Jewish*ness* is encoded within specific key Jewish American films—films which, while made by Jewish American film-makers, are accessible to—and indeed intended for—a mainstream, and therefore not neces-sarily a Jewish, audience. I emphasize the 'ness' in 'Jewishness' to move the humanistic analysis of popular cinema from what the director intended to the way that different audiences interpret the production. It is a way to get at Jewish meanings which may be different from literal meaning, which tends to be defined by mainstream or Christian standards.

Coding is here recognized as a kind of cultural bilingualism wherein, while the films are on the surface fully comprehensible to all potential audience members, Jewish and non-Jewish, certain discourses will be directed to and more immediately understood by those who have esoteric knowledge of Jewish American culture. Through a consideration of various types of cinematic encodedness—of language, of customs, and of music—I will investigate the emergent Jewishness of these films.[2]

Coding and Cultural Studies

Within the discourses of cultural studies, Stuart Hall has noted that all communication is in some way encoded:

Before [the] message can have an 'effect' (however defined), satisfy a 'need' or be put to a 'use', it must first be appropriated as a meaningful discourse and be meaningfully decoded. It is this set of decoded meanings which have an 'effect', influence, entertain, instruct or persuade, with very complex perceptual, cognitive, emotional, ideological or behavioural consequences. (Hall 1980: 130)

These are the most general and pragmatic levels of reception: when both sender and receiver share a cultural base, when they both claim membership of a particular group, the clarity of textual transmission increases. Through this implied shared cultural identity other forms of discourse have the potential to be transmitted. This is not to say such further discourse is necessarily in contradiction with the surface-level discourse, but that when the encoder–decoder relationship is predicated upon shared cultural values the transmission process is less ambiguous. What Hall calls *equivalence* (Hall 1980: 131), I further specify as *cultural* equivalence: 'What are called "distortions" or "misunderstandings" arise precisely from the *lack of equivalence* between two sides in the communicative exchange. Once again, this defines the "relative autonomy" but "determinateness" of the entry and exit of the message in its discursive moments' (Hall 1980: 131; emphasis in original).

Hall hypothetically identifies three positions for the decoding of the transmitted text: (1) the *dominant-hegemonic position*, 'when the viewer takes the connotated meaning . . . full and straight, and decodes the message in terms of the reference code in which it has been encoded'; (2) the *negotiated code*, which recognizes the operation of hegemonic encoding, and further connects the connotative message to a larger, globally operational superstructure; and (3) the *oppositional code*, whereby the receiver 'detotalizes the message in the preferred code in . . . order to retotalize the message within some alternative framework of reference' (Hall 1980: 136–8). Here lies an implicit problem within the discourse of cultural studies, and one which other scholars (noted below) endeavour to resolve: Hall identified that there are only two possibilities of discursive positioning within hegemony: either one is aligned with the ideological position of the dominant cultural order or one is in opposition to it. This automatically precludes the existence of non-oppositional yet non-hegemonic cultural positions, such as ethnic identification. This is not to say that ethnic identity is, in essence, non-oppositional, but Hall's schema only allows for essential positioning. Ethnic identities, as decoding positions, are, I propose, much more fluid. Benshoff and Griffin, in their application of Hall's schema to the study of ethnicity and race in American cinema, offer the following amendments:

When producers and readers share aspects of the same culture, texts are more easily decoded or understood . . . however, not every reader is going to take (or make) identical meanings from the same text. Depending upon their own cultural positioning, different people may decode texts in different ways . . . Readings that decode a text in accordance with how it was encoded are said to be dominant readings. On the other side of the spectrum are oppositional readers, which actively question the ideological assumptions encoded in a text. Most readings lie somewhere in between these two extremes. Negotiated readings resist some aspects of what has been encoded, but accept others. Frequently, members of minority groups have social standpoints that differ from those encoded in mainstream texts, and sometimes this allows such individuals to perform readings that are more regularly negotiated or oppositional. (2004: 17)[3]

Mikhail Bakhtin's view, in further contrast to Hall's more rigid schema, is that the reception of cultural texts must be seen as polyphonous: 'a plurality of voices which do not fuse into a single consciousness, but rather exist on different registers and thus generate dialogical dynamism' (Stam 1991: 262). In this view, the multifaceted experiences of cultural audiences operate within a pluralistic reality; each different audience member, with his or her own cultural background and experience, is going to approach texts differently. Some may in fact be, as Hall argued, unaware of the hegemonic operation, others may agree with this operation, and still others may in fact be opposed to it. But Hall's approach disregards the existence of the polyphonous audience, whose experience may not fall into any of his categories of unaware, supportive, or oppositional.[4]

To develop Hall's idea of coding/decoding in a way which takes account of the esoteric and exoteric understandings of culture outlined above, I will use Joan Radner and Susan Lanser's more concrete analysis of the operation of coded meanings in cultural texts, shifting the signifier from 'woman' to 'Jewish'. Radner and Lanser are trying to identify the techniques that women use to exclude men from their private discourse. An analogous operation is observable in Jewish culture wherein Jewish cultural texts exclude non-Jews. Radner and Lanser explain the operation of coding thus:

Coding occurs in the context of complex audiences in which some members may be competent and willing to decode the message, but others are not. In other words, coding presumes an audience in which one group of receivers is 'monocultural' and thus assumes that its own interpretation of messages is the only one possible, while the second group, living in two cultures, may recognize a double message—which also requires recognizing that some form of coding has taken place. (1993: 3)

In terms of the present discussion the assumption here is that Jewish audiences are going to have a different understanding of the cultural dynamics in operation within specific film texts than non-Jewish ones. In many respects, this latter 'monocultural' audience will, like Hall's 'negotiated code' audience, interpret any divergence from their own cultural experience through the lens of the dominant world-view which their group represents. Coding is thus defined by Radner and Lanser as 'the expression or transmission of messages potentially accessible to a (bicultural) community under the very eyes of a dominant community for whom these same messages are either inaccessible or inadmissible' (1993: 3).

It should be further noted that this kind of coding is multi-layered: if we take, for example, *Half the Kingdom* (Francine Zukerman and Roushell Goldstein, 1989), a documentary film about Jewish women, a non-Jewish woman may empathize with or understand the coded discourse within the film as a woman, but not as a Jew. Likewise, a Jewish man watching the film may understand the cultural discourse of Judaism, but not catch the coded feminist discourse. Discussing this 'multiplicity of traditions', folklorist Barre Toelken states that 'the probability that most people belong to more than one . . . group is a consideration that must remain central in the study of [cultural] dynamics; it requires us to recognize that a given person may have a wide repertoire of potential traditional dynamic interactions, each of which is set in motion by particular live contexts' (1979: 72).

For such a variety of group memberships to exist requires a 'cultural bilingualism'. Members of the ruled classes must be fluent in the dominant culture as well as in the culture of their own community, 'because dominated people need this knowledge to survive' (Radner and Lanser 1993: 2). Furthermore, plurality does not exist within multicultural contexts: hegemony, at one very basic level, denies the existence of Bakhtin's polyphonous cultural expression, as it presumes a degree of equality. Any culture different from the dominant one—in ideology, in praxis, in belief system—is inherently subservient. Radner and Lanser note that parallel cultural spheres do not exist as equals, but in a dominant/subservient relationship (1993: 2). For example, as 'culturally neutral' as a phrase like 'Season's Greetings' or 'Happy Holidays' may appear, it is encoded by hegemony and often decoded as 'Merry *Christmas*'. Liberal ideologies may strive towards multicultural equality, but in reality one culture tends to dominate; the material existence of ethnic communities within cultural or national borders, and their often accompanying assertions of multiculturalism based on that material existence, is evidence of resistance to such hegemony.

In order for ethnic identity to persist, these groups must continually renegotiate their own identity in opposition to the dominant culture within which they

exist. Hall's argument implies that the alternative frameworks of these interpretative communities are governed by some kind of oppositional consensus—that all
resisting groups are in agreement in what Raymond Williams called 'alternative
hegemony—a new predominant practice and consciousness' (1976: 118). Radner
and Lanser offer a more precise reconfiguration of this cultural operation:

> In using the concept *women's cultures*, we do not mean to suggest that women share a
> universal set of experiences or any essentially 'female' understanding or worldview.
> Rather, we understand gender itself to be constructed through the social relations of
> particular communities. We assume, therefore, that women's experiences, material cir-
> cumstances, and understandings—hence women's identities—vary from culture to
> culture, community to community, and individual to individual. (1993: 2)

By replacing 'women' with 'Jewish', we can observe a similar dynamic in operation: that, although we cannot refer with any accuracy to 'the' Jewish community, we can assume that Jewish 'experiences, material circumstances, and
understandings', although differing from group to group, will share some kind of
commonality, even if only the opposition to the cultural hegemony.

It is worth noting here some fundamental differences between how Stuart
Hall and Radner and Lanser understand the concept of coding. Within Hall's
schema, the text itself is not much more than a medium by which the governing
culture maintains itself. Individuals are either in a purely denotative position
with respect to the texts of the dominant culture or, if they are sensitive to the
subtleties of connotation, they support or oppose it. But this schema is predicated
on the idea of a monolithic cultural industry that denies the possibility of resistance by sub-groups at the level of production. Hall only recognizes resistance at
the reception level; Janice Radway characterizes his view in negative terms:

> Because readers are present in this theory as passive, purely receptive individuals who
> can only consume the meanings embodied within cultural texts, they are understood to
> be powerless in the face of ideology. The text's irreducible givenness prevents them
> from appropriating its meanings for their own use just as it thwarts any desire on their
> part to resist its message. . . . In this theory of mass culture, ideological control is
> thought to be all-pervasive and complete as a consequence of the ubiquity of mass
> culture itself and of the power of individual artifacts or texts over individuals who can do
> nothing but ingest them. (Radway 1984: 6)

To reduce the process of cognition and meaning-making within popular culture to a simplistic binary opposition between acceptance and rejection, Radway
comments, is 'to petrify the human act of signification, to ignore the fact that
comprehension is actually a process of making meaning, a process of sign production where the reader actively attributes significance to signifiers on the basis
of previously learned cultural codes' (1984: 7). In her study of female readers of
romance novels, Radway demonstrates that the ideology within popular culture
can be interpreted in a multitude of ways.

Radner and Lanser offer a different paradigm. They likewise suggest a tripartite schema, but in this case the emphasis is not on the text, but on the cultural producer—the encoder. Hall subdivides his schema into connotative and denotative codes; Radner and Lanser divide theirs into complicit, explicit, and implicit codes. They define complicit and explicit coding as follows: 'In complicit coding, an unwitting receiver has no idea an act of coding is taking place; in explicit coding, any receiver knows the code exists, even if she or he cannot crack it' (Radner and Lanser 1993: 6). In both these modes of coding, ethnographic investigations are required in order to assess the rhetorical function of the codes themselves, that is, to understand these systems of encoding and decoding from an insider perspective.

At a further level codes exist which Radner and Lanser identify as 'implicit': 'precisely those acts whose very codedness is arguable' (1993: 6). The centrality of implicit coding is that the sender may be unaware of anything but a denotative message in the text. It is this level that requires intensive textual analysis. It must be borne in mind, however, that:

the suggestion of implicit coding remains an act of inference—one that has potential consequences for individuals and communities and therefore should not be made without care. Who is to say whether coding has taken place in a given context? Who is to say what the decoded meaning is? What are the relations of power in which such judgements are made? If coding is a strategy adopted (consciously or not) for concealment, what will be the consequences of uncovering an act of coding? These are not merely academic questions; they involve the safety, reputations, and well-being of individual[s] . . . and entire communities. (Radner and Lanser 1993: 9)

More contentious within Radner and Lanser's paradigm is their notion of 'risk', wherein they distinguish between groups at 'risk' and groups at 'play':

By situations of *risk* we mean those occasions when the code has been adopted to provide safety or freedom rather than simply pleasure or play. Coding may be undertaken for a variety of purposes, not all of them involving real or perceived danger to the encoder or the encoding community . . . Such cases involve a 'bicultural' context but not necessarily an operant context of dominance; there is thus no need to suppress the fact that coding might be embarrassing or uncomfortable but not of serious consequence. (1993: 4–5; emphasis in original)

Although all communication is coded by virtue of the fact that language itself is a series of signifiers, members of smaller communities within a larger hegemony can communicate among themselves by means of cultural codes that may or may not be observable or comprehensible to the wider society. Some of these codes are explicit, understood as coded even if the code cannot be cracked, while others are complicit, understood within the community itself as significant markers of identity or meaning, and of which outsiders may not be aware.

Irving Howe observed that, when Jewish comics of the early television age used Yiddish expressions, they encoded them as 'waving to the folks back home' (cited in Shandler 1994: 20). Shandler also notes that within later American popular culture, which supports a kind of bland generic ethnicity as opposed to specific ethnic expression rooted in the lived experiences of cultural groups, ethnic audience members try to identify their own countrymen:

> Some characters who would appear to be beyond ethnicity are open to the projections of viewers' idiosyncratic assertions. *Star Trek*'s Science Officer Mr. Spock is a perfect example. When I worked on a screening and discussion series on ethnic portraiture on prime-time television for the Jewish Museum of New York in 1991, Spock came up several times in discussion. Author Jewelle Gomez, who was the series discussant for science fiction programs, noted that many African Americans identified with Spock, who was stigmatized as 'other' because of his skin color and his multiracial background (his mother a human, his father a Vulcan). Charlie Chin, then of the Chinatown History Museum, told me that many Asian Americans feel an affinity for Spock—skin color again, as well as those slanted eyebrows, while the character's Vulcan logic was under-stood as the equivalent of Confucian philosophy. I, of course, explained to them that Jews lay claim to Spock as a figure of their own sense of 'otherness' and 'between-two-worldliness'—besides, the actor who plays him is Jewish, his Vulcan hand salute is derived from the gesture made by *kohanim* when they offer a priestly benediction, he works for the Federation (rabbis love to point this out) and—as I have been told by a member of the Jewish Science Fiction Society—if Vulcan logic is symbolic of anything, surely it must be Talmudic sophistry! (Shandler 1994: 20; see also Zurawik 2003)

It is my contention that coding does occur within feature fiction films, specifically within ethnic cinema, as a means of intra-group communication. Coding excludes non-members from a complete understanding of the cinematic text. By utilizing a variety of linguistic, paralinguistic, and musical signifiers, ethnic cinema conveys to members of particular groups, not necessarily a contra-dictory message to that understood by a general audience, but certainly a more holistic textual, and therefore cultural, one.

By code, I do not necessarily mean a subversive message, 'hidden' within the text to avoid the kind of physical risk Radner and Lanser warn of; but I do mean that genres such as film, which use a medium of mass communication that gives a wide audience access to the narrative, encode certain levels of meaning in order to avoid the risk of alienating their mainstream audience while at the same time communicating to non-dominant groups. A film aimed specifically at an ethnic or limited market has less need for such coded messages. Likewise, more special-ized films—for example documentaries such as *Half the Kingdom* or *Shoah* (Claude Lanzmann, 1985) or American low-budget independent films such as Joan Micklin Silver's *Hester Street* (1975) or *Crossing Delancey* (1988) are less likely to use coded messages. Both documentaries and small, independent films tend to have more specialized audiences, and so are less likely to need to encode their ethnic specificity to the same degree as films which receive wider and general release.

Linguistic Coding

A number of sociolinguists have noted that, although Hebrew remains the official language of Jewish religion, Yiddish is a language of Jewish culture, specifically for Ashkenazi Jews (Fishman 1965: 1–11). Elsewhere, I have noted the centrality of Yiddish for some Jews as a way of determining a film's Jewish identity (Koven 1999: 157–97). Speaking in a counter-hegemonic language, which for a North American presupposes any language other than English, explicitly distances anyone who does not speak that language. Many people within the English-speaking West actively eschew non-English-language films, even those using English-language subtitles. There is an assumption, frequently made, that only those who speak a specific national/cultural language are interested in that nation/culture's cinema.

Radner and Lanser point out that one of the coding strategies operating in women's culture is 'distraction': 'Usually distraction involves creating some kind of "noise", interference, or obscurity that will keep the message from being heard except by those who listen very carefully or already suspect it is there' (1993: 15). Jewish cinema can use language in this way in order to avoid risk and deflect attack by discouraging potentially antagonistic audiences from attending. While Jansen's use of 'esoteric' refers to how a group sees itself, his definition of folklore studies also reflects how a group thinks *others* see it (Jansen 1965: 46); seen in this context, this kind of linguistic distraction is a means of framing or presenting explicitly Jewish content based on assumed fears about what non-Jewish reactions might be to it.

For example, the prologue to *Schindler's List* shows, in colour as opposed to the monochrome cinematography of the majority of the movie, an Orthodox family (signified by their clothes and the men's *peyos*) reciting the Kiddush which begins the *shabbes* meal. This liturgy, recited with a glass of wine in hand, which is familiar even to Jews with only a cursory knowledge of Judaism, is in Hebrew. Jews understand the religious context of Hebrew; among North American *cultural* Jews (that is, non-practising, or secular, and likely Ashkenazi), the only time one is likely to come into contact with Hebrew is in the religious context. Taking a scene like this from *Schindler's List*, presented in another language without the benefit of subtitles, out of the context of an English-language movie, demonstrates how this 'distracting' technique of coding operates. As we watch it, Jewish difference is audible, and denies those not conversant with Jewish prayer the textual meaning of the scene. In Radner and Lanser's terms this is an *explicit* code since for the non-Jewish audience the language is not immediately understandable and they must resort to other (e.g. visual) codes within the cinematic frame in order to comprehend what is going on. Even Jews who are not fluent in Hebrew, and who may not understand the *words* of the prayer, are likely to recognize, at least, that it is in Hebrew. There is no assurance that non-Jews would even recognize the language, let alone the words' meaning

Films in modern Hebrew (that is, films made in Israel) or in Yiddish, even if supplied with subtitles which allow non-Hebrew or Yiddish speakers to feel less 'distracted' by the unfamiliar language, do not give the audience full immersion in the cultural experience of the language, or the culture whence that language emerges. As I have noted in a study of the Toronto Jewish Film Festival, each year the festival screens at least one classic Yiddish-language film. One of the festival participants commented on the importance of understanding the language that cannot be translated in subtitles: 'some of the things that weren't translated at all were absolutely hilarious . . . it has so much more taste and feeling to it when you understand it from that perspective' (Koven 1999: 213). Self-proclaimed 'Yiddisholugist' and writer Leo Rosten has likewise noted the near-impossibility of translating Yiddish into English, since the language is so closely tied in to the culture itself:

To translate is to re-create portions of a culture to someone not raised in that culture. To translate Yiddish is to translate an entire style of life, a construct of perceptions, a complex system of values, subtleties of thinking and feeling which are embedded in the history of European Jews and the life of their descendants. (Rosten 1968: 4)

Or course, this is true for any language, not just Jewish languages. But within these Jewish languages, Yiddish and Hebrew, is encoded the cultural history of the people, and one must understand the culture for the language to be decoded. Furthermore, there is a strong gender basis to the ideological definition of Yiddish as the *mamaloshen* (mother tongue) of Ashkenazi Jews. As Rosten noted, 'Hebrew was the father's language, since the holy books were in Hebrew, and only Jewish males were taught to read. Yiddish became known as "the mother's tongue", the language of the home' (1968: 223). Of course, some women were taught Hebrew too, and many different languages use the idiom 'mother tongue', but I use Rosten's comments here to make at least a rhetorical division between the languages of the synagogue and the home. Charles Ferguson has observed the distinction between the high literary forms of a language and the more vernacular, dialect-based speech patterns, and the code-switching between the two (what he calls 'diglossia'):

among speakers . . . adults use L [low forms of speech, or dialect] in speaking to children and children use L in speaking to one another. As a result, L is learned by children in what may be regarded as the 'normal' way of learning one's mother tongue. H [high forms of speech] may be heard by children from time to time, but the actual learning of H is chiefly accomplished by the means of formal education, whether this be traditional . . . schools, modern government schools, or private tutors. (Ferguson 1972: 239)

Given Ferguson's schema, it seems apparent that Hebrew is H, and Yiddish is L for Ashkenazi Jews. But even beyond understanding the language, and therefore the culture itself, for some just hearing the language spoken, even when they cannot understand it, is a significant action enabling them to feel culturally connected (Koven 1999: 214).

For example at the 1997 Toronto Jewish Film Festival the Yiddish-language film screened was *Tkies khaf* (The Vow; Henryk Szabó, 1937). It was an unprecedented success. Helen Zukerman, the director of the festival, tells the story:

> when I sat in the theatre [on] Sunday, and people's reaction to *The Vow*—I couldn't believe it! I expected 250 people to show up. Maybe 300 people. [The show sold out— over 900 people.] So in the office, when ticket sales were happening, I look at the ticket sales, and thought 'this is really interesting'. But then I thought 'well, they're coming to see it cause it's a new version that I happened to get', and all that stuff. When I sat in the theatre, I didn't expect to watch that whole film. I wanted—I started watching it because I wanted to see if the print was any good. And the people were so involved. I sat there and watched this film. And when the wedding happened, and everybody started clapping [and shouting *mazel tov!*]—I mean, if I had been sitting with Ginger [Mittleman— the festival administrative assistant], I would have gotten up and *danced*. I thought, this is unbelievable. This is a whole generation—and in the audience, where people were laughing, I would suggest that half of them could speak Yiddish because they were laughing in different places. So you figure 300 and some odd people could speak Jewish and the others didn't. But the people who couldn't were *so* into it. They left, they *loved* it. (Koven 1999: 213–14)

Despite only some of the audience at this screening having linguistic competence in the Yiddish language, there was a tremendous demand for 'authentic' cultural products in that language. Not only did *Tkies khaf* sell over 900 tickets, on Zuckerman's own estimate maybe half that audience actually spoke Yiddish. But the cultural communion created by screening this pre-Holocaust artefact of European Ashkenazi culture transcended the linguistic hindrances. When, unprompted, the entire 900-strong audience shouted *Mazel tov!* when the glass was smashed during the wedding scene that concludes the film, and literally began dancing in the aisles, something more than watching a film was occurring.

The *Schindler's List* sequence described above, although in Hebrew, is still within the context of an American-produced, English-language film. It exists within the film as a culturally significant linguistic moment. Within North American films, it is these isolated moments of spoken Yiddish or Hebrew that are the norm. In Mel Brooks's *Blazing Saddles* (1973), African American sheriff Bart (Cleavon Little) remembers his family crossing the frontier in a wagon train when he was a child. At one point they meet a tribe of Native Americans, whose chief is played by Brooks himself. In addition to speaking the pidgin English that characterizes Native American stereotypes in Hollywood Westerns, Brooks's chief also speaks in Yiddish. Film scholar Lester Friedman observed that in this

sequence it 'seems comically appropriate that the West's most conspicuous outsider, the Indian, should speak in the tongue of history's traditional outsider, the
Jew' (1982: 228). Yet this Yiddish-language joke can only be decoded *as* Yiddish
for those who know the language; *what* Brooks speaks is not framed as anything
other than 'not-English'. In fact, when the film was released in 1974 the television
advertisement promoting it said that in Brooks's version of 'the Old West' 'the
Indians' spoke 'German'. Returning to Radner and Lanser's idea of 'distraction',
publicly identifying the language as German creates a sense of 'noise' around the
Jewish content of the film, allowing the Jewish content to be encoded and alleviating the risk of the film being seen as 'too Jewish'. If one has already identified the
language as German, then the Indian ceases to be necessarily Jewish, and
remains abstractly 'Other', much like Bart's African American family.

Stereotyping, though, can also be considered a form of implicit encoding:
Radner and Lanser refer to 'indirection' as a strategy which women frequently
use in order to communicate their 'feminist messages', and cite women's use of
metaphor as a means of discussing forbidden subject areas (1993: 16). Within
Jewish cultures, if we see self-stereotyping as a metaphorical activity, those stereotypes then function as a strategy of indirection for the Jewish discourse deeply
encoded within a film. Two recent films have created tremendous controversy
regarding their stereotypical presentation of Jewish figures, despite the fact that
both were made by Jews: *Suzy Gold* (Richard Cantor, 2004) and *When Do We Eat?*
(Salvador Litvak, 2005). A consideration of both films, their controversies and
their use of stereotypes, would need a full separate discussion, but we should at
least note here that there has been little consideration of the use of cultural stereotypes as metaphorical 'indirection' in contemporary Jewish culture. What we see
in these criticisms, even fleetingly, is the fear that the 'non-Jewish' world might
get the wrong impression that 'Jews' are really like these characters. Such a
perception reflects something of a crisis within this Jewish culture.

The Coding of Customs

Non-Jews can see, and enjoy, the depiction of Jewish customs within a film
without fully understanding their ritual significance. It is worth reiterating that
while Jewish spectators are likely to see such customs as a natural part of a scene,
non-Jews do not necessarily even 'see' the actions portrayed. One can safely
assume, for example, that at least some non-Jews were in the audience for *Tkies
khaf*, and whether or not they were aware of the traditions of Ashkenazi weddings
they were presumably caught up in the overall celebratory atmosphere the
screening created. But certain customary meanings may not be so readily open to
non-members of the group.

In the Polish-made Yiddish-language film *A brivele der mamen* (A Letter to
Mother; Joseph Green, 1938), the Berdichevski family attempts to fulfil the

Passover requirements by conducting a *seder*. But patriarch Duvid (Alexander Stein) has left the family to seek his fortune in America, and his chair at the head of the table is left empty. Duvid functions as a 'structured absence' in the sequence: his patriarchal influence is felt in the failure of the *seder* to run effectively. Traditionally, the (re)telling of the Jews' Exodus from Egypt at Passover is initiated through a series of four questions. At one narrative juncture, when the youngest son, Arele (Irving Bruner), is to ask these questions, he breaks down in tears because his father is not there to answer them. In Ashkenazi tradition, if the father is not able to answer the questions, then the Passover *seder* cannot be completed and the family cannot fulfil the commandment to retell the story of the Exodus from Egypt. While the liturgy for the Passover *seder* is relatively fixed and in the vernacular, thereby allowing anyone to read from the Haggadah to complete the ritual, to *A brivele*'s 1936 audience, the absent father-figure would have been profoundly felt. This is the more esoteric understanding of the impact of Duvid's absence from the rite.

In *Leon, the Pig Farmer* (Vadim Jean and Gary Sinyor, 1993), the strictly kosher Leon (Mark Frankel) from north London discovers that not only is he the product of artificial insemination, but, due to a lab error, the sperm used to conceive him belonged to Brian Chadwick (Brian Glover), a pig farmer from North Yorkshire. Leon travels to Yorkshire to meet his biological father and his family. Once there, he begins to feel homesick, but the Chadwicks decide to try and behave a bit more like his Jewish family. The result is a montage of clips that point out the stereotypical differences between Christian and Jewish cultures. Because the narrative of the sequence is built upon learning the codes of Ashkenazi Jewish culture, the cultural items themselves are obvious, but there is a further level of meaning that is esoteric.

The sequence begins with the removal of the decorative pigs' heads that Brian has on the mantelpiece. A framed picture of Leon replaces one of the heads, reflecting the cultural stereotype of Jewish parents who are overly proud of their children. A small Israeli flag replaces another. An ornate chandelier replaces an antique lighting fixture, looking quite incongruous with the rural motifs of the Chadwick farm, reflecting the stereotype of conspicuous consumption among parvenu Jews. This montage of visual gags leads up to a visual 'punch line': the Chadwick's son Keith (Sean Pertwee) is lying in bed reading Philip Roth's *Portnoy's Complaint* with one hand, while with the other hand he mimes gripping some invisible object and looks under his bedcovers.

While there is nothing specifically Jewish about reading, or indeed masturbating, in bed, the connection with Roth, and the placing of this scene at the end of a series of cultural icons which suggest a more elevated aspect of Judaism, successfully creates a visual joke about Jewishness. It offers an example of Radner and Lanser's 'complicit coding': there is no masturbation joke without understanding the complicit encoding of Roth as an author who wrote about masturbation (particularly in that novel), or the stereotype of the sexually obsessed young Jewish male. If the previous icons in the montage could be taken seriously— the objection to pigs, the pride of the family, the State of Israel, and finally the material wealth of the parvenu—this final gag deflates the joke to its most absurd and banal. 'Contemporary Jewish literature' is satirically reduced to a 'masturbation how-to book'. This combination of specific icons operates as the locus for cultural meaning, and is, I would argue, essential to an understanding of cinematic coding. There is another shot in *Leon*, a benign moment focusing on the Chadwicks' dinner table. We have seen this beautiful hardwood table prior to this shot, but now it is covered with a white tablecloth. Two dark candlesticks with white candles burning in them, a bottle of wine, and bread are all on the table. The Chadwicks each have a crystal/glass wine cup in front of them, but it is the placement of a silver wine goblet at the centre of the table which appears significant, and changes the entire meaning of the table setting. In this scene, rather than any specific icon holding Jewish iconographical meaning it is the mix of these signs which points to the scene's emergent Jewish*ness*. The shot tracks to the right, in order to reveal someone walking in the front door, but this camera movement reveals that the bread is in fact under a challah-cover, further particularizing the table setting as Jewish. The characterization of Keith in *Leon* also offers an example of Radner and Lanser's 'implicit coding', where the existence of the code is arguable: Keith is studying to be a cordon bleu chef, and in an earlier sequence attempts to turn chicken soup into some kind of *nouvelle cuisine*. Perhaps the most infamous moment in *Portnoy's Complaint* is Portnoy's confession that he used a piece of liver to masturbate: 'My first piece I had in the privacy of my own home, rolled around my cock in the bathroom at three-thirty—and then had again on the end of a fork, at five-thirty, along with the other members of that poor innocent family of mine. So. Now you know the worst thing I have ever done. I fucked my own family's dinner' (Roth 1967: 34). The image of 'liver' returns in *Leon* a few minutes after we see Keith reading Roth's book. While at the dinner table, eating chopped liver, Leon chastises the Chadwicks for 'just fulfilling stereotypes. You don't understand the fundamental concept of guilt. Without guilt it's meaningless. "Guilt" isn't a word—it's a way of life.' Keith replies: 'I think I do—understand the concept of guilt. I just realized—I uh—used pig's liver.' At the explicit level, the humour comes from the accidental violation of the kosher laws; but the implicit level could be a pointed reference to the liver in Roth's novel.

Another of the encoding techniques which Radner and Lanser identify as 'complicit' is that of 'incompetence': that when someone appears to be inept at a specific task they may in fact be demonstrating their resistance to it (Radner and Lanser 1993: 20). Jews may interpret the Chadwicks' 'incompetence' at reproducing the codes of Jewish behaviour as resistance to understanding Jewish culture in anything other than its stereotypical manifestation; as Leon himself comments, 'you're just fulfilling stereotypes'. The Chadwicks do not understand the cultural concepts that lie beneath the surface of the manifested cultural traits. The incompetence with which the Chadwicks reproduce the codes of Jewish culture expresses their implicit resistance to the changes Leon requests, except at the most superficial (stereotypical) levels. Textually, we see Brian Chadwick's resentment on his face as he takes down his pig-head plaques from over the mantelpiece. As Radner and Lanser noted above, one of the problems in identifying the encoded complicit discourse is that it may reveal cultural aspects the members of the culture would rather not have revealed. Jewish paranoia about the motives or sincerity of non-Jewish interest in Jewish culture beyond the stereotypical is perhaps not something most Jews would like revealed; it is something we would rather keep to ourselves, even subconsciously. Although in some respects many of these clips could be classified as more iconographic than 'customary', it is the customary use of these icons that is significant for the encoding of a certain kind of Jewish identity.

Musical Coding

Music also has strong cultural associations, and to be aware of those associations reveals a deeper level of meaning in the cinematic text. In *Annie Hall* (Woody Allen, 1977), Alvy (Woody Allen) and his friend Max (Tony Roberts) are walking down a Manhattan street. Alvy, as usual, is ranting—this time about the anti-semitism he experiences everywhere he goes. To prove this to his friend he tells him the following anecdote:

You know, I was in a record store—listen to this—so I know—there's this big, tall, blonde, crew-cutted guy and he's looking at me in a funny way and smiling. And he's saying 'Yes, we have a sale this week on Wagner.' Wagner, Max! Wagner! So I know what he's really trying to tell me. Very significantly! Wagner.

Knowledge that the German composer Richard Wagner was both a vehement antisemite and Hitler's favourite composer is not Jewish per se, but it is significant within Jewish experience to think that someone suggesting Wagner to you is also aware of the cultural associations the composer evokes. The joke about selling an album by an antisemitic composer to a Jew can only work if one is aware that Wagner was antisemitic, and much appreciated in the Third Reich. Those associations are 'complicit'—if one is unaware of them, one is unaware even that a joke is being told.

Fiddler on the Roof (Norman Jewison, 1971) is also informative. The film is able implicitly to encode its Jewish discourse through a technique that Radner and Lanser identify as 'trivialization':

Trivialization involves the employment of a form, mode, or genre that the dominant culture considers unimportant, innocuous, or irrelevant. When a particular form is conventionally nonthreatening, the message it carries, even if it might be threatening in another context, is likely to be discounted or overlooked. (1993: 19)

Fiddler on the Roof's depiction of the Old World Jewish family, with its gender inequality and the patriarchal discourse of Tevye (Chaim Topol), the father, at its centre, can be expressed through a 'trivial' genre, the musical.[5] The opening sequence of the film, the musical number 'Tradition', encodes the narrative world we are about to spend the next three hours within as one based on tradition, a cultural aesthetic which might have been discordant in 1970s United States, a period where the traditional values were being challenged. Although, within the narrative of the film, Tevye eventually learns to accept certain modern practices, including intermarriage, rejection of the *shadchan*, and leaving home to emigrate to America, this acceptance is presented with a kind of melancholy over the loss of these traditions. The imposition of modernization on the traditional Jewish family and its reluctant acceptance is a fairly serious topic to discuss. But within the context of a 'trivial' genre like the musical it can be encoded for those with the cultural background to decode it.

Finally, returning again to *Schindler's List*, there is a sequence of intense musical coding. This sequence, which depicts the liquidation of the Kraków ghetto, is shot from Schindler's perspective, high on a nearby hill. Schindler watches in horror as the Nazis massacre the Jews in the streets. Instead of using clichéd, 'dramatic' music, composer John Williams utilizes the Jewish lullaby 'Oyf'n pripetshok' sung by the Li-Ron Herzeliya Children's Choir. For those who are familiar with the tune it is not just a lullaby but a musical code of Jewish continuity, for in the repeated line, 'And the rabbi teaches all the little ones all their *alef beis* or ABCs' is a signifier of tradition or intergenerational learning and, by extension, persistence. At a very basic level, there is a tonal juxtaposition between the images of carnage and this softly sung lullaby. This act of juxtaposition is itself a technique of implicit coding according to Radner and Lanser (1993: 13), where it attempts to encode a further message. The irony is also textual: 'Oyf'n pripetshok', which translates from Yiddish as 'In the Hearth/Fireplace', is a song about the safety of home and the family hearth, while the images show the destruction of Jewish households. Maurice Yacowar refers to Spielberg's irony in using this song as a 'cruel inversion' (1994: 43): the smoke from the family 'hearth' becomes the smoke from Auschwitz's furnaces. But at a more personal and anecdotal level, although *Schindler's List* is a moving film, it was this sequence that really upset me, not so much because of the violence of the images but because of the music. 'Oyf'n pripetshok' is the one lullaby I remember my mother singing to me as a small child, and that cultural association, of feeling safe in a mother's arms as a small child, compounded by having the song sung by a children's choir, created an even stronger juxtaposition with the violent images, where mothers were helpless in protecting their children. I happened to mention my reaction to this sequence to my grandmother, and her reply was that it was the one song most Jews remember their mothers singing to them. The tonal contrast between the innocent children singing and the horror of the images is observable to anyone paying attention, allowing the audience to feel that they understand what is going on emotionally within the sequence. But the linguistic level of understanding the Yiddish of the song presents a more exclusive degree of irony, the one that Yacowar refers to as 'cruel'. And yet a third level, more inchoate, more profound, also opens up: the personal and familial associations of that memory of one's own childhood and those feelings of safety at the 'hearth'. Any scholar with the where-withal to research the lyrics of 'Oyf'n pripetshok' can access that second level of signification, but only those with the memory of one's family and the songs sung around the cradle can reach the third level.

Decoding Texts

Decoding Jewish discourse within popular cinema involves a high level of inter-pretation. Radner and Lanser have identified several techniques by which women, and by a switch of signifiers Jews, can encode their discourse—that is, encode Jewish messages even without knowing such messages are being com-municated. Identifying the use of such techniques as appropriation, juxtaposi-tion, distraction, indirection, and incompetence positions the scholar to uncover culturally specific messages that are 'appropriate' only for esoteric consumption.

These films are not necessarily 'oppositional' in Hall's schema; neither is read-ing industrially produced cinematic texts such as *Schindler's List*, *Exodus*, or *Fiddler on the Roof* as Jewish to read 'oppositionally'. A view that is not reflexive of the dominant cultural view is not necessarily oppositional. This binary position-ing of being aligned with either the hegemonic order or opposed to it seems artificial and simplistic. It may sometimes be true, but the syllogism cannot be applied in all cases.

Radner and Lanser's quasi-Bakhtinian approach to 'bicultural' readings of texts (polyphony by any other name) seems to be more grounded in a cultural reality than Hall's approach. For any message to be received there needs to be someone to encode and someone to decode that message. Linguistic codes them-selves are not always sufficient for the direct communication of data; cultural specificity frequently precludes things other than language, although not exclud-ing it. Put differently, Jews are in a better position, or are more likely, to have a fuller understanding and appreciation of Jewish texts by virtue of their cultural experiences, expectations, and understandings of the codes within which that culture manifests itself.

Notes

1   I am using the term 'esoteric' here, and throughout this essay, as Jansen uses it within folklore studies: 'The esoteric applies to what one group thinks of itself and what it supposes others think of it' (Jansen 1965: 46). See also Narvaez 1992 for the relationship between folklore and cultural studies.

2   The concept of 'Jewishness' is problematic: not only does it refer to both the cultural and religious practices of 'Jews', but further specification is required to distinguish between Ashkenazi, Sephardi, and Middle Eastern Jewish cultures. The term 'Jewish' becomes even more complex, in so far as I am using it here to refer to my own experiences, as someone from the Ashkenazi Jewish 'cultural' (as opposed to 'religious') tradition whose experience of the culture comes primarily from a North American context. By rights, I should refer explicitly to the 'Ashkenazi-based, (North) American Jewish cultural reading', but I have used 'Jewish' here as a shorthand to my own Jewish experiences, culturally ethnocentric though they may be.

3   Or as folklorist Robert Klymasz noted, 'it is the dominant, mainstream culture itself that dictates and furnishes the appropriate escape mechanisms and makes available the various generative tools and productive vehicles with which to reshape and refine the old folklore legacy. In effect, then, the reconstructed folklore complex allows its assorted carriers and enthusiasts to indulge in a fantasy of ethnic separateness and individuality without transgressing the limits and patterns prescribed and sanctioned by the surrounding . . . culture' (1973: 139).

4   Roland Barthes, Hall's mentor, understood the polysemic nature of textual analysis: 'The interpretation demanded by a specific text, in its plurality, is in no way liberal: it is not a question of conceding some meanings, of magnanimously acknowledging that each one has its share of truth; it is a question, against all in-difference, of asserting the very existence of plurality, which is not that of the true, the probable, or even the possible' (Barthes 1974: 6).

5   I use 'trivial' here in the sense that Radner and Lanser do, to mean a non-threatening and easily dismissed form, rather than to imply criticism.

References

BARTHES, ROLAND. 1974. *S/Z: An Essay*, trans. Richard Miller. London.

BENSHOFF, HARRY M., and SEAN GRIFFIN. 2004. *America on Film: Representing Race, Class, Gender, and Sexuality at the Movies*. London.

FERGUSON, CHARLES A. 1972. 'Diglossia'. In Pier Paolo Giglioli, ed., *Language and Social Context: Selected Readings*, 232–51. Harmondsworth.

FISHMAN, JOSHUA A. 1965. 'Yiddish in America', *International Journal of American Linguistics*, 32: 1–11.

FRIEDMAN, LESTER D. 1982. *Hollywood's Image of the Jew*. New York.

HALL, STUART. 1980. 'Encoding/Decoding'. In Stuart Hall, Dorothy Hobson, Andrew Love, and Paul Willis, eds, *Culture, Media, Language: Working Papers in Cultural Studies, 1972–79*, 128–38, 294–5. Boston.

JANSEN, WILLIAM WUGH. 1965. 'The Esoteric-Exoteric Factor in Folklore'. In Alan Dundes, ed., *The Study of Folklore*, 43–52. Englewood Cliffs, NJ.

KLYMASZ, ROBERT B. 1973. 'From Immigrant to Ethnic Folklore: A Canadian View of Process and Tradition', *Journal of the Folklore Institute*, 10: 131–9.

KOVEN, MIKEL J. 1999. 'An Ethnography of Seeing: A Proposed Methodology for the Ethnographic Study of Popular Cinema.' Ph.D. thesis, Memorial University of Newfoundland.

NARVÁEZ, PETER. 1992. 'Folkloristics, Cultural Studies and Popular Culture', *Canadian Folklore canadien*, 14(1): 15–30.

RADNER, JOAN N., and SUSAN S. LANSER. 1993. 'Strategies of Coding in Women's Cultures'. In J. N. Radner, ed., *Feminist Messages: Coding in Women's Folk Culture*, 1–30. Urbana, Ill.

RADWAY, JANICE A. 1984. *Reading the Romance: Women, Patriarchy, and Popular Literature*. Chapel Hill, NC.

ROSTEN, LEO. 1968. *The Joys of Yiddish*. New York.

ROTH, PHILIP. 1967. *Portnoy's Complaint*. New York.

SHANDLER, JEFFREY. 1994. 'Is There a Jewish Way to Watch Television? Notes from a Tuned-In Ethnographer', *Jewish Folklore and Ethnology Review*, 16(1): 19–22.

STAM, ROBERT. 1991. 'Bakhtin, Polyphony, and Ethnic/Racial Representation'. In Lester D. Friedman, ed., *Unspeakable Images: Ethnicity and the American Cinema*, 251–76. Urbana, Ill.

TOELKEN, BARRE. 1979. *The Dynamics of Folklore*. Boston.

WILLIAMS, RAYMOND. 1976. *Keywords: A Vocabulary of Culture and Society*. New York.

YACOWAR, MAURICE. 1994. 'Schindler's Film', *Queen's Quarterly*, 101(1): 35–47.

ZURAWIK, DAVID. 2003. *The Jews of Prime Time*. Waltham, Mass.

Contributors

Simon J. Bronner is Distinguished University Professor of American Studies and Folklore at the Pennsylvania State University, Harrisburg, where he is lead scholar of the campus's Holocaust and Jewish Studies Center. He is the author and editor of over twenty-five books, including the *Encyclopedia of American Folklife* (2006), *Following Tradition: Folklore in the Discourse of American Culture* (1998), and *Manly Traditions: The Folk Roots of American Masculinities* (2005). He edits the Material Worlds series for the University Press of Kentucky and has published in Jewish cultural studies in the *Journal of Modern Jewish Studies, Jewish History, Yiddish, Markers*, and *Chuliyot: Journal of Yiddish Literature*. As well as editing the Littman Library's Jewish Cultural Studies series, he leads the Jewish Folklore and Ethnology section of the American Folklore Society. He has received the Mary Turpie Prize from the American Studies Association and the Wayland D. Hand Prize and Peter and Iona Opie Prize from the American Folklore Society for his scholarship and educational leadership.

Olga Gershenson is Assistant Professor in the Department of Judaic and Near Eastern Studies at the University of Massachusetts at Amherst. She holds degrees from the Urals State University in Russia, the Hebrew University of Jerusalem, and the University of Massachusetts. She is the author of *Gesher: Russian Theatre in Israel: A Study of Cultural Colonization* (2005) and co-editor of a special issue of the *Journal of International Women's Studies* (2005) on gendered construction of space. She has also published on Jewish cultural studies in the *Journal of Modern Jewish Studies, Multilingua*, the *Western Journal of Communication*, the *Journal of International Communication*, and others.

Bea Hollander-Goldfein is Director of the Transcending Trauma Project (TTP) at the Council for Relationships, a non-profit outpatient therapy centre and educational institution, which is in the Division of Couple and Family Studies, Department of Psychiatry and Human Behavior, Jefferson Medical College in Philadelphia, Pennsylvania, where she holds the positions of Clinical Assistant Professor and Director of the Post-Graduate Certificate Program in Marriage and Family Therapy. In addition, as Director of TTP she has been awarded the Joseph D. Meranze Fellowship in Trauma Studies. She received her doctorate in psychology from Teachers College, Columbia University, New York City, and subsequently expanded her training to include certification in marriage and family therapy.

Miriam Isaacs is Visiting Associate Professor of Yiddish Language and Culture in the Joseph and Rebecca Meyerhoff Center for Jewish Studies and the Department of

Germanic Studies, University of Maryland, College Park. She is the author of *Yiddish in Orthodox Communities* (2004), published in Yiddish and French. She has also published essays on Yiddish in the *Journal of Sociolinguistics* and the *International Journal of the Sociology of Language*, and chapters in Leonard Greenspoon (ed.), *Yiddish Language and Culture: Then and Now* (1998), D. B. Kerler (ed.), *The Politics of Yiddish: Studies in Language, Literature and Society* (1998), Ilana Abramovitch and Sean Galvin (eds), *The Jews of Brooklyn* (2000), and Alan L. Berger and Naomi Berger (eds), *Second Generation Voices: Reflections by Children of Holocaust Survivors and Perpetrators* (2001).

Hannah Kliger is Senior Adviser to the Chancellor and Professor of Communication and Jewish Studies at the Pennsylvania State University, the Abington College, where she has also been Associate Dean for Academic Affairs. Kliger has also served as Associate Dean for Graduate Studies and Senior Research Investigator at the University of Pennsylvania's Annenberg School for Communication, and as Associate Dean for Education at MCP Hahnemann University (now Drexel) School of Public Health. From 1985 until 1997 she was a faculty member at the University of Massachusetts, Amherst. She is also an Academic Fellow of the Psychoanalytic Center of Philadelphia, applying psychoanalytic ideas to understanding organizational dynamics and leadership. The National Endowment for the Humanities and the American Council of Learned Societies have recognized Professor Kliger for her scholarly and curricular initiatives. Her publications focus on the communicative practices and communal organizations of minority groups. In addition to her book, *Jewish Hometown Associations and Family Circles in New York* (1992), she has authored numerous articles on communication and culture in immigrant communities.

Mikel J. Koven is Senior Lecturer at the University of Worcester, where he is head of the Film Studies programme. He received his Ph.D. in folklore from Memorial University of Newfoundland (Canada). He is the author of *La Dolce Morte: Vernacular Cinema and the Italian Gallo Film* (2006) and *Blaxploitation Cinema* (2001). He edits the journal *Contemporary Legend* for the International Society for Contemporary Legend Research, and he co-edited a special issue of *Western Folklore* on 'Folklore and Film'. He serves on the editorial boards of *Participations* and *Critical Studies in Television*. He also serves on the advisory board of the Jewish Cultural Studies series.

Sergey R. Kravtsov is a researcher at the Center for Jewish Art, at the Hebrew University of Jerusalem. Born in Lviv, Ukraine, he was trained as an architect at the Lviv Polytechnic University. He received his doctoral degree in architectural history from the Institute for the Theory and History of Architecture in Moscow in 1993, and moved to Israel in 1994. In 2000 he received the Mordechai Narkiss Prize for the three-dimensional computerized documentation of synagogue architecture. He has published essays in *Treasures of Jewish Galicia: Judaica from the Museum of Ethnography and Crafts in Lvov, Ukraine* (1996), the *Journal of the Society of Architectural Historians* (2005), and *Architectura* (2005).

Judith Lewin is Associate Professor of English and is affiliated with the programmes on Women's and Gender Studies and Religious Studies. She has received awards from the National Foundation for Jewish Culture, the Leo Baeck Institute of New York, and Hadassah–Brandeis Institute. Her publications are concerned with the issue of gender and representation, especially of Jewish women in nineteenth-century literature. She has published articles about the Jewish character Rebecca in Walter Scott's *Ivanhoe* in *ANQ: A Quarterly Journal of Short Articles, Notes, and Reviews, Nashim: A Journal of Jewish Women's Studies and Gender Issues*, and *Jewish Culture and History*. She has also written about twenty-first-century novels by Jewish American women writers in 'Diving into the Wreck: Binding Oneself to Judaism in Contemporary Jewish Women's Fiction', for *Shofar: An Interdisciplinary Journal of Jewish Studies*.

Ted Merwin is Assistant Professor of Religion and Judaic Studies at Dickinson College in Carlisle, Pennsylvania, where he also directs the Milton B. Asbell Center for Jewish Life. While serving since 2000 as theatre columnist for the New York *Jewish Week*, the largest-circulation Jewish newspaper in the United States, he has also published widely in both academic journals and mainstream newspapers and magazines. His first book, *In Their Own Image: New York Jews in Jazz Age Popular Culture*, was published in 2006.

Jascha Nemtsov is a pianist and musicologist born in Magadan, Russia. He graduated with distinction from the Leningrad Conservatory in 1986, and moved to Germany in 1992. In 2004 he earned his doctorate with a dissertation on 'The New Jewish School in Music'. Dr Nemtsov has been a member of the School of Jewish Studies at the University of Potsdam since 2002. The focus of his research is Jewish art music and Jewish composers of the twentieth century. As a pianist he has recorded more than twenty CDs of solo and chamber music works.

Emilie S. Passow is an Associate Professor in the Department of English and Philosophy and the Judaic Studies Program at Drexel University, Philadelphia, where she is also Co-Director of the certificate programme in humanities, health sciences, and society. Dr Passow has given Medical Humanities Grand Rounds at the major medical institutions in Philadelphia and is Visiting Lecturer in Medical Humanities at Thomas Jefferson Medical College. She is also an observer on the Thomas Jefferson Ethics Committee and a researcher for the Transcending Trauma Project sponsored by the Council for Relationships, an affiliate of

Thomas Jefferson University. Dr Passow lectures and writes primarily on topics in Judaic studies and narrative, and medicine. Many of these activities have been sponsored by grants from the Pennsylvania Humanities Council, the National Endowment for the Humanities, and the National Institutes of Health.

Holly A. Pearse teaches religious studies at Wilfred Laurier University, Waterloo, Ontario, where she is completing her Ph.D.; her MA was in religious studies with a special focus on ancient Jewish literature. She has published research in *Hinge: A Journal of Contemporary Studies*, and has helped organize conferences on interdisciplinary arts at Wilfred Laurier University.

Ilana Rosen is a senior lecturer in the department of Hebrew literature at Ben-Gurion University, and specializes in the study of Jewish oral lore from central and eastern Europe, particularly Jewish memories of the inter-war period and the Holocaust. She completed her Ph.D. in the Folklore Program of the Hebrew Literature Department of the Hebrew University of Jerusalem. Her major publications include: *There Once Was . . . The Oral Lore of the Jews of Carpatho-Russia* (Hebrew) (1999), which focuses on the inter-war period; *Sister in Sorrow: A Journey to the Life Histories of Female Holocaust Survivors from Hungary* (first published in Hebrew in 1993; English edition forthcoming from Wayne State University Press); *'In Auschwitz We Blew the Shofar': Carpatho-Russian Jews Remember the Holocaust* (Hebrew) (2004); and *Hungarian Jewish Women Remember the Holocaust: An Anthology of Life Histories* (2004), a selection of previously unpublished documented life histories.

Joachim Schlör is Professor of Jewish–Non-Jewish Relations at the University of Southampton. He is the author of *Das Ich der Stadt. Debatten über Judentum und Urbanität* (2005), *Memorial to the Murdered Jews of Europe* (2005), *Tel-Aviv: From Dream to City* (1999), and *Nights in the Big City: Paris, Berlin, London, 1840–1930* (1998). He is also an editor of *Deutscher, Jude, Europaer Im 20. Jahrhundert. Arnold Zweig und das Judentum* (2003). He has received fellowships in Jewish cultural studies from the Internationales Forschungszentrum Kulturwissenschaften, Collegium Budapest, and the Institute for German History at Tel Aviv University.

Elly Teman received her Ph.D. in anthropology at the Hebrew University of Jerusalem. Her doctoral thesis is an ethnography of surrogate motherhood arrangements in Israel from the perspectives of the anthropology of reproduction and medical anthropology. She has published articles in *Medical Anthropology Quarterly*, *Women's Studies Quarterly*, and *Symbolic Interaction*. Dr Teman has received the Herbert Blumer Award for 2005 from the Society of Symbolic Interaction of the American Sociological Association, the Raphael Patai Prize from the Jewish Folklore section of the American Folklore Society, and the Elli Köngäs-Maranda Prize from the Women's Folklore Section of the American Folklore Society. Her other honours include the Faye Kaufman Prize in Excellence from the Canadian Friends of the Hebrew University and the Golda Meir Fellowship award from the Golda Meir Foundation, Israel. In 2007 she received the Rothschild Foundation Postdoctoral Fellowship and took up a post as postdoctoral scholar at the University of California, Berkeley.

Index